# Java: Data Structures and Programming

Springer
*Berlin*
*Heidelberg*
*New York*
*Barcelona*
*Budapest*
*Hong Kong*
*London*
*Milan*
*Paris*
*Singapore*
*Tokyo*

Liwu Li

# Java:
## Data Structures
## and Programming

**With 44 Figures**
**Including CD-ROM**

Springer

Professor Liwu Li
University of Windsor, School of Computer Science
401 Sunset, Windsor, Ontario N9B 3P4
Canada

E-mail: liwu@cs.uwindsor.ca

Library of Congress Cataloging-in-Publication Data
Li, Liwu.
   Java: data structures and programming/Liwu Li.
   p. cm.
   Includes bibliographical references and index.
   ISBN 3-540-63763-X (hardcover: alk. paper)
   1. Java (Computer program language)  2. Data structures
(Computer science)   I. Title.
QA76.73.J38L5 1998
005.7`3--dc21                              98-25666  CIP

ISBN 3-540-63763-X Springer-Verlag Berlin Heidelberg New York

© Springer-Verlag Berlin Heidelberg 1998
Printed in Germany

The use of designations, trademarks, etc. in this publication does not imply, even in the absence of a specific statement, that such names are exempt from the relevant protective laws and regulations and therefore free for general use.

*Cover Design:* Künkel + Lopka, Heidelberg
*Printing:* Mercedesdruck, Berlin
*Binding:* Lüderitz & Bauer, Berlin
Printed on acid-free paper   SPIN 10655386   45/3142   5 4 3 2 1 0

# Preface

This book is written for practitioners of software development and for students of computer science who are interested in using the Java language to construct data structures. The book assumes general knowledge of computer programming but no experience of Java programming or object modeling for the readers. It introduces the Java language and object model by going through examples of data modeling.

The book emphasizes programming skills for developing various types of data structure and fundamental techniques for complexity analysis. The programming skills are necessary for software development. The analysis techniques are needed to ensure performance of programs. The author has been responsible for teaching a data structure course for years. The book carries out his expectations for proficiency in both programming and complexity analysis from students.

Several features of the book distinguish it from other books on data structures. A challenge for the book is relating the complexity analysis to the Java Virtual Machine, which isolates Java programmers from platform issues. The book devotes a chapter to discuss the structure of Java class files and the Java Virtual Machine. The book presents the problem of maximum flow and implements algorithms in Java to evaluate maximum flow for networks. It introduces persistent data structures, which may be included by some practitioners in their projects.

As a faculty member of School of Computer Science at University of Windsor, the author acknowledges the opportunity of teaching and research provided by the university. The author is grateful for encourages the author received from his colleagues and students while the book was prepared.

The whole process of the book preparation was consistently supported by Dr. Hans Wössner, Executive Editor, Computer Science Editorial I at Springer-Verlag. The author is particularly grateful for the careful reviewing arranged by Springer-Verlag, which helped removing some weaknesses from the manuscript of the book. J. Andrew Ross, English Copy Editor, and Peter Strasser, Production Editor at Springer-Verlag, gave valuable suggestions and comments on the manuscript.

The author is solely responsible for any errors in the book. Comments on the book are welcome. The author can be reached at liwu@cs.uwindsor.ca.

## Overview

The Java language is widely accepted for software development due to its portability, type safety, security, and other interesting features. It is attractive for Web applications. For quality software, we often need to design customized data structures for different applications. Data structures are indispensable components of software systems to support functionality of the systems and for efficient storage, retrieval, and manipulation of information. The book is an introduction to programming object-oriented data structures in Java.

Object-oriented programming languages are founded on an object model. The skill of object-oriented analysis and the knowledge of the Java language are necessities for Java data structure programmers. The book presents the Java object model for application analysis and the Java language for data structure programming.

The success of Java is attributable to the Java Virtual Machine (JVM). Here we present the JVM as an abstract machine like a traditional Turing or random access machine. To take the full advantage of the Java language, the book relates the analysis of programs and data structures with the JVM.

The book presents common data structure classes in Java. The data structures include linear linked lists, trees, graphs, and networks.

Most non-trivial applications need data persistence and/or data transportation. Java provides a mechanism for object serialization and deserialization. The book presents the Java serialization mechanism and introduces an approach to serializing data structures for efficient storage and transportation.

## Contents

The book is divided into four parts:

- Part I introduces Java programming. It shows how Java supports the object concepts and how to apply the Java constructs for data modeling. It presents the Java language and the Java standard data structure classes. The first part of the book consists of Chapters 1, 2, 3, and 4.
- Part II presents the JVM as an abstract machine. It relates the analysis of data structures with the JVM. It introduces basic notions for algorithm analysis and applies the notions for Java programs. The second part consists of Chapters 5 and 6.
- Part III presents classes for linear linked lists, trees, graphs, and networks. This part dedicates one chapter for each of the data structures. It consists of Chapters 7, 8, 9, and 10.
- Part IV presents the classes and interfaces of the Java serialization mechanism. It shows how to apply the mechanism to generate efficient serial representations of data structures. The part consists of Chapters 11 and 12.

The book leaves some exercises in the running text. The exercises are relevant to the discussed topics. Some of the exercises are programming exercises. The book presents assignments at the end of some chapters. The assignments can be used to practice the topics or notions presented in the chapters.

## Roadmaps

We present a roadmap for each part of the book in the following. The roadmaps guide reading by interests.

Part I of the book looks at how to apply object-oriented concepts in application analysis and how to construct Java programs. It presents the Java object model by studying a simplified supermarket. It introduces the Java language and the standard Java data structures. Graphics user interfaces (GUIs) should be used for users to enter data into data structures and retrieve data from a system. Part I shows how to construct GUIs.

As shown in Fig. 1, Chapters 1 and 2 are relatively independent from each other. Chapter 1 introduces Java constructs with examples. Chapter 2 presents the Java language. A reader may start Java programming by reading Chapter 1 and then going to Chapter 3 without reading Chapter 2. Chapter 4 presents the Java data structure classes. It extends the functionality of the Java language.

Part I is for self-containment of the book. A reader who is familiar with the Java language and has sufficient Java programming experience can skip the part. The part assumes some computer programming experience for readers. A reader with no experience of object-oriented programming or knowledge of object-oriented languages may find the part helpful.

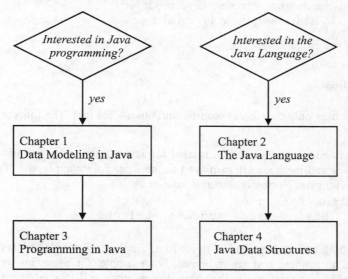

**Fig. 1** Roadmap for Part I

As shown in Fig. 2, Chapter 6 is based on Chapter 5, which presents the JVM as an abstract computational model. Chapter 5 discusses the various types of JVM instructions with respect to time and space requirement. Chapter 6 introduces the notion of analysis for algorithms and data structures that are implemented in Java. It lays the foundation for designing efficient data structures and algorithms in Java.

Chapters 7, 8, 9, and 10 in Part III are independent from each other. They present different types of data structure. A reader may read the chapters in any order. However, the inherent complexity of the data structures increases from Chapters 7 to 10. For example, a student may find reading Chapter 7 is easier than first reading other chapters. Reading Chapter 7 helps understand other chapters. Chapter 10 presents advanced algorithms for maximizing network flows. An instructor may skip the chapter in a junior undergraduate course.

Part III analyzes some algorithms implemented in Java as well as presenting data structure classes. It discusses the correctness and efficiency of the Java programs. This part is the core of the book. Readers can apply and adapt the classes in their programs.

In Part IV, Chapter 11 introduces the Java serialization mechanism. Chapter 12 depends on Chapter 11. It discusses how to serialize data structures.

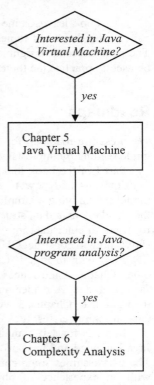

**Fig. 2** Roadmap for Part II

## Font Use

The book uses only two fonts – courier and times – for text. The fonts are used as follows:

- The fixed width courier font is used for Java source code. Specifically, Java classes and methods are displayed in the font. For example, the Java source code for class *Person* is shown in courier as

```
Class Person {
    String name, address, telephone;
}
```

- Running text is displayed in times font. Emphasized words and Java expressions in running text are italicized. For example, the identifier for instance variable *name* defined in the above *Person* class is displayed as *name* in the running text.

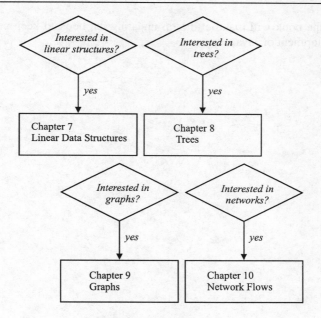

**Fig. 3** Roadmap for Part III

## Programs

All the Java source code listed inside the book is included in the CD of the book. The Java classes can be copied to a hard-drive disk and compiled with the Java compiler. For example, the Java file *Customer.java* for Example 1.1 can be compiled by issuing command

> *javac Customer.java*

in the directory the contains the file. After compilation, the main method in the class can be executed with command

> *java Customer*

Compiled bytecode for the example classes is also included in the CD. A reader can run a compiled main method before compiling the source code.

The Java source code was prepared with Sun's JDK 1.1, which includes a Java compiler and a runtime system. Visit Sun's Web site at http://java.sun.com for information on the latest release of Sun's JDK for a platform. Because of backward compatibility, the source code provided in the CD of the book can be compiled and run with later releases of Sun's JDK. The

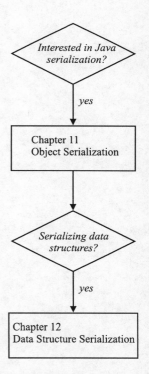

**Fig. 4** Roadmap for Part IV

author of the book will make efforts in updating the book to keep pace with the rapid development of Java.

# Table of Contents

# Part I
# Java Programming

*- Data modeling in Java*
*- The Java language*
*- Programming in Java*
*- Java data structure classes*

# Chapter 1
# Data Modeling in Java

Object technology for software development has a sound engineering foundation. Its core is a simple, natural object model, which consists of object-oriented concepts. It focuses on objects. It creates reusable designs and components for software development. It facilitates abstraction to handle the complexity of large software systems. Compared with other programming paradigms, programming with object technology has the benefits of improved software productivity and quality. Object technology requires a different way of thinking about software decomposition, production, and organization.

The Java programming language is an object-oriented language. It supports the major object-oriented concepts, which include object, class, and class inheritance. An object-oriented program works by creating objects. An *object* aggregates data and methods. Other objects communicate with it by invoking the methods. The basic programming unit in an object-oriented language like Java is a *class*. Programmers construct classes, which are used to compose Java programs. An object is an instance of a class. Each class, except class *Object*, in Java inherits the software defined in another class. The *Object* class defines common behaviors for objects created by Java programs. In this chapter, we present the Java object model by discussing the object-oriented concepts.

A Java programming environment includes a compiler, an interpreter, and a run-time library. The Java compiler translates the source code of a Java program into a sequence of bytecode instructions, which can be executed by the interpreter on the Java Virtual Machine. The Java Virtual Machine defines an interface between Java bytecode and computer. Its implementations for different platforms are called Java runtime systems. The Java Virtual Machine makes it possible to run the same Java bytecode on any platform. Thus, "write once, run anywhere" is no longer merely a wish of software developers. Java makes it become a reality.

To understand object-oriented programming in Java, we need answer some basic questions: How objects are represented in computer? How methods in objects are invoked? How classes are organized? The questions may have different answers for different object-oriented languages. Here, we answer the questions for the Java language. Particularly, we present the Java object model and discuss the notions of

- *object* supported by Java and how to store data with objects,
- *class* and how objects are created from classes,
- *class inheritance* and how classes are organized into an inheritance hierarchy,

- *interface*, which is used to support multiple inheritance in Java, and
- *polymorphism*, which allows the execution of overriding methods by invoking an overridden abstract method.

Since this is a book on data structures, we shall emphasize data distribution among objects in a program. A Java program for a simplified supermarket can be found at the end of the chapter. Running examples in this chapter extract source code from the program. Classes in the examples can be compiled with the Java compiler into class files. The main methods in the generated class files can run on Java runtimes.

# 1.1 Objects and Classes

## 1.1.1 The Notion of Object

### 1.1.1.1 Real-World Entities

A computer program can create an object to represent a tangible entity or an intangible concept or process in the real world. An entity such as a customer has attributes and behaviors. An abstract concept such as a triangle has properties and formulas. The formulas evaluate the properties. A process such as a chemical reaction has a state. Nature laws and rules dominate the state transition. They describe the behaviors of the chemical reaction. Entities, concepts, and processes in the real world can be represented with objects in object-oriented programs. An object created by a program has fields and methods. The values stored in the fields describe the object's state. The methods prescribe the object behavior.

An object created by a program is a component allocated in a computer memory. It encodes data and information. Specifically, its fields, which are represented with named or indexed variables, store the data and information. For example, a customer object created in a computer can use variables *name*, *address*, *telephone*, *balance*, and *orders* to record the data for a customer. When a Java program creates a customer object, a Java runtime system is responsible for allocating memory space for the variables. Similarly, a triangle object in a computer uses variables to record the values of its properties such as the degrees of its angles and the lengths of its sides. A chemical process object records its state with variables such as *starting_time*, *temperature*, *volume*, and *pressure*.

An object created by an object-oriented program belongs to some class, which defines methods as well as variables for the object. The methods of an object can be invoked to run on the object. Consider an object of class *Customer*, which defines methods *getOrder* and *addOrder*. We assume that an object of class *Order* can be used to keep the data of an order placed by a customer. Method *getOrder*() can be invoked for the customer object to retrieve an order that was placed by the customer. Method *addOrder(Order order)* can be invoked to add an order, represented with the *order* parameter, for the customer. The method may simply insert the order object referenced by parameter *order* into a data structure that keeps order objects for the customer. The method may also increase the balance of the customer according to the order.

### 1.1.1.2 Data and Object

A variable in an object represents a named or indexed field in the object. The terms variable and field are used as synonyms in Java. A variable may hold a primitive value. For instance, the *balance* field in a customer object may hold floating-point value 55.60, which is represented with 55.60*f* in Java with type suffix *f* for *float* value. (Java constants will be discussed in Section 2.1.2.3.)

An object may use a variable to hold a reference to an object as well. The referenced object stores data. By using references, we can distribute related data among objects.

Let us consider the supermarket. A customer object uses a variable named *orders* to reference an array of outstanding orders placed by the customer. The array and orders are objects. Elements in an array are anonymous, indexed variables. Each element in the *orders* array can hold a reference to an order object. An order object uses variable *receiver* to hold a reference to a customer object, which represents a customer who is the receiver of the order in the real world. An order object uses another variable named *items* to hold (the reference to) an array of ordered items. Thus, the data for the supermarket is distributed among objects.

We use Fig. 1.1 to illustrate the objects for the supermarket, which is interested in customers, orders, and the merchandise it sells. We use rounded rectangles to represent objects, and arrows to represent references. Note that the customer objects use a variable named *orders* to hold a reference to an orders array. Each order object uses variable *items* to hold a reference to an array of items. An element of the *items* array references an item, which encapsulates a reference to a type of merchandise and an integer variable named *quantity*. The item object created by the Java application represents an order item line. It stores data about the order item line.

We can retrieve data from an object-oriented program by following references to objects. For example, we can navigate the diagram in Fig. 1.1 to read the information

> John Smith has a balance of $55.60.
> Tom David has an order for two units of cheese and one unit of
> milk to be delivered to himself.

This type of information is crucial for the operation of a supermarket.

Each of the rounded rectangles in Fig. 1.1 represents an object, which can be created with a Java program. Each of the fields in the objects can be filled with a primitive type value such as a float or with a reference to an object such as a string, array, or customer object. Upon completion of this chapter, a reader is expected to be able to create the objects displayed in Fig. 1.1, store the data into the objects, and retrieve the above information from the objects.

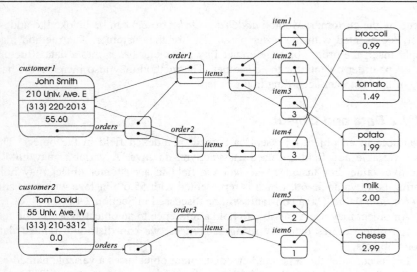

**Fig. 1.1** Storing data in objects for a supermarket

**Exercise 1.1** By following Fig. 1.1, answer the question of how much the supermarket should charge John Smith for the two orders placed by him.

**Exercise 1.2** Suppose the supermarket is also interested in storing the information about its employees in a computer. What fields should an employee object contain, and what names should be used for the fields?

A Java program uses classes to define data representation for objects, one class for each kind of objects. A class declares variables for storing values of primitive types and for holding references to objects. It may also define variables to hold (references to) arrays. In Java, an array is an object with indexed elements. Each element holds a value or a reference. The following example describes a class that can be used to model the customer data shown in Fig. 1.1.

**Example 1.1** In Java, a class is used to describe the data for one kind of objects. The data stored in customer objects can be specified with the following class definition.

```
class Customer {
     String name, address, telephone;
     float balance;
     Order[] orders;
}
```

In the above Java source code, keyword *class* is used to introduce class name *Customer*. The Java standard class *String* is an object type, and *float* is a primitive type. A type may refer to a primitive type such as *float* or a class name such as *Customer*, *Order*, and *String*. In the above Java source code, identifier *Order* represents a class, which will be defined shortly. The declaration

```
Order[] orders;
```

declares variable *orders* with array type *Order*[], which is composed of class name *Order* and brackets []. The variable *orders* can hold a reference to an array of *Order* objects.

In summary of the discussion, the class *Customer* defines five variables – *name, address, telephone, balance,* and *orders.* When an object of the class is created, each of the variables is allocated a slot in the computer memory. We can place a reference to a string into one of the fields *name, address,* and *telephone,* a *float* number into the field *balance,* and a reference to an array into the field *orders.*                                                                                      □

A class in a Java program may define a main method to start a computation. A main method is declared as

*public static void main(String[] args).*

The identifiers *public, static,* and *void* are keywords in Java. The method name *main* is reserved for the main method of a class. The parameter *args* represents the array of command-line arguments, which are encoded in strings. More than one class in a Java program may contain main method, which can be used to test the classes (unit testing).

In the following example, we add a main method into the *Customer* class defined in Example 1.1. In the main method, we apply operator *new* to create a customer object in expression *new Customer().* In Java, assignment operator is =. The following statement in the main method declares a variable named *customer1* with class *Customer,* creates a customer object, and assigns (the reference to) the created object to variable *customer1.*

```
Customer customer1 = new Customer();
```

The Java expression *"The first customer: " + customer1* in the main method applies operator + to concatenate string *"The first customer: "* and a string representation of object *customer1.* The arithmetic addition operator + is overloaded with string concatenation operation in Java.

**Example 1.2** (Continuation of Example 1.1) The following definition of the *Customer* class includes a main method, which declares two local variables, *customer1* and *customer2.* The main method uses the *new* operator to create two *Customer* objects and assigns them to the local variables. Thus, the local variables will hold (references to) customer objects.

```
class Customer {
    String name, address, telephone;
    float balance;
    Order[] orders;
    public static void main(String[] args) {
        Customer customer1 = new Customer();
        Customer customer2 = new Customer();
```

```
customer1.name = "John Smith";
customer1.address="210 Univ. Ave. E";
customer1.telephone="(313) 220-2013";
customer1.balance = 55.60f;
customer1.orders = new Order[5];

System.out.print("The 1st customer: "
                      + customer1 + "\n");
System.out.print(
          "The 1st customer's name: ");
System.out.println(customer1.name);
System.out.print("The 2nd customer: "
                      + customer2 + "\n");
    }
}
```

The main method assigns constants to four fields in object *customer1*. Then, it uses operator *new* to create an array of five elements and assigns the array to variable *orders*. The statement

```
System.out.print("The 1st customer: "
                      + customer1 + "\n");
```

invokes method *print* to print a string on the standard output device, which is represented by expression *System.out*.                              □

In Java, a field in an object occupies at most two words in memory. It is large enough to hold an object reference or a primitive value such as an integer. A reference is similar to an address in memory or a pointer in the C language. But, Java does not support memory address or pointer. An object created with the *new* operator is placed in a heap. The execution of the *new* operator returns a reference to the created object. The reference can be assigned to a named variable such as *customer1* or an element of an array such as *orders*[0]. The expression *orders*[0] represents the first element of array *orders*. It can reference an order object. For simplicity, we say "assign a customer object to variable *customer1*", which really means "place a reference to the customer object into variable *customer1*". We can interpret the sentence "assign an order object to array element *orders*[0]" similarly.

**Exercise 1.3** Add statements into the main method in Example 1.2 to place meaningful values into the fields of object *customer2*.

To compile and run the class *Customer* defined in Example 1.2, we also need class *Order* and other classes that are used by classes *Customer* and *Order*. The following example defines these classes. It presents a complete Java program, which can be compiled and executed.

**Example 1.3** (Continuation of Example 1.2) The following classes model the data shown in Fig. 1.1. They can be used to create the objects illustrated in Fig. 1.1. The Java source code can be placed in a file named *Customer.java*. Then, we can compile the file with the Java compiler and execute the main method of class *Customer* with a Java runtime system. (The source code was tested with Sun's JDK Java compiler and runtime system, which are invoked with command *javac* and *java*, respectively.)

```java
class Customer {
    String name, address, telephone;
    float balance;
    Order[] orders;

    public static void main(String[] args) {
        Customer customer1 = new Customer();
        Customer customer2 = new Customer();

        customer1.name = "John Smith";
        customer1.address="210 Univ. Ave. E";
        customer1.telephone=" (313) 220-2013";
        customer1.balance = 55.60f;
        customer1.orders = new Order[5];

        System.out.print("The 1st customer: "
                             + customer1 + "\n");
        System.out.print(
                  "The 1st customer's name: ");
            System.out.println(customer1.name);
        System.out.print("The 2nd customer: "
                             + customer2 + "\n");
    }
}

class Order {
    Customer receiver;
    Item[] items;
}

class Item {
    Merchandise item;
    int quantity;
}

class Merchandise {
    String name;
    float price;
}
```

□

The above examples show that a variable such as *address* in a class is declared with a type such as *String*. An array type such as *Order*[] is denoted with a type *Order* and a pair of brackets []. A variable declaration does not mean object creation. We can create an object with operator *new* and assign it to a variable so that the variable holds a reference to the created object.

**Exercise 1.4** The main method of class *Customer* in Example 1.3 prints the *name* field stored in object *customer1* on the standard output. Add statements into the method to print the address and telephone number of *customer1*. Also add statements to assign values to the fields in object *customer2* and print the fields.

### 1.1.1.3 Method and Object

The above discussion concentrates on the data stored in objects. An object has behavior. It encapsulates methods to define its behavior. The methods can access and change the data in the object. They can perform operations and computations for the object.

In a program, an object may need to access or change the value stored in a field of another object. Some methods of an object are dedicated to retrieve or reset the data fields of the object. They are called accessers and mutaters, getters and setters, or get and set methods. A programming style advocated by Java is to access and modify fields in an object through the accessers and mutaters of the fields. We can use the methods to restrict access to and protect the integrity of the data stored in the object. Another advantage of the programming style is the possibility of changing the data representation of an object without breaking existing programs that access the data in the object. The following example improves class *Customer* by defining get and set methods in the class.

**Example 1.4** (Continuation of Example 1.3) We now add several methods into the class *Customer* defined in Example 1.3. The methods are dedicated to retrieving and resetting the values of variables. The improved class *Customer* is shown as follows. Most of the accessers simply return the value of an instance field, and mutaters set an instance field with an argument value. The *getOrder* method tests the existence of the *orders* array before it accesses the elements of the array. Method *addOrder* creates the *orders* array if the array does not exist. After the array is created, it is assigned to field *orders* and the field no longer holds *null*. The methods are invoked in the main method of class *Customer*.

```
class Customer {
    String name, address, telephone;
    float balance;
    Order[] orders;
    String getName() { return name; }
    void setName(String name) { this.name = name;}
    String getAddress() { return address; }

    void setAddress(String address) {
        this.address = address;
    }
}
```

```java
String getTelephone() { return telephone; }

void setTelephone(String telephone) {
    this.telephone = telephone;
}

float getBalance() { return balance; }

void setBalance (float balance) {
    this.balance = balance;
}

Order getOrder() {
    if (orders == null) return null;
    Order temp_order;
    for (int i = 0; i < orders.length; i++){
        if (orders[i] != null) {
            temp_order = orders[i];
            orders[i] = null;
            return temp_order;
        }
    }
    return null;
}

boolean addOrder(Order order) {
    if (orders == null) orders = new Order[20];
    for (int i=0; i < orders.length; i++){
        if (orders[i] == null) {
            orders[i] = order;
            return true;
        }
    }
    return false;
}

public static void main(String[] args) {
    Customer customer1 = new Customer();
    Customer customer2 = new Customer();

    customer1.setName("John Smith");
    customer1.setAddress("210 Univ. Ave. E");
    customer1.setTelephone("(313) 220-2013");
    customer1.setBalance(55.60f);
    Order order = new Order();
    order.receiver = customer1;
    customer1.addOrder(order);
```

```
        System.out.print("The 1st customer name: ");
        System.out.println(customer1.getName());
        System.out.print(
                "The order receiver name: ");
        System.out.println(customer1.getOrder().
                        receiver.getName());
        System.out.println("The 2nd customer: " +
                        customer2);
    }
}
```

To execute the main method of the above class, we need classes that are used by the above class. Specifically, we can place the above class and classes *Order*, *Item*, and *Merchandise*, defined in Example 1.3, into file *Customer.java*. The file is a compilation unit, which can be compiled.    □

We have applied several features of the Java language in the above example. The features are explained as follows.

- A Java method declares a return type, a method name and a sequence of parameters, which may be empty. For instance, the *Customer* class uses declaration

```
    boolean addOrder(Order order)
```

to specify the primitive type *boolean* as return type, *addOrder* as method name, and a parameter named *order* for method *addOrder*. If a method does not return any value, keyword *void* is used to specify the return type. The body of a method is a sequence of statements that is enclosed between a pair of curly braces { and }.

- By assigning keyword *null* to a variable, we indicate that the variable references no object, i.e., the variable does not hold a valid reference. We can test whether a variable or an array element, say *orders[i]*, holds a valid object with a comparison expression such as

    *orders[i] == null*,

which evaluates to *true* only if the array element *orders[i]* does not contain a valid object reference.

- In method *setName(String name)*, parameter *name* conflicts with field *name* defined in class *Customer*. The parameter *name* hides (shadows) the field *name* in the body of the method. In the method body, the field defined in class *Customer* is represented with *this.name*, where keyword *this* is used to represent the current object for which the method is invoked. For example, when the method is invoked for *customer1* with statement

```
    customer1.setName("John Smith");
```

the keyword *this* in the *setName* method body represents *customer1*. Thus, the *setName* method sets the *name* field in the *customer1* object with a reference to string *John Smith*.

- We use keyword *return* in a method to terminate an execution of the method. The *return* statement may return a value from the execution.

- In the for loop

```
for (int i = 0; i < orders.length; i++) {
    if (orders[i] == null) {
        orders[i] = order;
        return true;
    }
}
```

we declare a local integer variable *i*, which is visible (available) only in the for loop, and initialize it with 0. The for loop tests condition *i < orders.length*. If the test results in *true*, the loop body and statement *i++* are executed. (Statement *i++* increases local variable *i* by 1.) The process of test and execution is repeated until the loop condition becomes *false*. After the loop, the local variable *i* no longer exists.

The length of an array is fixed when the array is created with operator *new*. In an object of class *Customer*, we use an array named *orders* with 20 elements to store orders. The range of the element indexes in the array is 0, 1, ..., 19. Adding an order object into the non-existing element *orders*[20] will result in a runtime error. A vector is a standard data structure in Java. In Section 4.2, we shall learn that a vector can automatically expand its capacity as objects are added into the vector. We can also shrink a vector so that the vector will not contain empty elements. Adding more objects into a vector never causes overflow problem. You may want to change the representation of field *orders* in customer objects to a vector. The change requires modify the bodies of methods *getOrder* and *addOrder*, but not their signatures. It will not break any program that accesses the *orders* field through methods *getOrder* and *addOrder*.

### 1.1.1.4 Object Analysis

The traditional structured programming approach focuses on the functions of an application. It recognizes procedures and designs algorithms for the procedures. It decomposes the functionality of the procedures in a top-down manner and combines the solutions to subprocedures bottom-up. It uses data structures, which are shared by the procedures and subprocedures, to support the procedures.

Object-oriented analysis is an important phase in object-oriented software development. It emphasizes the data rather than functions that manipulate the data. Object-oriented analysis presents a different way to decompose an application. It looks at the problem-domain entities that are to be maintained in a computer. By identifying nouns mentioned by the users of an application, we can identify some objects to be created by the program.

**Example 1.5** By analyzing a supermarket such as the one described in Fig. 1.1, we can identify the nouns customer, order, and merchandise. Thus, we can find the interesting objects customer, order, and merchandise. These objects correspond to classes *Customer*, *Order*, and *Merchandise*, presented in Example 1.3.

To represent the data for the supermarket in a Java program, we define fields for the objects. For example, to store the information on a customer, we need variables *name, address,* and *telephone.* To support the operation of the supermarket, we also need a float variable to record the balance of a customer and an array of orders to keep the outstanding orders placed by the customer. Therefore, we need variables *balance* and *orders* in a customer object.

After identifying objects and fields for the objects, we can design methods to access and manipulate the data stored in the objects. Methods are responsible for performing operations on the objects. For instance, the method *getOrder* applied for a customer object returns an order placed by the customer. The method *addOrder* can be invoked for a customer object to add an order into the *orders* array referenced by the object.                                ☐

**Exercise 1.5** Assume our supermarket is also interested in storing employee information in a computer. In Exercise 1.2, we designed fields for employee objects. What methods should an employee object have in order to support the operation of the supermarket?

## 1.1.1.5 Design and Implementation

By an object-oriented analysis of an application, we can discover objects and understand interactions between the objects. Then, we design classes for the objects. We need a data representation and a set of methods for each type of object. When designing and implementing an application, we can ask two different questions for each object:

- *what* the object does, and
- *how* the object does it.

Users of the object are interested in what the object can do. They may not care about how the object does it. The first question is important for both the users and the designer of the object class. The designer and programmer of the object must answer the second question as well. They design variables and data structures to store data in the object. They select or design algorithms for processing the data when they implement the class for the object.

In the object-oriented languages C++ and Eiffel, an operation for an object is implemented with a function, a procedure, or a routine, which is called a method in Java. Conceptually, the method is tightly coupled with the object. It is defined in the class of the object. All the objects in the class share the method. The compiled methods of the class are available in the runtime environment. When a method in a class is invoked for an object of the class, the compiled method is executed. For instance, when expression *customer1.setName*("*John Smith*") is evaluated, the method *setName* defined in class *Customer* is executed for object *customer1*. During the execution, keyword *this* in the method body refers to the object for which the method is invoked. In the current case, keyword *this* refers to object *customer1*. Thus, the method sets the *name* filed of *customer1* with a reference to string *John Smith*.

In object-oriented software engineering, the term *contract* has been used to abstract object behaviors. The *signature* of a method consists of the method name and the number and types of parameters of the method. In Java, the contract of an object is described with the signatures of public methods, publicly available fields, and the semantics of the methods and fields as defined in the class of the object.

**Example 1.6** (Continuation of Example 1.4) Class *Customer* can be abstracted with the following method signatures and return types.

```
String getName()
void setName(String name)
String getAddress()
void setAddress(String address)
String getTelephone()
void setTelephone(String telephone)
float getBalance()
void setBalance (float balance)
Order getOrder()
boolean addOrder(Order order)
```

A document can be used to describe the functionality of the methods. We can invoke the methods for a customer object to access and modify variables in the object. We can hide the variables of class *Customer* from the users of the class. □

In Java, a class is the fundamental unit of software. The development of an application includes designing classes for the application. We design the contracts of classes before implementing the classes. The contracts can be used to guide constructing and testing the classes. The design of a class contract is affected by many factors. For example, if many users will reuse a class, the class should be designed with generality and flexibility, and it should be well documented. If a class is only useful for one other class and it is short, it can be embedded in the latter class and its methods can be private. We shall introduce inner classes in Section 2.5, which are useful for data structure design and implementation.

**Exercise 1.6** In Exercise 1.5, you already decided data fields and methods for employee objects. Describe the return types and signatures of the methods.

After designing classes, programmers who construct the classes must ensure appropriate data representation and correct implementation of methods. The programmers select data structures for representing data and choose algorithms for implementing the methods. They also need to understand the complexity of the methods, which measures the time and space required by the methods at runtime. The topic of time and space complexity analysis will be covered in Chapter 6. Standard Java data structure classes will be described in Chapter 4. Common data structures will be introduced in the third part of the book.

The Java language supports in line document, which can be used to describe class, field, and method. An in line document consists of documentation comments. A documentation comment can be placed in the front of a class, a field, or a method in Java source code. It is used to explain the class, the use of the data field, or the functionality of the method. A documentation comment is started with symbol /** and ended with symbol */.

Java provides an automated tool, named *javadoc*, to extract documents from the source code of classes. The generated documents can be viewed with Internet browsers. Cross-references can be placed in a documentation comment. The *javadoc* tool converts cross-references to hyperlinks in the generated documents.

In the following example, we add documentation comments in class *Customer*. For readability, we should avoid cluttering a class with unnecessary comments. For instance, since declarations

```
String telephone;
float balance;
```

are self-explaining, we do not need comments for the variables.

**Example 1.7** (Continuation of Example 1.5) Class *Customer* can be documented as follows. Accessers and mutaters can be used to hide data fields. An object-oriented programming style is to place methods before data fields so that users of the class can see the contract of the class as early as possible. The following presentation of class *Customer* follows the style. It includes a documentation comment for each method.

```
/** Class Customer represents customers for a
 *    supermarket. A customer object keeps the
 *    name, address, telephone number, balance,
 *    and orders placed by the customer.
 *    @author Liwu Li
 *    @see Order, Merchandise
 */
class Customer {
    /** main method: Tests class Customer by
     *    instantiating the class and initializing
     *    data fields for a created object of the
     *    class.
     */
    public static void main(String[] args) {
        Customer customer1 = new Customer();
        Customer customer2 = new Customer();

        customer1.setName("John Smith");
        customer1.setAddress("210 Univ. Ave. E");
        customer1.setTelephone("(313) 220-2013");
        customer1.setBalance(55.60f);
        customer1.orders = new Order[5];

        System.out.println(
                "The 1st customer: " + customer1);
        System.out.print(
                "The 1st customer's name: ");
```

```java
        System.out.println(customer1.getName());
        System.out.println(
                "The 2nd customer: " + customer2);
}

/** Retrieves the name of the customer. */
String getName() { return name; }

/** Sets the name field of the customer
 *   with a string.
 */
void setName(String name) {
    this.name = name;
}

/** Retrieves the address of the customer. */
String getAddress() { return address; }

/** Sets the address field of the customer
 *   with a string.
 */
void setAddress(String address) {
    this.address = address;
}

/** Retrieves the telephone number of the
 *   customer.
 */
String getTelephone() { return telephone; }

/** Sets the telephone field of the customer
 *   with a string.
 */
void setTelephone(String telephone) {
    this.telephone = telephone;
}
/** Retrieves the balance of the customer. */
float getBalance() { return balance; }

/** Sets the balance field of the customer
 *   with a float value.
 */
void setBalance(float balance) {
    this.balance = balance;
}

/** Retrieves an order placed by the
```

```
    *     customer. If no outstanding order
    *     placed by the customer, returns null.
    */
    Order getOrder() {
        if (orders == null) return null;
        Order temp_order;
        for (int i=0; i < orders.length; i++){
            if (orders[i] != null) {
                temp_order = orders[i];
                orders[i] = null;
                return temp_order;
            }
        }
        return null;
    }

    /** Adds a new order for the customer. If
    *     the addition is successful, returns
    *     true; returns false otherwise.
    */
    boolean addOrder(Order order) {
        if (orders == null)
            orders = new Order[20];
        for (int i=0; i < orders.length; i++){
            if (orders[i] == null) {
                orders[i] = order;
                return true;
            }
        }
        return false;
    }

    String name, address, telephone;
    float balance;
    Order[] orders;
}
```

□

**Exercise 1.7** Add accessers and mutaters into classes *Order*, *Item*, and *Merchandise*. Also add documentation comments into the classes. Use Java utility *javadoc* to create documents from the classes.

## 1.1.2 Methods

### 1.1.2.1 Method Invocation

In a Java program, we request an object to perform an operation by invoking a method of the object. In object-oriented programming community, method invocation is called message sending, and the object that is requested to execute the method is called the message receiver or receiving object. In Java, dot notation . is used to connect the receiving object and invoked method name, which is followed by a sequence of arguments. The syntax of method invocation is

$$receivingObject.methodName(arg_1, ..., arg_k)$$

where $k$ may be equal to 0. For instance, we can use expression

```
customer1.getBalance()
```

to invoke method *getBalance* of object *customer1*. The method invocation has an empty argument sequence. The expression returns a *float* value. Note that the dot notation can also be used to qualify a field. For example, we use expression

```
customer1.name
```

in Example 1.3 to denote the *name* field of object *customer1*. The expression is used in statements

```
customer1.name = "John Smith";
System.out.println(customer1.name);
```

to assign or retrieve the field.

As shown in the above examples, a method may return a value of a primitive type or (the reference to) an object of a class. The return type must be declared with the method declaration. If a method does not return any value, use keyword *void* as return type. If a method is declared to return a valid value, which is a primitive value or an object, the method body must use keyword *return* to return a value of the primitive type, an object in the class, or the *null* reference. For example, the following method is in class *Customer* of Example 1.7. The method has return type *boolean*. The method body returns either *true* or *false*.

```
boolean addOrder(Order order) {
    if (orders == null) orders = new Order[20];
    for (int i=0; i < orders.length; i++){
        if (orders[i] == null) {
            orders[i] = order;
            return true;
        }
    }
    return false;
}
```

In an object-oriented program, a method is associated with an object or a class. The body of a method of an object may invoke a method for the same object. In this case, the receiving object is referred to with keyword *this* in the body of the invoking method. We illustrate the use of the specific object reference *this* in the following example.

**Example 1.8** (Continuation of Example 1.7) The method *addOrder* defined in class *Customer* adds an order object into array *orders* encapsulated in a customer object if there is an empty element in the array. We now modify the method with a restriction that a customer cannot place a new order if the customer has a balance over $1000. The modified method is shown in the following. It invokes method *getBalance* of *this* object to retrieve the balance of the current object. The *float* value returned by method *getBalance* is used to decide whether an order object, referenced with parameter *order*, can be added to the *orders* array.

```
/** Adds a new order for the customer if the
 *    customer owes a balance less than $1000. If
 *    the addition is successful, returns true;
 *    otherwise returns false.
 */
boolean addOrder(Order order) {
    if (this.getBalance() >= 1000) return false;
    if (this.orders == null)
        this.orders = new Order[20];
    for (int i=0; i < orders.length; i++){
        if (orders[i] == null) {
            orders[i] = order;
            return true;
        }
    }
    return false;
}
```

In a method body, the receiving object referenced by *this* is often omitted. For instance, we can replace the first conditional statement in the above method with statement

```
if (getBalance() >= 1000) return false;
```

□

In the above example, we use the special reference *this* for the receiving object of a method invocation. The keyword *this* can be omitted from an expression if *this* denotes the receiving object of a method invocation. It may be used as the argument of a method invocation as well. It cannot be omitted if it is used as a method argument.

In Java, a method can return a primitive value or an object reference. For a method to evaluate multiple values and return them, we can define a class to encapsulate the values. The method can create an object of the class, place computed values into the object, and return the object. Another approach to returning multiple values is to create an array, use the array elements to hold the multiple values, and return the array. A method that returns an array can be found in Example 1.10.

### 1.1.2.2 Method Overloading

In a Java class, several methods may share the same name, and the method name is *overloaded*. Methods that share the same name must differ in the numbers and/or types of parameters. The feature of Java is known as *method overloading*. The different methods with the same name in a class can implement different operations.

**Example 1.9** (Continuation of Example 1.8) In class *Customer* defined in Example 1.8, we use method *getOrder*() to retrieve an order object from the *orders* array in a customer object. The customer who should receive an order may not be the same as the customer who placed the order. We introduce two new methods into class *Customer* to retrieve an order that will be received by a specified customer. The three methods that overload the *getOrder* method name are shown as follows.

```
/** Retrieves an order placed by the customer.
 *    If no outstanding order placed by the
 *    customer, returns null.
 */
Order getOrder() {
    if (orders == null) return null;
    Order temp_order;
    for (int i=0; i < orders.length; i++){
        if (orders[i] != null) {
            temp_order = orders[i];
            orders[i] = null;
            return temp_order;
        }
    }
    return null;
}


/** Retrieves an order to be received by a
 *    named customer. If no such an order,
 *    returns null.
 */
Order getOrder(String name) {
    if (orders == null) return null;
    Order temp_order;
    for (int i=0; i < orders.length; i++){
        if (orders[i] != null &&
            orders[i].receiver.name.equals(name)){
            temp_order = orders[i];
            orders[i] = null;
            return temp_order;
        }
    }
```

```
        return null;
    }

    /** Retrieves an order to be received by a
     *    specified customer. If no such an order,
     *    returns null.
     */
    Order getOrder(Customer receiver) {
        if (orders == null) return null;
        Order temp_order;
        for (int i=0; i < orders.length; i++){
            if (orders[i] != null &&
                orders[i].receiver == receiver) {
                temp_order = orders[i];
                orders[i] = null;
                return temp_order;
            }
        }
        return null;
    }
```

The first *getOrder* method returns an order that was placed by the current customer. The second *getOrder* method returns an order that will be delivered to a customer with a given name. It uses expression *orders[i].receiver.name. equals(name)* to compare the *name* field of a customer object with argument *name*. The third *getOrder* method returns an order to be delivered to a given customer. It uses expression *orders[i].receiver == receiver* to compare the receiver of an order with the argument *receiver*.                                □

Each pair of overloading methods with the same name in a class must be different in the number and/or types of their parameters. They cannot differ only by their return types. For example, we cannot have two methods declared as

> *Order getOrder(String name)*
> *Order[] getOrder(String name)*

in a class since they differ only in return type. The following example shows how to retrieve orders that will be delivered to a customer.

**Example 1.10** (Continuation of Example 1.9) We expand class *Customer* described in Example 1.9 with the following methods, which retrieve the orders that are to be delivered to a named or specified customer. The methods overload method name *getOrders*.

```
    /** Retrieves orders to be received by a named
     *    customer.
     */
    Order[] getOrders(String name) {
        if (orders == null) return null;
        Order[] temp_orders =
                        new Order[orders.length];
```

```
        int j = 0;
        for (int i = 0; i < orders.length; i++)
        if (orders[i] != null &&
                orders[i].receiver.name.equals(name))
            temp_orders[j++] = orders[i];
        Order[] orders = new Order[j];
        for (int i = 0; i < j; i++)
            orders[i] = temp_orders[i];
        return orders;
    }

    /** Retrieves orders to be received by a customer
    */
    Order[] getOrders(Customer receiver) {
        if (orders == null) return null;
        Order[] temp_orders =
                        new Order[orders.length];
        int j = 0;
        for (int i=0; i < orders.length; i++)
        if (orders[i] != null     &&
                orders[i].receiver == receiver)
            temp_orders[j++] = orders[i];
        Order[] orders = new Order[j];
        for (int i = 0; i < j; i++)
            orders[i] = temp_orders[i];
        return orders;
    }
```

□

## 1.1.2.3 Parameter Passing

Parameters of Java methods are call-by-value parameters, or simply value parameters. When an invoked method is executed, a local variable is created for each parameter of the method. Before the method is executed, the parameter variable is initialized with the value of the actual argument. Specifically, if the actual argument is of a reference type, the parameter variable is initialized with the argument reference. Thus, the actual argument and the parameter variable reference the same object. In the method body, we can access and modify the referenced object through the parameter variable. Changing the parameter variable in the method body does not change the value of the actual argument. There is a similar relationship between a parameter variable and an actual argument of a primitive type.

The following example illustrates the argument passing mechanism of Java. It changes a parameter variable named *order* in a method body. The change to the parameter has no effect on the value of the argument variable used by the invoking method.

**Example 1.11** (Continuation of Example 1.4) Let us modify method *addOrder* (*Order order*) defined in class *Customer* in Example 1.4. The modified method checks if the *receiver* field of an argument order holds the *null* reference. If the field holds *null*, the field is set with the reference to the current customer. The method supports the common-sense rule that if a customer places an order but does not mention a different receiver for the order, the customer should be the receiver of the order.

In the modified *addOrder* method, we reset parameter *order* with *null* after its value is placed in array *orders*.

```
/** Adds an order for the customer. If the order
 *    does not have a receiver, sets the receiver
 *    with the customer.
 */
boolean addOrder(Order order) {
    if (order.receiver == null)
        order.receiver = this;
    if (orders == null) orders = new Order[20];
    for (int i = 0; i < orders.length; i++) {
        if (orders[i] == null) {
            orders[i] = order;
            order = null;
            return true;
        }
    }
    order = null; return false;
}
```

We now use a main method, presented below, to testify the Java argument passing mechanism. Since parameter *order* in method *addOrder* is implemented with a local variable, which is not the actual argument, an execution of the statement

```
order = null;
```

in the above method body does not affect the value of argument *order1* for method invocation *addOrder*(*order1*). Therefore, the main method prints

     *The receiver of order1 is John Smith*

In other words, after the execution of invoked method *addOrder*(*order1*), local variable *order1* still holds its initial value, which is a valid reference to an order object.

```
public static void main(String[] args) {
    Customer customer1 = new Customer();
    customer1.name = "John Smith";
    Order order1 = new Order();
    customer1.addOrder(order1);
    System.out.print("The receiver of order1 is "
                        + order1.receiver.name);
}
```

After adding the above *addOrder* and *main* methods into class *Customer* presented in Example 1.4, one can compile class *Customer* and run the main method.                                                                                □

## 1.1.3 Objects and Classes

Each object in a Java program is an instance of a class. It is created by instantiating the class. A class represents a kind of objects that have the same data representation and perform the same set of methods. The objects are the instances of the class. Conceptually, a class such as *Customer* or *Employee* represents a group of real-world entities.

A *value* is either a primitive type value or an object of a class. For example, an *int*, *float*, *char*, or *boolean* value is a primitive (type) value, an instance of class *Customer* or *Employee* is an object. In the above examples, we see that a customer object can be created with expression *new Customer()*.

Arrays are objects. An array is created with the *new* operator, a primitive type or a class name, and an integer length. For instance, expression *new int*[20] creates an array with 20 elements and returns a reference to the created array. The created array is allocated in the memory. The allocated space also contains a field named *length*, which is initialized with 20. The reference to the created array can be assigned to a variable. For instance, statements

```
int[] integers = new int[20];
Object integers1 = new int[20];
```

declare variables *integers* and *integers1* with types *int*[] and *Object*, respectively. The statements create array objects and assign the created arrays to the variables. The type of both arrays is *int*[]. Since an array is an object, it can be assigned to variable *integers1* declared with class *Object*. The following statement declares an array variable of type *Customer*[], creates an array, and assigns the array to the variable.

```
Customer[] customers = new Customer[15];
```

After the statement is executed, variable *customers* holds the reference to an array of 15 elements, each of which can hold (a reference to) a customer object.

We can apply method *instanceof* to test if an object is an instance of a class. For example, the following code prints message *The customers array is an instance of type Customer*[].

```
Customer[] customers = new Customer[15];
if (customers instanceof Customer[])
        System.out.println("The customers array is"
        + " an instance of type Customer[]");
```

We regard a class as a representation of its instances. A class provides a *protocol* of public methods and public variables for its instances. Other objects interact with the instances of the class through the public methods and variables in the protocol.

**Exercise 1.8** Design and implement methods for the classes *Order*, *Item*, and
   *Merchandise*, which are presented in Example 1.4. Test each of the classes
   with a main method.

# 1.2 Classes

## 1.2.1 Members of Classes

### 1.2.1.1 Instance Field and Class Field

A class in a Java program defines fields and methods, which are called *members*
of the class. In the above examples, class *Customer* declares fields to store information on customers. The field declarations do not include the modifier *static*.
The fields are called non-static fields, non-static variables, instance fields, or instance variables.

   When an instance of a class is created, each instance variable of the class is
incarnated once. The instance field in the created object is used to hold a specific
value for the object. For example, variables *name*, *address*, *telephone*, *balance*,
and *orders* are instance variables of class *Customer*. As shown in Fig. 1.1, a customer object uses the instance fields to hold particular values for a customer.

   In addition to instance fields, which are encapsulated in objects, a class may
have properties relevant to the class. We can define class-level fields, which are
called class fields or class variables, in the class. Since Java uses keyword *static* to
specify class fields, class fields are also called static fields or static variables. For
instance, the average salary attribute is a property of all employees. We can define
static field *averageSalary* in class *Employee* to keep the value of average salary.

   In the following example, we add a static field named *allCustomers* in class
*Customer*. Class *Vector* is a standard Java data structure class, which will be discussed in Section 4.2. The class field *allCustomers* references a vector, which can
hold the customer objects that have been created.

**Example 1.12** (Continuation of Example 1.1) We now add a static variable named
   *allCustomers* into class *Customer* presented in Example 1.1. The class variable is declared with class *Vector*. The following code imports class *Vector*
   from package *java.util*, declares static variable *allCustomers*, creates a vector,
   and assigns the created vector to the static variable.

```
import java.util.Vector;
class Customer {
    String name, address, telephone;
    float balance; Order[] orders;
    static Vector allCustomers = new Vector();
}
```

□

The existence of a static field in a class does not depend on the existence of objects of the class. Even when no instance of the class has been created, the static field exists and it stores a value, default or explicitly assigned. For instance, when no employee object exists, the value of class variable *averageSalary* of class *Employee* should be equal to 0. When a class is loaded by a Java runtime system, class fields defined in the class are initialized with default values. For example, the default value of static field *allCustomers* is *null*, which indicates no vector has been assigned to the field. Then, the assignment statement in class *Customer* in Example 1.12 is evaluated to create a vector, which is assigned to the static field.

### 1.2.1.2 Instance Method and Class Method

A class may define methods to perform computation for the class. For example, accessing or modifying the static field *allCustomers* is a responsibility of class *Customer*. The accesser and mutater of static field *allCustomers* are class methods. A class method is specified with keyword *static*. It is also called a static method. A method that is not declared with keyword *static* is an instance method or a non-static method.

In the following example, we define static methods for adding and removing customer objects for static field *allCustomers* in class *Customer*.

**Example 1.13** (Continuation of Example 1.12) We add two class methods into the class *Customer* presented in Example 1.12. Class method *addCustomer* (*Customer customer*) adds an object referenced by parameter *customer* into the data structure referenced by class variable *allCustomers*. Class method *removeCustomer*(*String name*) removes a customer object that has a specified name from the data structure. These methods are declared with keyword *static*.

```
import java.util.*;
class Customer {
    String name, address, telephone;
    float balance;
    Order[] orders;
    static Vector allCustomers = new Vector();

    /** Adds a new customer object into
     *     allCustomers.
     */
    static void addCustomer(Customer customer){
        allCustomers.addElement(customer);
    }

    /** Removes a named customer object from
     *     allCustomers.
     */
    static Customer removeCustomer(String name) {
```

```
        Customer customer;
        Enumeration total=allCustomers.elements();
        while (total.hasMoreElements()) {
            customer =(Customer)total.nextElement();
            if (customer.name.equals(name)){
                allCustomers.removeElement(customer);
            return customer;
            }
        }
        return null;
    }
}
```

&#9633;

The source code in Example 1.13 contains the import statement

```
import java.util.*;
```

and class *Customer*. The statement uses character * to denote all the class names defined in package *java.util*. The keyword *import* means introducing the names defined in package *java.util* to the current compilation unit, which contains the import statement. Thus, we can use a simple name of a class such as *Vector* rather than a qualified name *java.unit.Vector* in the compilation unit.

Class *Vector* defines instance method *elements*(), which returns an enumeration of elements in a vector. The method *hasMoreElements*() of an enumeration tests if any more elements are left in the enumeration. If the test returns *true*, method *nextElement*() can be used to enumerate the next element from the enumeration. By repeatedly applying methods *hasMoreElements* and *nextElement* for the enumeration, we can enumerate all the elements in the vector.

**Exercise 1.9** Define a class *Employee* that consists of instance fields and two class fields. One of the instance fields is named *salary*. Class field *allEmployees* is of type *Vector*, and class field *averageSalary* is of *float*. In the main method of class *Employee*, create several employee objects and add the employee objects into the *allEmployees* vector. Each time an employee is created, initialize the *salary* field of the object with a float and update the *averageSalary* class variable.

In the above example, we use the statement

```
static Vector allCustomers = new Vector();
```

to declare static field *allCustomers*, create a vector, and initialize the static field with the created vector. A class may have one or several static initialization blocks, which are executed in sequence when a Java runtime system loads the class. A static initialization block uses keyword *static* to introduce a sequence of statements, which is enclosed between a pair of curly braces. Static initialization blocks can be used to initialize static fields in the class. We use the following example to illustrate static block.

**Example 1.14** (Continuation of Example 1.13) The definition of class *Customer* in Example 1.13 is equivalent to the following definition. In Example 1.13, we use an initialization clause in the declaration of static variable *allCustomers*. Here, we use a static block to initialize the static variable.

```java
import java.util.*;
class Customer {
    String name, address, telephone;
    float balance;
    Order[] orders;
    static Vector allCustomers;
    static { allCustomers = new Vector(); }

    /** Adds a new customer object into
     *    allCustomers.
     */
    static void addCustomer(Customer customer){
        allCustomers.addElement(customer);
    }

    /** Removes a named customer object from
     *    allCustomers.
     */
    static Customer removeCustomer(String name) {
        Customer customer;
        Enumeration total =allCustomers.elements();
        while (total.hasMoreElements()) {
            customer= (Customer)total.nextElement();
            if (customer.name == name) {
                allCustomers.removeElement(customer);
                return customer;
            }
        }
        return null;
    }
}
```

□

**Exercise 1.10** Add a static method *numberOfCustomers*() into class *Customer* defined in Example 1.14. The method returns the total number of customer objects that are kept in vector *allCustomers*. (Hint: invoke method *size*() for the vector to return the number of objects stored in the vector)

## 1.2.2 Object Creation

### 1.2.2.1 Constructors

A class may define constructors to initialize newly created instances of the class. Constructors are not methods. They are used for initializing instance fields of newly created objects. A constructor of a class has the same name as the class. It has a parameter list, which may be empty. It introduces a sequence of statements, enclosed between a pair of braces, as its body. A constructor body may be empty. A constructor does not return any value. Its body may use a return statement to terminate its computation.

When a Java runtime system creates an instance of a class, it automatically initializes the instance fields of the new object with default values. Then, a constructor of the class is invoked for the new object. If a class definition does not contain any constructor, the Java compiler provides a default constructor, which has no parameter and which does nothing. For instance, an execution of the expression *new Customer()* in the main method in Example 1.3 will invoke the default, no-argument constructor of class *Customer*.

A class may define several constructors, which have different signatures. The following example presents multiple constructors for class *Customer*. The Java compiler uses the number and types of actual arguments of a constructor invocation to decide which constructor of the class to execute.

In the beginning of a constructor body, we can use an expression like *this(argumentList)* to invoke a constructor defined in the same class. The Java compiler uses the number and types of the arguments in the argument list to decide a constructor to execute. The following example shows how to invoke constructor to avoid repeated code.

**Example 1.15** (Continuation of Example 1.13) We now add several constructors into class *Customer* defined in Example 1.13. The first constructor has no argument. It does nothing with an empty body. The next two constructors use arguments to initialize instance fields in a newly created object. The third constructor invokes the second with expression *this(name, address, telephone)*.

```
import java.util.*;
class Customer {
    String name, address, telephone;
    float balance;
    Order[] orders;
    static Vector allCustomers = new Vector();

    Customer() { }
    Customer(String name, String address,
                        String telephone) {
        this.name = name;
        this.address = address;
```

```
            this.telephone = telephone;
    }

    Customer(String name, String address,
                String telephone, float balance) {
        this(name, address, telephone);
        this.balance = balance;
    }

    /** Adds a new customer object into
    *   allCustomers
    */
    static void addCustomer(Customer customer){
        allCustomers.addElement(customer);
    }

    /** Removes a named customer object from
    *   the total collection
    */
    static Customer removeCustomer(String name) {
        Customer customer;
        Enumeration total= allCustomers.elements();
        while (total.hasMoreElements()) {
            customer =(Customer)total.nextElement();
            if (customer.name == name) {
                allCustomers.removeElement(customer);
                return customer;
            }
        }
        return null;
    }

    static public void main(String[] args) {
        Customer customer = new Customer(
                "John Smith", "Windsor, Ontario",
                "555-2341", 100f);
        System.out.println(customer.name);
    }
}
```

☐

## 1.2.2.2 Constructor Invocation

To create an object of a class, we apply the *new* operator and invoke a constructor
of the class. The invoked constructor may be the default constructor, which has no
argument. For example, in the main method of class *Customer* in Example 1.3, we

invoke the default constructor of class *Customer* in the initialization clause of the statement

```
Customer customer1 = new Customer();
```

which applies operator *new* to create a new customer object and invokes the default no-argument constructor *Customer()* for the created customer object. Another example of using constructor is the statement

```
static Vector allCustomers = new Vector();
```

in class *Customer* in Example 1.15. The no-argument constructor *Vector()* of class *Vector* is invoked for a created vector object. In the same example, the expression

```
new Customer("John Smith", "Windsor, Ontario",
                         "555-2341", 100f)
```

invokes a constructor in class *Customer* to initialize four instance fields for the created customer object.

In C++, a constructor can be invoked like an ordinary function. In Java, we cannot invoke a constructor to perform something other than initializing a newly created object. For example, the last two constructors of class *Customer* in Example 1.15 set instance fields with actual arguments. They cannot be invoked to reset the instance fields in an existing customer object. In the following exercise, we define methods that can reset fields in customer objects.

**Exercise 1.11** Add two instance methods that have signatures

```
    reset(String name, String address,
               String telephone)
    reset(String name, String address,
               String telephone, float balance)
```

into class *Customer* in Example 1.15. The methods reset instance fields of customer objects with given argument values.

Java classes do not support destructor, which can be used by a C++ class to release resources seized by an object before the memory space of the object is reclaimed by a computer. A Java runtime system has a garbage collection mechanism, which claims objects that are not referenced by any object in the active methods. The garbage collection is automatically started when more memory is needed by the Java runtime system.

# 1.3 Class Inheritance

## 1.3.1 Java Subclassing Mechanism

One of the major features of object orientation is *class inheritance*, or simply inheritance, which enables a new class to inherit the variables and methods defined in an existing class. Class inheritance is implemented by a subclassing mechanism supported by the Java compiler. Different object-oriented programming languages support different subclassing mechanisms, which imply different levels of complexity and flexibility. The subclassing mechanism of Java has some novel features.

Java supports *single* inheritance only; i.e., each class has at most one direct superclass. As a matter of fact, only the predefined class *Object* in Java has no superclass. Each other class in a Java program has exactly one (direct) superclass. Single inheritance means a class can directly inherit only one class. In Java and other object-oriented programming languages, inheritance is transitive; i.e., a class may inherit inherited variables and inherited methods from a class.

The single-inheritance feature of Java may not be as flexible or powerful as a multiple-inheritance mechanism, which is supported by C++. For example, we may need a class called *EmployeeCustomer* for our supermarket to record information on a person who is an employee as well as a customer of the supermarket. In a language that supports multiple-inheritance, we can let the new class *EmployeeCustomer* inherit both classes *Employee* and *Customer*. In Java, a new class such as *EmployeeCustomer* can specify only one class, either *Employee* or *Customer* but not both, to inherit.

In Java, *class Object* provides the common behavior for all objects. Every class inherits class *Object* directly or indirectly. Class *Object* is the universal type for all objects. A variable that is declared with class *Object* may reference any object of any class. It can hold a reference to an array as well. The elements of an array declared with *Object*[] are regarded as unnamed, indexed variables of type *Object*. They can hold arrays or objects of any classes.

The direct inheritance relationship between a pair of classes is specified with keyword *extends*. When a class inherits another class, we say that the former class extends the latter, the former is called a *subclass* of the latter, and the latter the (direct) *superclass* of the former. The keyword *extends* is used in the subclass definition to introduce the direct superclass name. Assume class *Person*, which describes persons, and a subclass named *Employee* of class *Person*. The inheritance relationship between classes *Person* and *Employee* is declared in class *Employee* with an *extends* clause

```
class Employee extends Person
```

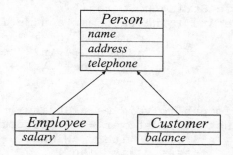

**Fig. 1.2** A class inheritance hierarchy

Similarly, we can let class *Customer* to extend class *Person*. The inheritance relationships are shown in Fig. 1.2, where instance variable names are also displayed.

We now implement the classes illustrated in Fig. 1.2 in Java. In the following example, classes *Employee* and *Customer* extend class *Person*. Thus, the instance variables defined in class *Person* are inherited by classes *Employee* and *Customer*.

A class may override an inherited method by defining a method with the same signature as the inherited method. When the method is invoked for the class or instance of the class, the overriding method will be executed.

**Example 1.16** The following three classes imply the inheritance hierarchy shown in Fig. 1.2. By default, class *Person* inherits class *Object*. Class *Customer* inherits instance fields *name*, *address*, and *telephone* from class *Person*. A constructor of class *Customer* initializes the instance fields. The constructor is tested with a main method in class *Customer*.

```java
class Person {
    String name, address, telephone;
}

class Employee extends Person {
    float salary;
}

class Customer extends Person {
    float balance;

    Customer(String name, String address,
             String telephone, float balance) {
        this.name = name; this.address = address;
        this.telephone = telephone;
        this.balance = balance;
    }

    public String toString() {
        return ("The customer's name is " +
                name + ",\n" + "address is " +
                address +",\n"+"telephone is "+
                telephone+",\n" +"balance is "+
                balance + ".");
    }
    static public void main(String[] args) {
        Customer customer = new Customer(
            "John Smith", "Windsor, Ontario",
            "555-2341", 100f);
        System.out.println(customer);
    }
}
```

In addition to the instance variables *name, address,* and *telephone* inherited from class *Person,* class *Customer* defines instance variable *balance,* a constructor, and two methods. The method *toString* concatenates values in the instance fields of a customer object. After placing the three classes in three separate files and compiling class *Customer,* we can execute the main method of class *Customer,* which displays

> *The customer's name is John Smith,*
> *address is Windsor, Ontario,*
> *telephone is 555-2341,*
> *balance is 100.0.*

When method *println(customer)* is invoked for object *System.out* with argument *customer,* it invokes the *toString* method for the object *customer* to create a string, which is displayed by the *println* method. Class *Object* defines method *toString().* Class *Customer* inherits the *toString* method from its superclass *Person,* which inherits *Object.* But, class *Customer* redefines the method to override the inherited one. □

**Exercise 1.12** Delete method *toString()* from class *Customer* presented in Example 1.16. Then, compile the class and run the main method of the class. (Note: This time, the *toString* method defined in class *Object* is invoked for argument *customer* in expression *println(customer).*)

By suing inheritance relationships, classes in a Java program form a tree structure, which is called a class inheritance hierarchy or simply an inheritance hierarchy. The hierarchy is rooted at class *Object.* When a class is compiled, its superclass is compiled automatically if the superclass has not been compiled yet. A class that is being compiled may use other classes to declare variables, return types, and parameters. For example, class *Customer* in Example 1.15 uses class *Order* to declare instance variable *orders* in statement

```
Order[] orders;
```

The used classes will be searched for and compiled automatically by the Java compiler. The Java library includes compiled standard classes such as *Object* and *String.* The library classes will not be compiled again when they are used in a Java program.

## 1.3.2 Access Control

### 1.3.2.1 Packages

Java classes are organized into packages. A large software system in Java can be divided into subsystems. Each subsystem provides specific functionality and is implemented with a package. Packages can be used to avoid class name clashes. Two packages can use the same name for two different classes. A class can be used to define subclasses and declare variables, return types, and parameters. It can be used to create objects. A class or a member of a class in a package may not be accessed from another package. The programmer of a package can control the accessibility of the software in the package.

A class in a package is accessible from another package only if the class is specified with the access modifier *public*, which is a keyword in Java. For example, a public class in a package can be imported into another package. Then, we can use the imported class name in the importing package to declare variables, create objects, declare return and parameter types for methods. Note that in the above examples, we have not used access modifier for any class. The classes in the above examples can be accessed only by code in the same package. In the following example, we add modifier *public* to the classes *Employee* and *Customer* so that the two classes can be used outside the package that contains the classes.

A Java compilation unit, which is a file with file name suffix *java*, may contain at most one public class and several classes that are not public. When a compilation unit is compiled, the Java compiler generates a file with suffix *class* for each of the classes contained in the compilation unit. In the following example, we place class *Person* and public class *Employee* in one file, and public class *Customer* in another file. After compiling both files, we have three class files.

A package constructed by a programmer consists of one or more compilation units. In a compilation unit, we declare the package name with keyword *package*. The package declaration must be in the very beginning of the file. It indicates that the classes and other software elements in the compilation unit belong to the named package.

A package may be a subpackage of another package. The name of a subpackage is qualified with the containing package name. For example, the subpackage *java.lang* is in package *java*. A package name in a package declaration may be a simple identifier such as *person* or qualified with package names such as *java.lang*.

A compilation unit in a subpackage declares the fully qualified subpackage name, which includes containing package names. For example, the subpackage *transaction* of package *supermarket* can be declared with

```
package supermarket.transaction;
```

in the beginning of the compilation units that belong to subpackage *transaction*.

A Java runtime system supports an unnamed package. When a compilation unit that does not declare any package name is compiled, the Java compiler places the generated class files into an unnamed package. In the above examples, class files are placed in unnamed packages.

A host machine may support multiple unnamed packages. Due to the possible interaction between public classes in the unnamed packages and between unnamed and named packages, it is recommended that classes should be placed in named packages unless a program is small or a project is in the beginning stage.

Packages are organized in directories in a host file system. The Java interpreter searches the directories specified with environment variable *classpath* for a class file. To place a package in a directory, create a subdirectory with the name of the package in the directory, place the compiled class files of the package into the subdirectory. You may insert the path name of the directory to environment variable *classpath*.

Java standard class files are compacted into a compressed file for efficiency. The compressed file includes the class files of package *java.lang*, which are automatically imported to any Java compilation unit by the Java compiler, and that of package *java.util*. The full names of classes in package *java.util* must be imported to a compilation unit before the compilation unit can use the class names, which are not qualified with package names.

**Example 1.17** We now present two compilation units, one contains classes *Employee* and *Person*, the other contains *Customer*. The compilation units are contained in a directory. The classes *Employee* and *Customer* are specified with access modifier *public*. Both compilation units declare package *person*. Therefore, all the three classes belong to package *person*. Before compiling class *Customer* and running the main method of the class, the class files *Person.class* and *Employee.class* should be placed into a subdirectory named with *person* in the current directory.

The contents of the first compilation unit are

```
package person;
public class Employee extends Person {
    float salary;
    Employee(String name, String address,
             String telephone, float salary) {
        this.name = name;
        this.address = address;
        this.telephone = telephone;
        this.salary = salary;
    }

    public String toString() {
        return ("The employee's name is " +
                name + ",\n" + "address is " +
                address + ",\n" + "telephone is "+
                telephone + ",\n" +"salary is " +
                salary + ".");
    }
}

class Person {
    String name, address, telephone;
}
```

The contents of the second compilation unit are

```
package person;
public class Customer extends Person {
    float balance;
    Customer(String name, String address,
```

```
                         String telephone, float balance) {
        this.name = name;
        this.address = address;
        this.telephone = telephone;
        this.balance = balance;
    }

    public String toString() {
        return ("The customer's name is " +
                name + ",\n" + "address is " +
                address +",\n"+"telephone is "+
                telephone +",\n"+"balance is "+
                balance + ".");
    }

    static public void main(String[] args) {
        Employee employee = new Employee(
                "John Smith", "Windsor, Ontario",
                "555-2341", 40000f);
        System.out.println(employee);
    }
}
```

The Java compiler generates class files *Person.class*, *Employee.class*, and *Customer.class* from the above two files. Since both classes *Employee* and *Customer* are in the same package, class *Employee* can be used to declare variable *employee* and create an object in the main method of class *Customer*. The expression *println(employee)* in the main method invokes the *toString* method defined in class *Employee* for the *employee* argument.      □

## 1.3.2.2 Access Modifiers

A class in a compilation unit can be declared with the *public* access modifier. A public class can be used outside its containing package as a superclass, a variable type, a return type, or a parameter type. The fully qualified class name should be used outside its containing package unless the class has been imported into a package that uses the class. If a class is not declared as *public*, it has the default access mode and it can be accessed only in the package that contains the class.

A method or field in a class can be declared with one of three access modifiers – *public*, *protected*, and *private*. The implication of the modifiers is described as follows.

1. *public*: A public field or method is accessible wherever the class is accessible. For example, a public instance variable of an object can be reset and a public instance method can be invoked where the class of the object can be used. A public field or method is inherited by a subclass as a public field or method in the subclass.

2. *protected*: A protected field or method of a class is inherited by subclasses of the class as protected. It is accessible from subclasses, which may not be in the same package, and from the code in the same package.

3. *private*: A private field or method of a class is accessible only from the code in the same class.

In addition to the public, protected, and private access modes, there is a default access mode for members of a class. If no access modifier is used for a variable or method in a class, the variable or method can be used only in the classes in the same package, and the member has a *package access* mode.

Constructors are not methods. A constructor also has an access mode. It may be declared with *public* or *private*.

**Exercise 1.13** Add appropriate access modifiers for the classes and their members in Example 1.3. Compile and run the main method defined in class *Customer*. (A main method in a class must be declared with keywords *public* and *static* and with signature *main(String[])*.)

### 1.3.2.3 final *Classes and Methods*

We can declare a class with keyword *final* to prevent other classes to extend it. For example, the Java standard class *String* in package *java.lang* is a final class. No other class can extend it. Class *String* cannot have a subclass.

In a subclass of a class, we may define a method with the same signature as an inherited method. The new method overrides the inherited one. For example, the class *Person* in Example 1.17 inherits method *toString* from its superclass *Object*. Subclass *Employee* of class *Person* overrides the inherited method with a new definition. The overriding method concatenates field values into a string, which is returned by the method.

We may prevent subclasses of a class from overriding a method of the class by using keyword *final* for the method. A final method of a class cannot be overridden by subclasses of the class.

## 1.3.3 Abstract Method, Abstract Class, and Interface

### 1.3.3.1 Abstract Method and Abstract Class

In the above examples, each method has a body. A method is *abstract* if it does not have a body, i.e., if it does not have a sequence of statements that is enclosed between a pair of curly braces. A class as well as a method may be declared abstract. If a class contains an abstract method, the class must be declared as abstract.

An abstract class can be used to represent a generic notion or a general kind of entities in the real world. For example, we may use an abstract class to represent the generic concept employee. Payments for different types of employee are calculated with different formulas. A manager has an annual salary, a salesperson may be paid by the hour. The *Employee* class may specify an abstract instance method named *getSalary*(), which will be implemented in the subclasses of class *Employee*.

The format of an abstract method declaration is

*modifiers* **abstract** *returnType methodName(parameterList)*;

where *abstract* is a keyword of Java. The modifiers may include access modifier *public* or *protected* and other keywords such as *synchronized*. An abstract class is declared with keyword *abstract*. The following example presents an abstract class and an abstract method.

**Example 1.18** We now present three classes – abstract class *Employee* and its subclasses *Manager* and *SalesPerson*. Class *Employee* defines abstract instance method *getSalary*(), which is implemented in the subclasses.

The following compilation unit in file *Employee.java* contains classes *Employee* and *Person*.

```
package employee;
/** Abstract class Employee. Its subclasses
*    implement abstract method getSalary().
*/
public abstract class Employee extends Person {
    public abstract float getSalary();
}
class Person {
    String name, address, telephone;
}
```

The next compilation unit in file *Manager.java* contains class *Manager*.

```
package employee;
/** Class Manager extends Employee and
*    implements method getSalary().
*/
public class Manager extends Employee {
    float annualSalary;
    public float getSalary() {
        return annualSalary;
    }
}
```

The last compilation unit is in file *SalesPerson.java*. It contains class *SalesPerson*. It uses some comments, introduced with symbol //, to describe source code. The Java compiler will ignore comments.

```
package employee;
/** Class SalesPerson extends Employee
*    and implements method getSalary().
*/
public class SalesPerson extends Employee {
```

```
float hourRate;
//number of working hours per week
int hours;

SalesPerson () {
   hourRate = 12f; hours = 38;
}

public float getSalary() {
   // assume 50 working weeks per year
   return hourRate * hours * 50;
}

public String toString () {
  return ("The sales person's name is "+
          name +",\n" + "address is " +
          address + ",\n" + "telephone is " +
          telephone + ",\n" + "salary is " +
          getSalary() + ".");
}

static public void main(String[] args) {
   SalesPerson sperson = new SalesPerson();
   sperson.name = "John Smith";
   // part-time employee
   sperson.hours = 24;
   System.out.println(sperson);
}
}
```

The above three compilation units can be compiled. To build the *employee* package, create a subdirectory named *employee* in the current directory. The *employee* directory corresponds to the *employee* package. Compile *Employee.java* and place the class files *Person.class* and *Employee.class* into the *employee* directory. Then, one can compile files *Manager.java* and *SalesPerson.java* and run the main method of class *SalesPerson*. When the main method of class *SalesPerson* is executed, the Java interpreter prints the following message on the standard output.

*The sales person's name is John Smith,*
*address is null,*
*telephone is null,*
*salary is 14400.0.*

□

### *1.3.3.2 Interface*

A class defines variables and methods. The value in a variable at runtime is a part of the current state of the class or that of an object of the class. The statements in the body of a method can access and change the state. A class defines what the class and its instances can do by defining static and instance methods. A class implements a specification.

Java uses notion *interface* to support pure specification. An interface specifies constants and/or abstract methods. It contains no variable field. It does not provide body for any method. For example, we shall present an interface called *Customer-Interface*, which declares a float constant *BALANCE_LIMIT* and two abstract methods, *setBalance(float balance)* and *getBalance()*.

Like a class, an interface is a software component in a package. A programmer constructs an interface in a compilation unit. No interface can be instantiated to create an object. A class or interface can inherit an interface, which is the super-interface. The class or interface is called a subclass or subinterface of the inherited interface. A non-abstract class that inherits an interface must implement all the methods specified in the interface. A class can explicitly inherit (extend) at most one class. It can inherit (implement) multiple interfaces. The keywords *extends* and *implements* are used in a subclass to introduce a superclass and a series of superinterfaces, respectively.

We shall define a class called *EmployeeCustomer*, which represents persons who happen to be an employee and a customer of our supermarket. As shown in Fig. 1.3, the class, denoted as *EmployeeCus*, inherits class *Employee* and implements interface *CustomerInterface*, which is denoted as *CustomerInt*. The class is a subclass of class *Employee* and interface *CustomerInterface*, which are super-class and superinterface, respectively.

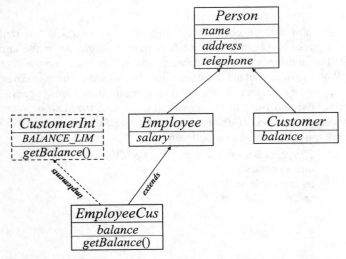

**Fig. 1.3** Class inheritance hierarchy with classes and interface

The syntax of an interface is

> *accessModifier* **interface** *interfaceName* **extends** *interfaceList* {
>     *constantDeclarations*
>     *abstractMethods*
>
> }

where *interface* is a keyword of Java, *accessModifier* and *extends* clause are optional. The *accessModifier* must be *public* if it is present. We use *interfaceList* in the above syntax to denote a list of interface names separated by commas. The interface inherits the constants and abstract methods of the superinterfaces. The following example presents interface *CustomerInterface*.

An instance of a class is also regarded as an instance of an interface that the class implements. For example, objects of class *EmployeeCustomer* can be regarded as instances of interface *CustomerInterface*.

An interface can be used as a type to declare variables. The declared variables can hold references to objects of the classes that implement the interface. For example, we can use interface *CustomerInterface* to declare a variable, use class *EmployeeCustomer* to create an object, and assign the object to the variable.

The following example illustrates the notion of interface. For simplicity, the interface and classes are included in one compilation unit of an unnamed package. The interface and classes have package access mode. A more flexible design of the interface and classes is presented in Section 1.4.

**Example 1.19** The following compilation unit includes classes *Person*, *Employee*, *Customer*, and *EmployeeCustomer*. It defines interface *CustomerInterface*. The inheritance hierarchy of the classes and interface is shown in Fig. 1.3. Class *Person* implicitly inherits class *Object*, which is not displayed in Fig. 1.3.

```
class Person {
    String name, address, telephone;
}

class Employee extends Person {
    float salary;
    float getSalary() {
        return salary;
    }
}

class Customer extends Person {
    float balance;
    Customer() { }

    Customer(String name, String address,
                String telephone, float balance) {
        this.name = name;
        this.address = address;
```

```java
            this.telephone = telephone;
            this.balance = balance;
        }

    public String toString() {
        return ("The customer's name is " +
                name + ",\n" + "address is " +
                address + ",\n" + "telephone is " +
                telephone + ",\n" + "balance is " +
                balance + ".");
        }
}

interface CustomerInterface {
    static final float BALANCE_LIMIT = 1000f;
    abstract float getBalance();
}

class EmployeeCustomer extends Employee
                    implements CustomerInterface {
    float balance;
    EmployeeCustomer() { }

    EmployeeCustomer(String name, String address,
                String telephone, float salary,
                float balance){
        this.name = name;
        this.address = address;
        this.telephone = telephone;
        this.salary = salary;
        this.balance = balance;
    }

    /** Implements method getBalance inherited
     *   from interface CustomerInterface
     */
    public float getBalance() { return balance; }

    public String toString() {
        return("The employee customer's name is "
                + name + ",\n" + "address is "
                + address + ",\n" + "telephone is "
                + telephone + ",\n" + "salary is "
                + getSalary() + ",\n" + "balance is "
                + getBalance() + ".");
    }
```

```
static public void main(String[] args) {
    CustomerInterface customer = new
            EmployeeCustomer ( "John Smith",
            "Windsor, Ontario", "555-2341",
            50000f, 100f);
    System.out.println(customer);
    }
}
```

When the main method of class *EmployeeCustomer* is executed, the Java interpreter prints the following message on the standard output.

> *The employee customer's name is John Smith,*
> *address is Windsor, Ontario,*
> *telephone is 555-2341,*
> *salary is 50000.0,*
> *balance is 100.0.*

□

### 1.3.3.3 Multiple Inheritance

The subclassing mechanism of Java supports only single inheritance. When a programmer develops a new class, the class can explicitly extend at most one class. It is illegal in Java to inherit two or more classes in the definition of a class. Java uses interfaces to abstract classes. A class can declare multiple interfaces as its superinterfaces. The restriction on inheritance of multiple classes in Java reduces both the complexity of the compiler and the possibility of conflict between inherited method implementations. It also limits the expressiveness of the Java language. For example, the class *EmployeeCustomer* cannot inherit the software from both existing classes *Employee* and *Customer*. Java uses interfaces to compensate the disadvantage of single inheritance. A class can inherit methods from a class and inherit abstract methods from multiple interfaces, which have no implementation. It implements the inherited abstract methods by itself.

As shown in the above example, the instances of a class that implements an interface are regarded as instances of the interface. The interface can be used as a type to declare variables to hold (references to) instances of the class.

## 1.3.4 Polymorphism

Java has predefined primitive types such as *int* and *boolean*. Classes and interfaces are used as types as well. Java is a strongly typed language. Each variable is declared with a type, which is a primitive type, a class name, or an interface name. Each object is created with a class. To assign an object to a variable, the object class must be compatible with the variable type; i.e., the class must inherit the class or interface that was used to declare the variable. Types are also required for return value, method parameter, and array element.

The type system of a Java program is flexible. The *polymorphism* feature of Java is indispensable for many applications. It means a single object may have several types. For example, an *EmployeeCustomer* object is created with class *EmployeeCustomer*, which extends class *Employee*. The object is an instance of class *Employee* as well as an instance of class *EmployeeCustomer*. Since class *EmployeeCustomer* implements interface *CustomerInterface*, an *EmployeeCustomer* object can be regarded as an instance of interface *CustomerInterface*. If a variable is declared with class *Employee* or interface *CustomerInterface*, a reference to the *EmployeeCustomer* object can be placed in the variable.

Polymorphism makes it possible to invoke a generic behavior for objects of various types. Particularly, a generic behavior can be invoked for the objects in a data structure. Each of the objects executes a specific method that implements the generic behavior. For example, we may maintain a collection of employee objects in a data structure. The generic behaviors of employee objects include retrieving salary with method *getSalary()*. In the Java program of Example 1.18, both classes *Manager* and *SalesPerson* extend the abstract class *Employee* but implement the method *getSalary()* differently. Objects of class *Manager* and *SalesPerson* are instances of class *Employee*. We can place the objects of the two classes in an array created with element type *Employee*. By invoking method *getSalary()* for each of the elements of the array, we retrieve the salaries of all the objects in the array. We use the following example to illustrate the use of generic behavior, which is supported by polymorphism.

**Example 1.20** (Continuation of Example 1.18) Let us create a file named *Employee.java* and place the three classes defined in Example 1.18 into the file. Remove the *public* modifier from the declaration of classes *Manager* and *SalesPerson*.

We add a main method, shown below, into the abstract class *Employee* in file *Employee.java*. The method creates an array to hold three *Employee* objects. One of the objects is a manager; the other two are *SalesPerson* instances. The average salary of the employees is evaluated by retrieving their salaries with the *getSalary()* method.

```
public static void main(String[] args) {
    Employee[] employees = new Employee[3];
    employees[0] = new Manager();

    SalesPerson sperson = new SalesPerson();
    sperson.hours = 100;
    employees[1] = sperson;

    sperson = new SalesPerson();
    sperson.hours = 20;
    employees[2] = sperson;

    float sum = 0f;
    for (int i=0 ; i < employees.length; i++)
        sum += employees[i].getSalary();
```

```
System.out.println("The average " +
               "salary of the employees is " +
               (sum / employees.length));
}
```

After compiling class *Employee*, an execution of the main method prints the following message on the standard output.

*The average salary of the employees is 24000.0*

□

# 1.4 A Supermarket Application

We now present classes and an interface to support transactions of the assumed supermarket. The classes integrate the source code shown in the above examples. The classes and interface are organized into an inheritance hierarchy shown in Fig. 1.4. (Class *Object* is automatically imported from package *java.lang.*) The classes *Person, Employee, Manager, SalesPerson*, and *EmployeeCustomer* specify data representation for persons, employees, managers, sales persons, and customers who are employees of the supermarket. The class *EmployeeCustomer* implements interface *CustomerInterface*, which is a specification of the behavior of customers. Class *Customer* defines the data and behavior for customers of the supermarket.

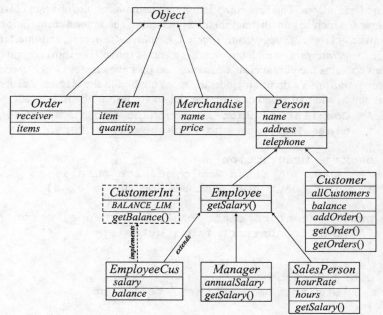

**Fig. 1.4** The classes and interface for the supermarket

The classes and interface are placed in package *transaction*, which supports customer order handling. We expect that the classes *Employee* and *Customer* are useful for other operations of the supermarket too. These classes are declared with modifier *public*. Other classes have the package access mode.

In public class *Customer*, we define accessers and mutaters for instance and class fields. We hide the fields by declaring them with modifier *private*. The methods for accessing and changing the *orders* array in a customer object are

> *addOrder(Order order)*
> *getOrder()*
> *getOrder(String name)*
> *getOrder(Customer receiver)*
> *getOrders(String name)*
> *getOrders(Customer receiver)*

where parameter *name* represents an order receiver's name and *receiver* represents a customer who is the receiver of order(s) to be retrieved.

Class *Customer* defines a static field *allCustomers*, which holds a vector of customer objects. The vector can be modified with class methods *addCustomer* (*Customer customer*) and *removeCustomer(String name)*. The *addCustomer* method adds a customer object into vector *allCustomers*, and *removeCustomer* deletes a customer object with a give name from the vector.

**Example 1.21** Package *transaction* consists of three compilation units, which are listed as follows. The first compilation unit contains public abstract class *Employee*, which has an abstract method *getSalary*. The second compilation unit contains classes *Manager*, *SalesPerson*, *EmployeeCustomer*, and interface *CustomerInterface*, which have package access mode. The third compilation unit contains the public class *Customer* and package classes *Order*, *Item*, and *Merchandise*. We do not include any main method in the classes. Readers are invited to add main methods into the classes for testing them.

```
/* Compilation unit 1: contains public abstract
 *   class Employee and package class Person.
 */
package transaction;
/** Abstract class Employee. Its subclasses
 *   implement abstract method getSalary().
 */
public abstract class Employee extends Person {
    public abstract float getSalary();
}

class Person {
    String name, address, telephone;
}


/* Compilation unit 2: contains classes
 *   Manager, SalesPerson, EmployeeCustomer and
```

```
 *   interface CustomerInterface.
 */
package transaction;
/** Class Manager for representing managers. */
class Manager extends Employee {
    float annualSalary;
    public float getSalary(){return annualSalary;}
}
/** Class SalesPerson for representing sales
 *   persons.
 */
class SalesPerson extends Employee {
    float hourRate;
    int hours;
    SalesPerson () { hourRate = 12f; hours = 38; }

    public float getSalary() {
        return hourRate * hours * 50;
    }

    public String toString () {
        return ("The sales person's name is "
                + name + ",\n " + "address is "
                + address + ",\n " + "telephone is "
                + telephone + ",\n " + "salary is "
                + getSalary() + ".");
    }
}


/** Class EmployeeCustomer for representing
 *   employees who are also customers.
 */
class EmployeeCustomer extends Employee
            implements CustomerInterface {
    private float salary;
    private float balance;
    EmployeeCustomer() { }

    EmployeeCustomer(String name, String address,
                String telephone, float salary,
                float balance){
        this.name = name;
        this.address = address;
        this.telephone = telephone;
        this.salary = salary;
        this.balance = balance;
    }
```

```java
      void setBalance(float balance) {
         this.balance = balance;
      }

      /** Implements method getBalance inherited
      *   from interface CustomerInterface.
      */
      public float getBalance() { return balance; }

      void setSalary(float salary) {
         this.salary = salary;
      }

      public float getSalary() { return salary; }

      public String toString() {
         return("The employee customer's name is "
               + name + ",\n" + "address is "
               + address + ",\n" + "telephone is "
               + telephone + ",\n" + "salary is "
               + salary + ",\n" + "balance is "
               + balance + ".");
      }
}

interface CustomerInterface {
      static final float BALANCE_LIMIT = 1000f;
      abstract float getBalance();
}
/* Compilation unit 3: public class Customer */
package transaction;
import java.util.*;
public class Customer {
      private static Vector allCustomers =
                                    new Vector();
      /** Adds a customer object into allCustomers*/
      public static void addCustomer(
                        Customer customer) {
         allCustomers.addElement(customer);
      }

      /** Removes a named customer object from
      *    allCustomers.
      */
      public static Customer removeCustomer(
                                    String name) {
```

```
        Customer customer;
        Enumeration total =allCustomers.elements();
        while (total.hasMoreElements()) {
           customer =(Customer)total.nextElement();
           if(customer.name.equals(name)){
            allCustomers.removeElement(customer);
            return customer;
           }
        }
        return null;
}

/** Retrieves the name of the customer. */
public String getName() { return name; }

/** Resets the name field of the customer
*    with a string.
*/
public void setName(String name) {
    this.name = name;
}

/** Retrieves the address of the customer. */
public String getAddress() { return address; }

/** Resets the address field of the customer
*    with a string.
*/
public void setAddress(String address) {
    this.address = address;
}

/** Retrieves the telephone number of the
*    customer.
*/
public String getTelephone() {
    return telephone;
}

/** Resets the telephone field of the customer
*    with a string.
*/
public void setTelephone(String telephone){
    this.telephone = telephone;
}

/** Retrieves the balance of the customer. */
```

```java
public float getBalance() { return balance; }

/** Resets the balance field of the customer
 *    with a float value.
 */
void setBalance(float balance) {
   this.balance = balance;
}

/** Retrieves an order placed by the customer.
 *    If no outstanding order for the customer,
 *    returns null.
 */
public Order getOrder() {
   if (orders == null) return null;
   Order temp_order;
   for (int i = 1; i < orders.length; i++){
      if (orders[i] != null) {
         temp_order = orders[i];
         orders[i] = null;
         return temp_order;
      }
   }
   return null;
}

/** Retrieves an order placed by the customer
 *    for a named customer. If no such
 *    outstanding order, returns null.
 */
public Order getOrder(String name) {
   if (orders == null) return null;
   Order temp_order;
   for (int i=1; i < orders.length; i++){
      if (orders[i] != null &&
        orders[i].receiver.name.equals(name)){
         temp_order = orders[i];
         orders[i] = null; return temp_order;
      }
   }
   return null;
}

/** Retrieves an order placed by the customer
 *    for a customer. If no such outstanding
 *    order, returns null.
 */
```

```java
public Order getOrder(Customer receiver) {
   if (orders == null) return null;
   Order temp_order;
   for (int i = 1; i < orders.length; i++){
      if (orders[i] != null &&
        orders[i].receiver == receiver) {
         temp_order = orders[i];
         orders[i] = null;
         return temp_order;
      }
   }
   return null;
}


/** Retrieves orders to be received by a named
 *    customer.
 */
public Order[] getOrders(String name) {
   if (orders == null) return null;
   Order[] temp_orders =
                   new Order[orders.length];
   int j = 0;
   for (int i=0; i < orders.length; i++)
      if (orders[i] != null &&
         orders[i].receiver.name.equals(name))
        temp_orders[j++] = orders[i];
   Order[] orders = new Order[j];
   for (int i = 0; i < j; i++)
      orders[i] = temp_orders[i];
   return orders;
}


/** Retrieves orders to be received by a
 *    customer.
 */
public Order[] getOrders(Customer receiver) {
   if (orders == null) return null;
   Order[] temp_orders =
                   new Order[orders.length];
   int j = 0;
   for (int i=0; i < orders.length; i++)
      if (orders[i] != null &&
            orders[i].receiver == receiver)
        temp_orders[j++] = orders[i];
   Order[] orders = new Order[j];
   for (int i = 0; i < j; i++)
```

```java
                    orders[i] = temp_orders[i];
            return orders;
        }

        /** Adds a new order for the customer if the
         *   customer owns a balance less than
         *   BALANCE_LIMIT. If the addition is
         *   successful, returns true; returns false
         *   otherwise.
         */
        public boolean addOrder(Order order) {
            if (getBalance() >=
                    CustomerInterface.BALANCE_LIMIT)
                return false;
            if (orders == null) orders = new Order[20];
            for (int i = 1; i < orders.length; i++){
                if (orders[i] == null) {
                    orders[i] = order;
                    return true;
                }
            }
            return false;
        }

        private String name, address, telephone;
        private float balance;
        private Order[] orders = new Order[20];
    }

class Order {
    Customer receiver;
    Item[] items;
}

class Item {
    Merchandise item;
    int quantity;
}

class Merchandise {
    String name;
    float price;
}
```

□

**Exercise 1.14** Modify class *Customer* to let the class inherit interface *Customer-Interface*.

# 1.5 Summary

The Java object model and its implementation are described in this chapter. The model consists of a set of object-oriented concepts for analysis and design of applications. The fundamental concept is an object. In a Java software system, objects are used to organize and store data. Methods are associated with objects. They access and manipulate data in objects. A method implements a desired computation. The design of a method depends on data structures. Another important concept of the object model is that of a class, which is the implementation unit of software. Classes define data representations and methods for objects. A class describes a kind of objects. A programmer constructs classes by declaring variables and developing methods. Classes can be shared between programmers and reused in different projects.

The other two fundamental concepts of the Java object model are class inheritance and polymorphism. In a Java program, each class, except class *Object*, is a subclass of an existing class. A class inherits the software from its superclass. Class *Object* defines the common behavior for objects. Since a class is a direct or indirect subclass of class *Object*, its instances have the common behavior. Some methods of class *Object* should be overridden in classes. For instance, the *toString* method of class *Object* is adapted in classes *Customer* and *Employee* of Example 1.17 to access the data in a customer or employee object.

To reduce complexity of the Java compiler and to avoid the inheritance of conflicting members from different sources, Java does not allow direct inheritance of multiple classes. However, Java supports inheritance of multiple interfaces, which abstract classes. An interface contains abstract methods with no implementation. An interface can be used as a type to declare variables, which can reference objects of classes that implement the interface.

# Assignment

We have used a supermarket as example to illustrate how to use object-oriented concepts to model an application. You are asked to use the Java object model to study the data required by a university administration system. Implement the identified classes in Java. Use main methods in the classes to test the classes.

# Chapter 2
# The Java Language

The Java language is a general-purpose programming language for platform-independent software development. As described in *Java White Papers* (Sun Microsystems, Inc.), "Java is simple, object-oriented, distributed, interpreted, robust, secure, architecture-neutral, portable, high-performance, multithreaded and dynamic."

Programmers for the Internet regard Java as a tool to create *applets*, which are mini-applications capable of running inside Web pages. After a Java applet is downloaded to a client browser, it may perform tasks without using resources from the server. Java is also a valuable programming language for distributed network environments.

For software developers who may not depend on networks, Java helps them produce bug-free code. It offers features like automated garbage collection, type-safe references, and multithreading to ease the task of developing robust, reliable, and complex software systems. The features make it easier to construct readable and manageable software.

Java has novel features such as exception handling, object reflection, and inner class to make programming simpler and easier. The objects created in a Java program can tell information about themselves. Control transfers in a Java program can be based on various types of information, including exceptions. The inner class feature of the Java language brings the structure of a Java program closer to a real-world application that the program models.

This chapter introduces the fundamental constructs of the Java language. It discusses some novel features of the language that are useful in data structure design and implementation. Specifically, we shall present

- the basic elements of Java programs, which include tokens, expressions, and statements;
- the control transfer mechanism of Java, which is supported by various types of statement and an exception handling mechanism;
- the object reflection model for querying objects; and
- the notion of inner class, which allows adapter and service classes to be embedded in classes that demand their functions.

# 2.1 Basic Elements of Java Program

## 2.1.1 White Space and Comment

### 2.1.1.1 White Space

A new line character, a return character, or a return character followed by a line feed character terminates a line in a Java program. The three types of line terminator are treated as white spaces. Other white spaces include the space character, horizontal tab, and form feed character.

  Any number of white spaces can be inserted between Java program elements for improved readability. A statement or a block of statements may span several lines. The Java compiler ignores extra white spaces.

### 2.1.1.2 Comment

There are three types of comment in Java programs.

- A *C-style comment* starts with symbol /* and ends with */. It may span several lines.
- A *C++-style comment* starts with symbol // and ends with a line terminator.
- A *documentation comment* starts with symbol /** and ends with */. As shown in Example 1.7, a documentation comment may span several lines.

The Java compiler ignores comments when it compiles source code. An automatic tool such as *javadoc* can collect documentation comments from the source code of classes into HTML documents.

## 2.1.2 Token

### 2.1.2.1 Token and Unicode

Syntactical symbols in a Java program that are not white spaces or comments are tokens. Specifically, a *token* is a keyword, identifier, literal, separator, or operator. To satisfy international language programming, characters in comments, identifiers, string literals, and character constants are expressed in Unicode, which is an international standard character set. A Unicode character is 16 bits (2 bytes) long. Unicode character set is large enough for major international languages.

  The first 128 Unicode characters represent ASCII characters. Elements other than comments, identifiers, string literals, and character constants in Java programs are formed with ASCII characters. Particularly, keywords and operator names are formed with ASCII characters.

## 2.1.2.2 Keyword and Identifier

Some sequences of ASCII letters are reserved keywords, which cannot be used as identifiers. The Java language specifies fifty keywords, which include *class*, *public*, *protected*, *private*, *extends*, and *implements*. The names of primitive types are *char*, *boolean*, *byte*, *short*, *int*, *long*, *float*, and *double*, which are keywords. Keywords *this* and *super* are used to represent the current object in a method body, which is running for the current object. Keywords *const* and *goto* are reserved but not in use.

An *identifier* is a sequence of Java letters and digits started with a letter. The Java letters include the underscore _, dollar sign $, ASCII letters A–Z, a–z, and other Unicode letters. The Java digits include decimal digits 0–9. Examples of identifiers are *Customer*, *String*, *item$1*, $\pi$, and *customer1*. The dollar sign $ has been used by Java compiler to generate internal identifiers. It should be used rarely in source code.

## 2.1.2.3 Literal

A *literal* is a token that represents a primitive value, a constant string, or the *null* reference. It cannot be changed. A primitive value can be an integer, a floating-point number, a boolean literal, or a character. In a Java program, we can explicitly specify a constant and assign it to a variable of the same type.

An integer literal is of type *int* or *long*. An integer value with suffix *l* or *L* is a *long*; otherwise, the integer value is an *int*. For example, 17, 0x11, and 021 are integer literals of type *int*; 17L, 0x11L, and 021L are literals of type *long*. All the literals are equal to the decimal value 17. An integer literal can be decimal such as 17 or –17, which is started with a non-zero decimal digit. It can be a hexadecimal such as 0x11 or –0X11, which has a prefix 0X or 0x. It can be octal such as 021 or –021, which is started with digit 0.

A floating-point number (literal) may have a whole-number part, a decimal point, a fractional part, and an exponent. To distinguish a *float* literal from a *double*, suffix *f* or *F* is appended at the end of a float number. For example, the following are *float* literals

     1.0f    1.e0f    0.1e1f    10e–1f   .1e+1f

all of which represent the same value; the following are *double* literals

     1.0    1.e0    0.1e1    10e–1   .1e+1

which are equal with each other.

A boolean literal is either *true* or *false*. The two literals are the only values of boolean expressions.

A character literal is a character or an escape sequence enclosed between a pair of single quotes. It represents a unique character of type *char*. For example, *'a'*, *'\n'*, and *'\177'* are character literals. Some non-graphic characters, the single quote, double quote, and backslash are represented by *escape sequences* in string literals. A 16-bit Unicode character constant can be represented with *'\uXXXX'*, where *XXXX* is the hexadecimal Unicode encoding of the character.

A string literal is a sequence of characters that is enclosed by a pair of double quotes. For example, *""*, *"A customer"*, and *"\n"* are string literals.

The null reference is represented by the literal *null*.

### 2.1.2.4 Separator

Separators are also called punctuators. A Java separator is one of the following symbols

   (   )   {   }   [   ]   ;   ,   .

The dot separator . can be used to qualify a field in an object or class with a variable or class name. For instance, expression *customer1.name* is used in Example 1.3 to denote a field in a customer object. The dot separator can also be used to invoke a method for an object or class. For instance, we use expression *customer1.setName("John Smith")* to invoke the *setName* method for a customer object in Example 1.4.

### 2.1.2.5 Operator

Java provides 37 built-in operators to denote comparison, arithmetic, increment, decrement, bitwise, and other operations. A Java programmer can define new methods but not operators.

The symbol = is an assignment operator. The assignment operators

   +=   −=   *=   /=

are infix operators. They perform a binary arithmetic operation +, −, *, or / with two operands and, then, assign the result to the variable on the left-hand side of the operator. A numeric operand is subject to numeric promotion for a binary arithmetic operation. The increment operator ++ and decrement −− operator can be applied to a numeric variable to increase or decrease the variable by 1.

Tokens <, >, <=, >=, !=, and == are relational operators for comparison. Logical operations are represented with operators ! (negation), & (conjunct), | (disjunct), && (shortcut conjunct), and || (shortcut disjunct). Given a logical expression *b1 && b2*, if the value of operand *b1* is *false*, the value of the expression can be determined as *false* and the subexpression *b2* will not be evaluated. For expression *b1 & b2*, both subexpressions *b1* and *b2* must be evaluated even if *b1* is equal to *false*. A similar difference exists between the disjunct operators | and ||.

# 2.2 Flow of Control

## 2.2.1 Statement

A *statement* in a Java program instructs the computer to perform some operation for achieving an effect. The operation may incur a transfer of control to another statement. A statement may be a composite one, which contains statements. A statement does not have a value. It is different from an expression. A value is expected from an expression.

Here, we describe several types of statement, including expression statement, block, if, switch, while, do, and for statements. We also discuss throw and try statement, which are related to exception handling, and the synchronization statements for multithread programming. A statement is terminated with a semicolon ;. Particularly, an empty statement is a statement terminated immediately by a semicolon.

An execution of a composite statement may encounter a control transfer statement such as *break, continue*, or *return* and the execution may complete normally. An execution of a statement may encounter an exceptional condition that prevents a normal completion and the statement completes *abruptly*.

### 2.2.1.1 Expression Statement

An expression in a Java program can be used as a value. Its evaluation may have side effects. Some expressions can be used as statements. The following are expression statements

```
customer1 = new Customer();
customer2 = customer1;
balance += 12;
balance++;
new Customer();
```

A method invocation usually returns a value. It is an expression. A method invocation can be used as a statement as well. For example,

```
System.out.println("The 1st customer: "
                                    + customer1);
customer1.setAddress("210 Univ. Ave. E");
```

are statements; the first invokes method *println* and the second invokes *setAddress*.

### 2.2.1.2 Block

A *block* is a compound statement that uses a pair of curly braces { and } to enclose a sequence of statements. For example, the following are two blocks

```
{ }
{ Order temp_order; temp_order = new Order(); }
```

The first block contains no statement. The second block contains two statements, one is a local variable declaration, the other an assignment.

A variable declared inside a block hides or shadows the same named field of the enclosing class but conflicts with the same named variable declared in an enclosing block. The shadowing is legal. The conflicting results in a compilation error. A local variable exists only in the block where it is declared; i.e., outside the block, the variable is not available.

The body of a method is a block. A (local) variable declaration can appear anywhere in a method body. An instance or class field of a class is automatically initialized with a default value when the instance is created or when the class is loaded. A local variable must be initialized before it is used.

The following example presents variations of class *Customer* to illustrate the hiding and scope rules of variables.

**Example 2.1** A local variable can be defined only once within a block. The main method in the following class declares local variable *name* twice. The second declaration is in an embedded block. It conflicts with the first one in the enclosing block. Therefore, the class cannot be compiled.

```
class Customer {
    /** Tests the effect of local variable
     *   declaration. The program is invalid
     *   due to the second declaration of local
     *   variable name.
     */
    public static void main(String[] args) {
        Customer customer = new Customer();
        String name = "John Smith";
        {
            //illegal redeclaration
            String name = "Tom David";
            customer.name = name;
            System.out.println(
            "The customer's name : "+customer.name);
        }
    }
    private String name;
}
```

We correct the main method by changing the second declaration of local variable *name* to an assignment. The following class can be compiled. It prints *The customer's name: Tom David.*

```
class Customer {
    /** Tests the effect of local variable hiding.
     *   The program is valid. The local variable
     *   name hides the instance field name.
     */
    public static void main(String[] args) {
        Customer customer = new Customer();
        String name = "John Smith";
        {   name = "Tom David";
            customer.name = name;
            System.out.println(
            "The customer's name: "+customer.name);
        }
    }
}
```

```
        private String name;
}
```

The following class demonstrates a local variable scoping rule. In the main method, the second declaration of local variable *name* is legal since the first is already out of its scope. The method can be compiled. It prints

> *The customer's name: Tom David*
> *The customer's name: John Smith.*

```
class Customer {
    /** Tests the scope of local variable. The
     *   program is valid. Outside the inner
     *   block, the local variable name defined
     *   in the inner block no longer exists.
     */
    public static void main(String[] args) {
        Customer customer = new Customer();
        {   String name = "Tom David";
            customer.name = name;
            System.out.println(
            "The customer's name: "+ customer.name);
        }
        // legal redeclaration
        String name = "John Smith";
        customer.name = name;
        System.out.println(
            "The customer's name: "+ customer.name);
    }
    private String name;
}
```

◻

A declaration may declare several variables in sequence. A declared variable may have an initialization clause. For example, the following statement declares two variables with type *Customer*, the first is assigned with a *Customer* object.

```
Customer customer1 = new Customer(), customer2;
```

**Exercise 2.1** Add a constructor into the second or third version of class *Customer* in Example 2.1. The constructor has signature *Customer(String name)*. It assigns instance field *name* with argument *name*. (Hint: see Example 1.4)

## 2.2.1.3 *if Statement*

An if statement implements a conditional transfer of control. Its syntax is

> *if* (*boolean_expression*) *statement1*
> *else statement2*

Control is transferred to the first statement if the boolean expression evaluates to *true*; otherwise, the second statement is executed. The *else* part of an if statement is optional. The statements *statement1* and *statement2* may be if statements.

Two consecutive occurrences of *if* parts may be followed by an *else* part. The *else* is bound to the most recent *if* part that has no matching *else*. To avoid confusion, use braces to change the association of *if-else* pairings. We use the following example to illustrate the *if-else* pairing rule.

**Example 2.2** The following method is equivalent to the same named method presented in Example 1.8. It tests whether a customer's balance is over $1000. If the test results in *true*, the method returns *false*. Otherwise, the argument *order* is added into array *orders*.

```
boolean addOrder(Order order) {
    if (getBalance() < 1000) {
        if (orders == null) orders = new Order[20];
        for (int i = 0; i < orders.length; i++)
            if (orders[i] == null) {
                orders[i] = order;
                return true;
            }
    }
    else System.out.println(
        "The customer has outstanding balance.");
    return false;
}
```

□

### 2.2.1.4 switch Statement

The syntax of a switch statement is

> **switch** (*expression*) {
>     **case** $l_1$: *statements*
>     **case** $l_2$: *statements*
>
>     ...
>
>     **case** $l_k$: *statements*
>     **default**: *statements*
> }

where *expression* evaluates to an integer or a character, case labels $l_1$, $l_2$, ..., $l_k$ are integer or character constants. The default clause

> **default**: *statements*

uses keyword *default* to introduce a sequence of statements. It is optional. An execution of the switch statement first evaluates *expression*, which returns an integer or character called *switch value*. Then, it compares the switch value with the case labels in sequence. If the switch value is equal to a case label, it executes the labeled statements. The default clause is entered when the switch value is not equal to any of the labels $l_1$, $l_2$, ..., $l_k$.

When the switch value matches a case label, the flow of control falls through the statements starting from the labeled statement. To stop the execution at a statement, place a break statement before the statement. When the break statement is encountered, the flow of control skips the remaining statements in the switch statement. We use the following example to illustrate control falling through and the break statement.

**Example 2.3** The following main method uses a switch statement to test decimal digits and English letters. It indicates whether or not the first character in the first argument of a command is a digit, a lowercase or uppercase letter.

```
public static void main(String[] args) {
    char ch = args[0].charAt(0);
    switch(ch) {
        case '0': case '1': case '2': case '3':
        case '4': case '5': case '6': case '7':
        case '8': case '9':
            System.out.println(
                "The character is digit " + ch);
            break;

        case 'a': case 'b': case 'c': case 'd':
        case 'e': case 'f': case 'g': case 'h':
        case 'i': case 'j': case 'k': case 'l':
        case 'm': case 'n': case 'o': case 'p':
        case 'q': case 'r': case 's': case 't':
        case 'u': case 'v': case 'w': case 'x':
        case 'y': case 'z':
            System.out.println(
             "The char is lowercase letter " + ch);
            break;

        case 'A': case 'B': case 'C': case 'D':
        case 'E': case 'F': case 'G': case 'H':
        case 'I': case 'J': case 'K': case 'L':
        case 'M': case 'N': case 'O': case 'P':
        case 'Q': case 'R': case 'S': case 'T':
        case 'U': case 'V': case 'W': case 'X':
        case 'Y': case 'Z':
            System.out.println(
             "The char is uppercase letter " + ch);
            break;

        default: System.out.println("The character"
            + " is neither a digit nor a letter.");
    }
}
```

When the main method is executed, if the first character in the first command-line argument, denoted with *args*[0], is *A*, it prints

> *The char is uppercase letter A*

If the last break statement is removed from the above method, the method will print

> *The char is uppercase letter A*
> *The character is neither a digit nor a letter.*

due to the control falling-through feature of the switch statement.                    □

**Exercise 2.2** Write a switch statement that tests if an integer variable, say *count*, holds integer 100, 200, or 300 and prints the integer value.

## 2.2.1.5 for Loop

A for loop contains statements for variable initialization, a boolean expression for loop control, statements for variable updating, and a body. The syntax is

> *for* (*init_statements* ; *boolean_expression* ; *updating_statements*)
>     *statement*

The statements in *init_statements* or *updating_statements* are separated with commas. When the for loop is executed, the *init_statements* are executed in sequence. Then, the body *statement* is repeated each time *boolean_expression* evaluates to *true*. After each repetition of the loop body, *updating_statements* are executed in sequence before *boolean_expression* is evaluated again.

All the three components inside the pair of parentheses are optional. For example, the for loop

> *for* ( ; ; ) *statement*

has no control boolean expression, which is default to *true*. The above loop is equivalent to

> *for* ( ; *true* ; ) *statement*

An execution of the above loop can be terminated only by *statement*, which may incur an exception or execute a control transfer statement such as break or return.

In Example 2.2, we use for loop

```
for (int i = 0; i < orders.length; i++)
    if (orders[i] == null) {
        orders[i] = order;
        return true;
    }
```

to search for an empty element in array *orders*. The loop stops either by condition $i \geq orders.length$ or by an execution of statement *return true*.

## 2.2.1.6 while and do Loop

In an application, we may need to repeat a block of statements as long as a boolean condition remains true. The repetition can be implemented with a while or do loop. A while loop has syntax

> *while* (*boolean_expression*) *statement*

A do loop has syntax

> *do* *block*
> *while* (*boolean_expression*)

For the while loop, *boolean_expression* is evaluated first; if it evaluates to *true*, the *statement* is executed. The process repeats until *boolean_expression* evaluates to *false*. The do loop executes *block* and then evaluates *boolean_expression*. If *boolean_expression* evaluates to *true*, *block* is repeated. The do loop is equivalent to

> *block*
> *while* (*boolean_expression*) *block*

The while loop can be expressed with for loop

> *for* (; *boolean_expression*; ) *statement*

which has empty initialization and increment statement lists. It terminates when the value of *boolean_expression* becomes *false* or a break or return statement in *statement* is executed.

## 2.2.1.7 break and continue Statements

As shown in Example 2.3, a break statement can be placed in a switch statement. When the break statement is encountered at runtime, the remaining part of the switch statement is omitted and the control exits the switch statement.

A break statement can be placed in a for, while, or do loop as well. When the break statement in a loop is encountered at runtime, the remaining part of the loop is omitted and the control exits the loop.

A break statement may specify a label. A break statement containing no label will break the closest switch statement or loop that encloses it. To break an outer enclosing loop, label the outer loop and use the label in the break statement. The following example illustrates break statement that contains a label.

**Example 2.4** The following method in class *Customer* searches for an order that includes a given type of merchandise. It uses two loops, one embedding the other. The outer loop goes through the elements of the *orders* array in a customer object. If an element *orders*[*i*] of array *orders* references an order object, the inner loop goes through the elements of the *items* array in the order object. When an item object that contains the given type of merchandise is found in the inner loop, a break in the inner loop is used to stop the outer loop, which is labeled with *probing*.

```
public Order getOrder(Merchandise p) {
    if (orders == null) return null;
    Order temp_order = null;
```

```
probing: for (int i=0; i<orders.length; i++) {
    if (orders[i] != null &&
                        orders[i].items!=null)
        for (int j = 0;
                j < orders[i].items.length; j++)
        if (orders[i].items[j] != null
            && orders[i].items[j].item == p) {
                temp_order = orders[i];
                break probing;
            }
    }
    return temp_order;
}
```

The above method is for illustrating a break statement with label. As suggested by Exercise 2.3, the method can be simplified.                    □

In a for, while, or do loop, we can use a continue statement to skip statements in the loop and repeat the loop. A continue statement is coded in one of the forms

  *continue*;
  *continue aLabel*;

where *continue* is a keyword of Java and *aLabel* is a label of a loop that includes the continue statement. The first statement instructs the computer to skip the remaining statements in the closest loop and restart the loop. The second requests to restart a loop that includes the continue statement and that is labeled with *aLabel*.

**Exercise 2.3** The method *getOrder*(*Merchandise p*) in Example 2.4 can be simplified by eliminating the label. Change the method by substituting a return statement for the break statement.

## 2.2.2 Exception Handling

An *exception* is used in a Java program to signal a runtime unexpected condition. Exception handling in computer programming is essentially a special type of control transfer from an erroneous or exceptional spot to an exception handler. The Java exception handling mechanism consists of the following components:

- A class inheritance hierarchy rooted at class *Throwable*, which is extended by classes *Exception* and *Error*. Class *RuntimeException* is a subclass of *Exception*. The top part of the hierarchy is shown in Fig. 2.1. Each exception is an object of a class in the hierarchy.
- The contract of a method includes a set of exception classes the instances of which the method body may throw. Specifically, keyword *throws* is used in the method declaration to introduce the exception classes. The throws clause is optional in a method declaration.

- A try construct, which defines a block from which exceptions can be thrown and which defines exception handlers for thrown exceptions. An exception handler is implemented as a catch clause in Java.
- A *throw* operator for throwing exceptions in method bodies and try blocks.

An exception is an object of a subclass of class *Throwable*. By convention, an exception thrown at runtime is a direct or indirect instance of one of the three classes *Error*, *RuntimeException*, and *Exception*. The three classes categorize exceptions by severity and checkability.

The instances of classes *Error* and *RuntimeException* represent unrecoverable errors and severe runtime exceptions, respectively. For example, the exception class *LinkageError* is a direct subclass of *Error*. A *LinkageError* signals an unrecoverable error that the dependency of a class on another class cannot be satisfied. Classes *ArithmeticException* and *SecurityException* extend class *RuntimeException*. When dividing by zero, an *ArithmeticException* is thrown. A security system signals a *SecurityException* when a program attempts to violate a security rule.

*Error* and *RuntimeException* may appear at any time during the execution of a program. They represent exceptions that are *unchecked* by the Java compiler. The instances of a class that extends class *Exception* or its subclass but not *RuntimeException* are *checkable*. For instance, class *InstantiationException* is a subclass of class *Exception*. An *InstantiationException* signals an attempt to create instance for an abstract class or interface. It is impossible to satisfy the request. The Java compiler can check the instantiation errors.

A method uses a throws clause to introduce checkable exception classes, the instances of which may be thrown from the method body. Assume a method declares an exception class in its throws clause. For an invocation of the method, the Java compiler checks that either the invocation is within a try block followed by a handler that intercepts exceptions in the exception class or the invoking method can throw exception in the class. The Java compiler ensures that a method body throws only exceptions of classes declared by the method.

We now use classes *Order*, *Item*, and *Merchandise*, introduced in Example 1.3, to illustrate Java exception handling. The *Order* class defines instance field *items*, which will hold an array of item objects. Each item encapsulates a merchandise object and an integer *quantity*. A customer may request to change the ordered *quantity* for a specified type of merchandise.

The following example defines a checkable exception class, which signals the absence of a specified type of merchandise in an order. The class extends class *Exception*. Its constructor invokes constructor *Exception(String reason)* of class *Exception* to encode a string as the exception reason in a created exception object.

**Example 2.5** We now extend class *Exception* to define class *NoSuchMerchandiseOrdered*. The new exception class has a constructor that accepts a merchandise argument and an integer argument.

```
class NoSuchMerchandiseOrdered extends Exception {
    public Merchandise p;
    public int newQuantity;
```

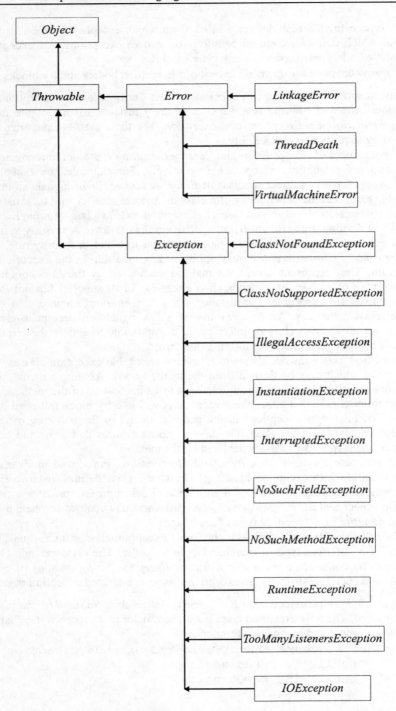

**Fig. 2.1** Exception class hierarchy

```
NoSuchMerchandiseOrdered(Merchandise m, int q)
{   super("No merchandise \""
        + m.name+"\" is ordered." );
    p = m; newQuantity = q;
}
}
```

The above class can be used as a checkable exception class by a method. Particularly, the class name *NoSuchMerchandiseOrdered* can be listed in the throws clause of a method so that the method body can throw instances of the class.                                                                                            □

As we said, the definition of a method may use keyword *throws* to introduce a sequence of exception class names. The exception classes must be checkable; i.e., the classes extend class *Exception* or its subclasses except *RuntimeException*. The following example shows a throws clause.

**Example 2.6** We now consider a method named *changeQuantity* that changes the quantity of an ordered item. We can declare the method with signature

```
void changeQuantity(Merchandise p,
                        int newQuantity)
```

which has no throws clause. The declaration indicates that the method will not throw checkable exception. Any checkable exception thrown by a statement in the method body cannot be thrown out of the method body. It must be handled by an exception handler in the method body.

The types of exception that can be thrown by a method are part of the contract of the method. An exceptional condition for method *changeQuantity* is that the merchandise type specified with parameter *p* cannot be found in the order object. If the method body does not process the exception, the method should declare the exception in its throws clause, and method *changeQuantity* can be declared as

```
void changeQuantity(Merchandise p,int newQuantity)
        throws NoSuchMerchandiseOrdered
```

Thus, the body of method *changeQuantity* can throw checkable objects of class *NoSuchMerchandiseOrdered* without catching and processing the exceptions.                                                                                            □

A programmer uses throw statements to throw exceptions. The syntax for exception throw statement is

> **throw** *anExceptionObject*;

where *throw* is a keyword of Java. An exception object thrown by a throw statement can be created with the *new* operator. For example, statement

```
throw new NoSuchMerchandiseOrdered(p, 25);
```

instantiates class *NoSuchMerchandiseOrdered* with a merchandise object *p* and integer 25 and throws the created exception object.

A throw statement may be included in a try block, which is followed by catch clauses. A catch clause specifies a type of exception that it is willing to intercept and handle. Following the catch clauses, an optional finally clause can be used to introduce a block that is always executed before the try construct is terminated normally or abruptly. A general syntax for the try construct is described as follows.

> *try* block
> *catch*(*ExceptionType*$_1$ $e_1$) { *statements* }
>   ...
> *catch*(*ExceptionType*$_k$ $e_k$) { *statements* }
> *finally* { *statements* }

where $k \geq 0$, *try*, *catch*, and *finally* are keywords of Java.

When the above try construct is encountered at runtime, the try block is executed until either the block is exited normally or an exception is thrown and the control exits from the block abruptly. In the latter case, the catch clauses are examined in sequence to find a parameter type *ExceptionType*$_i$ such that the thrown exception is of type *ExceptionType*$_i$. If such a parameter type is found, *statements* in the catch clause

> *catch*(*ExceptionType*$_i$ $e_i$) { *statements* }

are executed, and the remaining catch clauses are omitted.

The Java exception handling mechanism adopts a termination model. After a catch clause following a try block intercepts and handles an exception thrown from the try block, the control of flow will leave the try construct. If no catch clause intercepts an exception thrown from the try block, the exception will be percolated into an enclosing try construct to look for an intercepting catch clause.

A normal statement like a return statement as well as an exception may cause control exiting from a try construct. If the try construct has a finally clause, the statements in the finally clause are executed before the control is transferred away from the try construct. The finally clause may clean up resources such as graphics resources and open files before the try construct completes.

The following example illustrates the try construct, exception throw statement, and catch clause.

**Example 2.7** We add two methods into class *Order* defined in Example 1.3.

Method *changeQuantity* changes the quantity of a type of merchandise for an order. In the normal situation, the order contains the type of merchandise in an item; otherwise, the method body throws a *NoSuchMerchandiseOrdered* exception. Method *findItem*(*Merchandise p*) tries to find a given type of merchandise in an order. If the mentioned type of merchandise cannot be found in the order, the method returns *null*.

```
class Order {
    Customer receiver;
    Item[] items;
    public void changeQuantity(Merchandise p,
                               int newQuantity)
            throws NoSuchMerchandiseOrdered {
        Item item = findItem(p);
        if (item == null)
```

```
            throw new
            NoSuchMerchandiseOrdered(p,newQuantity);
        item.quantity = newQuantity;
    }

    Item findItem(Merchandise p) {
        if (items == null) return null;
        for (int i= 0; i < items.length; i++)
            if (items[i]!=null && items[i].item== p)
                return items[i];
        return null;
    }
}
```

To test the exception handling facility, we add the following main method into class *Order*. The main method creates an order object and enters an item for a type of merchandise into the order. It uses a catch clause to intercept *NoSuchMerchandiseOrdered* exception. The catch clause prints a message to describe the failure of quantity change request.

```
public static void main(String[] args){
    Order order = new Order();
    order.items = new Item[3];

    Merchandise merchandise1 = new Merchandise();
    merchandise1.name = "tomato";
    merchandise1.price = 0.99f;
    Merchandise merchandise2 = new Merchandise();
    merchandise2.name = "potato";
    merchandise2.price = 0.19f;
    order.items[0] = new Item();
    order.items[0].item = merchandise1;
    order.items[0].quantity = 3;

    try {
        order.changeQuantity(merchandise1,4);
        order.changeQuantity(merchandise2,2);
    }
    catch(NoSuchMerchandiseOrdered e) {
        System.out.println("Merchandise "+ e.p.name
                    + " is not in the order.\n");
    }
}
```

An execution of the main method of class *Order* prints the following message on the standard output.

*Merchandise potato is not in the order.*

□

**Exercise 2.4** In the above example, instance method *findItem* (*Merchandise p*) of class *Order* returns *null* if merchandise *p* cannot be found in an order. Modify the method so that a *NoSuchMerchandiseOrdered* exception is thrown by the method when the specified merchandise *p* cannot be found in an order. Test your method by running the main method of Example 2.7.

## 2.2.3 Thread and Multithread Programming

### 2.2.3.1 Thread

Java supports multiple execution threads, which are lightweight processes. The multithread programming handles different tasks concurrently for a program. The Java standard library uses threads for I/O channel blocking and multimedia operations to increase interactive performance. For example, when the *repaint* method is invoked for a graphical user interface component, Java creates a thread for updating the screen and the control is returned to the caller (the invoker of the *repaint* method) immediately. Thus, the rest of the program continues independently of the repaint task.

The execution of a Java program is started as a thread. A thread may spawn threads. Each thread executes specified statements in sequence. Threads have priorities. When a thread is created, its priority is initialized with that of the creating thread and can be changed. All the live threads with the highest priority have the same chance to receive the processor. A thread may be marked as a daemon. A Java system exits when all threads that are not daemons have died. Threads can be placed in thread groups for security management.

Java supports thread synchronization. Keyword *synchronized* can be used to mark code block or method that should obtain a lock on an object before the block or method can run for the object. In synchronized methods and code blocks, the *wait* and *notify* methods can be used to coordinate threads by suspending or awaking threads.

### 2.2.3.2 Thread Creation

A thread is an instance of class *Thread* or its subclass. A thread is created with operator *new* and a constructor of class *Thread* or its subclass. Class *Thread* is defined in package *java.lang*. It implements interface *Runnable*. When a thread receives the processor, it starts or continues method *run*(). The execution of method *run* is automatic. We never need an explicit invocation of method *run*. The method *run* in class *Thread* does nothing. It should be overridden in a subclass of *Thread* with specific functionality.

There is another approach to creating a thread. Interface *Runnable* defines abstract method *run* only. We can define a class that implements interface *Runnable* and extends a class other than *Thread*. To create a thread that executes the *run* method of the *Runnable* class, create an instance of the class and pass the created

*Runnable* object as an argument to a constructor of class *Thread* to create a thread. When the created thread is started, it executes the *run* method defined in the *Runnable* class automatically.

A thread has a name, which is supplied or automatically generated at runtime when the thread is created. Multiple threads may have the same name.

Class *Thread* defines the following constructors to initialize a created thread:

> *Thread*()
> *Thread*(*Runnable*)
> *Thread*(*Runnable, String*)
> *Thread*(*String*)
> *Thread*(*ThreadGroup, Runnable*)
> *Thread*(*ThreadGroup, String*)
> *Thread*(*ThreadGroup, Runnable, String*)

A constructor of the class may receive a *Runnable* argument, which is the target running object of the created thread. It may accept a string argument for the name of a created thread. We may specify a group for the created thread. We use the following example to illustrate the creation of thread. It is the running example for this section.

**Example 2.8** The following compilation unit defines two classes – *Supermarket* and *GUI_thread*. Class *GUI_thread* extends class *Thread*. The main method of class *Supermarket* creates two instances of class *GUI_thread*. We assume the supermarket needs two GUIs open at the same time so that a sales person can enter data for two different customers at the same time. The *run* method in the thread class *GUI_thread* simply identifies each thread by printing its name.

```
class GUI_thread extends Thread {
    public GUI_thread(String name) {
        // invokes constructor Thread(String)
        super(name);
    }

    public void run() {
        System.out.println("GUI thread for "
                            + getName());
        try { sleep(100); }
        catch(InterruptedException e){}
    }
}

public class Supermarket {
    public static void main(String[] args) {
        GUI_thread cusGUI1 = new
                    GUI_thread("customer 1.");
        GUI_thread cusGUI2 = new
                    GUI_thread("customer 2.");
        cusGUI2.start();
```

```
            cusGUI1.start();
        }
    }
```

An execution of the main method of class *Supermarket* prints

> *GUI thread for customer 2.*
> *GUI thread for customer 1.*

□

**Exercise 2.5** Modify the above compilation unit by letting class *GUI_thread* implement interface *Runnable* and creating threads with constructor *Thread(Runnable, String)* in the main method of class *Supermarket*.

### 2.2.3.3 Thread State Transition

Class *Thread* defines instance methods to change the state of a thread. The possible states of a thread are *runnable, running, not running,* and *dead*. After a thread is created, it is runnable. By invoking method *start()* for a runnable thread, the thread becomes either running or not running. Specifically, if the processor is allocated to the thread, the thread executes its *run* method and it is in the running state. A running thread may be suspended or waiting for other threads to finish, and the thread is not running. A thread becomes dead after it exits method *run()* or after it executes method *stop()*. The state transitions for threads are described in Fig. 2.2.

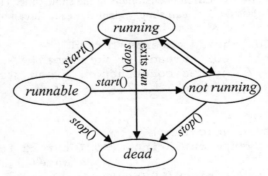

**Fig. 2.2** Thread state transitions

The following methods can be invoked for an object of class *Thread* or a subclass of the class. A subclass of *Thread* can be found in Example 2.8. In an explanation of a method, we use the term "this object" to mean an object for which the method is invoked. For example, in the explanation of method *start*, this thread refers to any thread like *cusGUI1* or *cusGUI2* created in Example 2.8.

| Signature | Semantics |
|---|---|
| `void start()` | Causes method *run()* to be invoked for this thread. This thread and the calling thread will run concurrently. |
| `static void sleep(long millis) throws InterruptedException` | Pauses the currently running thread for a number of milliseconds |
| `void stop()` | Causes this thread stops abnormally and a *ThreadDead* exception is thrown |
| `void suspend()` | Suspends the progress of this thread until it is resumed |
| `void resume()` | Resumes this thread |
| `static void yield()` | Causes the currently running thread to yield the processor to others |
| `void join() throws InterruptedException` | Waits for this thread to die |
| `void join(long millis) throws InterruptedException` | Waits for a number of milliseconds for this thread to die |
| `void interrupt()` | Interrupts this thread |
| `void destroy()` | Destroys this thread abnormally without cleanup |

Class *Thread* defines integer constants *MAX_PRIORITY*, *NORM_PRIORITY*, and *MIN_PRIORITY* to denote the maximum, default, and minimum priority that a thread may have. The constants are equal to 10, 5, and 1, respectively. The priority of a thread can be changed with method *setPriority*. The name of a thread can be changed at runtime with method *setName*. A thread may be changed to a daemon or a user thread by invoking method *setDaemon(boolean)*. These methods are described as follows.

| Signature | Semantics |
|---|---|
| `void setPriority(int newPriority)` | Sets this thread's priority to the smaller of a new priority and the maximum one permitted by security manager |
| `void setName(String newName)` | Changes this thread name if security permits |
| `void setDaemon (boolean on)` | Marks this thread as either a daemon or a user thread |

### 2.2.3.4 Accessers

Class *Thread* uses the following methods to access the state of a thread or static variables.

| Signature | Semantics |
|---|---|
| `boolean isAlive()` | Tests if this thread has been started but not stopped |
| `boolean isInterrupted()` | Tests if this thread has been interrupted |
| `static boolean interrupted()` | Tests if the current thread has been interrupted |
| `boolean isDaemon()` | Tests if this thread is a daemon thread |
| `String getName()` | Retrieves this thread's name |
| `int getPriority()` | Retrieves this thread's priority |
| `ThreadGroup getThreadGroup()` | Retrieves this thread's group |
| `void checkAccess()` | Determines if the currently running thread has permission to modify this thread. Exception *SecurityException* may be thrown by the method execution. |
| `String toString()` | Returns a string representation of this thread. The string includes this thread's name, priority, and group. |
| `static Thread currentThread()` | Returns the currently executing thread |
| `static int activeCount()` | Counts the active threads in the thread group |
| `static int enumerate(Thread[] threadArray)` | Collects active threads in this thread group and its subgroups into a thread array |

### 2.2.3.5 Thread Synchronization

Each object created in a Java runtime system is implicitly associated with a monitor. To coordinate data accesses, we can define an accesser or mutater in a critical object class and declare the method with keyword *synchronized*. A synchronized method locks an object before it can be executed for the object. If the object has been locked by a thread, another thread that requests to lock the object will be placed into the wait set associated with the object. Thus, at most one thread can execute the method for the object at a time. For example, if the field *accounts* is critical in a customer object, we declare method *setAccounts()* as *synchronized* so that only one thread can access or change the field in a customer object through the method at a time.

In a method, we can have a synchronized block with syntax

*synchronized*(*anObject*) *block;*

The block in the statement is executed only after the thread receives the monitor on the synchronized object.

Instance methods *wait()* and *notify()* are defined in class *Object*. They can be invoked to place a thread into waiting state or awake a waiting thread. The method *notifyAll()* can be issued to awake all waiting threads, which can then compete for normal processor scheduling. Methods *wait*, *notify*, and *notifyAll* defined in class *Object* will be discussed in Section 2.3.1.2.

# 2.3 Standard Java Classes

The Java standard library includes packages *java.lang*, *java.io*, *java.util*, and *java.awt*, which contain basic classes for the language, I/O, utilities, and window-ing toolkit. The names of classes and interfaces defined in package *java.lang* are automatically imported into a compilation unit when the Java compiler compiles the compilation unit. A compilation unit must explicitly import classes and inter-faces from other packages for using the class and interface names defined in the packages. We now discuss some classes in the Java standard library.

## 2.3.1 Class *Object*

### 2.3.1.1 Class Object – *Common Superclass*

Class *Object* defined in package *java.lang* is the root of the class hierarchy of any Java system. Every class has *Object* as a direct or indirect, explicit or implicit su-perclass. If a class does not declare a superclass in its definition, it has class *Object* as its direct superclass implicitly. Because of the superclass *Object*, all classes in a Java program inherit methods from class *Object*.

Class *Object* has only one constructor with signature *Object()* for creating new objects.

Since class *Object* is the superclass of all other classes, a variable declared with class *Object* can hold a reference to an object or an array of any type.

### 2.3.1.2 Common Behaviors of Objects

Class *Object* defines common behaviors for all objects with the following meth-ods. Many of the methods do nothing. They are provided to support polymorphism. They should be overridden in subclasses with useful functions. The methods can be applied to any object and array.

| Signature | Semantics |
|---|---|
| `boolean equals(Object)` | Compares this object with another for equivalence |
| `Object clone() throws CloneNotSupportedException` | Creates an instance of the class of this object and initializes the created object with values in this object. If the class does not implement interface *Cloneable*, an exception is thrown. |
| `int hashCode()` | Returns integer hash code for this object. Two equal objects must return the same hash code. |
| `String toString()` | Returns a string that represents this object. The method should be overridden in a user-defined class. |
| `Class getClass()` | Returns the runtime class of this object |
| `void finalize() throws Throwable` | A garbage collector calls the method before reclaiming this object. |

Class *Object* defines the following methods for thread synchronization. The method *wait* places a running thread in waiting state until it is awaken by *notify* or *notifyAll* issued by a running thread.

| Signature | Semantics |
|---|---|
| `void wait() throws InterruptedException` | Causes the thread that owns this object's monitor to give up the monitor and wait until it is awaken by *notify* or *notifyAll* |
| `void wait(long timeout) throws InterruptedException` | Causes the thread to wait until it is notified or after timeout |
| `void notify()` | Wakes up a thread waiting on this object's monitor |
| `void notifyAll()` | Wakes up all threads waiting on this object's monitor |

## 2.3.2 Class *String*

### 2.3.2.1 *String Creation*

Class *String* extends *Object* and implements interface *Serializable*. It is a final class, which cannot be extended. Instances of class *String* represent immutable character strings. After a *String* object is created, its contents cannot be changed. (Class *StringBuffer* supports mutable strings.)

A string constant such as *"abc"* is an instance of class *String*. For example, an execution of statement

```
if ("abc" instanceof String)
    System.out.println(true);
else System.out.println(false);
```

prints *true* on the standard output.

The following table includes some constructors of class *String*.

| Signature | Semantics |
|-----------|-----------|
| `String()` | Creates an empty string |
| `String(byte[])` | Creates a string with an array of bytes that encode platform native characters |
| `String(char[])` | Creates a string with a character array |
| `String(String)` | Creates a string with characters in a string |
| `String(StringBuffer)` | Create a string from a *StringBuffer* |

Java overloads the arithmetic addition operator + with concatenation operation for strings. When a string result is expected, operands of operator + are converted to strings through method *toString*. Then, the strings are concatenated to get the result. The operator + is implemented by the Java compiler through methods in class *StringBuffer*. Class *String* redefines method *toString* inherited from class *Object*.

| Signature | Semantics |
|-----------|-----------|
| `String + Object` | Returns a string by concatenating this string and string representation of an object |
| `String concat(String str)` | Returns a string by concatenating strings. |
| `String copyValueOf (char[])` | Creates a string from the characters in a character array |
| `String substring(int index1, int index2)` | Extracts a substring from *index1* to *index2*−1 in this string |

Class *String* overloads static method *valueOf* to convert values and objects into strings. The method argument can be a *boolean, char, char* array, or numeric value. For instance, statements

```
System.out.println(String.valueOf(new Object()));
System.out.println(String.valueOf(3.1415926f));
```

print *java.lang.Object@1ea737* and 3.1415925, respectively, which are string representations of an object and the float value 3.1415926f.

### 2.3.2.2 String Testing and Access

Class *String* includes methods for accessing individual characters in a string, comparing strings, and searching for or extracting a substring.

| Signature | Semantics |
|---|---|
| char charAt(int index) | Returns the character at *index* in this string |
| int compareTo(String anotherString) | Compares two strings lexicographically; returns a negative integer, 0, or a positive integer for less-than, equal-to, or greater-than |
| boolean equals(Object anObject) | Tests if two strings contain the same characters |
| boolean equalsIgnoreCase (String anotherString) | (case-insensitive *equals*) |
| byte[] getBytes() | Converts this string into a byte array according to platform character encoding |
| void getChars(int srcIndex1, int srcIndex2, char[] dst, int index) | Copies a substring of this string into a character array at given *index* |
| int hashCode() | Returns the hash code of this string |
| int indexOf(int ch) | Returns the index of the first occurrence of character *ch* in this string |
| int indexOf(int ch, int index) | Returns the index of *ch* at or after *index* in this string |
| int indexOf(String str) | Returns the index of the first occurrence of string *str* in this string |
| int indexOf(String str, int index) | Returns the index of the first occurrence of string *str* at or after *index* in this string |

| int length() | Returns the length of this string |
|---|---|
| boolean startsWith (String prefix) | Tests if this string starts with a string as prefix |
| boolean endsWith(String suffix) | Tests if this string ends with a string as suffix |

### 2.3.2.3 String Conversion

Instances of class *String* are immutable. The following methods create character arrays or strings from strings.

| Signature | Semantics |
|---|---|
| String replace(char oldChar, char newChar) | Creates a string by replacing occurrences of *oldChar* in this string with *newChar* |
| char[] toCharArray() | Creates a character array from this string |
| String toLowerCase() | Creates a new string by converting uppercase to lowercase |
| String toUpperCase() | Creates a new string by converting lowercase to uppercase |

## 2.3.3 Input/Output Streams

### 2.3.3.1 Class InputStream and OutputStream

A *stream* represents an ordered sequence of formatted data. In a program, we can create an input or output stream for the purpose of data input or output. A stream object has methods for reading from or writing to the stream. A stream isolates programmers from physical details of host file systems and memory data formats. The data may be in a byte array, a string buffer, or a disk file. We can access the data with uniform stream methods.

The Java standard library has a class for random access to files. The class implements stream methods for both input and output operations for files.

Package *java.io* defines standard stream classes. To use a stream class in the package, import the class from the package.

The basic stream classes are *InputStream* and *OutputStream*, which represent input and output streams of bytes. They are abstract classes.

### 2.3.3.2 Input Methods

The instance methods of class *InputStream* are described as follows. A subclass of *InputStream* must provide method *read*() to return the next input byte. Method *read*() returns −1 if the end of the stream is reached. Since class *InputStream* is abstract, we can use an instance of a subclass such as *FileInputStream* of class *InputStream* to encapsulate a file. Some of the methods throw *IOException* when an IO error occurs at runtime.

Method *mark*(*int limit*) marks the current position in an input stream. We can read ahead and reset the stream to the marked position with method *reset*(). Parameter *limit* specifies how many bytes we can read ahead without losing a marked position.

| Signature | Semantics |
|---|---|
| `int available() throws IOException` | Returns the count of bytes that can be read from this input stream |
| `void mark(int limit)` | Marks the current position in this input stream. The mark will be lost after moving beyond limit. |
| `int read() throws IOException` | Reads the next byte or returns −1 if the end of this input stream is reached |
| `int read(byte[] b) throws IOException` | Reads bytes from this input stream into byte array *b* and returns the number of the bytes placed in *b* |
| `void reset() throws IOException` | Repositions the stream to the latest marked position |
| `long skip(long n) throws IOException` | Skips *n* bytes, which are discarded, in this input stream and returns the number of actual bytes skipped |
| `void close() throws IOException` | Closes this input stream |

### 2.3.3.3 Output Methods

Some instance methods of class *OutputStream* are described as follows. A subclass of class *OutputStream* must provide a method for writing a byte of data to an output stream. Class *FileOutputStream* is a subclass of class *OutputStream*. We can create an instance of class *FileOutputStream* with statement

```
OutputStream f = new FileOutpuStream("myda.dat");
```
and invoke the methods for the output stream *f*.

| Signature | Semantics |
|---|---|
| `void write(int b) throws IOException` | Writes a byte to this output stream |
| `void write(byte b[]) throws IOException` | Writes an array of bytes to this output stream |
| `void flush() throws IOException` | Forces buffered bytes output |
| `void close() throws IOException` | Closes this output stream |

### 2.3.3.4 Subclasses of Class InputStream and OutputStream

Some subclasses of classes *InputStream* and *OutputStream* in package *java.io* are described as follows. The subclasses implement the methods of *InputStream* and *OutputStream* with the same semantics. They add features for flexibility and convenience in data input/output.

- *FilterInputStream* and *FilterOutputStream*: The classes encapsulate an *InputStream* called *in* or an *OutputStream* called *out*. Objects of the classes delegate input/output to stream *in* or *out*. The classes can be used to build a stream filter on top of a specified input or output stream. The constructor of class *FilterInputStream* requires an *InputStream* as argument to initialize variable *in*; *FilterOutputStream* requires an *OutputStream* to initialize *out*.
- *BufferedInputStream* and *BufferedOutputStream*: Class *BufferedInputStream* extends class *FilterInputStream* with variable *buf* to reference a byte array and variable *count* to count the valid bytes in the buffer. A position in a *BufferedInputStream* can be marked and reset. Constructors of class *BufferedInputStream* require an *InputStream* as argument.

  Class *BufferedOutputStream* extends class *FilterOutputStream* with two instance variables, *buf* and *count*. Constructors of class *BufferedOutputStream* require an *OutputStream* as argument.

  Buffer size can be specified with constructors of classes *BufferedInputStream* and *BufferedOutputStream*.
- *DataInputStream* and *DataOutputStream*: Class *DataInputStream* extends *FilterInputStream* and implements interface *DataInput*. A *DataInputStream* object reads data that was written with a *DataOutputStream* object. In addition to the *read* methods for reading bytes, class *DataInputStream* provides instance methods for reading primitive types such as *readInt*, *readDouble*, and *readLine*. The class defines method *readUTF* to read strings. The constructor of class *DataInputStream* requires an *InputStream* argument. For example, to read formatted data from file *myda.dat*, we can create a data input stream with code

```
InputStream inf = new FileInputStream("myda.dat");
DataInputStream din =new DataInputStream(inf);
```

Class *DataOutputStream* extends *FilterOutputStream* and implements interface *DataOutput*. In addition to the *write* methods for writing bytes, class *DataOutputStream* specifies instance methods *writeInt*, *writeDouble*, and *writeUTF*. The constructor of class *DataOutputStream* requires an *OutputStream* argument.

- Class *PushbackInputStream*: The class extends class *FilterInputStream* with instance variables *buf* and *pos*. Variable *buf* references a byte array that serves as a pushback buffer, and *pos* refers to the current position inside the buffer. The overloaded methods *unread* have signatures

  *unread(int ch)*
  *unread(byte[])*
  *unread(byte[] bytes, int beginIndex, int endIndex)*

for pushing back a character or a byte array. Constructors of class *PushbackInputStream* require an *InputStream* as argument. One may also specify the pushback buffer size as an argument in a constructor invocation.

The unread functionality of *PushbackInputStream* is used when reading ahead for a particular byte value. If the byte value is a part of the next data element, the byte must be pushed back before reading the next data element.

The following example illustrates the formatted input/output. It uses *read-Float* and *writeFloat* methods for input and output. Readers are invited to exercise *readUTF* and *writeUTF* methods for string input/output.

**Example 2.9** The following main method writes an array of float values through a *DataOutputStream* into a file and then reads the values with a *DataInputStream* from the file. It prints the values on standard output.

```
import java.io.*;
class TestDataIO {
    public static void main(String[] args) {
        try {
            OutputStream outf = new
                    FileOutputStream("myda.dat");
            DataOutputStream dout = new
                    DataOutputStream(outf);
            float[] floats = { 12f, 33.1f, 55.55f };
            for (int i = 0; i < floats.length; i++)
                dout.writeFloat(floats[i]);
            dout.close();
        }
        catch(IOException e) {return;}
        try {
            InputStream inf = new
                    FileInputStream("myda.dat");
            DataInputStream din = new
                    DataInputStream(inf);
            try { while (true)
                System.out.println(din.readFloat());
```

```
            }
            catch(EOFException e) { din.close(); }
        }
        catch(IOException e) { }
    }
}
```

Here we use an exception object in class *EOFException* to trigger method *close*, which closes a file. The exception is thrown when method *readFloat* is invoked for an empty stream.                                                    □

**Exercise 2.6** Modify the above main method by writing strings to file *myda.dat*. Read the strings from the file and print them on standard output.

## 2.3.3.5 Byte Array Streams

We may read from a byte array in the main memory. We can create a byte array input stream with the byte array as argument. Class *ByteArrayInputStream* extends *InputStream* with instance variables *buf*, *count*, *mark*, and *pos*. Variable *buf* references the byte array in the memory; *count* is the valid byte count in the array; *mark* is an index in the array; and *pos* is the current position index. A *ByteArray-InputStream* object uses methods *mark* and *reset* to mark the current position or reset the stream to a marked position.

Class *ByteArrayOutputStream* extends class *OutputStream* with instance variable *buf* and *count*. Variable *buf* references a byte array, which is used to store the output, and *count* records the number of valid bytes in the byte array.

When we need to write to a byte array, we can create a byte array output stream. The constructors of class *ByteArrayOutputStream* create a byte array and reference it with variable *buf*. In addition to the methods defined in class *Output-Stream*, class *ByteArrayOutputStream* defines method *toByteArray()* to return a new copy of the byte array referenced by *buf* and method *toString()* to convert the byte array into a *String*.

## 2.3.3.6 File Input/Output

In Java, a file can be associated with a stream for input or output. The stream is an instance of class *FileInputStream* or *FileOutputStream*. To perform both input and output for a file, open the file with a *RandomAccessFile* object. The information on the file can be encapsulated in an instance of class *File* or *FileDescriptor*. When class *FileInputStream*, *FileOutputStream*, or *RandomAccessFile* is instantiated, a *File*, a *FileDescriptor*, or a file name is required to denote a file or directory in the host file system. We now describe classes *File*, *FileDescriptor*, *FileInputStream*, *FileOutputStream*, and *RandomAccessFile* for file I/O.

The purpose of class *File* is to abstract file naming conventions of a host file system. An instance of the class represents a file or a directory in the host file system. It can be created with one of the constructors

*File(String path)*
*File(String directoryPath, String fileName)*
*File(File directoryObject, String fileName)*

The following methods can be applied to a file object to test the status of a file or directory in a host file system. For example, the file object can be created with the statement

```
File f = new File("Examples\\Chapter2");
```

where we use backslash \ to connect names *Examples* and *Chapter2* in Windows. UNIX uses slash / as file name separator.

| Signature | Semantics |
|---|---|
| `String getPath()` | Returns the path name encapsulated in the file object |
| `String getAbsolutePath()` | Returns an absolute path to this file |
| `boolean exists()` | Tests if the file represented by this object exists in the host file system |
| `boolean canWrite()` | Tests if the application can write to this file |
| `boolean canRead()` | Tests if the application can read from this file |
| `boolean isFile()` | Tests if the object does not represent a directory |
| `boolean isDirectory()` | Tests if the object represents a directory |
| `long length()` | Returns the length of the file represented by this object; returns 0 if the file does not exist |
| `boolean equals(Object obj)` | Compares two file objects based on their pathnames |

The following instance methods can be used to create, delete, or manipulate files and directories in a file system. The security manager of a Java runtime may prevent applications from invoking the methods.

| Signature | Semantics |
|---|---|
| `boolean mkdir()` | Creates a directory with the pathname in this file object |
| `boolean mkdirs()` | Creates a directory with the pathname in this file object; creates parent directories if necessary |

| | |
|---|---|
| `boolean delete()` | Deletes the file represented by this file object |

The methods in the following table access *File* objects. Assume a *File* object that represents a directory. The *File* object can list the names of files and directories in the directory that can be accepted by a *filter*, where *filter* is an instance of interface *FilenameFilter*. The operation is implemented with method *list(FilenameFilter filter)*. The interface *FilenameFilter* defines method

   *boolean accept(File dir, String name)*,

which determines whether the *name* of a file or directory is accepted. The parameter *dir* represents a file object, for which method *list(filter)* is invoked. For example, to accept files with suffix *class*, we can use an argument *filter* that references an object in the following class.

```
class JavaClassFileFilter
                        implements FilenameFilter {
      public boolean accept(File dir, String s) {
         return s.endsWith(".class");
      }
}
```

| Signature | Semantics |
|---|---|
| `String[] list()` | Lists files and directories in the directory specified by this file object |
| `String[] list(FilenameFilter filter)` | Lists files and directories in the directory specified by this file object that can be accepted by a filter |
| `int hashCode()` | Computes hash code for this file object |
| `String toString()` | Gives the path name encapsulated in this file object |

Class *FileDescriptor* represents a handle to an open file in a file system or a handle to an open socket for network connection. It defines class variables *in*, *out*, and *err* to represent the standard input, output, and error stream. Applications should not create their own file descriptors. A file descriptor is returned from a file stream. The class has an instance method to test whether an instance represents a valid open file or socket, and a method to enforce synchronization of all system buffers for a device.

Class *FileInputStream* extends class *InputStream*. An instance of class *FileInputStream* is a stream for reading data from a file in a file system. The file can be represented with a *File* or a *FileDescriptor* object. Constructor signatures of class *FileInputStream* are

   *FileInputStream(String path)*
   *FileInputStream(File)*

*FileInputStream*(*FileDescriptor*).

Class *FileInputStream* implements the methods of class *InputStream*. The instance method *getFD*() applied to a *FileInputStream* returns a *FileDescriptor* handle for the file represented by the stream.

Class *FileOutputStream* extends class *OutputStream*. An instance of the class is a stream for writing data to a file in a file system. Constructor signatures of class *FileOutputStream* are

*FileOutputStream*(*String path*)
*FileOutputStream*(*File*)
*FileOutputStream*(*FileDescriptor*).

Class *FileOutputStream* implements methods of class *OutputStream*. Method *getFD*() applied to a file output stream returns a *FileDescriptor* handle to the file.

Class *RandomAccessFile* extends class *Object* and implements interfaces *DataOutput* and *DataInput*, which are implemented by classes *OutputStream* and *InputStream*, respectively. An instance of class *RandomAccessFile* represents a file for random accesses. It supports reading and writing data of Java types as well as bytes. For example, the class defines methods *readInt*, *readDouble*, *readLine*, *readUTF*, *writeInt*, *writeDouble*, and *writeUTF*. The instance method *seek*(*long*) can be used to position an underlying file where the next read or write will occur.

Constructors of class *RandomAccessFile* are

*RandomAccessFile*(*File fileObject*, *String mode*)
*RandomAccessFile*(*String name*, *String mode*),

where the *mode* string can be *"r"* for read-only and *"rw"* for both read and write. For example, we can create a random access file with statement

```
RandomAccessFile raf = new
                RandomAccessFile("myda.dat", "rw");
```

The following example illustrates the use of random access file. It associates a data file with a *FileOutputStream* object. Then, it opens the file with a random access file object. It reads and writes the file through the random access file object.

**Example 2.10** The following method writes three float constants to a file through a file output stream named *dout*. Then, it associates the file with a random access file named *raf*. It reads the file, replaces the first float in the file with another float, and reads the modified file again.

```
import java.io.*;
class TestRandomDataIO {
    public static void main(String[] args) {
        try {
            OutputStream outf = new
                    FileOutputStream("myda.dat");
            DataOutputStream dout = new
                    DataOutputStream(outf);
            float[] floats = { 12f, 33.1f, 55.55f };
            for (int i = 0; i < floats.length; i++)
                dout.writeFloat(floats[i]);
```

```
                dout.close();
          }
          catch(IOException e) {return;}
          try {
             RandomAccessFile raf = new
                RandomAccessFile("myda.dat", "rw");
             try {
              while (true)
              System.out.print(raf.readFloat()+"\t");
             }
             catch(EOFException e) {
                System.out.println();
             }

             raf.seek(0L); raf.writeFloat(21f);
             raf.seek(0L);
             try {
              while (true)
              System.out.print(raf.readFloat()+"\t");
             }
             catch(EOFException e) {
                System.out.println(); }
          }
          catch(IOException e) { }
       }
    }
```

An execution of the above class prints

| 12.0 | 33.1 | 55.55 |
|------|------|-------|
| 21.0 | 33.1 | 55.55 |

□

**Exercise 2.7** Modify the above method by changing the third float in file *myda.dat*.

## 2.3.4 Wrapper Classes

Some Java data structures such as a vector store objects but not primitive values. To store primitive values in the data structures, we can wrap the values with objects and store the wrappers in the data structures. Java has built-in wrapper classes for wrapping values of primitive types.

### 2.3.4.1 Class Boolean

An instance of class *Boolean* wraps a value of primitive type *boolean*. It consists of a single field of type *boolean*. The class provides methods to convert a *boolean* value to a string and vice versa. The constructors of class *Boolean* are

> *Boolean(boolean)*
> *Boolean(String)*

for wrapping a *boolean*. The string argument should be either *"true"* or *"false"*. For example, expression *Boolean("false")* returns an object of class *Boolean*, which wraps boolean value *false*.

The following methods, except static method *valueOf*, access the data encapsulated in a *Boolean* object. The *valueOf* method converts a string to a *Boolean*.

| Signature | Semantics |
|-----------|-----------|
| boolean booleanValue() | Returns the boolean value in this object |
| static Boolean valueOf (String s) | Creates a *Boolean* object with string *s*, which is either *"true"* or *"false"* |
| String toString() | Returns string *"true"* or *"false" for* this *Boolean* object |
| int hashCode() | Returns hash code of this *Boolean* |
| boolean equals(Object obj) | Compares two *Boolean* objects based on truth values |

### 2.3.4.2 Class Character

An instance of class *Character* wraps a value of primitive type *char*. It consists of a single field of type *char*. It can be created with constructor

> *Character(char)*.

Class *Character* provides static methods for testing characters and converting characters into different forms. For example, *isLetter(char)*, *isJavaLetter(char)*, *isLetterOrDigit(char)*, *isUpperCase(char)*, *isLowerCase(char)*, *isJavaIdentifierStart(char)*, and *isJavaIdentifierPart(char)* test if a *char* argument is a letter, a Java letter, a letter or digit, an upper case letter, a lower case letter, a legal starting letter for Java identifiers or in Java identifiers. Given a *char* value, class *Character* has methods to decide its equivalent numeric value and other values.

### 2.3.4.3 Numeric Value Wrappers

Class *Number* is an abstract class. It is the superclass of classes *Byte*, *Short*, *Integer*, *Long*, *Float*, and *Double* for wrapping numeric values. For an object of class *Number*, we can apply methods *byteValue()*, *shortValue()*, *intValue()*, *longValue()*, *floatValue()*, and *doubleValue()* to return a *byte*, *short*, *int*, *long*, *float*, or *double* value. The methods are implemented by subclasses of class *Number*. They may involve conversions and truncations. All the numeric classes *Byte*,

*Short, Integer, Long, Float,* and *Double* have similar behavior. We use class *Byte* to illustrate the classes.

Class *Byte* extends class *Number* with a private instance variable *value* to hold a *byte.* Constructors

> *Byte(byte value)*
> *Byte(String s)*

of class *Byte* use a *byte* or the string representation of a byte to initialize the *value* field of a created *Byte* object. For example, expression *Byte(*12) wraps value 12 in an object of class *Byte* and returns the object.

Class *Byte* has class methods for converting a string into a *byte* value or a *Byte* object. The methods may have an optional integer argument as conversion radix. The default radix is 10.

Class *Byte* provides instance methods *byteValue(), shortValue(), intValue(), longValue(), floatValue(), doubleValue(),* and *toString()* to return a *byte, short, int, long, float, double,* or string based on the value of the instance field *value.*

# 2.4 Reflection Model

## 2.4.1 Java Core Reflection API

The Java reflection model is implemented with the Java core reflection API (application programming interface). It supports introspection of loaded classes and objects created at runtime. It also supports performing dynamically decided operations for objects, object creation and modification, and invocation of methods on behalf of an object or array. The Java reflection model satisfies applications that need to access definitions of public members of runtime objects and definitions of classes by accessing class files at runtime.

The Java reflection uses classes *Class, Array, Field, Method,* and *Modifier* to represent object types, arrays, fields, methods, and modifers. A running program can manipulate the instances of the classes. It can access the definition information on the objects and classes and access the actual data in them. The API defines interface *Member* to describe members, which are fields and methods, of classes. Class *Modifier* uses integers to encode Java language modifiers for classes and members. It has class methods to decode integers to modifiers.

A *Method* object describes a method in a class or interface. The reflected method may be a class or instance method, which may be abstract. Its method *invoke(Object, Object[])* can be used to invoke the method for an object with an array of objects as arguments. Example 3.6 uses the Java object reflection to retrieve a *Method* object from the class of an object. The method is invoked for the object and given arguments.

## 2.4.2 Class *Class*

An instance of class *Class* represents a Java type, which is a class, an interface, or a primitive type. Since an array type such as *int*[] or *Customer*[] is a type, it is also represented by an instance of class *Class*. The Java primitive types such as *int* and *float* are represented by predefined *Class* objects that have the same names as the primitive types. These *Class* objects are accessed by expressions *Boolean.TYPE*, *Character.TYPE*, *Byte.TYPE*, *Short.TYPE*, *Integer.TYPE*, *Long.TYPE*, *Float. TYPE*, and *Double.TYPE*, which access constant *TYPE* defined in the wrapper classes. Keyword *void* is regarded as the only value of type *Void.TYPE*.

For a fully qualified class or interface *name*, an execution of static method *forName*(*name*) of class *Class* locates, loads, and links the named class or interface. It returns an instance of class *Class*. For example, the source code

```
try {
    Class classObj = Class.forName("Customer");
}
catch(ClassNotFoundException e){
    System.out.println("Customer can't be loaded.");
}
```

can be used to load class *Customer*.

An instance of class *Class* represents a type. It responds to method *newInstance*() for creating an object of the type. The method does what operator *new* and a no-argument constructor do. Class *Class* defines instance methods for testing if an instance of *Class* represents an interface, an array type, or a primitive type. It also defines instance methods for retrieving the type name, declared modifiers such as *public* and *static*, superclass and superinterfaces, declared fields, declared methods and constructors, and other features in the underlying type.

Class *Class* is in package *java.lang*. Subpackage *java.lang.reflect* actually defines all other classes of the core reflection API. They must be imported before the reflection classes can be used in a program. Classes of exceptions thrown by reflection methods are defined in package *java.lang*.

## 2.4.3 Classes *Field*, *Method*, and *Constructor*

A *member* in a class or interface is either a variable or a method. An object of interface *Member* represents a member. The interface *Member* is implemented by classes *Field*, *Method*, and *Constructor*. It defines methods *getDeclaringClass*(), *getName*(), and *getModifiers*() for retrieving a class, a string, or modifiers that describe a member in a class or interface.

An instance of class *Field* encapsulates information on a field of a class or interface. Methods *getField*, *getFields*, *getDeclaredField*, and *getDeclaredFields* of class *Class* can be used to retrieve a public field or fields in a class. Using an object as argument, method *get* invoked for a *Field* object can retrieve the actual value from the field in the object. Typed access methods such as *getBoolean* and *getInt* retrieve formatted values from fields of objects. We can place a value into a field in an object with method *set(Object targetObj, Object value)*. Similarly, methods *setBoolean* and *setInt* can place a boolean or integer into a field.

An instance of class *Method* encapsulates the information on a method of a class or interface. Method *getMethod, getMethods, getDeclaredMethod*, or *getDeclaredMethods* invoked for a class object returns a public method or methods.

We use the following example to show how to load a class and how to retrieve a method from the class.

**Example 2.11** The following try construct loads class *Customer* and retrieves public method *setAddress(String address)* from the class object. The method *forName* declares *ClassNotFoundException* to throw, and *getMethod* declares *NoSuchMethodException*. Since the try construct intercepts the two types of exceptions, the following code can be added to a method that does not throw the exceptions.

```
try {
    Class cus_class =Class.forName("Customer");
    Class str_class =
                Class.forName("java.lang.String");
    Class[] types = new Class[1];
    types[0] = str_class;
    Method method1 = cus_class.getMethod(
                        "setAddress", types);
    System.out.println(method1);
}
catch(ClassNotFoundException e) {
    System.out.println("Class Customer or "
                    + "String can't be loaded.");
}
catch(NoSuchMethodException e) {
    System.out.println("Method setAddress "
                        +"can't be accessed.");
}
```

□

**Exercise 2.8** Use a try construct to retrieve instance field *name* from class *Customer*. (For a successful retrieval, instance variable *name* must be a public variable.)

An instance of class *Method* can perform the method represented by the object with method *invoke(Object targetObj, Object[] args)*. If the name of the represented method is *methodName*, an execution of the *invoke* method is equivalent to the method invocation

   *targetObj.methodName(args)*.

Thus, we can dynamically construct a method name, retrieve the method from a class, and invoke (dispatch) the method for an object. In Section 3.4.2, we show how to apply the Java reflection to dynamically dispatch a method.

An instance of class *Constructor* represents a constructor of a class. We can retrieve a *Constructor* object from a class object and invoke method *newInstance* for the *Constructor* object to create a new instance of the class. The receiving object of method *newInstance* is the *Constructor* object. The constructor body uses the arguments of method *newInstance* invocation.

**Exercise 2.9** Use a try construct to retrieve the no-argument constructor from class *Merchandise*. Invoke the constructor to create an object of class *Merchandise*. (If you cannot retrieve the constructor, add modifier *public* to the constructor.)

# 2.5 Inner Classes

## 2.5.1 Scopes of Classes

In the above examples, classes are defined as members of compilation units. Therefore, the classes are members of packages. The *scope* of a class is the range where it plays roles in object creation and variable declaration. It is based on where the class resides. The latest release of the Java language allows classes to be defined not only as members of packages but also as members of classes, as components of statements, and as ingredients of expressions. It also permits nameless (anonymous) class definitions. Programmers can define the *inner classes* as well as top-level classes. Java actually removes any restriction on reasonable placement of classes in programs. The inner class feature of Java helps model applications and structure fields, methods, and classes inside classes.

A class can be defined as a static member of a top-level class with keyword *static*. A static member class of a top-level class is another top-level class. An interface can be placed in a top-level class as well. The collection of top-level classes in a Java program consists of the classes that are package members and static members of top-level classes. Thus, a program has a hierarchical organization of top-level classes. We can place logically related secondary top-level classes in a top-level class.

The non-top-level classes defined in classes are called *inner classes*. A difference between a top-level class and an inner class is whether an enclosed class knows its enclosing class. A top-level class cannot directly use the instance variables specified in the classes that enclose it. Instead, it can define an instance field to hold an object of a top-level class that encloses it and access the instance fields of the object. An instance of an inner class is associated with the current instance of an enclosing class. The inner class can directly access the instance variables defined in its enclosing class.

An inner class may be placed in another inner class. It may use the private instance variables of a class that encloses it. An inner class may have a series of current instances, one for each of its enclosing inner classes and one for the closest top-level class that encloses it. The inner class knows the instance variables of all the current instances.

The notions of inner class and secondary top-level class are based on two views:

- We can place the definition of a class in another class like the declaration of a static or instance variable in a class. Thus, the class is defined as a member of the other class.
- The creation of an object relies on only the *new* operator and the body of a class. We can use the expression

  **new** *superclassName*(*parameterList*) *innerClassBody*

to create an object of an anonymous class. The anonymous class inherits a class or interface named *superclassName* in the above expression. The anonymous class body represented with *innerClassBody* in the above expression can use parameters declared in *parameterList*.

In the following example, we illustrate several types of class in a compilation unit. Some classes in the file are package members. Some are inner classes. We also show how to use the classes to declare variables and create objects.

**Example 2.12** The following compilation unit can be compiled and executed. It contains several types of classes:

- package member classes named *OuterClass* and *PackageClass*. They are top-level classes.
- class member class named *TopLevelClass* in class *OuterClass*. Because class *TopLevelClass* is contained in a top-level class and is declared with *static*, it is a (secondary) top-level class.
- class member classes named *InnerClass1* and *InnerClass2*, which are inner classes. Class *InnerClass1* is a non-static member of class *Outer-Class*. One of the definition of inner class name *InnerClass2* is a member of class *InnerClass1*, the other a member of class *TopLevelClass*.
- anonymous inner classes, one inheriting *InnerClass1* and the other inheriting *PackageClass*.

```
import java.util.*;
// package member OuterClass
public class OuterClass {
    public static void main(String[] args) {
        OuterClass obj = new OuterClass();
        TopLevelClass obj1 = new TopLevelClass();
        System.out.println(obj1);
        Object innerObj = obj.create(obj);
        System.out.println(innerObj);
    }
    // uses InnerClass1
    InnerClass1 innerObj1 = new InnerClass1();
```

```java
Object create(final OuterClass argObj) {
    OuterClass outerObj = new OuterClass();
    /* uses InnerClass1 to create object,
     *  which is attached to argObj
     */
    InnerClass1 innerObj2 =
                argObj.new InnerClass1();
    System.out.println(argObj + "\n" +
                innerObj1 + "\n" + innerObj2);

    /* anonymous inner class that inherits
     *  InnerClass1
     */
    return new InnerClass1() {
        public String toString() {
         return "Anonymous inner class method.";
        }
    }
}

// class member inner class InnerClass1
class InnerClass1 {
    Object obj1;
    // inner class InnerClass2
    class InnerClass2 {
        Object obj2;
    }

    // uses InnerClass2
    InnerClass2 obj3 = new InnerClass2();

    public String toString() {
        return obj3.toString();
    }
}

// top-level class TopLevelClass
static class TopLevelClass {
    Object obj1;
    // inner class of TopLevelClass
    class InnerClass2 {
        Object obj2 = new PackageClass() {
            // anonymous inner class body
            int i = 20;
            public String toString(){
                return
                ("TopLevelClass.Innerclass2@"+i);
```

```
                    }
                }; // end of object creation
            }
        }
    }

    // a top-level class, which is a package member
    class PackageClass {
        String name;
        Object obj1;
        public static void main(String[] args) {
            // use secondary top-level class
            OuterClass.TopLevelClass o = new
                        OuterClass.TopLevelClass();
            System.out.println(o);
        }
    }
```

                       □

In the above example, we do not show any inner class that is declared in a block or method body. In a block or method body, we can define classes as well as local variables. These classes are inner classes.

## 2.5.2 Data Organization and Adapter Classes

In a Java program, we can implement a data structure with a class and define the element type for the data structure with an inner class in the class. For example, class *Order* in Example 1.3 uses class *Item* to declare array *items*. Since class *Item* is useful only for orders, we can define class *Item* as a member of class *Order*. Thus, the logical relation between order and item is maintained in the class structuring.

In the design of a class, we may deliver a service offered by the class through another class. The latter class is usually called an *adapter* of the former. For example, we may need to enumerate the items contained in an order object. An adapter for class *Order* can be used to generate an enumeration for an order object. Since an adapter needs access to the instance fields of the order object, it is better to place the adapter class inside the *Order* class.

The following example illustrates two uses of inner class. First, we move class *Item* into class *Order*. The declaration of an item array in class *Order* will use the inner class *Item*. Secondly, we define an adapter class called *Enumerator*, which enumerates items in the *items* array for an order object. Both classes *Item* and *Enumerator* are inner classes of class *Order*.

**Example 2.13** The following class, class *Order*, contains class *Item* as a member class. It uses the class *Item* to declare an array referenced by instance variable *items*. It also defines the adapter class *Enumerator* to enumerate the items in the array. Class *Enumerator* implements interface *Enumeration* by defining methods *hasMoreElements* and *nextElement*. Since a field of class *Item* is declared with class *Merchandise*, we also include the class *Merchandise* within the compilation unit. We test the classes with a main method in class *Order*.

```java
import java.util.*;
public class Order {
    Customer receiver;
    Item[] items;
    class Item {
        Merchandise item;
        int quantity;
    }

    class Enumerator implements Enumeration {
        int pos = 0;
        public boolean hasMoreElements() {
            if (items == null) return false;
            for (int i = pos; i < items.length; i++)
                if (items[i] != null) return true;
            return false;
        }

        public Object nextElement() {
            for (; pos < items.length; pos++)
                if (items[pos] != null)
                    return items[pos++];
            throw
                new NoSuchElementException("No item");
        }
    }

    public Enumeration elements() {
        return new Enumerator();
    }

    public static void main(String[] args) {
        Order order1 = new Order();
        order1.items = new Item[20];
        order1.items[2] = order1.new Item();
        Enumeration total = order1.elements();
        Item temp_item;
        while (total.hasMoreElements()) {
            temp_item = (Item) total.nextElement();
            System.out.println(temp_item);
        }
    }
}
```

```
class Merchandise {
    String name;
    float price;
}
```

□

**Exercise 2.10** In Example 2.13, the main method invokes method *println*() in a while loop. What will the while loop print on the standard output, and why?

## 2.6 Summary

The Java language is object-oriented. A program written in Java is composed of classes and interfaces. A class defines fields, methods, and/or classes. In this chapter, we introduce the various types of token for class definition and various types of statement to compose class definitions and method bodies.

The control transfer statements of the Java language include block, if statement, switch statement, for loop, while loop, and do loop. Inside a loop or a switch statement, we may use a break statement to skip the loop or the remaining part of the switch. In a loop, we may use a continue statement to skip the remaining part of the loop and start the next repetition of the loop.

In Java programming, exceptions are extensively used to transfer control to code that handles exceptional conditions. The Java exception handling mechanism categorizes exceptions into checkable and non-checkable exceptions. A method may declare checkable exceptions that it throws and throw the checkable exceptions from its body. When the method is invoked, either the calling method declares that it throws a checkable exception that is thrown by the invoked method or the calling method intercepts the checkable exception thrown by the invoked method with an exception handler. The Java compiler checks checkable exception declaration, throwing, and handling. Using exception handling may create readable and maintainable Java programs.

This chapter also discusses multithread programming, which improves the interactive performance of a program. Multiple threads are coordinated with the synchronization mechanism of Java. Specifically, we can declare synchronized methods and blocks with keyword *synchronized*. We can invoke methods *wait* and *notify* to coordinate consumers and producers with object monitors.

The Java standard library includes classes *Object*, *String*, and I/O classes. Class *Object* provides common behaviors for objects created by Java programs. The common behaviors include methods for thread synchronization. Class *String* represents immutable strings of characters. It provides methods for accessing and manipulating strings. Most I/O classes are streams, which hide the complexity of a file system with simple, uniform stream operations. A file can be randomly accessed and changed through class *RandomAccessFile*, which is not a stream class. But, the class implements interfaces *DataInput* and *dataOutput*, which include most of the stream methods.

The reflection model of the Java language makes it possible to access object fields and dispatch methods dynamically based on runtime information. The Java reflection model allows a program to determine the definition information of classes and that of members in the classes. It benefits not only system programmers who develop tools such as debugger but also application programmers.

A new feature of the Java language is an inner class, which can be placed in a class that logically includes it. Inner classes can be used to implement adapter classes so that an adapter class can reside inside the class it serves and access the fields of the enclosing class. Inner classes will be used to define data structure classes in the book.

# Assignment

In the assignment of Chapter 1, you are asked to analyze and implement a university administration system in Java. Identify several possible exceptional conditions for the instance methods in the system, define checkable exception classes for the exceptional conditions, and use the exceptions in the instance methods.

# Chapter 3
# Programming in Java

Java is regarded by the software industry as one of the most promising general-purpose programming languages. It eases the task of developing robust, reliable, readable, and manageable software systems. For Internet programmers, Java can be used to write applets, which are displayed by Internet browsers. For other developers, Java has features such as network and database APIs (Application Programming Interfaces) to satisfy various applications. The software industry is still exploring the potential of Java programming. The Java language is evolving as well.

Java provides a standard class, class *Applet*, to support Web programming. The class has a standard API for Internet browsers.

Graphical user interface (GUI) is indispensable for software systems. Java has standard classes to support graphics and GUI construction. The Abstract Windowing Toolkit (AWT) is the Java graphics library. It supports primitive graphical operations and GUI construction. The graphics and GUIs generated with AWT may not look as nice as those generated with some platform-dependent native graphics toolkits. But AWT ensures platform independence and maximum portability. It is Internet-oriented. Different operating systems and Internet browsers can reliably display graphics developed in Java.

In this chapter, we discuss Java programming from the standpoint of application developer. We describe the notions of applet and application, and show how to develop applets and standalone applications. We also study graphics and GUI construction in Java. To understand how a GUI interacts with users, we present the event delegation model of Java. Several utility classes of Java that are useful for data structure analysis are discussed. Since we are concerned with the performance of data structures in terms of speed, we present a benchmarking method to evaluate the performance of Java code. The method depends on the Java reflection model.

This chapter focuses on the following topics of programming in Java.

- Applet construction. All useful applets are instances of subclasses of the standard class *Applet*, which is in package *java.applet*. Class *Applet* specifies a standard interface for Internet browsers and applet viewers to run applets. A programmer extends class *Applet* to define data representation, specify visual presentation, and prescribe behavior for applets. We look at the standard methods of applet classes and discuss how to use Web pages to display applets.
- Graphical operations such as drawing rectangles, ovals, text, and images and filling shapes on screen. In Java, all the graphical operations are performed

through objects of class *Graphics*. We look at graphical operations and graphics attributes to control colors, fonts, and painting modes for the graphical operations.

- GUI construction and the event delegation model. A GUI is composed of components, which are objects of component classes. To interact with users, GUI components handle events, which are generated by users, other components in GUIs, and the operating system. Java event model has evolved from a simple one to the flexible event delegation model. Java has deprecated the simple model. We discuss the event delegation model.
- Several utility classes in the Java standard library. The classes include *System*, *Math*, and *Random*. We also apply the Java core reflection API to develop a benchmarking utility, which can be used to decide the time spent by the execution of an instance method.

Most examples in this chapter are related to the supermarket discussed in Chapter 1. Particularly, we shall create an application to keep customer objects for the supermarket. The application has a GUI, which allows a user to enter new customer information, read existing customer data, and delete selected customers.

# 3.1 Java Programs

## 3.1.1 Applet Programming

### 3.1.1.1 Applets

An *applet* is a mini-program associated with a World Wide Web page. A local or remote Java-enabled browser displays an applet in a Web page by invoking methods of the applet. When the browser comes across the applet, the applet is loaded and started. When it leaves the page, the applet is stopped. A browser may temporarily leave an applet and then reenter it when a user scrolls the Web page up and down. A user of the Web page browser can interact with the applet. The applet may display multimedia information.

An applet is different from a standalone application in several ways. An applet is a special type of visible panel, which has a width and a height. An applet has no main method but a set of standard methods. The standard methods include *init*, *start*, *stop*, and *paint*. A browser invokes the standard methods. An applet is not in control of the thread of its execution. (In the methods, an applet may create threads for time-consuming jobs such as animation. An applet has control over the created threads.) An applet is not created with a constructor. A browser invokes method *init* for one-time initialization when it creates an applet. An Internet browser regards an applet as untrusted code and places security restrictions on applets with a security manager. For example, applets cannot read or write local files.

### 3.1.1.2 Displaying Applets

An applet is defined with a subclass of class *Applet*. An applet class is compiled with the Java compiler before a browser can display the applet. A browser downloads the compiled class file from a server, which may be the local computer on which the browser is run. To include an applet in a Web page written in HTML, use an *<APPLET>* tag to specify attributes for the applet. The attributes include class file name, applet size, and optional parameters used by the applet methods. An Internet browser uses the file name to download the applet class file from server. It executes the compiled applet methods on the local computer.

Some attributes of an applet must be specified in a Web page. The required attributes include *CODE*, *WIDTH*, and *HEIGHT*. Attribute *CODE* specifies the class file name of the applet. If the class file is not in the same directory as the Web page document, attribute *CODEBASE* must be used to introduce the path to the directory that contains the class file at server. Attributes *WIDTH* and *HEIGHT* specify the width and height of the applet panel when the applet is displayed. We can specify a parameter name and value on the Web page in the syntax

    *<PARAM NAME=parameterName VALUE=value>*.

Multiple parameters may be specified for a Web page.

The following example shows an HTML file that can be loaded and displayed by a browser. After changing the value of attribute *CODE*, an applet viewer such as the *appletviewer* of Sun's JDK can use the HTML document to display the applets described in this chapter. You may change the size of the applet to accommodate components.

**Example 3.1** The following is an HTML Web page document. It introduces the required attributes and a parameter for an applet with the *<APPLET>* tag. The applet is embedded in a paragraph of the Web page body. It specifies parameter name *MAX_LINES* and value "10" (a string) from the parameter.

```
<HTML>
<HEAD>
<Title>Customer List</Title>
</HEAD>
<BODY>
Please enter a customer information
or select a customer.
<P>
<APPLET CODE="CustomerList.class"
WIDTH=150 HEIGHT=200>
<PARAM NAME="MAX_LINES" VALUE="10">
</APPLET>
</BODY>
</HTML>
```

          □

An applet viewer like *appletviewer* is different from an Internet browser. It needs only the attributes and parameters between a pair of tags *<APPLET>* and *</APPLET>*. For example, the HTML code

```
<APPLET CODE="CustomerList.class"
              WIDTH=150 HEIGHT=200>
<PARAM NAME="MAX_LINES" VALUE="10">
</APPLET>
```

can be used to start *appletviewer*.

The following table illustrates the possible attributes of an applet for displaying the applet with a Web browser or applet viewer. The values of attributes *WIDTH*, *HEIGHT*, *VSPACE*, and *HSPACE* of an applet panel are expressed in pixels. We use URL to abbreviate the term *uniform resource locator*.

| Name | Value |
|------|-------|
| CODEBASE | The URL of the applet class file (optional) |
| ARCHIVE | A list of archive files, each containing classes and resources for loading together (optional) |
| CODE | The applet class file name, relative to the *CODEBASE* URL. One of attributes *CODE* or *OBJECT* is required. |
| OBJECT | The file name of the serial representation of the applet (discouraged to use) |
| ALT | Text to be displayed when the browser cannot run a Java applet (optional) |
| NAME | A name for the applet instance (optional) |
| WIDTH | Initial width to display the applet panel in pixels |
| HEIGHT | Initial height |
| ALIGN | A specification of alignment for the applet panel (optional) |
| VSPACE | The vertical space above and below the applet panel in browser (optional) |
| HSPACE | The horizontal space at the left of the applet panel (optional) |

### 3.1.1.3 Applet States

An applet is an instance of class *Applet*, which defines a standard interface between applets and Web browsers. Applet viewers also understand the interface. The methods in class *Applet* do nothing. A programmer of an applet extends class *Applet* and overrides the inherited methods in the subclass to introduce behavior for applets. Class *Applet* has a constructor *Applet()*, which is actually useless for a programmer.

After a browser loads an applet class and creates an instance of the class, the browser is responsible to change the state of the applet object by invoking the following methods for the applet. As we already mentioned, the methods are overridden in subclasses to include meaningful operations.

| Signature | Semantics |
|---|---|
| `void init()` | Called when an applet is loaded. It can perform initialization for this applet such as thread creation and image loading. |
| `void start()` | Called when an applet becomes visible. It can start animations and other threads. |
| `void stop()` | Called when this applet is temporarily invisible or before it is destroyed. It should stop time-consuming activities such as animations and interactive threads. |
| `void destroy()` | Called before this applet is about to be reclaimed. It can perform resource clean-ups. |
| `void paint(Graphics g)` | Called when a browser should draw this applet (inherited from class *Component*) |
| `void update(Graphics g)` | Updates this applet by completely redrawing it (inherited from class *Component*) |
| `void repaint()` | Called when this applet should be redrawn. It calls *update* method for this applet. (inherited from class *Component*) |

**Example 3.2** We now extend class *Applet* with a class named *CustomerList*, an instance of which is shown in Fig. 3.1. The *init* method of class *CustomerList* creates two buttons labeled with *Add* and *Remove*. It adds the buttons onto the applet. It also creates a list for the applet to display strings. The count of visible lines in the list is retrieved from applet parameter *MAX_LINES* with statement

```
int lines = Integer.parseInt
                  (getParameter("MAX_LINES"));
```

The *init* method initializes the list with a couple of strings.

After class *CustomerList* is compiled, an applet viewer such as *appletviewer* of Sun's JDK can load the HTML document shown in Example 3.1 and display the applet as shown in Fig. 3.1.

```
import java.applet.*;
import java.awt.*;
public class CustomerList extends Applet {
    public void init() {
        Button addButton = new Button("Add");
        add(addButton);
        Button removeButton = new Button("Remove");
        add(removeButton);
        int lines = Integer.parseInt(
                getParameter("MAX_LINES"));
        List CustomerNames =new List(lines, false);
```

```
            CustomerNames.addItem("John Smith");
            CustomerNames.addItem("Tom David");
            add(CustomerNames);
        }
    }
```

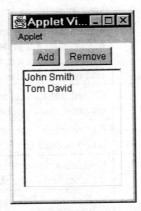

**Fig. 3.1** An applet with two buttons and a list

A browser invokes the *init* method only once for an applet. The *start* method is invoked each time the applet becomes visible. As suggested in the next exercise, method *start* can also do initialization like method *init*. Moving initialization to method *init* may avoid unnecessary repetitions of the initialization.

**Exercise 3.1** Add a method with signature

```
    public void start()
```

into the *CustomerList* class presented in Example 3.2. Move the list creation and item addition statements to the *start* method body. Compile the class and view it with an applet viewer such as Sun's *appletviewer*.

### 3.1.1.4 Applet Accessers

An applet is embedded in a Web page. The following instance methods of class *Applet* can be invoked for an applet to access and affect its environment.

| Signature | Semantics |
|---|---|
| AppletContext getAppletContext() | Returns a handle to this applet's context, which allows querying and affecting the document that contains the applet |
| String getAppletInfo() | Returns a string that describes this applet |

| String getParameter (String name) | Returns the value of the named parameter from this applet's Web page |
|---|---|
| URL getCodeBase() | Returns the URL of this applet |

Class *Applet* defines the following instance methods for applets to function properly. The methods resize an applet itself, play audio clips, and show message in a Web browser status box. An applet may perform graphical operations, which will be discussed in Section 3.2.1.3.

| Signature | Semantics |
|---|---|
| boolean isActive() | Determines if the applet is active (An applet is marked active after the *start* method is called, and inactive after *stop* is called.) |
| void resize(int width, int height) | Resizes this applet with given width and height |
| void play(URL url) | Plays the audio clip stored at a URL |
| void showStatus (String msg) | Displays a status message in this applet's context |

## 3.1.2 Application Programming

### 3.1.2.1 The main *Method*

Class *Applet* inherits AWT class *Panel*, which inherits AWT class *Component*. An applet is actually a GUI component displayed by a browser, which is a special GUI. An applet is embedded in an HTML document. The document provides attribute and parameter values for the applet. A standalone application does not have the support of a Web page browser or applet viewer. The Java interpreter starts the execution of an application from the main method defined in a class of the application. A main method must be defined with signature

```
public static void main(String[] args).
```

A main method accepts an array *args* of strings that encode command-line arguments. The main method body accesses the arguments with array elements *args*[*i*].

Because of the difference between an applet and an application, an application must create a main window if it uses a GUI. It must accept arguments from the *args* parameter of the main method. The following example illustrates an application equivalent to the applet presented in Example 3.2.

**Example 3.3** The following compilation unit contains public class *CustomerList* and class *GUI*. The main method of class *CustomerList* uses statement

```
int lines = Integer.parseInt(args[0]);
```

to decode the first command-line argument, which is represented by array element *args*[0], into an integer. Then, the integer is passed to a constructor of class *GUI* as argument. The constructor is invoked to create a frame for GUI. The frame is packed with its components and displayed.

The constructor of class *GUI* uses a panel to organize the Add and Remove buttons. A panel uses a flow layout, which is an instance of class *FlowLayout*, by default. A flow layout lays components from left to right. It opens a new line if it needs. (An applet uses flow layout by default.) A frame uses border layout by default. As we shall see in Section 3.3.2, a border layout divides the area of a window into five parts. Here, the main method adds the panel into the north division of the frame.

The constructor of class *GUI* creates a list and places the list into the center division of the frame.

The compilation unit can be compiled, and the main method of class *CustomerList* can be executed. For example, after placing the code into file *CustomerList.java*, we can compile the file and issue command *java CustomerList 10* to run the main method of class *CustomerList*. The execution displays a window similar to the one shown in Fig. 3.1 with no title or Applet menu.

```
import java.awt.*;
public class CustomerList {
    public static void main(String[] args){
        int lines = Integer.parseInt(args[0]);
        GUI mainWindow = new GUI(lines);
        mainWindow.pack();
        mainWindow.show();
    }
}


class GUI extends Frame {
    GUI(final int lines) {
        Panel p = new Panel();
        Button addButton = new Button("Add");
        p.add(addButton);
        Button removeButton = new Button("Remove");
        p.add(removeButton);
        add(p, "North");
        List CustomerNames =new List(lines, false);
        CustomerNames.addItem("John Smith");
        CustomerNames.addItem("Tom David");
        add(CustomerNames, "Center");
    }
}
```

□

### 3.1.2.2 Application Design and Construction

Object-oriented software development emphasizes the separation of business logic from data presentation (views). In the above example, the business logic will be implemented in class *CustomerList*, class *GUI* supports data presentation. We have not created any business logic in the class *CustomerList* yet.

An application may implement business rules and operations to manipulate data. The business logic is based on domain-specific knowledge. It is different from a GUI layout or a presentation mechanism.

An application may use several GUIs to present information and/or interact with users. In a modern programming language like Java, predefined component classes are used to construct GUI's. Due to the availability of component libraries, GUI construction is no longer the time-consuming part of application development.

Java provides GUI component classes in package *java.awt*. Some of the classes represent containers such as frame and panel. Some represent basic components such as button and list. As shown in the above two examples, the development of a GUI consists of creating component objects, laying out containers, and adding component objects into the containers.

The GUIs and business logic are glued together with an event handling mechanism. Different languages support different event handling mechanisms. The latest Java event handling mechanism is based on an event delegation model. The deprecated predecessor of the model is simple but inefficient. The above two examples do not have any event handling. For instance, a GUI displayed by the application in Example 3.3 cannot accept a user's exit request. A detailed discussion of the event delegation model will be delayed until Section 3.3.3. An example that expands class *CustomerList* with window closing event handling can be found in Section 3.3.3.1.

# 3.2 Graphics Programming in Java

## 3.2.1 Class *Graphics*

A Java program uses objects of class *Graphics* to organize graphics attributes and render graphics on windows. Before performing a graphical operation such as drawing a rectangle, you can inquire the current values of graphics attributes and change them. All drawings and fillings in Java go through the graphics objects. A graphics (object) can be requested to draw figures, fill shapes, display images, and draw texts in different fonts. A graphics can be used to control color for graphical operations as well.

A graphics is known as a graphics context in other graphics toolkits. It uses instance fields to represent graphics attributes such as the current component on which graphical operations operate on, current color, current font, etc. Class

*Graphics* is an abstract class defined in package *java.awt*. It extends class *Object*. It is extended by classes for drawing on components in screens or on off-screen images.

We can create a copy of a graphics by invoking one of the methods

```
create()
create(int x, int y, int width, int height)
```

for the graphics. The first method is abstract in class *Graphics*. The second depends on the first. It sets the new origin at point (*x*, *y*). It defines a new clipping region, which is the intersection of the clipping region stored in the receiving graphics object with the rectangle that is at point (*x*, *y*) with dimension (*width*, *height*).

After using a graphics, the graphics should be disposed of by invoking method

```
dispose()
```

which actually disposes of system resources used by the graphics. The disposed system resources do not include the memory allocated for the graphics. It is the responsibility of the garbage collector of a Java runtime system to reclaim memory from unreachable objects.

## 3.2.2 Graphics Attributes

Class *Graphics* defines methods for inquiring and setting graphics attributes. The attributes are applied for graphical operations.

The following table includes methods that retrieve the current attribute values from a graphics. The methods can be invoked for a graphics object.

| Signature | Semantics |
|---|---|
| `Shape getClip()` | Returns an object representing the current clipping area |
| `Rectangle getClipBounds()` | Returns the rectangle of the current clipping area |
| `Color getColor()` | Returns the current color from this graphics context |
| `Font getFont()` | Returns the current font |
| `FontMetrics getFontMetrics()` | Returns the font metrics object of the current font |
| `FontMetrics getFontMetrics(Font f)` | Returns the font metrics object for a font object |

Class *Graphics* defines instance methods for setting clipping area, color, and font attribute values in a graphics object. The following table includes methods that can be used to set the drawing and painting mode for a graphics.

| Signature | Semantics |
|---|---|
| `void setPaintMode()` | Sets the painting and drawing mode in this graphics object with overwriting the destination with current color |
| `void setXORMode(Color c)` | Sets the painting and drawing mode with XOR mode to alternate pixels between the current color and color *c* |

## 3.2.3 Graphical Operations

The graphical operations supported by graphics objects include drawing, filling (painting), rectangle area copying, and image drawing. The following table describes some graphical operations applied for a graphics object, which represents a screen or an off-screen image.

| Signature | Semantics |
|---|---|
| `void copyArea(int x, int y, int w, int h, int dx, int dy)` | Copies a rectangle area and places the copy down by *dx* and right by *dy* pixels |
| `void clearRect(int x, int y, int w, int h)` | Fills a rectangle area with background color |
| `void drawRect(int x, int y, int w, int h)` | Draws the shape of a rectangle using the current color |
| `void fillRect(int x, int y, int w, int h)` | Fills a rectangle area using the current color |
| `void drawOval(int x, int y, int w, int h)` | Draws a circle or oval limited with a rectangle with the current color |
| `void fillOval(int x, int y, int w, int h)` | Fills a circle or oval specified with a rectangle with current color |
| `void drawArc(int x, int y, int w, int h, int a1, int a2)` | Draws an arc along an oval starting at angle *a1* and ending at angle *a1+a2*. The oval is limited with a rectangle. |
| `void fillArc(int x, int y, int w, int h, int a1, int a2)` | Fills an area bounded by an arc |

| | |
|---|---|
| `void drawLine(int x1, int y1, int x2, int y2)` | Draws a line between points $(x1, y1)$ and $(x2, y2)$ |
| `void drawPolygon(int[] x_array, int[] y_array, int length)` | Draws a closed polygon with the x-values and y-values |
| `void drawPolyline (int[] x_array, int[] y_array, int length)` | Draws an open polyline with the x-values and y-values |
| `fillPolygon (int[] x_array, int[] y_array, int length)` | Fills closed polygon specified with the x-values and y-values. |
| `void drawString (String str, int x, int y)` | Draws a string at $(x, y)$ with current font and color |
| `boolean drawImage (Image img, int x, int y, ImageObserver obj)` | Draws image at $(x, y)$ and informs observer on the image conversion progress |

When the Java interpreter invokes instance method *paint*(*Graphics g*) of class *Applet*, it provides an instance of class *Graphics* as argument *g*. Another way to get the graphics associated with an applet is invoking method *getGraphics*() for the applet. We can use the graphics to perform graphical operations described in the above table on the applet panel.

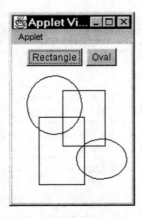

**Fig. 3.2** Rectangle and oval drawings on an applet

The following example applies graphics methods to set XOR mode and draw rectangles and ovals on an applet. As shown in Fig. 3.2, you can choose to draw either a rectangle or an oval by clicking the Rectangle or Oval button. Then, drag mouse on the applet to draw a rectangle or oval. Before the mouse button is released, the rectangle or oval to be displayed is highlighted. After the mouse button is released, the rectangle or oval is displayed with the current foreground color.

**Example 3.4** The following compilation unit defines class *RectsOvals* by extending class *Applet*. Class *RectsOvals* overrides only the method *init* of class *Applet*. The method *init* places two buttons onto the applet panel for user to choose drawing either rectangle or oval. A user draws by dragging the mouse. When the user presses the mouse button inside the applet, the starting point of drawing is recorded in variables *x* and *y*. While the mouse is dragged, the last point is recorded in variables *last_x* and *last_y* and a temporary shape is drawn in highlighted color (XOR mode). When the mouse button is released, the start and end points are used to draw either a rectangle or an oval in paint mode.

We define four adapter inner classes in class *RectsOvals*. Two inner classes implement interface *ActionListener*; the other two extend classes *MouseAdapter* and *MouseMotionAdapter*, respectively. The *ActionListener* classes are responsible for handling button-clicking events for the two buttons. Specifically, when a button is clicked, the *actionPerformed* method of the associated adapter class is executed. The extended *MouseAdapter* and *MouseMotionAdapter* classes are anonymous. The extensions provide methods for handling mouse press, release, and move events. They draw a rectangle or an oval based on the value of boolean variable *rectOrOval*. (Detailed discussion of event handling can be found in Section 3.3.3.)

```
import java.applet.*;
import java.awt.*;
import java.awt.event.*;
import java.util.*;

/** Applet for drawing rectangle and ovals. */
public class RectsOvals extends Applet {
    private int x, y, last_x, last_y;
    private Graphics g;
    private boolean rectOrOval;

    /** Applet init method, which adds
    *    (1) two buttons for user to choose
    *        drawing rectangle or oval,
    *    (2) the instance of an anonymous
    *        ActionListener to each button, which
    *        responds to the button clicking event,
    *    (3) the instance of anonymous
    *        MouseListener to the applet, which
    *        responds to mouse press and release,
```

```
 *    (4) the instance of anonymous
 *        MouseMotionListener to the applet,
 *        which responds to mouse drag.
 */
public void init() {
  g = this.getGraphics();
  Button rectButton =new Button("Rectangle");
  add(rectButton);
  rectButton.addActionListener
                      (new ActionListener() {
  // inner class body
  public void actionPerformed(ActionEvent e){
    rectOrOval = true;
  }
  });

  Button ovalButton = new Button("Oval");
  add(ovalButton);

  ovalButton.addActionListener(
                      new ActionListener() {
  public void actionPerformed(ActionEvent e){
    rectOrOval = false;
  }
  });

  this.addMouseListener(new MouseAdapter() {
     public void mousePressed(MouseEvent e) {
        x = last_x = e.getX();
        y = last_y = e.getY();
        // highlighted drawing
        g.setXORMode(Color.red);
        draw();
     }
     public void mouseReleased(MouseEvent e){
                 // erase temporary drawing
        draw();
        last_x = e.getX();
        last_y = e.getY();
        // draw in paint mode
        g.setPaintMode();
        draw();
     }
  });
  this.addMouseMotionListener(new
                     MouseMotionAdapter() {
    public void mouseDragged(MouseEvent e) {
```

```
                    // erase temporary drawing
                    g.setXORMode(Color.red);
                    draw();
                    last_x = e.getX(); last_y = e.getY();
                    // temporary rect or oval
                    draw();
            }
        });
    }

    /** Draws either a rectangle or oval based
     *    on boolean variable rectOrOval.
     */
    void draw() {
        if (rectOrOval) g.drawRect(
            Math.min(x, last_x),Math.min(y, last_y),
            Math.abs(x -last_x),Math.abs(y-last_y));
        else g.drawOval(Math.min(x, last_x),
                        Math.min(y, last_y),
                Math.abs(x - last_x),
                Math.abs(y - last_y));
    }
}
```

□

# 3.3 GUI Construction

The construction of a graphical user interface (GUI) consists of creating the components of the interface, positioning the components in the interface, and programming the components to handle events. In this section, we discuss the three aspects of GUI construction.

User interface components are objects of classes. Java provides component classes in package *java.awt*. Some of the classes define top-level windows, others define parts for GUIs. We shall study the user interface component classes in Section 3.3.1.

Java has a set of predefined layout managers for component containers. A layout manager is an object of a layout class. It is used to control the layout of components in a component container. A panel and an applet have a flow layout manager by default. A frame has a border layout by default. We shall discuss the layout classes in Section 3.3.2.

Event handling mechanism associates business logic with user interfaces. We introduce the event delegation model of Java, which is flexible and efficient, in Section 3.3.3.

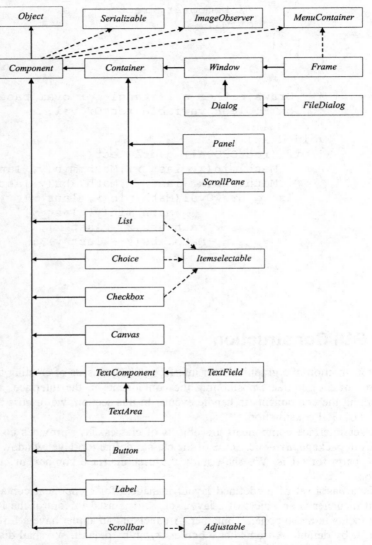

**Fig. 3.3** The class hierarchy of GUI component classes

## 3.3.1 GUI Components

The GUI component classes are organized in package *java.awt*. They are used to create various types of component. The class inheritance hierarchy of GUI components is shown in Fig. 3.3. It is rooted at class *Component*, which extends class *Object* and implements interfaces *ImageObserver*, *MenuContainer*, and *Serializable*.

Class *Component* is an abstract class for specifying user interface components. It defines methods for the normal behavior of GUI components. Some methods allow a GUI to communicate with users and access operating system resources.

The following table includes methods of class *Component* for event handling. Events generated by a component are delivered to listeners. For example, a component event is a special type of event. It is sent to component event listeners that are registered for the event source. Class *Component* defines methods to register various types of listener for GUI components. It has methods for deregistering listeners, which are not shown here. It also provides methods for a component to decide to receive or refuse some types of events. Class *Frame* is a subclass of *Component*. The methods can be invoked for a frame created with expression *new Frame()*. The first five methods require a listener argument, which is to be registered.

| Signature | Semantics |
|---|---|
| void addComponentListener(ComponentListener l) | Registers a component event listener for this component to send component events to the listener |
| void addFocusListener (FocusListener l) | Registers a focus event listener to send focus events to it |
| void addKeyListener (KeyListener l) | Registers a keyboard event listener to send keyboard events to it |
| void addMouseListener (MouseListener l) | Registers a mouse event listener to send mouse events to it |
| void addMouseMotionListener(MouseMotionListener l) | Registers a mouse motion event listener to send mouse motion events to it |
| void enableEvents(long eventsToEnable) | Enables the component to receive the events specified with an event mask |
| void disableEvents (long eventsToDisable) | Disables the component to receive the events specified with an event mask |
| void dispatchEvent (AWTEvent e) | Dispatches an event to the component or its sub components |

Class *Component* provides the following methods for a component to determine its position on a screen and test whether it contains a point.

| Signature | Semantics |
|-----------|-----------|
| `Point getLocation()` | Returns the current location of this component |
| `boolean contains(int x, int y)` | Tests if point $(x, y)$ is in this component |

Class *Component* provides the following graphics methods for GUI components. A graphics object is associated with each GUI component. We can retrieve the graphics by sending message *getGraphics()* to a component. A component has graphics attributes. We can query or set the attribute values. The following table lists graphics attribute accessers but not mutaters. The mutaters set the attributes with values.

| Signature | Semantics |
|-----------|-----------|
| `Graphics getGraphics()` | Retrieves the graphics object of this component |
| `Color getForeground()` | Retrieves the current foreground color |
| `Color getBackground()` | Retrieves the background color |
| `Rectangle getBounds()` | Retrieves the bounding rectangle of this component |
| `Component getComponentAt (int x, int y)` | Returns subcomponent that contains point $(x, y)$ |
| `Font getFont()` | Retrieves the font of this component |
| `FontMetrics getFontMetrics(Font font)` | Retrieves the font metrics object for a font |
| `int checkImage(Image image, ImageObserver observer)` | Retrieves the status of an image construction in this component |

Class *Component* provides the following methods for a component to paint, repaint, show, hide, or arrange its layout.

| Signature | Semantics |
|-----------|-----------|
| `void paint(Graphics g)` | Paints this component using a graphics |
| `void repaint()` | Repaints this component |

| void setVisible (boolean b) | Shows or hides this component |
|---|---|
| void doLayout() | Lays out this component |

Abstract class *Container* extends class *Component* with methods to keep track of subcomponents in a component. Class *Window* extends class *Container* to represent top-level windows that have no border or menu bar. It can be used to implement a pop-up window. It can generate window events for window listeners. Class *Frame* extends *Window*. It represents top-level windows of standalone applications. A frame displays a title and a border. The classes *Dialog* and *FileDialog* are used to communicate with users for input/output. Classes *Panel* and *ScrollPane* represent generic containers for user interfaces.

A component object is created with the *new* operator and a constructor. For example, the following statements create a frame titled *Customers*, which is assigned to variable *topLevelWindow*. The default size of a frame is 0 by 0. A frame must be resized before it can be displayed on the screen. The method *show* of a frame displays the frame.

```
topLevelWindow = new Frame("Customers");
topLevelWindow.resize(200, 300);
topLevelWindow.show();
```

Component classes *List*, *Choice*, and *Checkbox* in package *java.awt* extend class *Component* and implement interface *ItemSelectable*, which defines methods to support item selection by users. We use the following Java source code to illustrate a list creation and item addition for the list. The first statement creates a list with 10 visible items and with multiple selection enabled. Then, strings *John Smith* and *Tom David* are added into the list.

```
customerList = new List(10, true);
customerList.add("John Smith");
customerList.add("Tom David", 1);
```

Class *Canvas* extends class *Component*. Its instances represent GUI components on which we can draw by invoking graphical operations.

Package *java.awt* has component classes for text input and display. The components are represented by classes *TextComponent*, *TextField*, and *TextArea*. They allow users to edit text. An object of class *TextField* displays only a single line. A *TextArea* allows multiple lines.

The classes *Label*, *Choice*, *Button*, and *Scrollbar* extend class *Component*. A *Label* can be placed beside another component such as a *Choice* or *List* in a GUI. A list of choices in a *Choice* object can be pulled down for user to select a choice. A *Button* can be pressed to trigger some action. A *Scrollbar* can be added to a component such as a frame. Its appearance and behavior are adjustable. We use the following code to illustrate class *Button*. The code creates a button, which is then added to the frame *topLevelWindow*. The string argument in the *Button* constructor is used to label the button.

```
addButton = new Button("Add");
topLevelWindow.add(addButton);
```

## 3.3.2 Layout Classes

Package *java.awt* contains layout manager classes to arrange components in a container. It defines layout manager interfaces that abstract behaviors of layout objects. The layout manager interfaces in the package *java.awt* are *LayoutManager* and *LayoutManager2*; the latter inherits the former.

The layout classes in package *java.awt* are *FlowLayout*, *BorderLayout*, *GridLayout*, *GridBagLayout*, and *CardLayout*. They extend class *Object*. Classes *FlowLayout* and *GridLayout* implement interface *LayoutManager*. Classes *BorderLayout*, *GridBagLayout*, and *CardLayout* implement interface *LayoutManager2*.

A flow layout manager is used to layout buttons and other types of component from left to right in a container. It starts a new line when no more components can be placed in the same line. By default, each line is centered. A flow layout manager is created with expression *new FlowLayout(int align, int hGap, int vGap)* with optional parameters. The parameter *align* specifies a left, center, or right alignment, parameter *hGap* specifies a horizontal gap in pixels between contained components, and *vGap* a vertical gap between lines. The following statement creates a new panel and assigns a flow layout manager to the panel. It uses the no-argument constructor of class *FlowLayout*.

```
Panel p = new Panel(new FlowLayout());
```

A border layout organizes the components in a container into five divisions (bags), named *North*, *South*, *East*, *West*, and *Center*, of the container area. The borders between divisions are invisible. A division will have width and/or height equal to 0 if the division contains no component. To add a component to a container that has a *BorderLayout* manager, specify a division for the component. The divisions implied by a border layout manager are shown in Fig. 3.4. The following code adds a button labeled *Add* into the south division of a top-level frame.

```
Button addButton = new Button("Add");
topLevelWindow.setLayout(new BorderLayout());
topLevelWindow.add(addButton, "South");
```

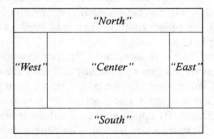

**Fig. 3.4** Border layout divisions in a container

A grid layout manager lays out components in the cells of rows and columns. A grid bag layout is more flexible than a grid layout manager. It does not require components to be of the same size. A component may occupy several grids. It is associated with a *GridBagConstraints*, which specifies how the component is laid out.

A container with a card layout manager contains several cards, only one of which is visible. The methods *first*, *last*, and *next* of the card layout manager object can be invoked to flip through the cards.

The following example places GUI components into the north, center, and south divisions of a frame. The GUI layout is shown in Fig. 3.5. Specifically, it places labels and text fields into a panel and adds the panel into the north division. It adds a label and a list into the center division. It adds two buttons labeled with *Add* and *Remove* into the south division.

**Example 3.5** We now create a class named *GUI* to represent the GUI shown in Fig. 3.5. Class *GUI* extends class *Frame* so that an instance of the class is a top-level window. A constructor *GUI(String title, int lines)* accepts a title for the created window and an integer for the count of visible lines in a list component inside the window.

The border layout of the GUI contains three panels, which are in north, center, and south, respectively. The north panel is created with a *GridLayout* manager. It consists of three rows, each row accommodates two components – a label and a text field. The center panel contains a label and a list. The count of visible lines in the list is set with the second argument of the *GUI* constructor *GUI(String title, int lines)*. The south panel contains two buttons labeled with *Add* and *Remove*.

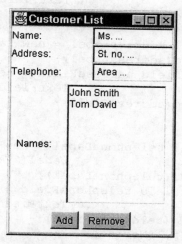

**Fig. 3.5** The layout of a GUI

The main method of class *CustomerList* can be started with command *java CustomerList 10* with argument *10*. The argument is denoted with expression *args*[0] in the main method.

```
import java.awt.*;
public class CustomerList  {
    public static void main(String[] args){
        int lines = Integer.parseInt(args[0]);
        GUI mainWindow = new
                    GUI("Customer List", lines);
        mainWindow.pack();
        mainWindow.show();
    }
}

class GUI extends Frame {
    /** constructor with list count as parameter*/
    GUI(int lines) {
        /* Creates a panel and replaces default
        *    layout manager with a grid of 3 rows
        *    and 2 columns.
        */
        Panel p = new Panel(new GridLayout(3, 2));

        Label nameLabel = new Label("Name:");
        p.add(nameLabel);
        TextField nameField = new
                    TextField("Ms. ...");
        p.add(nameField);

        Label addressLabel = new Label("Address:");
        p.add(addressLabel);
        TextField addressField = new
                    TextField("St. no. ...");
        p.add(addressField);


        Label telephoneLabel = new
                    Label("Telephone:");
        p.add(telephoneLabel);
        TextField telephoneField = new
                    TextField("Area ... ");
        p.add(telephoneField);
        add(p, "North");

        p = new Panel();
        Label namesLabel = new Label("Names:");
        p.add(namesLabel);
```

```
List customerNames = new List(lines,false);
customerNames.setSize(100, 50);
customerNames.addItem("John Smith");
customerNames.addItem("Tom David");
p.add(customerNames);
add(p, "Center");

p = new Panel();
Button addButton = new Button("Add");
p.add(addButton);
Button removeButton = new Button("Remove");
p.add(removeButton);
add(p, "South");
}

/** constructor with frame title and list
 *  count parameters.
 */
GUI(String title, int lines) {
    this(lines);
    setTitle(title);
}
}
```

The above compilation unit can be compiled and the main method of class *CustomerList* can be executed. An execution of the main method displays a window as shown in Fig. 3.5. To terminate the execution and, thus, banish the GUI from the screen, issue command Ctrl+C from keyboard.       □

The above example does not elaborate the layout of the GUI. As suggested by the next exercise, you can tune the layout with a grid bag layout manager. A discussion of the grid bag layout manager is beyond the scope of this book.

**Exercise 3.2** A grid layout manager of class *GridLayout* is used for a panel in Example 3.5. A grid bag layout manager, represented by class *GridBagLayout*, lets a component occupy more than one grid of a panel. Replace the grid layout manager with a grid bag layout manager in Example 3.5 and rearrange the text fields in the GUI. Compile the GUI class and run its main method.

## 3.3.3 Event Delegation Model

### 3.3.3.1 Event Delegation Model Overview

The latest event handling mechanism of Java is based on an *event delegation model*. It involves three types of parties: an *event* is propagated from its *source* to the event *listeners*. An event is an object in a class derived from class *EventObject*. An event source is typically a user interface component. It generates or *fires* events. A listener is usually an "adapter" for a user interface component or a business object. The authority of event handling is delegated to the adapter. A listener can be the GUI component or the business object itself and, thus, we can save an intermediate adapter class.

A listener class implements a listener interface. For example, class *WindowAdapter* in package *java.awt.event* is a window listener class. It implements interface *WindowListener*. The interface defines methods for responding to window events. The methods are invoked implicitly. We can define a listener class called *GUICloser* for receiving window closing event as follows.

```
class GUICloser extends WindowAdapter { ... }
```

To register an instance of the class *GUICloser* for a frame object, invoke method *addWindowListener* with a *GUICloser* argument for the frame. The statement

```
f.addWindowListener(new GUICloser());
```

creates a window listener and registers it for frame *f*. Thus, frame *f* becomes the source of window events for the listener of class *GUICloser*.

To handle window closing event, listener class *GUICloser* redefines inherited method *windowClosing(WindowEvent e)* so that if the ID of a received window event *e* is *WINDOW_CLOSING*, the method executes *System.exit*(0). The method is defined as follows.

```
public void windowClosing(WindowEvent e) {
    if (e.getID() == WindowEvent.WINDOW_CLOSING)
        System.exit(0);
}
```

A user can request for closing window *f* by double clicking the control box of frame *f*. The event will be accepted by the registered *GUICloser* listener. The listener handles the event with the *windowClosing* method. Thus, frame *f* is closed by the event.

We expand class *GUI* presented in Example 3.5 with window closing event handling. The following example adds an anonymous class into class *GUI*. The anonymous class has essentially the same function as the class *GUICloser* described above.

**Example 3.6** (Continuation of Example 3.5) The following compilation unit expands Example 3.5 with an anonymous event listener class, which is a subclass of class *WindowAdapter*. The anonymous class redefines method *windowClosing(WindowEvent e)* so that if event *e* is a closing request, the application exits. The compilation unit imports package *java.awt.event*, which contains event listener interfaces and adapter classes.

```
import java.awt.*;
import java.awt.event.*;
public class CustomerList {
    public static void main(String[] args){
        int lines = Integer.parseInt(args[0]);
        GUI mainWindow = new GUI
                ("Customer List", lines);
```

```
        /* registers an instance of anonymous
         *  window event listener class
         */
        mainWindow.addWindowListener(new
                                WindowAdapter() {
        public void windowClosing(WindowEvent e){
        if (e.getID() ==WindowEvent.WINDOW_CLOSING)
           System.exit(0);
        }
        });

        mainWindow.pack();
        mainWindow.show();
    }
}

class GUI extends Frame {
    /** constructor with list count as parameter*/
    GUI(int lines) {
        Panel p = new Panel(new GridLayout(3, 2));
        Label nameLabel = new Label("Name:");
        p.add(nameLabel);
        TextField nameField = new
                                TextField("Ms. ...");
        p.add(nameField);

        Label addressLabel = new Label("Address:");
        p.add(addressLabel);
        TextField addressField = new
                        TextField("St. no. ...");
        p.add(addressField);


        Label telephoneLabel = new
                        Label("Telephone:");
        p.add(telephoneLabel);
        TextField telephoneField = new
                        TextField("Area ... ");
        p.add(telephoneField);
        add(p, "North");

        p = new Panel();
        Label namesLabel = new Label("Names:");
        p.add(namesLabel);
        List customerNames =new List(lines, false);
        customerNames.setSize(100, 50);
        customerNames.addItem("John Smith");
```

```
        customerNames.addItem("Tom David");
        p.add(customerNames);
        add(p, "Center");

        p = new Panel();
        Button addButton = new Button("Add");
        p.add(addButton);
        Button removeButton = new Button("Remove");
        p.add(removeButton);
        add(p, "South");
    }

    /** constructor with frame title and list
     * count parameters.
     */
    GUI(String title, int lines) {
        this(lines);
        setTitle(title);
    }
}
```

□

## 3.3.3.2 Event Objects

The Java packages *java.awt* and *java.awt.event* include predefined event classes for the AWT event delegation model. The event classes inherit class *EventObject*, which extends class *Object*. AWT events are instances of class *AWTEvent* and its subclasses. Class *AWTEvent* is in package *java.awt*. It extends class *EventObject*. Other AWT event classes are defined in package *java.awt.event*. They are classified as low-level and semantic events. The inheritance hierarchy of AWT event classes is shown in Fig. 3.6.

Class *EventObject* defines instance variable *source* of type *Object* to encode event source. It defines instance method *getSource()* to retrieve the event source.

Class *AWTEvent* defines *long* constants to mask event. The constants can be combined with bitwise OR operator |. An AWT component can use the masks to enable or disable events that the component receives. The constants include *ACTION_EVENT_MASK*, *WINDOW_EVENT_MASK*, *ITEM_EVENT_MASK*, *TEXT_EVENT_MASK*, *KEY_EVENT_MASK*, *MOUSE_EVENT_MASK*, and *MOUSE_MOTION_EVENT_MASK*. An *AWTEvent* object can be created with constructor *AWTEvent(Object source, int id)*. Class *AWTEvent* defines instance method *getID()* to retrieve the ID of an event and *consume()* to consume an event.

A *low-level event* represents an input or window event. For example, component events include resizing, moving, and getting focus; input events include key press and release, mouse click, press, movement, and release. The low-level AWT event classes are subclasses of class *ComponentEvent* shown in Fig. 3.6.

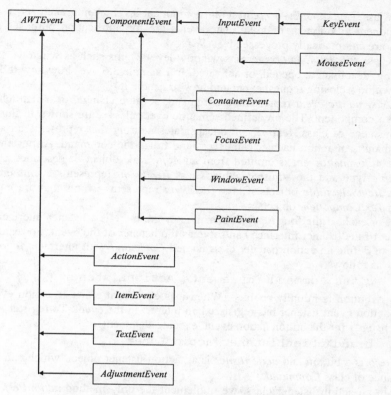

**Fig. 3.6** The hierarchy of AWT event classes

Class *ComponentEvent* represents component-level events such as component move and resize. The events are automatically handled by AWT internally. Their presence is for notification purpose only.

Class *FocusEvent* represents focus changes, either temporary or permanent. A temporary focus change happens for a component when the containing window is deactivated or hidden. A permanent focus change happens when the user uses the Tab key to move focus away from a component or when another component receives focus by executing method *requestFocus*().

Class *InputEvent* represents component-level input events, which can be consumed before a normal processing. For example, by consuming a button click event, the clicked button will not be activated. The instance method *consume*() in class *InputEvent* can be invoked to consume an input event. Classes *KeyEvent* and *MouseEvent* extend class *InputEvent*. They represent events generated from keyboard or mouse. A *KeyEvent* encloses information on the pressed key. It also encloses information on whether modifier keys are pressed when the key is pressed. A *MouseEvent* can distinguish mouse up, down, drag, and move.

Class *ContainerEvent* represents component-level events such as a child component addition or removal. The events are for notification purposes only. They are automatically processed by AWT.

Class *WindowEvent* represents window-level events such as window closed, closing, deactivated, opened, or activated. In Example 3.6, we show how to listen to a window closing request event and how to handle it.

A *semantic event* represents a command, a value change, or a state change from a component. The predefined semantic event classes are shown in Fig. 3.6. An instance of class *ActionEvent* encapsulates a string that represents an action command. An action listener can access and fulfill the command. An instance of class *AdjustmentEvent* is emitted from an *Adjustable* object. It describes an *Adjustable* type and the adjusted value. Class *ItemEvent* represents events emitted from *ItemSelectable* objects. Class *TextEvent* represents events that are emitted from *TextComponent* objects.

For each of the four types of semantic event, there is a listener interface. An object of the listener interface can serve as the listener of the event. For example, we can define an action listener class named *Command* with interface *ActionListener* as follows.

```
class Command implements ActionListener { ... }
```

A button is initially enabled. When it is clicked, it emits an action event if any action event listener has registered an interest in the event. To register an action listener for the button action event, execute statement

```
b.addActionListener(actionLsner);
```

where *b* is a button and *actionLsner* is an action listener object, which can be an instance of class *Command*.

In an action listener class, we implement the only method *actionPerformed* specified in interface *ActionListener*. The method signature is

```
public void actionPerformed(ActionEvent e).
```

The method in the action listener class handles the action event. It may use the data in a business object and run business logic.

Example 3.7 applies listener interface *WindowListener*. The interface defines seven abstract methods for various window action events. We extend class *WindowAdapter*, which implements all the seven methods with empty method bodies. The subclass is named *GUICloser*. It redefines method *windowClosing* with system exit when a window emits a window closing event.

**Example 3.7** The following compilation unit defines class *App*, inner classes *Command* and *GUI*. Class *Command* is an action listener class. A *Command* object handles action event fired by button clicking. It simply prints a message on the standard output. It shows that when the *Add* button is clicked, the button clicking event triggers an action. It shows a similar message when the *Remove* button is clicked.

A *GUI* object displays a top-level window referenced with local variable *f*. It invokes method *addWindowListener* to register a *GUICloser* object for the top-level window *f*. Thus, when a user of the GUI requests for closing the top-level window, the application exits.

```java
import java.awt.*;
import java.awt.event.*;
public class App {
    public void add() {
        System.out.println("Add ...");
    }

    public void remove() {
        System.out.println("Remove...");
    }

    static public void main(String[] args) {
        App app = new App();
        GUI gui = new GUI(app);
    }
}

class Command implements ActionListener {
    static final int ADD = 0;
    static final int REMOVE = 1;
    int id;
    App app;

    public Command(int id, App app) {
        this.id = id;
        this.app = app;
    }

    public void actionPerformed(ActionEvent e){
        switch(id) {
            case ADD: app.add(); break;
            case REMOVE: app.remove(); break;
        }
    }
}

class GUI {
    public GUI(App app) {
        Frame f = new Frame("Untitled");
        f.setLayout(new BorderLayout());
        f.setSize(200, 150); // preferred size
        f.addWindowListener(new GUICloser());

        Command addCmd = new
                    Command(Command.ADD, app);
        Command removeCmd = new
                    Command(Command.REMOVE, app);
```

```
        Panel p = new Panel(new FlowLayout());
        Button b;
        p.add(b = new Button("Add"));
        b.addActionListener(addCmd);
        p.add(b = new Button("Remove"));
        b.addActionListener(removeCmd);
        f.add(p, "South");

        List l;
        f.add(l = new List(), "Center");
        l.add("John Smith");
        l.add("Tom Smith");
        l.addActionListener(removeCmd);

        f.pack();
        f.show();
    }

    class GUICloser extends WindowAdapter {
        public void windowClosing(WindowEvent e) {
        if (e.getID() ==WindowEvent.WINDOW_CLOSING)
            System.exit(0);
        }
    }
}
```

□

**Exercise 3.3** Inner class *GUICloser* in Example 3.7 is a member of class *GUI*. It is used only once in the program. It is suitable for an anonymous inner class. Replace the inner class *GUICloser* in class *GUI* with an anonymous class that extends class *WindowAdapter* in the parameter of method *addWindowListener*.

### 3.3.3.3 Event Listeners

The event delegation model of Java uses various AWT listener types to discriminate AWT events. The listener types are specified with listener interfaces. Typically, an event listener interface defines a method dedicated to each event type that the listener can handle. For example, interface *ActionListener* defines method *actionPerformed* for handling action events. Interface *WindowListener* defines methods *windowActivated*, *windowClosed*, *windowClosing*, *windowDeactivated*, *windowDeiconified*, *windowIconified*, and *windowOpened* for receiving and handling different events that are related with windows.

For a program to handle a specific type of event, the program implements a listener interface that accepts the event. Some interfaces such as *ActionListener* defines only one method. Others define multiple methods. Java AWT library provides adapter classes to implement some interfaces that specify multiple abstract methods. For example, class *WindowAdapter* implements interface *WindowListener* by implementing all the methods specified in the interface. But each method in the class does nothing. If a program is interested in only one or a couple of events, the program can extend the adapter class and redefine only one or two methods. For example, Example 3.7 extends class *WindowAdapter* and overrides method *windowClosing* only.

Class *Component* defines methods to register event listeners for applets and GUI components. Specifically, the class introduces methods *addComponentListener*, *addFocusListener*, *addKeyListener*, *addMouseListener* and *addMouseMotionListener* to register listeners for GUI components. For example, statements

```
f.addWindowListener(new WindowAdapter(){ ... });
b.addActionListener(addCmd);
b.addActionListener(removeCmd);
l.addActionListener(removeCmd);
```

register listener objects for components. (Here we omit the body of an anonymous *WindowListener* class in the first statement. The class body may be the same as the body of class *GUICloser* in Example 3.7.) When an event happens in a component, a listener object interested in the event executes its dedicated method to handle the event. Particularly, method *windowClosing* responds to a window closing request event, and *actionPerformed* responds to an action event.

### 3.3.3.4 An Application with Event Handling – CustomerList

Here, we illustrate how to glue the business logic and GUI together with event listeners. The following example defines class *CustomerList* to hold customer objects for our supermarket. It uses a GUI with layout shown in Fig. 3.5. A user of the application can enter the name, address, and telephone number of a customer into text fields. Then, by clicking the *Add* button, an action event handler creates a customer object and adds it to the customer list. The user can delete a customer object from the application by selecting the customer name in the customer list and clicking the *Remove* button. Thus, the application keeps a dynamical list of customer objects for the supermarket.

The following example expands Example 3.6 with event handling classes. Particularly, we add two anonymous action listener classes to handle the customer add and remove events. The two action listeners are registered for the Add and Remove buttons, respectively.

**Example 3.8** (Continuation of Example 3.6) The following compilation unit defines a standalone application. Class *CustomerList* uses a vector referenced by variable *customers* to keep track of customer objects. Its constructor creates a *GUI* object, which is referenced with local variable *mainWindow*.

Class *GUI* uses the same components as in Example 3.6 to construct GUI. It adds two action listener classes, one is for the *Add* button clicking event, the other for the *Remove* button. When the *Add* button is clicked, the action listener creates a new customer object, instantiates the customer with texts in the text fields, adds the customer to vector *customers*, and inserts the

customer name into list *customerNames*. When the *Remove* button is clicked,
the action listener for the button retrieves the index of the selected name in
the *customerNames* list. The action listener removes the selected customer
object from vector *customers* and eliminates the name from the *customer-
Names* list.

When the main method of class *CustomerList* is executed, it displays a
window like the one shown in Fig. 3.5 without the two strings in the names
list. Then, a user can enter customers into the customer list, select and delete
customers from the list.

```java
import java.awt.*;
import java.awt.event.*;
import java.util.Vector;
public class CustomerList  {
    static public void main(String[] args) {
        new CustomerList();
    }

    private final Vector customers = new Vector();
    private final int LINE_COUNT = 10;

    public CustomerList() {
        GUI mainWindow = new GUI
                    ("Customer List", LINE_COUNT);
        mainWindow.addWindowListener
                        (new WindowAdapter() {
        public void windowClosing
                        (WindowEvent e) {
        if (e.getID()==WindowEvent.WINDOW_CLOSING)
            System.exit(0);
        }
        });

        mainWindow.pack();
        mainWindow.show();
    }

    /** Member class GUI for user interaction. */
    class GUI extends Frame {
        private final TextField
        nameField = new TextField("Ms. ..."),
        addressField = new TextField("St. no. ..."),
        telephoneField =new TextField("Area-code .."); 
        private final List customerNames = new
                            List(LINE_COUNT);
        private final Button
                addButton = new Button("Add"),
                removeButton = new Button("Remove");
```

```
/** GUI constructor with visible line count
 *   as parameter.
 */
GUI(int lines) {
    /* creates a panel and replaces default
     *  layout manager with a grid of 3 rows
     *  and 2 columns.
     */
    Panel p = new Panel(new GridLayout(3, 2));

    Label nameLabel = new Label("Name:");
    p.add(nameLabel);
    p.add(nameField);
    Label addressLabel = new Label("Address:");
    p.add(addressLabel);
    p.add(addressField);
    Label telephoneLabel =
                    new Label("Telephone:");
    p.add(telephoneLabel);
    p.add(telephoneField);
    add(p, "North");

    /* creates a panel and places a label and
     *  a list referenced with instance variable
     *  customerNames into the panel.
     */
    p = new Panel();
    Label namesLabel = new Label("Names:");
    p.add(namesLabel);
    customerNames.setSize(100, 50);
    p.add(customerNames);
    add(p, "Center");

    /* creates a panel and places Add and
     *  Remove buttons into the panel.
     */
    p = new Panel();
    p.add(addButton);
    p.add(removeButton);
    add(p, "South");

    // registers action event listeners
    addButton.addActionListener(new
                        ActionListener() {
        public void actionPerformed
                        (ActionEvent e) {
            Customer cus = new Customer();
```

```
                    cus.name = nameField.getText();
                    cus.address = addressField.getText();
                    cus.telephone =
                              telephoneField.getText();
                    customers.addElement(cus);
                    customerNames.addItem(cus.name);
                 }
            });

            removeButton.addActionListener(new
                                ActionListener() {
               public void actionPerformed
                                (ActionEvent e) {
               int index = customerNames.
                                getSelectedIndex();
               if (index < 0) return;
               Customer cus = (Customer) customers.
                                elementAt(index);
               nameField.setText(cus.name);
               addressField.setText(cus.address);
               telephoneField.setText
                             (cus.telephone);
               customers.removeElementAt(index);
               customerNames.remove(index);
                 }
            });
         }

         /** constructor with frame title and list
          *    count parameters.
          */
         GUI(String title, int lines) {
            this(lines);
            setTitle(title);
         }
      } // end of class GUI
   } // end of class CustomerList

   class Customer {
      String name, address, telephone;
   }
```

□

**Exercise 3.4** Add one more button labeled with *Show* to the south division of the *GUI* frame in Example 3.8. When the button is clicked, the name, address, and telephone number of a customer selected in the names list are displayed in the text fields.

# 3.4 Utility Classes and Object Reflection

## 3.4.1 Utility Classes – *System*, *Math*, and *Random*

### 3.4.1.1 Class System

The Java standard library class *System* provides standard input, output, and error streams. In the above examples, we often apply the method *println(String)* for object *System.out* to print a string on the standard output device. The constants *in*, *out*, and *err* defined in class *System* represent the standard input, output, and error console devices. The class *System* provides access to properties of underlying operating system and means of loading files and libraries. It has a method for quickly copying a portion of an array. It has static methods for system security manager.

Class *System* is defined in package *java.lang*. It is automatically imported into any compilation unit at compilation time.

The native static method *currentTimeMillis()* of class *System* returns the difference, measured in milliseconds, between the current time and midnight, January 1, 1970 UTC. We shall use the expression

```
System.currentTimeMillis()
```

to retrieve the current time.

### 3.4.1.2 Class Math

Class *Math* defines static methods for basic numeric functions such as exponential, logarithmic, square root, and trigonometric functions. For example, we use static methods *abs* and *min* to evaluate the absolute value of an integer and select the smaller one of two integers in Example 3.4. Since these methods are static methods, they are invoked for the class. For instance, expression *Math.abs($x - last\_x$)* returns the absolute value of the difference between variables $x$ and $last\_x$.

Numeric functions in class *Math* produce the same results as algorithms written in C in the Freely Distributable Math Library (fdlibm) by following Java floating-point arithmetic rules. The library is available at http://netlib.att.com/.

An invocation of static method *random* of class *Math* returns a pseudo-random number between 0.0 and 1.0 with double precision.

Class *Math* is defined in package *java.lang*. It is automatically imported to a compilation unit when the compilation unit is compiled.

### 3.4.1.3 Class Random

An instance of class *Random* represents a stream of pseudo-random numbers. It uses a 48-bit seed of type *long*. A *Random* object is instantiated with constructor *Random()* or *Random(long seed)*. The seed of a *Random* can be set with method *setSeed(long newSeed)*. Methods *nextFloat* and *nextDouble* returns the next pseudo-random real number between 0.0 and 1.0 with single or double precision. Methods *nextInt* and *nextLong* return the next pseudo-random integer or long.

Class *Random* is defined in package *java.util*. To use the simple name *Random* in a compilation unit, the unit must import the qualified class name *java.lang.Random*.

## 3.4.2 Method Benchmarking

We now present a class named *Evaluator* and a static method named *benchmark* in the class. The method can determine the time spent by the execution of a public instance method. Specifically, a method invocation expression

$obj.methodName(arg_1, ..., arg_k)$;

can be replaced with code

$Object[]$ $args = new$ $Object[k]$ $\{arg_1, ..., arg_k\}$;
$Evaluator.benchmark(obj,$ "$methodName$", $args$);

to invoke method *methodName* for *obj*. The method *benchmark* will print the time in milliseconds taken by an execution of method *methodName*.

The static method *benchmark* is based on the object reflection API of Java. It uses object *obj* to retrieve its class. Then, it uses the types of arguments $arg_1, ...,$ $arg_k$ and method name *methodName* to retrieve an object of class *Method* from the class of *obj*. As described in Section 2.4.1, we can invoke the *Method* object for *obj* in the *benchmark* method.

**Example 3.9** The following class, class *Evaluator*, defines static method *benchmark* to evaluate the time spent by a method execution for an object. It applies the Java core reflection API to retrieve the class of the object. Then, it uses the method name and argument types to retrieve a *Method* object, which represents the named method. It returns the time spent by the method execution.

Class *Method* imposes some limitation on the *benchmark* method. The *benchmark* method uses a method name and types of arguments to retrieve a *Method* object. The Java reflection API does not take class inheritance into account when it tries to find the *Method* object. An argument $arg_i$ used in method *benchmark* invocation must have the same declaration and runtime types.

Class *Evaluator* overloads method *benchmark*. The second *benchmark* method has an integer parameter *count*. It repeatedly executes the evaluated method for *count* times and sums the time for the executions.

Since Java reflection API is defined in package *java.lang.reflect*, class *Method* is imported from the package in the following compilation unit.

```
import java.lang.reflect.Method;
import java.awt.event.*;
public class Evaluator {
    public static long benchmark(Object obj,
        String methodName, Object[] args) {
```

```
            return Evaluator.benchmark
                         (obj, methodName, args);
    }

    public static long benchmark(Object obj,
        String methodName, Object[] args,
        int count) {
      Class objClass = obj.getClass();
      Method method;
      try {
        Class[] argsTypes = new
                        Class[args.length];
        for (int i = 0; i < args.length; i++){
          argsTypes[i] = args[i].getClass();
        }
        method = objClass.getMethod
                      (methodName, argsTypes);
      }
      catch(NoSuchMethodException e) {
        System.out.println("The method " +
              methodName + " does not exist.");
        return -1; }
      catch(Exception e) { return -1; }
      long totalTimeMillis = 0;
      try {
        long start, finish;
        for (int i= 0; i < count; i++){
          start = System.currentTimeMillis();
          method.invoke(obj, args);
          finish = System.currentTimeMillis();
          totalTimeMillis += finish - start;
        }
      }
      catch(Exception e) { return -1; }
      return totalTimeMillis;
    }
}
```

□

**Exercise 3.5** Create a class that defines two public instance methods: one constructs an array of pseudo-random integers, the other sorts the array. Use a main method in the class to determine the time required by each of the two methods. The main method may invoke the *benchmark* method of class *Evaluator*.

## 3.5 Summary

Java is a versatile programming language for Internet programming and for standalone application development. In this chapter, we discuss the difference between applet and application. We learn how to construct applets and how to use an HTML document to invoke an applet. We also discuss applet API methods, which are automatically invoked by Internet browsers and applet viewers. A useful applet is an instance of a subclass of class *Applet*. The subclass redefines the applet API methods to introduce meaningful operations.

We discuss how to perform graphical operations in applets and applications. Class *Graphics* is responsible for organizing graphics attributes and performing graphical operations. The graphical operations include drawing, filling, image creation, and image printing.

Class *Graphics* is in package *java.awt*. Other classes in the package can be used to create GUIs. Particularly, class *Frame* represents top-level windows. We can use layout managers to arrange components in a container component such as a frame or a panel. We learn how to use the flow, border, and grid layout managers to organize subcomponents in container components.

Event handling is the glue between a GUI and the business logic of an application. Here, we discuss the event delegation model of Java. We show how to use adapter classes to implement event listeners, which handle events.

Several utility classes are useful for data structure analysis. We introduce the Java standard classes *System*, *Math*, and *Random*. Based on the Java reflection API, we present a benchmarking method, which can be used to evaluate the time required by an instance method invocation.

## Assignment

In the assignment of Chapter 2, you were asked to implement an application. Design and implement one or several GUIs for the application.

# Chapter 4
# Java Data Structure Classes

An object-oriented program uses objects to store data. How to organize the objects in data structures depends on the desired functions of the program. Traditional problems for data structures remain important in the context of object-oriented programming. For example, to support search for customer object, various data structures are available for keeping customer objects. We may need to insert objects into and delete objects from a large collection of objects. A good structure of the objects is crucial to perform search, insertion, and deletion operations. The available data structures are suitable for different applications and have different performance.

An advantage of object-oriented programming (OOP) over procedural programming is that an object-oriented program can create flexible and reusable new types. A class can be used as a type for variables and for elements of data structures. OOP makes it easier to structure the data for an application.

Object-oriented programming languages provide common data structures in libraries. Some of the data structures are not available in any procedural languages. Other data structure classes provide more functions than their counterparts in a procedural language like C or Pascal. A programmer can customize an object-oriented data structure by extending it with new features and methods.

The standard Java library is designed for maximum productivity and portability. The support of data structures is an important part of the language design. The Java standard data structure classes are efficient and easy to use.

This chapter presents the data structure classes in the Java standard library. The classes include arrays, *Vector*, *Stack*, *Dictionary*, *Hashtable*, and *BitSet*. We discuss how to use the data structures from an application developer's standpoint. Specifically, we present

- The difference between the notions of array variable, array object, and array type. An array type is determined with a type for its elements. It can be used to declare array variables. An array variable may not reference any array object. After creating an array, we assign the reference to the array object to an array variable. We shall also discuss the notion of multi-dimensional array.
- Class *Vector*, which represents linear data structures that can dynamically increase or decrease capacity as needed. Like the elements of an array, the elements in a vector are indexed.
- Class *Stack*, which keeps objects in first-in first-out order. The class is a standard class. It extends class *Vector*.
- Interface *Enumeration*, which specifies a method for testing if any more elements in a data structure have not be enumerated and a method for retrieving

the next element. Class *Vector* has an instance method that returns an enumeration of the elements of a vector.

- A data structure called queue, which keeps objects in first-in first-out order. The data structure is not a standard class of Java. But its functionality has been implemented with class *Vector*. We define class *Queue* based on class *Vector*.

- Classes *Dictionary* and *Hashtable* for storing key-value pairs. A key is used to retrieve the associated value from a dictionary or a hash table. The performance of a hash table for data access can match that of an array. But the elements of an array must be accessed with integer indexes. A hash table can use any object as a key.

- Class *BitSet* for keeping sets of bits. The bits in a bit set are packaged into bytes for space efficiency. A bit set can be used as a mask of conditions.

## 4.1 Arrays

### 4.1.1 Array Objects

#### 4.1.1.1 Array Variable and Creation

An array is a sequence of anonymous variables (components) of the same type. The components of an array are accessed through their zero-based indexes in the array. The size of an array is fixed when the array is created. Using an index out of the index range of the array incurs a runtime exception of class *ArrayIndexOutOfBoundsException*, which is an unchecked exception.

In Java, arrays are objects. Like other types of object reference, the reference to an array can be assigned to a variable that is declared with a compatible type. An array encapsulates data and methods. Arrays are objects of class *Object*. The methods defined in class *Object* can be invoked for arrays.

An array type is declared with a type name followed by a pair of brackets. For example, expressions *Customer*[], *Customer*[][], and *Object*[] are three array types. The type *Customer*[][] can be regarded as constructed with array type *Customer*[] and symbol []. An interface name such as *Serializable* can be used to define an array type such as *Serializable*[] or *Serializable*[][]. The type *Serializable*[][] uses array type *Serializable*[] as its component type. Note that an array type is a type, which can be used to declare variables or another array type.

In a Java program, we use the *new* operator, a type, and an integer size to create an array object. The size is enclosed between a pair of brackets. For example, statement

```
new Customer[20]
```

creates an array with twenty elements. An element of the array is an anonymous variable of type *Customer*. It is initialized with value *null* when the array is created. It can hold an object of class *Customer* or a subclass.

We can assign an array variable with reference to a created array. Assume class *Customer* extends class *Object*. A customer object is compatible with a variable of type *Object*. Therefore, a *Customer* array is compatible with an *Object* array variable. The following code declares array variable *customers* with type *Object*[], creates a *Customer* array, and assigns the variable *customers* with the reference to the created array.

```
Object[] customers;
customers = new Customer[20];
```

In an array variable declaration, brackets [] can be placed between the type name and the variable name or after the variable name. For example, the following two declarations are equivalent, both declare variable *customers*, which can reference an array of objects.

```
Object[] customers;
Object customers[];
```

As shown above, an array variable declaration is different from an array creation. An array (object) is created with the *new* operator, a type such as *Object*, and a length enclosed within brackets []. The memory space allocated for an array variable can be used to hold only a reference. As shown in Fig. 4.1a, after declaration

```
Object[] customers;
```

variable *customers* references nothing. If *customers* is a local variable, it does not hold *null* after its declaration. The memory for an array object has space for its components. After statement

```
customers = new Customer[20];
```

is executed, an array object is allocated in memory and the reference to the array is placed in variable *customers*. The effect of array creation is shown in Fig. 4.1b, where each element is assigned with a *null* reference by default. We can create a customer object and assign it to the third element of the array with statement

```
customers[2] = new Customer();
```

After the above statement is executed, the array shown in Fig. 4.1b is changed to that in Fig. 4.1c.

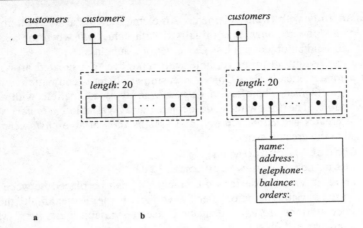

**Fig. 4.1** Array variable declaration and array creation

The type of an array variable may be different from the class of an array referenced by the variable. The source code

```
Object[] customers;
customers = new Customer[20];
```

can be compiled by the Java compiler. The type of variable *customers* is *Object*[]. The class of the array created by expression *new Customer*[20] is *Customer*[]. The above code is legal since class *Customer* extends class *Object*. The following assignment is illegal.

```
Customer[] customers;
customers = new Object[20];
```

An important property of an array is its length. When an array is created, its length is fixed. We can access the *length* field of an existing array. For example, the following code accesses the *length* field of array *customers*. The code prints the length *20* on standard output.

```
Customer[] customers = new Customer[20];
System.out.println(customers.length);
```

### 4.1.1.2 Array Element

An element in an array is represented with the array name and an index. The first element in an array referenced by a variable, say *customers*, is represented with *customers*[0], and the last element with *customers*[*customers.length* − 1]. If the array is created with class *Customer* as element type, the elements of the array are equivalent to variables of type *Customer*.

The reference in an element of an array can be accessed. The element can be assigned with a new value. For example, after statement

```
customers[3] = customers[2];
```

is executed, both elements *customers*[2] and *customers*[3] reference the same object or contain *null*. The statement retrieves from the third element of array *customers* and places the retrieved reference or *null* into the fourth element.

An interface can be used to create an array. For example, statement

```
Serializable[] serializables =
                    new Serializable[20];
```

creates an array with interface *Serializable* and assigns the array to variable *serializables*. Each element of the array is equivalent to a variable of type *Serializable*. It can hold an object of a class that implements interface *Serializable*. For example, class *String* implements interface *Serializable*. Statement

```
serializables[5] = new String();
```

creates an instance of class *String* and assigns it to the sixth element of array *serializables*.

## 4.1.2 Multi-Dimensional Array

### 4.1.2.1 Multi-Dimensional Array Types

Elements of an array may reference arrays. Java supports multi-dimensional arrays. For example, expression *Customer*[][] is a type, which represents two-dimensional arrays with element type *Customer*. The first dimension of the array expression represents an array of arrays. Generally speaking, an $n$-dimensional array can be regarded as an array of $(n-1)$-dimensional arrays.

A multi-dimensional array variable is declared with its element type followed by several pairs of brackets []. For instance, statement

```
Customer[][] customersByDepts;
```

declares variable *customersByDepts*, which may hold a reference to a two-dimensional array. The components in the first dimension reference arrays of customer objects. The elements in the second dimension reference customer objects or *null*.

Java uses the terms *component* and *element* differently for multi-dimensional arrays. An *element* of an $n$-dimensional array can hold a primitive value or a reference to an object that is not an array. A *component* of an $n$-dimensional array can hold a reference to an $(n-i)$-dimensional array for $1 \leq i \leq n-1$. The element type of a one-dimensional or a multi-dimensional array is a class, an interface, or a primitive type. For example, arrays created with expressions *new Customer*[20] and *new Customer*[10][20] both have element type *Customer*. For the 2-dimensional array, a component in the first dimension is indexed with an integer between 0 and 9. The component is an anonymous variable that references an array with 20 elements.

### 4.1.2.2 Fixed Multi-Dimensional Arrays

When we create a multi-dimensional array, we can allocate space for all the anonymous variables in the array. For example, statement

```
Customer[][] customersByDepts =
                        new Customer[5][20];
```

creates a two-dimensional array, which has 5 components, each references an array of 20 elements. Assume the components correspond to the departments of a supermarket. Each element can hold a reference to a customer object or *null*. The code

```
Customer[][] customersByDepts =
                        new Customer[5][20];
customersByDepts[2][0] = new Customer();
```

creates a new customer object and assigns it to the first element in the third component of array *customersByDepts*.

### 4.1.2.3 Variable Multi-Dimensional Arrays

In Java, when we create a multi-dimensional array, the sizes (lengths) of arrays in the last several dimensions may be omitted. For example, statement

```
Customer[][] customersByDepts = new Customer[5][];
```

creates a one-dimensional array with component type *Customer*[]. The created array has 5 components, each of which can be assigned with a one-dimensional array of customers. The Java code

```
Customer[][] customersByDepts = new Customer[5][];
customersByDepts[0] = new Customer[25];
customersByDepts[1] = new Customer[10];
```

assigns an array of length 25 to the first component of array *customersByDepts*, and an array of length 10 to the second component. The code models a situation that different departments of the supermarket may have different numbers of customers.

The *length* field of a component in a multi-dimensional array can be accesses. For instance, the statement

```
System.out.print(customersByDepts.length);
```

prints 5 on the standard output, where the variable *customersByDepts* refers to the same named variable in the above source code.

# 4.2 Vectors

## 4.2.1 Class *Vector*

### 4.2.1.1 Arrays and Vectors

Class *Vector* is a standard Java data structure class in package *java.util*. Like an array, a vector organizes its elements in a sequence. Elements of a vector are indexed.

A vector has a substantial difference from an array. Array is a fixed data structure. We cannot change the size of an array after the array is created. In an application, we may not know in advance the maximum number of objects to be stored. Overflow may happen for an array. Class *Vector* provides an array-like data structure that can expand and shrink dynamically in response to object insertions and deletions. The expansion is automatic.

Another difference between an array and a vector is about their element types. The elements of an array may hold values of a primitive type. For example, expression *new int*[20] creates an array with 20 integer elements. A *Vector* object can store objects of different types in its elements. To store integers in a vector, we wrap the integers with instances of class *Integer* and store the *Integer* objects in the vector. An array holds a homogeneous type of primitive values or objects. Its creation requires an element type. A vector does not have an element type other than *Object*.

An array is regarded as a low-level storage. A Java runtime system maps an array to a series of contiguous words in computer memory to allow fast access to its elements. An element of an array is referred to with a zero-based integer index. For example, the third element in one-dimensional array *customers* is represented with *customers*[2]. A vector is regarded as a high-level data structure. Its elements are retrieved with accessing methods such as *customers.elementAt*(2).

Class *Vector* extends class *Object*. It implements interfaces *Cloneable* and *Serializable*. Class *Vector* defines methods for inserting, removing, and searching for objects in vectors.

A vector object uses notion *size* to denote the number of objects actually stored in it. This integer quantity is different from the notion of storage capacity. A vector maintains a *capacity* and a *capacityIncrement* field. The *capacity* value is always greater than or equal to *size*. A vector increases its capacity in chunks of *capacityIncrement*. A vector is implemented with an array to keep objects. It has methods to reset the capacity. By setting a large capacity for a vector in advance, we can avoid reallocation of the underlying array when adding many objects into the vector.

### 4.2.1.2 Vector Creation

A vector is created with the *new* operator and a constructor of class *Vector*. The constructors of class *Vector* are

> *Vector*()
> *Vector*(*int capacity*)
> *Vector*(*int capacity, int increment*)

The first constructor uses a default initial capacity to allocate an array for a created vector. When the capacity of the vector is not enough to accommodate a new object, the capacity of the vector is doubled before the new object is inserted into the vector. By using the third constructor, we can specify the initial *capacity* and capacity *increment* for the created vector object. For example, we may create a vector to store customer objects as follows.

```
Vector customers  = new Vector(100, 10);
```

Note a difference between array and vector creations. An array creation expression such as *new int*[100] specifies an element type *int* for the created array. A vector creation does not specify an element type. You can regard the element type of vectors as *Object*.

A program may access or change the current capacity of a vector with the following instance methods of class *Vector*.

| Signature | Semantics |
|-----------|-----------|
| `int capacity()` | Returns the current capacity of this vector |
| `void ensureCapacity` `(int minCapacity)` | Ensures a minimum capacity by increasing the vector storage if necessary |

### 4.2.1.3 Vector Accessers and Mutaters

Class *Vector* defines the following instance methods to access the objects stored in a vector. A vector is an indexed sequential data structure. You can randomly access an element in a vector by using its index. You can also find the index of an object in a vector with method *indexOf*(*Object*), which returns −1 if the object is not in the vector. The following methods can be invoked for a variable that references a vector.

| Signature | Semantics |
|-----------|-----------|
| `Object firstElement()` | Returns the first object stored in this vector |
| `Object lastElement()` | Returns the last object |
| `Object elementAt(int index)` | Returns the object stored at an index in this vector |
| `Enumeration elements()` | Returns an enumeration of the objects in this vector |

| boolean contains (Object elem) | Tests if this vector contains an object |
|---|---|
| int indexOf(Object elem) | Searches for the first occurrence of an object in the vector; returns –1 if the object is not in the vector |
| int indexOf(Object elem, int index) | Searches for an occurrence of an object starting from a given index in this vector |
| int lastIndexOf (Object elem) | Searches for the last occurrence of an object in this vector |
| int lastIndexOf (Object elem, int index) | Searches backwards for an object starting from an index |

Class *Vector* defines the following methods to modify the contents of a vector. You can insert an element into a vector with method *insertElementAt(Object newElement, int index)* or replace an element with method *setElementAt(Object newElement, int index)*. The element insertion requires either reallocation of the underlying array in memory or shuffling some elements toward the end of the array to make room for the new element. Therefore, element insertion for a vector is expensive and should be limited. Removing an element in the middle of a vector causes element shuffling forward. It is expensive too.

| Signature | Semantics |
|---|---|
| void addElement (Object obj) | Adds an object to the end of this vector |
| void insertElementAt (Object obj, int index) | Inserts an object at an index so the size of this vector is increased by one |
| void setElementAt (Object obj, int index) | Sets a specified element of this vector with an object |
| void removeElementAt (int index) | Deletes an indexed element from this vector |
| boolean removeElement (Object obj) | Removes the first occurrence of an object from this vector |
| void removeAllElements() | Empty this vector |

Class *Vector* defines the following methods to test the state of a vector. Notion *size* refers to the number of objects that are actually stored in a vector, *capacity* refers to the storage capacity of the underlying array, which is at least as large as *size*.

| Signature | Semantics |
|---|---|
| `int size()` | Returns the number of objects stored in this vector |
| `boolean isEmpty()` | Tests if this vector stores no object |
| `void setSize(int newSize)` | Sets the size of this vector, which may add *null* references or discard valid references |
| `void trimToSize()` | Trims the capacity of this vector to its current size |

**Exercise 4.1** Create a vector with initial capacity 3, and then add four customer objects into the vector in the main method of class *Customer*.

### 4.2.1.4 Vector Replication

Class *Vector* defines the following instance methods to duplicate a vector or copy the references in a vector into an array. The objects referenced by the elements of the vector will not be replicated by the methods. Their references are copied from the vector to the clone vector or the target array.

| Signature | Semantics |
|---|---|
| `Object clone()` | Creates a clone of this vector and returns it |
| `void copyInto(Object anArray[])` | Copies the contents of this vector into an array, which must be at least as large as this vector size |

The following example illustrates the standard class *Vector*. It extends the class to store customer objects. It defines methods for accessing and inserting customer objects in a vector. Thus, the data structures of the extended class are typed data structures, which overcome a deficiency that class *Vector* has no element type.

**Example 4.1** The following class extends class *Vector* so that the elements in the vectors are of type *Customer*.

```
import java.util.Vector;
/** Customer vector, the elements reference
*    customer objects or null.
*/
class CustomerVector extends Vector {
    public void addCustomer(Customer cus) {
        addElement(cus);
    }
    public void insertCustomerAt(Customer cus,
                                 int index) {
```

```
      insertElementAt(cus, index);
   }

   public Customer firstCustomer() {
      return (Customer) firstElement();
   }

   public Customer lastCustomer() {
      return (Customer) lastElement();
   }

   public Customer customerAt(int index) {
      return (Customer) elementAt(index);
   }

   public static void main(String[] args) {
      CustomerVector customers =
                           new CustomerVector();
      customers.addCustomer(new Customer());
      System.out.println(customers);
   }
}
```

□

**Exercise 4.2** Extend class *Vector* to define a data structure for holding employee objects. The class *Employee* is defined in Example 1.16.

## 4.2.2 Interface *Enumeration*

Interface *Enumeration* is defined in package *java.util*. It declares two methods to enumerate through the elements in a data structure. The method *hasMoreElements*() returns a boolean to indicate if there are more elements in the data structure to be enumerated. The method *nextElement*() returns the next element if the enumeration has not been exhausted.

As indicated in Section 4.2.1.3, method *elements* of class *Vector* returns an enumeration for a vector. The enumeration can be used to go through objects contained in the vector. The following example uses the methods of interface *Enumeration* to visit all the customer objects stored in a customer vector.

**Example 4.2** The following main method can be substituted for the main method presented in Example 4.1. It creates a customer vector. The methods *hasMoreElements* and *nextElement* of interface *Enumeration* are applied repeatedly to retrieve balances of the customer objects. Note that the *balance* field of a customer object takes its default value 0.0 when the object is created. The method prints total balance 0.0 on the standard output.

```
   public static void main(String[] args) {
```

```
CustomerVector customers =
                        new CustomerVector();
customers.addCustomer(new Customer());
customers.addCustomer(new Customer());
float totalBalance = 0;
for (Enumeration e = customers.elements();
        e.hasMoreElements(); )
totalBalance += ((Customer)
                e.nextElement()).balance;
System.out.println(totalBalance);
}
```

□

## 4.2.3 Queues

A *queue* is a data structure that handles its elements in a first-in first-out (FIFO) manner. Assume that a customer comes in but he cannot be served immediately. We can place the customer in a waiting list, which is a queue.

The functionality of a queue is displayed in Fig. 4.2. To enforce the FIFO policy, a queue always adds a new element at its end, and removes an element from its front. For example, after invoking method *addCustomer(customer10)* for the queue in Fig. 4.2, object *customer10* will be placed at the end of the queue. Applying method *removeCustomer()* removes the front element *customer2* from the queue.

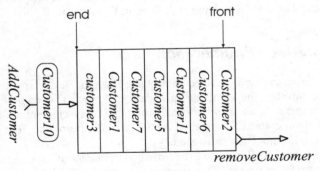

**Fig. 4.2** A queue with FIFO policy

The FIFO functionality of queue can be easily implemented with instance methods *addElement(Object obj)* and *removeElementAt(0)* of class *Vector*. As we learn in Section 4.2.1.3, method *addElement(Object obj)* adds object *obj* at the end of a vector, *firstElement()* retrieves the first element from a vector, and *removeElementAt(0)* removes the first element and decreases the size of the vector by 1. Thus, we can use an instance of class *Vector* as a queue.

The following example shows how to extend class *Vector* to define a queue for storing customer objects. The extended class introduces methods *addCusto-*

*mer*(*Customer cus*) and *nextCustomer*() to append a customer object to a queue or retrieve the front customer object from a queue. The methods are implemented with inherited methods *addElement* and *firstElement*.

**Example 4.3** The following class, class *CustomerQueue*, extends class *Vector* to store customer objects and support the FIFO policy. It defines methods *addCustomer*, *nextCustomer*, and *removeCustomer* for adding a new customer to the end of a customer queue, retrieving or removing the front customer.

Class *CustomerQueue* contains a main method for testing the FIFO property. After adding two customer objects into a customer queue, we remove a customer in the main method. Then, we retrieve a customer from the queue and print his name. Since the first customer will be removed first, the second customer name will be printed by the main method.

```java
import java.util.Vector;
/** CustomerQueue of customer objects
*/
class CustomerQueue extends Vector {
    public void addCustomer(Customer cus) {
        addElement(cus);
    }

    public Customer nextCustomer() {
        if (size() > 0)
            return (Customer) firstElement();
        return null;
    }

    public void removeCustomer() {
        if (size() > 0) removeElementAt(0);
    }

    public static void main(String[] args) {
        CustomerQueue customers =
                        new CustomerQueue();
        Customer cus = new Customer();
        cus.name = "John Smith";
        customers.addCustomer(cus);
        cus = new Customer();
        cus.name = "Tom David";
        customers.addCustomer(cus);
        customers.removeCustomer();
        System.out.println(customers.
                        nextCustomer().name);
    }
}
```

□

# 4.3 Class *Stack*

### 4.3.1 Class *Stack*

Class *Stack* in package *java.util* extends class *Vector* with instance methods to support last-in first-out (LIFO) policy. The data structures represented by class *Stack* are indispensable to process recursive definitions and procedures. For example, the computation of an arithmetic expression cannot be completed until subexpressions in the expression are evaluated. Arithmetic expressions require recursive computation. We can use a stack to keep uncompleted processes. Specifically, when a running process needs to evaluate a subexpression, the running process is halted, its state is placed onto a stack, and a process for evaluating the subexpression is dispatched. After the process for the subexpression is completed, the halted process is found at the top of the stack. We can resume the halted process.

The LIFO functionality of a stack is shown in Fig. 4.3. When a customer object is pushed onto a stack, it is placed on the top of the stack. When an object is removed from a stack, the top object of the stack is removed. The operations are traditionally called *push* and *pop*. After method *push(customer10)* is executed for the stack in Fig. 4.3, object *customer10* will be the new top element in the stack. If method *pop()* is invoked, object *customer2* will be removed from the stack and *customer6* becomes the new top.

The Java standard class *Stack* extends the traditional functionality of a stack with method *search(Object obj)*. The method searches the inside of a stack for an object. Class *Stack* inherits class *Vector*. By the discussion in Section 4.2.2, method *elements()* for a stack returns an *Enumeration* of the objects stored in the stack. The returned enumeration can respond to methods *hasMoreElements()* and *nextElement()*. We can use the enumeration to go through all the objects in the stack.

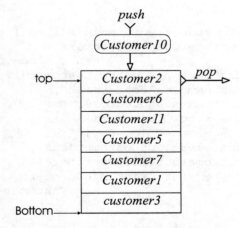

**Fig. 4.3** A stack of customer objects

## 4.3.2 Construction and Operations of Stacks

Class *Stack* defines constructor *Stack()*. A new stack can be created with expression *new Stack()*. A newly created stack is empty. Class *Stack* inherits the public and protected methods of class *Vector*.

The LIFO property of stack is supported with instance methods *push(Object obj)* and *pop()*. Method *push(obj)* places object *obj* on the top of a stack. Method *pop()* returns the top object of a stack and removes it from the stack. Method *peek()* of class *Stack* accesses the top element in a stack without removing it from the stack. The methods are described in the following table. They can be invoked for variable *customers* declared with the statement

```
Stack customers = new Stack();
```

| Signature | Semantics |
| --- | --- |
| `Object push(Object item)` | Places an object on the top of this stack |
| `Object pop()` | Returns the top object and removes it from this stack |
| `Object peek()` | Returns the top object of this stack without removing it |

Class *Stack* inherits methods of class *Vector*. It also defines the following stack accessers. The method *search(Object obj)* returns the index of argument *obj* in the stack if *obj* is in the stack; –1 otherwise. Method *empty()* tests if a stack is empty.

| Signature | Semantics |
| --- | --- |
| `int search(Object obj)` | Returns zero-based offset of *obj* from the top in the stack; returns –1 if *obj* is not in the stack |
| `empty()` | Tests if the stack is empty |

**Exercise 4.3** We extend class *Vector* to define a customer queue class in Example 4.3. Extend class *Stack* to define a customer stack.

# 4.4 Dictionary and Hash Tables

## 4.4.1 Class *Dictionary*

Class *Dictionary* in package *java.util* is abstract. It supports the storage of key-value pairs. Any non-null object can be used as a key. A dictionary uses the *equals(Object key)* method to decide whether two keys are the same.

Class *Dictionary* defines the following methods to add or remove keys and values. Particularly, method *put(key, value)* adds a key-value pair into a dictionary. The methods must be overridden by subclasses. We can declare a variable named *cusDictionary* with class *Dictionary* and assign it with a *Dictionary* object such as a hash table, which will be discussed in Section 4.4.3.

| Signature | Semantics |
|---|---|
| `Object put(Object key, Object value)` | Adds a key-value pair into this dictionary and returns the previous value for *key* |
| `Object get(Object key)` | Retrieves the value for a key from this dictionary; returns *null* if the key is not in this dictionary |
| `Object remove(Object key)` | Removes a key along with its value from this dictionary and returns the value |
| `Enumeration keys()` | Returns an enumeration of the keys in this dictionary |
| `Enumeration elements()` | Returns an enumeration of the values in this dictionary |

The following methods can be used to test the state of a dictionary. Method *size* counts the key-value pairs stored in a dictionary. Method *isEmpty()* answers whether a dictionary contains any key-value pair.

| Signature | Semantics |
|---|---|
| `int size()` | Returns the number of keys in this dictionary |
| `boolean isEmpty()` | Tests if this dictionary contains no key |

## 4.4.2 Hash Code

Class *Object* defines methods *hashCode()* and *equals(Object obj)*. The method *hashCode* uses the data in an object to evaluate a hash code, which is a long integer, for the object. A hash table uses the hash code of a key object to store and locate the object. The method *equals(Object obj)* decides whether the receiving object is equal to the object *obj*. If two objects are equal according to method *equals*, method *hashCode* must return the same hash code for them. That is, for any two objects *obj1* and *obj2*, if expression *obj1.equals(obj2)* returns *true*, the *long* integer values evaluated with expressions *obj1.hashCode()* and *obj2.hash-Code()* must be equal.

The definition of method *equals* in class *Object* regards two different objects as unequal. Method *hashCode* defined in class *Object* returns different values for different objects. The default behavior may not be suitable for some applications. For example, we may have two different objects representing the same person. In this case, the method *equals* should use the social security numbers of persons to determine whether two persons are equal each other. Class *Person* should override the default behavior of method *equals* inherited from class *Object*. If a class overrides the *equals* method, it should override method *hashCode* to ensure two equal objects return the same value with the *hashCode* method.

### 4.4.3 Class *Hashtable*

Class *Hashtable* in package *java.util* extends class *Dictionary*. It implements the abstract methods specified in class *Dictionary*. A hash table uses a table to store the key-value pairs. It maps a key to an index in the table by using the hash code of the key. The size of the underlying table is called the *capacity* of the hash table. The ratio between the number of stored keys and the capacity of the underlying table at runtime is called a *load factor* of the hash table.

The number of possible keys may be much more than the capacity of a hash table. For instance, the number of possible social security numbers is huge. But a supermarket needs to keep at most 200 employee objects in a hash table. It is possible that two different social security numbers are mapped to the same index in the underlying table; i.e., *hashing collision* is unavoidable. When hashing collision happens, the hash table must find a way to resolve it so that both keys can be stored in the table. The capacity and load factor of a hash table affect the chance of hashing collision. By increasing capacity, we can decrease load factor and reduce the chance of hashing collision.

At runtime, an instance of class *Hashtable* compares its load factor with a threshold, which is 0.75 by default. When the load factor is greater than the threshold, the capacity of the hash table is increased automatically.

### 4.4.4 Hash Table Creation

Class *Hashtable* defines constructors

    *Hashtable()*
    *Hashtable(int capacity)*
    *Hashtable(int capacity, float threshold)*

to create empty hash tables. The constructors may use an integer *capacity* as the initial capacity of the created hash table. If many key-value pairs are to be stored, create a hash table with a large initial capacity. In addition to a *capacity* parameter, a float value named *threshold* can be used in a constructor to override the default load factor. A larger load factor uses the memory space more efficiently but increases the possibility of hashing collision and decreases the performance of the hash table.

The statement

```
Hashtable employees = new Hashtable(300, 0.6f);
```

can be used to create a hash table with an initial capacity 300 and a load factor threshold 0.6. When the table is 60% full, it will be augmented automatically.

## 4.4.5 Accessers and Mutaters of Hashtables

Class *Hashtable* defines methods *get(Object key)*, *keys()*, and *values()*, which are inherited from class *Dictionary*, for accessing the values and keys in a hash table. It also defines methods for accessing a hash table and testing its state, which are described in the following table. We can declare variable *employees* with the statement

```
Hashtable employees = new Hashtable(300, 0.6f);
```

and invoke the methods for the variable.

| Signature | Semantics |
|---|---|
| `boolean containsKey (Object key)` | Tests if a key is stored in this hash table |
| `boolean contains (Object value)` | Tests if a value is stored in this hash table |
| `Object clone()` | Returns a clone of the hash table without cloning keys and values |
| `int size()` | Counts the keys stored in the hash table |
| `boolean isEmpty()` | Tests if this hash table does not store any key |
| `String toString()` | Returns a string representation of this hash table |

In Section 4.4.1, we describe the semantics of instance methods *put(key, value)* and *remove(key)* of class *Dictionary*. Class *Hashtable* implements the methods. In addition, class *Hashtable* defines the following methods to maintain hash tables.

| Signature | Semantics |
|---|---|
| `void clear()` | Clears all the key-value pairs from this hash table |
| `void rehash()` | Creates a larger hash table and rehashes the contents of this hash table into the new one |

We use the following example to illustrate the creation and management of a hash table. The hash table is assumed to hold employee objects as values. The social security number of an employee is used as the key to access the employee object. A programmer who uses class *Hashtable* is not concerned with hashing collision resolution. All she can do is to set the initial capacity and a load factor for a hash table creation.

**Example 4.4** The following class, class *Employee*, encapsulates a social security number and other information in each employee object. In the main method of class *Employee*, we create a hash table and reference it with variable *employees*. Then, we add employee objects into the hash table with social security numbers as keys. We retrieve one of the employee objects with a social security number. An execution of the main method prints *John Smith* on standard output.

```java
import java.util.Hashtable;
class Employee {
    String socialSecurityNumber;
    String name, address, telephone;
    public Employee() {}
    public Employee(String name, String address,
                    String telephone,
                    String socialSecurityNumber) {
    this.name = name; this.address = address;
    this.telephone = telephone;
    this.socialSecurityNumber =
                    socialSecurityNumber;
    }
    public static void main(String[] args) {
    // hash table creation
    Hashtable employees =
                    new Hashtable(300, 0.6f);
    Employee empee = new Employee("John Smith",
        "Windsor, Ontario", "519-555-4444",
        "3211234567");
        employees.put(empee.
                socialSecurityNumber, empee);
        empee = new Employee("Tom David",
            "New York, NY", "322-555-4444",
            "3211234765");
        employees.put(empee.
                socialSecurityNumber, empee);
    System.out.println(((Employee)
        employees.get("3211234567")).name);
    }
}
```

□

# 4.5 Class *BitSet*

## 4.5.1 Bit Sets

Class *BitSet* in package *java.util* extends class *Object*. It represents ordered sequences of bits. The elements of a *BitSet* are accessed through 0-based indexes. The storage required for a *BitSet* grows automatically when more bits are needed. It is more efficient to use a *BitSet* than an array or a vector of *booleans* for a large set of bits. The bits in a *BitSet* object are packed into bytes; each byte consists of eight bits.

Class *BitSet* defines constructors

> *BitSet*()
> *BitSet*(*int capacity*)

for creating bit sets. A constructor may use integer argument *capacity* to specify the initial capacity for a created *BitSet*.

In C/C++ programming, the bits of an integer can be used to keep on/off conditions. To extract bits from the integer, a mask must be created. Using a mask in C/C++ is error prone and difficult to understand. The class *BitSet* defines methods for performing bitwise logical operations *and*, *or*, and *xor*.

## 4.5.2 Accessers and Mutaters

Class *BitSet* defines the following methods for accessing and modifying the bits stored in a *BitSet*. The bits are zero-base indexed. The logical operations *and*, *or*, and *xor* change the bit settings in the first operand. The methods can be invoked for bit set variable *conditions* declared with the statement

```
BitSet conditions = new BitSet(10);
```

| Signature | Semantics |
|-----------|-----------|
| `void set(int index)` | Sets a bit at a given index |
| `boolean get(int index)` | Returns an indexed bit in the form of a *boolean* |
| `void clear(int index)` | Clears an indexed bit |
| `void and(BitSet set)` | Performs bitwaise AND for this bit set with another and return this bit set |
| `void or(BitSet set)` | Performs bitwise OR |
| `void xor(BitSet set)` | Performs bitwise XOR |
| `int hashCode()` | Evaluates the hash code of this bit set |

| `boolean equals(Object obj)` | Compares this bit set with another |
|---|---|
| `int size()` | Counts bits in this bit set |
| `String toString()` | Converts this bit set to a string |
| `Object clone()` | Creates a clone of this bit set |

## 4.6 Summary

This chapter introduces several standard Java data structure classes. An array can be regarded as a low-level data structure, which is mapped directly to memory cells for fast, random access. A vector is similar to an array. It is a high-level data structure, which is based on an array. When a vector needs more storage, a different array is automatically created and assigned to the vector.

Java provides interface *Enumeration* for enumerating elements of data structures. Different data structures implement the interface differently. The method *elements*() for a vector returns an enumeration of the objects stored in the vector. By repeatedly invoking methods *hasMoreElements*() and *nextElement*() for the enumeration, we can visit each object stored in the vector.

Two common data structures are stack and queue, which support LIFO (last-in first-out) and FIFO (first-in first-out), respectively. Queue is not a standard data structure in Java. We can implement a queue easily with a vector. Class *Stack* is a standard Java class. It uses the traditional operations *push* and *pop* to maintain the top of a stack.

Java standard classes *Dictionary* and *Hashtable* support the storage of key-value pairs. They provide methods for accessing the stored keys and values. Class *Hashtable* is a subclass of the abstract class *Dictionary*. It implements hashing tables with hash code of objects as keys.

Java class *BitSet* represents ordered sequences of bits. The bits in a bit set are indexed with first bit at index 0. They can be accessed or changed by using indexes. A bit set automatically increases itself when needed. It is more flexible to use a bit set than an array or vector of booleans.

# Part II
# Computation Analysis

- *Java Virtual Machine*
- *Complexity analysis*

# Chapter 5
# Java Virtual Machine

A compilation unit in a Java program contains classes and/or interfaces. The Java compiler compiles each class or interface into a class file, which is represented in a platform-independent binary format. A Java runtime system loads a class from the class file when it needs the class. It executes instructions in compiled methods loaded from class files.

The Java Virtual Machine (JVM) is the engine of the Java language. It is necessary for running Java programs. The instructions of a compiled Java program are not executed directly on the CPU of a hardware system. Instead, the JVM carries out the instructions. The JVM is the software interface between a compiled Java program and a hardware system. It can be regarded as a virtual processor from the standpoint of a Java programmer. It not only interprets the instructions of a compiled Java program but performs security verifications and other activities as well. It is the key to many distinctive features of Java such as portability and security.

Some of instructions on the JVM are similar with instructions on a real CPU. The instructions include arithmetic operations, flow control, and array element access.

Some of the JVM instructions represent high-level commands, each abstracting a computation done with a series of CPU instructions. The commands require other mechanisms of the JVM to support their functions. The high-level JVM instructions include method invocation, field access, and object creation. For example, the JVM has an instruction that creates multi-dimensional arrays. The implementation of the array creation instruction allocates memory and initializes array elements.

The specification of the JVM does not restrain memory layout for runtime data area and bytecode optimization, which are implementation-dependent. The JVM represents a high-level, object-oriented abstraction of computer systems. An implementation of the JVM is called a Java runtime system. A Java-enabled application such as an Internet browser has an embedded Java runtime system. By studying the JVM, we can understand the various mechanisms that support the Java features. It also helps us analyze the performance of programs and data structures written in Java.

In this chapter, we shall present

- A class file format. The Java compiler generates class files from the source code of classes. We describe the class file structure, which has substructures to encode variables, constants, and methods. The structure is necessary to support method execution.

- The instruction set of the JVM. A compiled method of a class consists of the instructions. The JVM loads a class file when it needs the class or a method of the class. It loads compiled methods from the class file. We describe the various types of instruction, their formats, and executions.
- The architecture of the JVM and its major components. The JVM is a software system for running Java programs. It interprets methods. It checks the requests of methods against security rules. It delegates necessary operations to the underlying operating system and hardware.

This chapter presents an overall description of Java runtime systems. It treats the JVM like a computational model such as a random access machine or a Turing machine. We shall emphasize the object-oriented abstraction of the JVM. The abstraction is rather involved. The knowledge of the JVM is necessary for understanding the performance of Java programs. It lays the basis for the time and space analysis of Java programs, which will be discussed in the next chapter.

A Java runtime system must follow the specification of the JVM so that a class file generated by a Java compiler can be loaded by all Java runtime systems. Java compilers may be different. They may apply different compilation and optimization techniques. Java runtime systems may be different as well. The following examples apply the Java compiler of Sun's JDK. The reader may use other compilers and utilities to repeat the examples.

# 5.1 Java Class Files

## 5.1.1 Class File Structure

The Java compiler compiles classes and interfaces to class files, one class file for each class and one for each interface.

A class file is a stream of bytes. A quantity larger than a byte is represented with multiple bytes in a class file. We shall use *u1*, *u2*, and *u4* to represent a 1, 2, or 4-byte quantities. In addition to *u1*, *u2*, and *u4* quantities, a class file contains several tables. Each table consists of one kind of structures. The structures are stored sequentially in a class file.

The types of structure stored in a class file are

- *cp_info* structure. A *cp_info* structure stores a symbolic reference or a constant. It may store a string constant, numeric value, full class name, field name, or method descriptor. It encodes its own length.
- *field_info* structure. A *field_info* structure describes a field of the class or interface. The represented field may be a static or instance field. The length of a *field_info* can be found in the structure.
- *method_info* structure. A *method_info* structure contains the description of a method defined in the class or interface. It contains the bytecode compiled from the method.

- *attribute_info* structure. An *attribute_info* structure describes an attribute of the class file or some component of the class file. For instance, the *SourceFile* attribute denotes the source file from which the class file was compiled.

A class file contains the following tables:

- *constant_pool* table, which consists of *cp_info* structures to encode constants and symbolic references that are referred to in the class file.
- *superinterfaces* table. The class or interface may have superinterfaces. The *superinterfaces* table contains the direct superinterface indexes in the *constant_pool* table.
- *fields* table, which consists of *field_info* structures for the fields of the class or interface.
- *methods* table, which consists of *method_info* structures for the methods of the class or interface.
- *attributes* table, which consists of *attribute_info* structures to describe attributes of the class file.

In addition to the above tables, several quantities in a class file describe the class or interface. Specifically, a class file includes a *u4* and several *u2* quantities. The *u4* quantity is named *magic* with value 0xCAFEBABE. Five of the *u2* quantities are named *minor_version*, *major_version*, *access_flags*, *this_class*, and *super_class*. The values of *minor_version* and *major_version* denote the minor and major versions of the Java compiler that generated the class file. The *access_flags* quantity indicates whether the class or interface is public, final, interface, and/or abstract. It uses a bit named *ACC_SUPER* to indicate which semantics of instruction *invokespecial* applies. The *this_class* and *super_class* quantities are indexes in the *constant_pool* table. The *constant_pool* entry at the *this_class* index represents the class or interface. The entry at index *super_class* represents the superclass of the class or interface. It refers to class *java.lang.Object* if the class file is generated from an interface.

A class file arranges the above described tables and quantities as follows. We use one line to describe a quantity or a table. The data type of a table or quantity is at the left, the table (array) or quantity name is on the right.

```
u4 magic
u2 minor_version
u2 major_version
u2 constant_pool_count
cp_info[1.. constant_pool_count−1] constant_pool
u2 access_flags
u2 this_class
u2 super_class
u2 interfaces_count
u2[0..interfaces_count−1] superinterfaces
u2 fields_count
field_info[0..fields_count−1] fields
u2 methods_count
```

method_info[0..methods_count–1] methods
u2 attributes_count
attribute_info[0..attributes_count–1] attributes

Note that each of the tables in a class file is preceded with an entry count. Each entry in a table encodes its own length. We shall detail the internal structures of the table entries later. The count and length information enables a Java runtime system to understand a class by reading the class file. We use the following example to illustrate the structure of a class file.

**Example 5.1** Let us examine the class file of the following class, class *Merchandise*. The class does not declare a superclass or implement an interface. By default, it extends class *java.lang.Object*. It defines private instance variable *name*. It defines accesser *getName* and mutater *setName* for the field. Since the class does not define a no-argument constructor, the Java compiler supplies a default no-argument constructor. Thus, we can find three compiled methods in the class file.

```
class Merchandise {
    private String name;
    String getName() { return name; }
    void setName(String name) {
        this.name = name;
    }
}
```

After compiling the class with Sun's JDK compiler *javac*, we get class file *Merchandise.class*. We can convert the binary file *Merchandise.class* to the more readable hexadecimal representation with program *dumpfile*, which is written in Java and listed in Appendix A. Program *dumpfile* converts a byte into two hexadecimal digits. The hexadecimal representation of file *Merchandise.class* is shown as follows. We separate the bytes into 16-byte blocks. The offset of each block in the class file is listed at the left side.

| *Offset* | | *Hexadecimal code* |
|---|---|---|
| 0x0000 | \| | CA FE BA BE 00 03 00 2D 00 18 07 00 11 07 00 15 |
| 0x0010 | \| | 0A 00 02 00 05 09 00 01 00 06 0C 00 0A 00 08 0C |
| 0x0020 | \| | 00 16 00 0F 01 00 14 28 29 4C 6A 61 76 61 2F 6C |
| 0x0030 | \| | 61 6E 67 2F 53 74 72 69 6E 67 3B 01 00 03 28 29 |
| 0x0040 | \| | 56 01 00 15 28 4C 6A 61 76 61 2F 6C 61 6E 67 2F |
| 0x0050 | \| | 53 74 72 69 6E 67 3B 29 56 01 00 06 3C 69 6E 69 |
| 0x0060 | \| | 74 3E 01 00 04 43 6F 64 65 01 00 0D 43 6F 6E 73 |
| 0x0070 | \| | 74 61 6E 74 56 61 6C 75 65 01 00 0A 45 78 63 65 |
| 0x0080 | \| | 70 74 69 6F 6E 73 01 00 0F 4C 69 6E 65 4E 75 6D |
| 0x0090 | \| | 62 65 72 54 61 62 6C 65 01 00 12 4C 6A 61 76 61 |
| 0x00a0 | \| | 2F 6C 61 6E 67 2F 53 74 72 69 6E 67 3B 01 00 0E |
| 0x00b0 | \| | 4C 6F 63 61 6C 56 61 72 69 61 62 6C 65 73 01 00 |
| 0x00c0 | \| | 0B 4D 65 72 63 68 61 6E 64 69 73 65 01 00 10 4D |
| 0x00d0 | \| | 65 72 63 68 61 6E 64 69 73 65 2E 6A 61 76 61 01 |
| 0x00e0 | \| | 00 0A 53 6F 75 72 63 65 46 69 6C 65 01 00 07 67 |
| 0x00f0 | \| | 65 74 4E 61 6D 65 01 00 10 6A 61 76 61 2F 6C 61 |

```
0x0100 |  6E 67 2F 4F 62 6A 65 63 74 01 00 04 6E 61 6D 65
0x0110 |  01 00 07 73 65 74 4E 61 6D 65 00 20 00 01 00 02
0x0120 |  00 00 00 01 00 02 00 16 00 0F 00 00 00 03 00 00
0x0130 |  00 14 00 07 00 01 00 0B 00 00 00 1D 00 01 00 01
0x0140 |  00 00 00 05 2A B4 00 04 B0 00 00 00 01 00 0E 00
0x0150 |  00 00 06 00 01 00 00 00 04 00 00 00 17 00 09 00
0x0160 |  01 00 0B 00 00 00 22 00 02 00 02 00 00 00 06 2A
0x0170 |  2B B5 00 04 B1 00 00 00 01 00 0E 00 00 00 0A 00
0x0180 |  02 00 00 00 07 00 05 00 06 00 00 00 0A 00 08 00
0x0190 |  01 00 0B 00 00 00 1D 00 01 00 01 00 00 00 05 2A
0x01a0 |  B7 00 03 B1 00 00 00 01 00 0E 00 00 00 06 00 01
0x01b0 |  00 00 00 01 00 01 00 13 00 00 00 02 00 12
```

The count value preceded each table and the length information in the table entries can be used to recognize the parts of the class file, which are described in the following table. We shall describe the entry structures of some tables later. We use the offsets of the beginning and ending bytes of a part to limit the part. The following table includes the part names and meaning.

| Offsets | Name | Meaning |
|---|---|---|
| 0x0000–0x0003 | *magic* | The *magic* value *0xCAFEBABE* for a Java class file |
| 0x0004–0x0005 | *minor_version* | The minor version number of the Java compiler that generated the class file; here, 0x0003 = 3 |
| 0x0006–0x0007 | *major_version* | The major version number of the Java compiler; here, 0x002D = 45 |
| 0x0008–0x0009 | *constant_pool_count* | Entry count of table *constant_pool*; here, 0x0018 = 24 (Entries of the table are indexed with 1, ..., *constant_pool_count*–1.) |
| 0x000A–0x0119 | *constant_pool* | A table of varying-sized structures for constants (Each structure contains its length information.) |
| 0x011A–0x011B | *access_flags* | Mask for the access modifiers of the class; here, 0x0020 |
| 0x011C–0x011D | *this_class* | Index in *constant_pool* for the class; here, 0x0001 = 1 |

| 0x011E-0x011F | *super_class* | Index in *constant_pool* for the superclass; here, 0x0002 = 2 |
|---|---|---|
| 0x0120-0x0121 | *interfaces_count* | Number of declared super-interfaces; here, 0x0000 = 0 (There is no *interfaces* table in the class file.) |
| 0x0122-0x0123 | *fields_count* | Number of fields of the class; here 0x0001 = 1 (The only field is *name*.) |
| 0x0124-0x012B | *fields* | The *fiedls* table; here, only one *field_info* structure for the instance variable *name* in the table |
| 0x012C-0x012D | *methods_count* | Number of methods in the class file; here, 0x0003 = 3, including the default instance initialization method supplied by the Java compiler |
| 0x012E-0x01B3 | *methods* | A table of *method_info* structures; here, three compiled methods for the class |
| 0x01B4-0x01B5 | *attributes_count* | The number of entries in the *attributes* table of class file; here, 0x0001 = 1 |
| 0x01B6-0x01BD | *attributes* | Table of *attribute_info* structures; here, only one *attribute_info* structure |

□

In the remainder of this section, we describe the structures *cp_info*, *field_info*, *method_info*, and *attribute_info*. Some of the structures contain substructures. The substructure specifications can be found in the document of the JVM specification.

**Exercise 5.1** The class *Merchandise* presented in Example 5.1 does not implement any interface. Modify the class by letting it implement an interface, say *Enumeration*. Compile the modified class and use the program *dumpfile* to generate a hexadecimal representation of the class file. Identify the *u2* quantity *interfaces_count* in the class file.

## 5.1.2 Constants in Constant Pool

### 5.1.2.1 Characters and Strings

A Java class file uses a *Utf8_info* structure to represent a string literal in table *constant_pool*. The Utf8 encoding of characters and strings is different from Unicode encoding. The Unicode of a character uses two bytes. Most identifiers used in a computer program consist of ASCII characters. An ASCII character is represented with one byte in Utf8 encoding. Thus, we can save half of the space required by Unicode encoding of ASCII characters. For a non-ASCII character, Utf8 encoding uses two or three bytes to encode the character.

The Utf8 encoding formats are shown in Fig. 5.1. In a *Utf8_info* structure, a character is represented with one byte if the character is in range \u0001 to \u007F, with two bytes if it is in range \u0080 and \u07FF, and with three bytes if it is in range \u0800 to \uFFFF. The byte or bytes in a Utf8 character representation use bits to identify a format. The auxiliary formatting bits are not part of the binary value of the character. They are shadowed in Fig. 5.1.

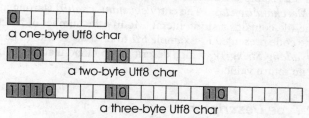

a one-byte Utf8 char

a two-byte Utf8 char

a three-byte Utf8 char

**Fig. 5.1** Utf8 representation of characters

A *Utf8_info* structure consists of three parts:

*u1 tag*
*u2 length*
*u1[length] bytes*

The *tag* value for a *Utf8_info* structure is equal to 0x01 = 1. The *u2* quantity *length* is the number of bytes in the *bytes* array, which stores the *Utf8* encoding of a string literal.

**Example 5.2** (Continuation of Example 5.1) One of the *Utf8_info* structures in table *constant_pool* of class file *Merchandise.class* starts at position 0x0024. The *u1* quantity at offset 0x0024 is the *tag* field, which is equal to 0x01 = 1, for a string literal. The next two bytes contain the length of the string, which is equal to 0x0014 = 20. We now introduce a Java method for reading Utf8 strings.

The following code uses the *readUTF* method of class *DataInputStream* to read a Utf8 string. The code opens file *Merchandise.class* and assigns the file to a *DataInputStream* object referenced by local variable *dataIn*. Then, the first 0x0025 = 37 bytes in the input stream are skipped over with method *skipBytes*(37). Now the first two bytes in stream *dataIn* denote the number of bytes that encode a string. Following the *length* field is the Utf8 encoding of the characters of the string.

```
FileInputStream fin =
        new FileInputStream("Merchandise.class");
dataIn = new DataInputStream(fin);
dataIn.skipBytes(37);
System.out.print(DataInputStream.readUTF(dataIn));
```

The last statement in the above code prints the Utf8 string starting at position 0x0025 in the class file *Merchandise.class* on the standard output. It actually prints expression

*()Ljava/lang/String;*

which consists of an empty parameter list, enclosed between a pair of parentheses, and the return type for a method. The expression is called a method descriptor. The descriptor indicates no argument and return type *java.lang.String*.                                                □

**Exercise 5.2** Example 5.2 describes constant pool entry *constant_pool*[7] in class file *Merchandise.class*. The entry *constant_pool*[9] starting at index 0x0041 in the file contains a string literal. Modify the number of bytes to be skipped in the code presented in Example 5.2 to read the literal. (The string literal is *(Ljava/lang/String;)V*, which describes a method that has a string parameter and no return value.)

## 5.1.2.2 Type Descriptors

A class file encodes types in strings. For instance, Example 5.2 reveals a string constant *Ljava/lang/String;*, which represents an object reference type. The class name *java.lang.String* is represented with *java/lang/String*, which is enclosed between letter *L* and semicolon *;* to denote a reference type. The reference type is used in method descriptor *()Ljava/lang/String;* as return type.

The possible types kept in the *constant_pool* table of a class file are primitive types, reference types, and array types. We now describe the type representations.

A class file uses characters *B, C, D, F, I, J, S,* and *Z* to denote primitive types *byte, char, double, float, int, long, short,* and *boolean*. It uses expression *L<classname>;* to represent a reference type, where *<classname>* is a class or interface name. It uses a left bracket *[* to denote one dimension in an array type. An array type is represented with a series of the dimension symbols followed by a type notation such as *B* or *Ljava/lang/String;*. For instance, expression *[[LCustomer;* denotes a two-dimensional array with element type *Customer*. Expressions *[B* and *[Ljava/lang/String;* denote a byte array and a string array, respectively.

### 5.1.2.3 Method Descriptors

A class file describes a method with a string, which is called the method descriptor. A method descriptor uses a pair of parentheses to enclose the method parameter types. The return type descriptor of the method follows the right parenthesis. If the method does not return a value, the return type descriptor is replaced with letter *V*. For instance, the descriptor of method *getName* of class *Merchandise* is *()Ljava/lang/String;*, and that of method *setName* is *(Ljava/lang/String;)V*.

### 5.1.2.4 Constant Pool Entrys

An entry in a *constant_pool* table uses a *u1* quantity as *tag*, which indicates the type of the entry. Its structure is

    u1 tag
    u1[] info

The possible types are *classRef, fieldRef, methodRef, interfaceMethodRef, string, integer, float, long, double, nameAndType*, and *Utf8*, which are represented by *tag* values 7, 9, 10, 11, 8, 3, 4, 5, 6, 12, and 1, respectively. Example 5.2 shows a *constant_pool* entry with *tag* 0x01 = 1.

The byte array *info* in a *constant_pool* entry encodes a structure. The following example uses three entries to illustrate the structure of the *info* array. The entries encode a symbolic class reference, a field reference, and a string constant, respectively.

**Example 5.3** (Continuation of Example 5.1) The first entry, *constant_pool*[1], in the *constant_pool* table of class file *Merchandise.class* starts at offset 0x000a. It has a tag 0x07 (*classRef*). The JVM specifies that the structure of a class reference constant is

    u1 0x07
    u2 classNameIndex

which can be represented as

    u1 0x07
    u1[2] info

Here, the class name index in the *constant_pool* table is 0x0011 = 17, i.e., the class name is the constant in entry *constant_pool*[17].

The entry *constant_pool*[17] starts at position 0x00be. We can find that the entry is a Utf8 string and the string length is 0x000B = 11. The structure of the entry is

    u1 0x01
    u1[2+0x000B] info.

By modifying the code in Example 5.2, we can print the string in *constant_pool*[17], which is *Merchandise*. Therefore, the symbolic reference stored in *constant_pool*[1] refers to class *Merchandise*.

Entry *constant_pool*[4] in class file *Merchandise.class* starts at position 0x0015. Its *tag* value is 0x09 (*fieldRef*). It encodes a field reference. The structure of a field reference is

> *u1 tag*
> *u2 classIndex*
> *u2 nameAndTypeIndex*

which contains the index of a class and the index of a field descriptor in *constant_pool*.

The *classIndex* value of entry *constant_pool*[4] is 0x0001 = 1. As we already learned, the entry *constant_pool*[1] is a *classRef* for class *Merchandise*. Class *Merchandise* owns the field. The *nameAndTypeIndex* denotes the index of the *nameAndTypeRef* of the field, which is 0x0006.

The constant pool entry *constant_pool*[6] starts at position 0x001f. It consists of

> 0C 00 16 00 0F

The *tag* value 0x0C = 12 indicates a *nameAndType* structure. The value 0x0016 = 22 indicates that entry *constant_pool*[22] contains the field name, and 0x000F = 15 indicates that then entry *constant_pool*[15] contains a description of the field type. We can read the Utf8 strings in the two entries and print *name* and *Ljava/lang/String;*.

By the discussion, entry *constant_pool*[4] references instance field *name* in class *Merchandise* declared with type *java.lang.String*.                □

With the above examples, we can see that a class file uses table *constant_pool* to store symbolic references and constants that are mentioned in the class.

## 5.1.3 The *code* Attribute in *method_info* Structure

As indicated in Section 5.1.1, a class file contains a *u2* quantity *methods_count* and a *methods* table. The Java compiler compiles methods into *method_info* structures and organizes the *method_info* structures in the *methods* table.

The format of a *method_info* structure is

> *u2 access_flags*
> *u2 name_index*
> *u2 descriptor_index*
> *u2 length*
> *attribute_info*[*length*] *attributes*

We explain the parts of structure *method_info* with method *getName* of class *Merchandise* as example. The *method_info* structure of the method starts at position 0x012e in class file *Merchandise.class*.

The *u2* quantity *access_flags* organizes bits for modifiers that are declared or implied for the method. It denotes access mode *public*, *private*, *protected*, or the default access mode. It records whether the method is static, final, or abstract. For example, the *access_flags* for method *getName* is 0x0000, which implies that the method has the default package access mode. The method is not static, not final, and not abstract.

The *name_index* part in a *method_info* structure is an index in the *constant_pool* table. The indexed entry contains the name of the method. For example, the *name_index* value in the *method_info* structure for method *getName* is 0x0014 = 20. We can verify that entry *constant_pool*[20] encodes string *getName*.

Like the *name_index*, the *descriptor_index* in a *method_info* structure is an index in *constant_pool*. The entry at the index contains a Utf8 string that describes the method. For example, the *descriptor_index* for method *getName* is 0x0007 = 7, and *constant_pool*[7] contains string *()Ljava/lang/String;*. As we already learned in Example 5.2, the method description *()Ljava/lang/String;* indicates an empty parameter list and return type *java.lang.String* for method *getName*.

The *length* part in a *method_info* structure specifies the number of attributes in the *attributes* table. A *method_info* structure contains at least a *code* attribute. For example, the *length* value for method *getName* is equal to 0x0001 = 1. The *attributes* table in the *method_info* structure of method *getName* contains only one attribute, which is the *code* attribute.

Each attribute in the *attributes* table of a *method_info* structure starts with a *u2* quantity and a *u4* quantity

> *u2 attribute_name_index*
> *u4 length*

For the *method_info* structure of method *getName*, *attribute_name_index* is 0x000B = 11. The entry *constant_pool*[11] encodes string *Code*, which is the attribute name. The *u4* quantity *length* is equal to 0x0000001D = 29, which implies that the code of method *getName* starts at offset 0x013c and ends at 0x0158.

The detailed format of a *code_attribute* structure is

> *u2 attribute_name_index*
> *u4 length*
> *u2 max_stack*
> *u2 max_locals*
> *u4 code_length*
> *u1[code_length] code*
> *u2 exception_table_length*
> *u8[exception_table_length] exception_table*
> *u2 attribute_counts*
> *attribute_info[attribute_counts] attributes*

The *code* array in a *code_attribute* structure is the compiled bytecode of the method. It consists of a sequence of JVM instructions. The elements of *exception_table* describe the exception handlers. The elements of *attributes* table are attributes for the method. There are predefined attributes such as *constantValue*, *LineNumberTable*, and *LocalVariableTable*.

The *code_attribute* structure of the *method_info* structure of method *getName* starts at position 0x0136 in class file *Merchandise.class*. Following the *u4* quantity *length*, we can find both the maximum operand stack size (*max_stack*) and the maximum number of local variables (*max_locals*) are 0x0001. The code length is 0x00000005. The byte code of method *getName* is

        2A B4 00 04 B0

We can decode the bytecode instructions of method *getName*. The bytes 2A, B4, and B0 represent operations *aload_0*, *getfield*, and *areturn*, respectively. The byte code of method *getName* represents the sequence of instructions

>    *aload_0*
>    *getfield* 0x0004
>    *areturn*

The instruction *aload_0* loads (the reference to) the object for which the method is invoked to an operand stack. Instruction *getfield* 0x0004 retrieves a field referenced with *constant_pool*[4] from the object. (As we discussed in Example 5.3, *constant_pool*[4] represents the *name* field of class *Merchandise*.) The instruction *areturn* returns the retrieved field value, which is an object. We shall learn JVM instructions in the next section.

For the *getName* method, the *exception_table_length* is 0x0000. Therefore, the *exception_table* does not exist in the *method_info* structure. The *attribute_counts* is equal to 0x0001. The only attribute has a name encoded in *constant_pool*[0x000E], which is *LineNumberTable*. The length of the attribute is 0x00000006.

**Exercise 5.3** Add a new method into the class *Merchandise*. Read the *method_info* structure of the new method.

# 5.2 Java Compilation

## 5.2.1 Instructions of the JVM

### 5.2.1.1 An Overview of Java Compilation

Like compilers of other languages, the Java compiler compiles statements in source code into instructions. But a real CPU cannot understand the instructions generated by the Java compiler. The instructions are accepted by Java runtime systems, which are software systems.

In the last section, we learned that a method is compiled to a *method_info* structure in a class file. The structure contains a series of bytes named *code*, which is a series of JVM instructions. Particularly, each instruction is started with a byte that represents an operation. The byte is called an *opcode*.

The byte representation of opcodes of instructions limits the length of opcodes with 8 bits. It limits the size of the instruction set of the JVM. Some data types have to be delegated to other types. For example, no instruction of the JVM supports arithmetic operation for primitive types *byte*, *short*, or *char*. Operands of these types are converted to *int* values before arithmetic operations are performed.

Java uses a standard class library to support programming for resources such as networks, windowing systems, threads, and file systems. A resource access is implemented with a class loading and a method invocation. The Java compiler compiles a resource access into an entry in the *constant_pool* table and a method invocation instruction in a *method_info* structure. The constant encodes the resource class name. The method invocation invokes a method of the resource class.

A method invoked in a Java program may be a native method, which acts as a gateway between the JVM and an operating system. A non-native method depends on Java runtime systems to execute the bytecode compiled from the method.

Currently, the JVM implements a reference to an object with a pointer to a handle that contains two pointers – one to the class of the object, the other to the object in memory. To retrieve a field from the object, it has to access the handle and then access the object. The extra indirection of handle access in the JVM slows down every field access.

The JVM is actually the specification of a software system. To satisfy portability, it has limited or no access to registers of a hardware system. It uses operand stacks in memory to perform operations. Operand stack accesses are slower than register accesses.

### 5.2.1.2 Instruction Format

The Java compiler compiles source code into bytecode instructions. A bytecode instruction has a one-byte opcode followed by zero or several operands. The opcode specifies an operation to be performed by the JVM. The number of operands depends on the opcode. An operand may be represented with one or several bytes. The JVM converts the bytes into the correct data for the operand. For instance, an instruction may need a 16-bit integer as an operand. The JVM uses the two bytes, denoted with *b1* and *b2*, that follows the opcode in the instruction to generate the desired 16-bit integer with formula $(b1 << 8) \mid b2$. The following example illustrates instruction operands.

**Example 5.4** Opcode 0xC5 represents the operation of creating a new multidimensional array. Its mnemonic is *multianewarray*. It requires a 16-bit index in the *constant_pool* table and an 8-bit quantity for the number of dimensions in the created array. The instruction format is

> *multianewarray b1 b2 dimension_count*

The JVM converts the first and second operands to the desired index $(b1 << 8) \mid b2$. The entry at the index in *constant_pool* table references a class or interface, which will be used as the element type of the created array. The operand *dimension_count* is an unsigned *byte*, which specifies the number of dimensions in the created array. The JVM is responsible for requesting an operating system to allocate memory for the created array and initializing the array elements with a default value.                                          ☐

A JVM instruction encodes operand type information within opcode. For a primitive type, there is a set of instructions that operate on operands of the type. For example, opcodes *iload* and *istore* represent *int* value transfer operations between operand stack and local variable. In opcode mnemonics, letters *b, s, c, i, l, f, d*, and *a* are used to denote types *byte, short, char, int, long, float, double*, and *reference*, respectively. For example, the opcodes *iadd, isub, imul, idiv, irem*, and *ineg* represent add, subtract, multiply, divide, remainder, and negate operations for *int* values. Opcode *iload* denotes an operation of pushing the value of an integer local variable onto an operand stack. Opcode *istore* pops the top integer out of an operand stack and stores the integer into a local variable. The popped operand must be an *int* value. We can replace the letter *i* in the above mnemonics with *l, f*, or *d* to represent operations on *long, float*, or *double* operands.

An advantage of using typed bytecode instructions is that no type checking is necessary for Java runtime systems. Thus, Java bytecode instructions can be executed more efficiently.

The set of primitive types supported by the Java language and the JVM instruction set are not orthogonal. The JVM provides different levels of supports for different operations and types. For example, there is no opcode for addition of *short* operands. The JVM automatically converts a *byte, short*, or *char* operand to an *int* before an operation like add is performed on the operand. Opcode *i2b, i2s*, or *i2c* converts an *int* value to a *byte, short*, or *char*.

In the specification of the JVM, a byte following an opcode may be an operand of the instruction. The operand is called an in line operand. An example of opcode that requires three in line operands can be found in Example 5.4. An operand of an instruction may be placed on the top of an operand stack before the instruction is executed. For instance, opcode *i2b* does not require in line operand. The instruction replaces an *int* (32-bit long) on the top of an operand stack with a *byte*. The following example shows a situation where a JVM instruction needs both in line operands and operands in an operand stack.

**Example 5.5** (Continuation of Example 5.4) The *multianewarray* opcode requires three in line operands, which are denoted with *b1, b2*, and *dimension_count*. The operand *dimension_count* represents the number of dimensions in the created array. The actual sizes for the dimensions of the created array are placed on an operand stack. Assume the created array has *m1* components for the first dimension, *m2* components for the second dimension, ..., and *mk* components for the *k*th dimension, where *k* = *dimension_count*. The *int* values *m1, m2, ..., mk* should be placed onto the operand stack in this order. When the *multianewarray* instruction is executed by a Java runtime system, the operand stack looks like

| mk |
| --- |
| ... |
| m2 |
| m1 |
| ... |

□

### 5.2.1.3 Bytecode Types

The JVM has instructions for arithmetic and logical operations, which are closely related to, but different from, machine instructions for arithmetic operations. It also supports high-level operations such as object and multi-dimensional array creations. We now describe the various types of the JVM instruction.

The JVM supports load and store operations with bytecode instructions. A load operation pushes a constant or a value in a local variable onto an operand stack. A store operation pops the top of an operand stack and places the top operand into a local variable. A load or store instruction encodes an operand type in opcode. For example, load instruction *aload n* pushes the reference stored in local variable indexed at $n$ in the local variable array onto an operand stack; load instruction *lload n* pushes the *long* value stored in local variables indexed at $n$ and $n+1$ onto an operand stack. Similarly, instruction *astore n* (*lstore n*) stores a reference (a *long*) to a local variable (two local variables) indexed at $n$ (at $n$ and $n+1$, respectively). The value to be stored is on the top of an operand stack.

The Java compiler compiles an arithmetic expression into a sequence of load and arithmetic instructions. Load instructions are used to push operand values onto an operand stack. Thus, when the JVM executes an arithmetic instruction, the operands for the operation are at the top of the operand stack. The execution takes operands from the top of the operand stack and pushes result onto the stack. A store instruction can be used to store the result to a local variable. For instance, the Java expression statement

```
i = i + j;
```

can be compiled to bytecode instructions

```
iload_1
iload_2
iadd
istore_1
```

Instructions *iload_1* and *iload_2* are equivalent to *iload 1* and *iload 2*, which load *int* operands from local variables at index 1 and 2, respectively. Instruction *iadd* adds the two top operands in operand stack. Instruction *istore_1* is equivalent to *istore 1*, which pops the top operand out of the operand stack and stores it into local variable indexed at 1.

As we mentioned earlier, the JVM provides different levels of support for different types of arithmetic operation. Particularly, the Java compiler converts arithmetic operations on *byte*, *short*, *char*, and *boolean* to that on *int*. Thus, the JVM needs to support only arithmetic operations on *int*, *float*, *long*, and *double* operands. The supported operations include add, subtract, multiply, divide, remainder, negate, bit shift, bitwise-OR, bitwise-AND, bitwise-XOR, and local *int* variable increment. For instance, instructions *ishl*, *lshl*, *ishr*, *lshr*, *iushr*, and *lushr* specify bit shift left, bit shift right, and logical shift right operations for *int* and *long* operands.

The JVM supports numeric type conversions. A type conversion instruction either widens or narrows its operand to derive a new numeric value. The format of the mnemonic of a type conversion instruction is *t2s*, where letters *t* and *s* represent numeric types such as *byte*, *char*, *short*, *int*, *long*, *float*, and *double*.

The widening conversions can convert *int* to *long*, *float*, and *double*, convert *long* to *float* and *double*, and convert *float* to *double*.

The narrowing conversions can convert *int* to *byte*, *short*, and *char*, convert *long* to *int*, convert *float* to *int* and *long*, and convert *double* to *int*, *long*, and *float*. A narrowing conversion may change the sign as well as losing precision of an operand.

The JVM supports operations that create an instance of a class, create an array with a primitive type or a reference type, and create a multi-dimensional array. It supports opcode that accesses a static or instance field. Some opcodes request loading or storing an element of an array. For instance, instruction *iastore* stores a value into an integer array. An operand stack contains the value, array reference, and element index for the operation. Instruction *iaload* loads an element of an array onto an operand stack. The operand stack contains the array reference and element index when the *iaload* instruction is executed. The length of an array can be retrieved with bytecode instruction *arraylength*, for which an array reference must have been placed on an operand stack. We can check whether an object is an instance of a class and whether a cast request can be fulfilled with JVM instructions.

An operand stack can be manipulated with bytecode instructions to pop, duplicate, or swap top operands on the stack. For instance, the instructions *pop*, *dup*, and *swap* can be used to pop, duplicate, and swap the top words of an operand stack.

The JVM can perform conditional and unconditional branches within a compiled method. The condition of a conditional branch depends on the top value(s) of an operand stack. For instance, instruction *if_icmpeq b1 b2* compares the two integer values at the top of an operand stack. If the two integers are equal, the instruction transfers control to an instruction with offset $(b1 << 8) | b2$ in the compiled method. Instruction *if_eq b1 b2* jumps to an instruction with offset $(b1 << 8) | b2$ from the instruction if the top integer is equal to 0. The conditional branch instructions *if_acmpeq b1 b2* and *if_acmpne b1 b2* compare two reference values in the top of an operand stack and transfer control if the references are equal or unequal.

The Java compiler uses different opcodes to encode different types of method invocation. It compiles an instance method invocation with opcode *invokevirtual*, interface method with *invokeinterface*, special method with *invokespecial*, and class method with *invokestatic*. A special method may be an instance initialization method named *<init>*, a private method, or a superclass method. For instance, the instance method invocation

    *m.setName("Cheese")*

can be compiled by the Java compiler to code

```
ldc #1 <String "Cheese">
invokevirtual #7
```

where entry *constant_pool*[1] in the class file holds string *Cheese* and *constant_pool*[7] holds a method descriptor. The instruction *ldc #1* pushes a reference to string *Cheese* onto the top of an operand stack. The instruction *invokevirtual #7* invokes method *setName* with argument in the operand stack.

The Java compiler uses instruction *athrow* to throw an exception. A reference to the exception object thrown can be found at the top of an operand stack. Each object has a monitor. The Java compiler uses instructions *monitorenter* and *monitorexit* to support the gaining or releasing of object monitor ownership. A reference to the involved object is at the top of an operand stack.

### 5.2.1.4 Textual Representation of Bytecode Instructions

The *javap* facility of Sun's JDK can list compiled methods. It presents a compiled method with opcode mnemonic and symbolic representations of operands. The syntax of the *javap* representation of an instruction is

    *<index> opcode_mnemonic* [*<operand1>* [*<operand2>* ...]]

The symbol *<index>* represents the offset of the instruction from the beginning of the compiled method. The *opcode_mnemonic* is the mnemonic of the instruction opcode. Some opcodes need in line operands. An in line operand may be a numeric constant, an index in the *constant_pool* table, or the index of a local variable of the method.

The *javap* facility uses the *<index>* values as targets of control transfer instructions. This representation is for readability. A JVM control transfer instruction uses the offset of the target instruction from the control transfer instruction as an operand.

The following example applies the *javap* facility to disassemble a class file. It uses option *–c* to disassemble methods.

**Example 5.6** (Continuation of Example 5.1) Issue command *javap –c Merchandise* in the directory that contains file *Merchandise.class*. The disassembled class file is

```
Compiled from Merchandise.java
synchronized class Merchandise
                        extends java.lang.Object
    /* ACC_SUPER bit set */
```

```
        {
            java.lang.String getName();
            void setName(java.lang.String);
            Merchandise();
        }
```

```
Method java.lang.String getName()
   0 aload_0
   1 getfield #4 <Field java.lang.String name>
   4 areturn
```

```
Method void setName(java.lang.String)
   0 aload_0
   1 aload_1
   2 putfield #4 <Field java.lang.String name>
   5 return
```

```
Method Merchandise()
   0 aload_0
   1 invokespecial #3
                    <Method java.lang.Object()>
   4 return
```

Class *Merchandise* does not define any constructor. The Java compiler supplies a default one, which invokes the constructor *Object*() of class *Object* before it returns. The default constructor is the last method in the above disassembled class file.                                                                    □

When the JVM executes an instance method invocation instruction, it allocates an array of local variables for the method invocation. Each element of the array uses one word. A *long* or *double* value requires two words in the local variable array. It is stored in two consecutive local variables in the array. The first element of the local variable array is reserved for the object for which the instance method is invoked. The following elements of the array store the arguments of the method invocation. The local variables declared in the method body and partial results of the method execution are also stored in the local variable array.

The Java compiler assumes a local variable array when it compiles a method invocation statement. It maps the *this* object, arguments, local variables declared by the method, and partial results to the indexed elements of the local variable array. The following example demonstrates the use of the local variable array.

**Example 5.7** The following instance method has an *int* parameter and declares two *int* local variables.

```
void experiment(int n) {
    int i, j;
    j = n;
    i = 100 + j;
}
```

The Java compiler compiles the method to the following code for Java runtime systems. The argument and local variables are indexed with 1, 2, and 3 in the assumed local variable array. The Java compiler uses instruction *iload_1* to load the argument to operand stack, *istore_3* to store the value to variable *j*.

```
Method void experiment(int)
  0 iload_1
  1 istore_3
  2 bipush 100
  4 iload_3
  5 iadd
  6 istore_2
  7 return
```

□

A value of type *long* or *double* occupies two consecutive elements of the local variable array. When a *long* or *double* value is loaded or stored, only the index of the first element is needed in the instruction. For example, instruction

```
lstore_3
```

can be used to store a *long* value that is on the top of the operand stack into the elements indexed at 3 and 4 in the local variable array.

We use the following example to show the difference between the treatment of a two-word value such as 100L and that of a one-word value 100. Comparing with Example 5.7, the following Java method performs operations on *long* rather than on *int* values.

**Example 5.8** The following Java method is the same as the method in Example 5.7 except parameter and local variables are of type *long*.

```
void experiment(long n) {
    long i, j; j = n; i = 100 + j;
}
```

The Java compiler compiles the method to the following code. The add operation requires *long* operands. The value 100L is loaded from entry *constant_pool*[4]. Argument *n*, local variables *i* and *j* occupy local variable 1 and 2, 3 and 4, 5 and 6, respectively. The result of the add operation is a *long*. The instruction *lstore_5* stores the result into the elements indexed at 5 and 6 in the local variable array. Thus, a *long* value is assigned to local variable *j*. Similarly, instruction *lstore_3* sets local variables indexed at 3 and 4.

```
Method void experiment(long)
   0 lload_1
   1 lstore 5
   3 ldc2_w #4 <Long 100>
   6 lload 5
   8 ladd
   9 lstore_3
  10 return
```

□

## 5.2.2 Arithmetic Operations

For each of the data types *int*, *long*, *float*, and *double* and for each of the arithmetic operations add, subtract, multiply, divide, and remainder, the JVM has an instruction to support the operation on operands of the type. For example, the opcodes for add, subtract, multiply, divide, and remainder operations on *int* operands are denoted with mnemonics *iadd*, *isub*, *imul*, *idiv*, and *irem*, which have bytecode values 96, 100, 104, 108, and 112, respectively. These binary arithmetic instructions use (consume) the top two or four elements in an operand stack and place result on the operand stack. For example, the code

```
bipush 100
iload_3
iadd
```

in Example 5.7 pushes constant 100 and the value of local variable *j* onto the top of an operand stack. Then, instruction *iadd* adds the two operands and places the sum on the top of the operand stack.

There is a negation opcode for each of the data types supported by the JVM. For instance, the opcode for *int* value negation is *ineg* (116). Instruction

```
ineg
```

negates the top operand of an operand stack.

The JVM provides bit-level operations for *int* and *long* values. The operations include arithmetic left and right shift, logical right shift, bitwise AND, OR, and XOR. For example, statement

```
n = n >> 3;
```

can be compiled to code

```
iload_1
iconst_3
ishr
istore_1
```

where *n* is a local variable indexed at 1 in the local variable array, instruction *iconst_3* places *int* value 3 on the operand stack, and instruction *ishr* performs a right shift.

## 5.2.3 Flow Controls

The JVM provides a variety of instructions for instruction switch. Some of the instructions do not have counterpart in the Java language. For example, currently keyword *goto* is not allowed to appear in Java source code. The JVM instruction *goto* followed by two bytes, *b1* and *b2*, can be used to jump to a bytecode in the same compiled method. The two bytes are used to compose the offset of the target instruction from the *goto* instruction.

The JVM has conditional branch instructions with branch conditions depending on the top value(s) of an operand stack. For example, instructions *ifeq*, *ifnull*, *iflt*, and *ifle* transfer control to a target instruction if the top of the operand stack is 0, *null*, less than 0, or less than or equal to 0. Some control transfer instructions also perform comparisons between the top two integers in the operand stack. For example, instruction *if_icmpeq* compares the top two values in the operand stack. The control is transferred to target instruction if the first value is equal to the second. Similarly, instructions *if_icmpne*, *if_icmplt*, *if_icmpge*, *if_icmpgt*, and *if_icmple* transfer control to a target instruction if the first value is not equal to, less than, greater than or equal to, greater than, or less than or equal to the second value.

Subroutine is a notion of the JVM. It can be regarded as a lightweight method. Instructions with opcodes *jsr* and *ret* can be used to jump to a subroutine and return from it. Exception handlers and *finally* clauses in Java programs are implemented with the instructions.

To support the translation of switch statement, the JVM provides two table-jump instructions; one uses the opcode *lookupswitch* and the other *tableswitch*. The instructions have a variable number of in line operands. Specifically, a *lookupswitch* instruction has a series of *match-offset* pairs following the *lookupswitch* bytecode. When the instruction is executed, the top value in an operand stack is compared with the *match* values in sequence. If the top value is equal to a *match* value, the coupled *offset* value is used to jump to a target instruction. A *tableswitch* instruction has a series of *offset* values. When the instruction is executed, the top value in an operand stack is used as an index in the *offset* sequence. The *offtset* at the index is used to find the target instruction.

## 5.2.4 Method Invocations

### 5.2.4.1 Types of Method Invocation Instruction

The JVM defines four types of instruction for invoking an

- instance method,
- class method,
- interface method, or
- special method.

The opcodes for the four types of instruction are *invokevirtual*, *invokestatic*, *invokeinterface*, and *invokespecial*.

In addition to an opcode, each method invocation instruction contains a method description, which identifies the class or interface for the invoked method, the method name, and its signature.

Operands for a method invocation instruction are placed onto an operand stack before the instruction is executed. The return result of the method invocation will be placed on the top of the operand stack. Thus, the operands in the operand stack are replaced by the result after the method invocation instruction is executed. The required operands for each type of method invocation instruction are detailed in the following sections.

An execution of a method is allocated with a private operand stack. The method may invoke a method. When the invoked method starts to execute, the JVM allocates a new operand stack for the execution. The JVM will place the return value from the invoked method on the operand stack owned by the invoking method.

### 5.2.4.2 Instance Method Invocation

The format of *invokevirtual* instruction for invoking an instance method is

    *invokevirtual <method_spec>*,

where *<method_spec>* is an index in the *constant_pool* table of a class file. The indexed entry in *constant_pool* holds a descriptor for the method.

We now use an example to illustrate the compilation of instance method invocation.

**Example 5.9** We now add a main method into the class *Merchandise* described in Example 5.1, and place statements

```
Merchandise m = new Merchandise();
m.setName("Cheese");
```

in the main method. The Java compiler compiles the second statement to code

```
aload_1
ldc #1 <String "Cheese">
invokevirtual #7
          <Method void setName(java.lang.String)>
```

Local variable at index 1 contains a reference to the merchandise object created by the first statement. The constant in entry *constant_pool*[1] contains the Utf8 string *Cheese*. Entry *constant_pool*[7] contains the descriptor of method *setName*. The instruction *aload_1* loads local variable at index 1 to operand stack. Instruction *ldc #1* loads the first entry from *constant_pool* to the operand stack. The method invocation instruction *invokevirtual #7* refers to entry *constant_pool*[7] for the description of method *setName*. It invokes the method for the merchandise object with argument *"Cheese"*.   □

The above example shows that the execution of an instance method invocation instruction requires the object for which the method is invoked and the arguments of the method invocation be placed onto the operand stack.

### 5.2.4.3 Class Method Invocation

The format of an *invokestatic* instruction for invoking a static method is

    *invokestatic <method_spec>*,

where *<method_spec>* is an index in the *constant_pool* table. The indexed entry describes the invoked method. Execution of an *invokestatic* instruction requires the arguments of the method invocation to be placed on the operand stack. It does not need an object as an operand. For instance, if a class method is represent by *constant_pool*[6], the class method can be invoked with statement

```
invokestatic #6
```

The instruction takes arguments from the operand stack.


### 5.2.4.4 Interface Method Invocation

The format of an *invokeinterface* instruction for invoking an interface method is

*invokeinterface <method_spec> n*

where *<method_spec>* is an index in the *constant_pool* table. The indexed entry describes the invoked method. The in line operand *n* is an unsigned 8-bit integer, which indicates that the top *n* words in the operand stack will be used for the method execution. The first word is a reference to an object for which the interface method is invoked. The following words contain the arguments for the method invocation. Execution of an *invokeinterface* instruction requires the object reference and arguments to be placed on the operand stack.

**Example 5.10** (Continuation of Example 2.13) We substitute the following main method for the main method in class *Order* presented in Example 2.13.

```
public static void main(String[] args) {
    Order order = new Order();
    Enumeration e = order.elements();
    for ( ; e.hasMoreElements(); ) {
        System.out.println(
                    e.nextElement().toString());
    }
}
```

Note that the expression *order.elements*() returns an object of class *Enumerator*, which implements interface *Enumeration*. Class *Enumerator* implements abstract method *hasMoreElements* inherited from the interface. The disassembled bytecode of method invocation expression *e.hasMoreElements*() is

```
aload_2
invokeinterface (args 1) #12
```

It uses instruction *aload_2* to load local variable indexed at 2 onto the operand stack. Thus, the reference in variable *e* is loaded onto the operand stack. The reference refers to an object of class *Enumerator*. It is the only operand required by the method invocation. Therefore, the number *n* of operands in the operand stack for the method invocation is 1. The value of *<method_spec>* is represented with #12. Entry *constant_pool*[12] in the *constant_pool* table contains a method description for the interface method *hasMoreElements*().                                                                              □

## 5.2.4.5 Special Method Invocation

An *invokespecial* instruction invokes a special method with format

$$\text{invokespecial} <method\_spec>$$

where *<method_spec>* is an index in the *constant_pool* table. The indexed entry describes the invoked method. A special method is an instance initialization method, an instance method inherited from superclass, or a private instance method.

An instance initialization method is named *<init>* in a class file. It is compiled from either an explicitly defined constructor or a default constructor provided by the Java compiler. The Java compiler compiles an instance creation expression such as *new Order()* to two pieces of code; the first piece allocates space for an object, the second invokes an instance initialization method for the object. Before the initialization method is executed, operands are placed onto the operand stack. The first operand is a reference to the newly created object. The remaining operands are the arguments for the constructor invocation.

We use the following example to illustrate the compilation of an object creation statement.

**Example 5.11** (Continuation of Example 5.10) Class *Order* defined in Example 2.13 does not define any constructor. The Java compiler supplies a default instance initialization method in the class file. The textual representation of the method is

```
Method Order()
    0 aload_0
    1 invokespecial #10<Method java.lang.Object()>
    4 return
```

which invokes the instance creation method of class *Object* with an *invokespecial* instruction.

The main method presented in Example 5.10 includes statement

```
Order order = new Order();
```

which creates a new object of class *Order* and assigns it to variable *order*. The Java compiler compiles the statement to code

```
0 new #2 <Class Order>
3 dup
4 invokespecial #9 <Method Order()>
7 astore_1
```

The *new* instruction creates a new object of class *Order*, which is represented by *constant_pool*[2]. A reference to the created object is placed on the top of the operand stack. The reference is duplicated in the operand stack by instruction *dup*. Then, the *invokespecial* instruction invokes the instance initialization method *<init>* described by *constant_pool*[9]. Finally, the above code stores the reference to the initialized object into local variable 1. Note that the default constructor *Order()* does not have any parameter. The *invokespecial* instruction needs only one operand, which is the reference to the newly created object. A copy of the reference is placed on the operand stack by the *dup* instruction. It is used by the constructor invocation. Finally, the original reference value is stored into local variable 1.          □

In an instance method of a class, we may use keyword *super* to invoke a method defined in the superclass of the class. The superclass method invocation expression is compiled to an *invokespecial* instruction. The *<method_spec>* operand of the *invokespecial* instruction refers to a superclass method. The JVM is responsible for resolving the method with a method defined in the closest superclass of the current class.

### 5.2.4.6 Recursive Method Invocation

An algorithm may be recursively defined; i.e., the algorithm applies itself for smaller problems. For example, the Fibonacci number $f(i)$ for integer $i \geq 0$ is defined by equations $f(0) = 0$, $f(1) = 1$, $f(i+2) = f(i+1) + f(i)$ for $i \geq 2$. It is recursively defined since the value $f(i+2)$ depends on $f(i+1)$ and $f(i)$. The following example uses a recursive method to evaluate Fibonacci numbers.

**Example 5.12** The following class, class *Fibonacci*, uses instance method *valueOf(int n)* to calculate the Fibonacci number $f(n)$. It includes a main method to test the method.

```
class Fibonacci {
    public static void main(String[] args) {
        Fibonacci f = new Fibonacci();
        System.out.println(
            "Fibonacci number for 4 is " +
            f.valueOf(4));
    }

    int valueOf(int n) {
        if (n < 0) return -1;
        if (n == 0) return 0;
        if (n == 1) return 1;
        return (valueOf(n-1) + valueOf(n-2));
    }
}
```

The method *valueOf(int n)* invokes itself in expression *valueOf(n−1) + valueOf(n−2)* with smaller arguments $n-1$ and $n-2$. The method is compiled to

```
Method int valueOf(int)
    0 iload_1
    1 ifge 6
    4 iconst_m1
    5 ireturn
    6 iload_1
    7 ifne 12
```

```
10 iconst_0
11 ireturn
12 iload_1
13 iconst_1
14 if_icmpne 19
17 iconst_1
18 ireturn
19 aload_0
20 iload_1
21 iconst_1
22 isub
23 invokevirtual #14<Method int valueOf(int)>
26 aload_0
27 iload_1
28 iconst_2
29 isub
30 invokevirtual #14<Method int valueOf(int)>
33 iadd
34 ireturn
```

The above compiled method invokes the same method referenced by *constant_pool*[14] with different operands. The *invokevirtual* instruction at offset 23 evaluates $f(n-1)$ and leaves a result on the operand stack. The *invokevirtual* instruction at offset 30 evaluates $f(n-2)$. The instruction *iadd* at offset 33 adds the two Fibonacci numbers and leaves the result $f(n)$ on the top of the operand stack.

When the JVM executes the *invokevirtual* instruction at offset 23, it uses the top two operands, one is a reference to *this* object and the other is integer $n-1$, in the operand stack and starts method *valueOf* from its beginning. The new execution of method *valueOf* has its own frame, which contains a private operand stack. Thus, the state of the execution cannot interfere or be interferred by its caller. The invoking method (caller) is synchronized to wait until a called method is complete. The JVM places the result returned by the called method on the top of the operand stack owned by the invoking method. The JVM processes the second recursive invocation of method *valueOf* at position 30 similarly.                                                             □

**Exercise 5.4** Example 5.12 uses a recursive algorithm to evaluate Fibonacci numbers. Add a non-recursive method named *valueOf1*(*int n*) in the above class to evaluate Fibonacci numbers.

# 5.3 Java Virtual Machine – An Abstract Machine

## 5.3.1 Java Runtime Systems

The JVM is an abstract specification of Java runtime systems. It does not specify implementation-related or platform-dependent details. Its functionality must be supported by all Java runtime systems to ensure portability and security. Here, we describe components of Java runtime systems that are required by the JVM.

### 5.3.1.1 Java Execution Engine

An execution engine executes the bytecode instructions compiled from a method. It can be implemented with an interpreter for the instructions. A just-in-time execution engine is different from a bytecode interpreter. It first compiles the bytecode of a compiled method to a native method, and then invokes the native method. It enables faster execution of the method than an interpreter.

A Java execution engine supports the JVM instructions. It can spawn multiple threads, which run independently. Multiple threads can be run on multiple processors. On a single-processor platform, time slices are assigned to threads to share the CPU.

An important feature of a Java execution engine is object orientation. The JVM instructions are designed with objects in mind. For example, the engine uses instruction *new b1 b2* to create an object, where the bytes *b1* and *b2* are used to index a class description in *constant_pool* table. A Java execution engine initializes instance fields with default values and specializes the created object with a special method invocation.

### 5.3.1.2 Class Loader and Security Manager

A Java runtime system treats class files from different sources differently. It may load class files from a local file system. It may load class files over the Internet with a class loader. A runtime system dynamically determines required class files. Then, it loads the class files to its memory, links the classes and interfaces with the runtime system, and initializes the classes and interfaces.

A runtime system defines security policies with a security manager. It defines the boundaries for Java programs. It limits some classes from accessing local resources and performing some activities.

When a runtime system loads an untrusted class file, it uses a verifier to check the format of the class file and verify consistency of the operand types. By default, a runtime system does not verify class files loaded from a local file system.

### 5.3.1.3 Thread, Multimedia, and Network Capabilities

A Java runtime system must implement the Java standard library. Some of the methods in the standard classes are native methods.

Java supplies a standard class, class *java.lang.Thread*, to support multi-thread programming. The Java compiler compiles most thread activities to *Thread* method invocations. The JVM specifies only two instructions for thread synchronization, which are *monitorenter* and *monitorexit*.

Similar with thread management, the JVM supports graphics, multimedia, and network capabilities through standard classes. The instruction set specified by the JVM does not support these capabilities directly. They are implemented with method invocations.

### 5.3.1.4 Memory Management

A Java runtime system is responsible for reclaiming objects that are not referenced by active methods. The JVM does not specify the garbage collection algorithm. A runtime system decides when and how to reclaim unused objects. A Java program does not have any direct control over memory management. The instruction set of the JVM does not provide any support for memory management either.

## 5.3.2 Objects and Types

### 5.3.2.1 Class Constant Pool

A *constant_pool* table in a class file holds symbolic references to classes, fields, and methods. A Java runtime system uses a *constant pool* in memory to organize the constants for a class. Like the *constant_pool* table in a class file, the constant pool of a class contains the symbolic references to fields, methods, classes, interfaces, and various types of literal such as numeric and string constants. The entries in a constant pool are ordered and accessed through indexes, which are 8-bit and 16-bit unsigned integers.

Constant pools are private data structures of loaded classes. They are associated with classes. No method of a class can access the constant pool of another class.

Symbolic references to fields, methods, and classes are dynamically resolved. When the execution of a method needs a field in a class or interface, the reference to the field is resolved, the referred class file is located, and the class is loaded from its class file if necessary. For instance, the instruction

```
invokespecial #10 <Method java.lang.Object()>
```

in Example 5.11 refers to the 10th entry in the constant pool of class *Order*. The entry actually contains a symbolic reference to the constructor of class *java.lang. Object*, which must be located and linked for the method invocation. Thus, the symbolic reference is converted to a reference or pointer to a runtime data structure that contains the compiled method.

The types of data structure in a constant pool stored by a Java runtime system include *CONSTANT_Class*, *CONSTANT_fieldref*, *CONSTANT_methodref*, *CONSTANT_Utf8* and primitive type values.

### 5.3.2.2 Primitive and Reference Types

A value operated by the JVM is of either a primitive type or a reference type. The primitive types are *byte*, *short*, *char*, *int*, *long*, *float*, *double*, and *returnAddress*. A *returnAddress* value is a pointer to a JVM instruction. Values of primitive type *boolean* are compiled to *int* values. A reference type is a class type, an interface type, or an array type. A value of a reference type is *null* or a reference to an instance of a class, an object of an interface, or an array.

Java is a strongly-typed language. The Java compiler makes type checking. The JVM assumes that each instruction in a class file receives the correct number of operands of correct types. The property of strong type makes it possible for the Java compiler to convert a general operator into a type-specific instruction. For instance, the Java compiler compiles add operator + in an expression to opcode *fadd* if the operands in the expression are floats. The Java compiler uses opcode *iadd*, *ladd*, *fadd*, or *dadd* to tell the JVM that the type of operands for an add operation is *int*, *long*, *float*, or *double*.

### 5.3.2.3 Words and Values

The JVM uses a *word* to abstract platform-specific data sizes. A word is used to hold a *byte*, *short*, *char*, *int*, *float*, *returnAddress*, or a reference. Two consecutive words are used to hold a *long* or *double* value. A data area used by a Java runtime system consists of words.

The runtime data area of a Java runtime system is called a *heap*, which stores all the objects created for the execution of a Java program. For example, an execution of the *new* instruction in a compiled method allocates memory space in the heap for a new object. All the threads created for the execution of a Java program share the heap. The area need not be contiguous in the main memory. The objects stored in the heap are subject to automatic storage management, commonly known as *garbage collection*.

## 5.3.3 Methods and Method Invocations

### 5.3.3.1 Method Types and Method Area

The JVM uses a *method area* to store compiled information and code. Specifically, a runtime system uses the method area to keep constant pools, field and method data, compiled code of methods and constructors. Threads created during the execution of a program share the method area.

Each class or interface has a constant pool in the method area. The constant pool contains constants and symbolic references to fields and methods. The symbolic references are resolved so that they point at the structures in the method area that represent the fields and methods.

Constructors of a class are used to instantiate newly created objects of the class. The Java compiler compiles constructors into methods named *<init>*, which are called *instance initialization methods*. Another type of initialization method is *class initialization method*, which is named *<clinit>*. A class initialization method is responsible for initializing a class or interface when the class or interface is loaded by a Java runtime system.

## 5.3.3.2 Java Stacks and Frames

Each thread has a private Java stack created when the thread is created. Each time a thread invokes a method, a frame is created for the method invocation. Before the thread executes the method, the JVM pushes the frame on the top of the Java stack owned by the thread. A frame contains an array of local variables and an operand stack. The local variable array holds actual arguments, local variables, and computation results for the invocation. If the invoked method is an instance method, the first element of the local variable array is reserved for a reference to the object for which the method is invoked. The operand stack is private to the current execution of the method.

When the execution of a method is complete, the JVM pops the frame from the Java stack of the thread. When a thread is dead, memory manager reclaims the Java stack.

At any time, a thread has only one current frame, which is at the top of the Java stack owned by the thread and represents a method execution. When the method execution is complete, the Java runtime system executes a return instruction of the method. The Java runtime system is responsible for placing the returned value onto the operand stack of the invoking method frame. Then, the frame of the completed method invocation is discarded and the frame beneath becomes the current frame. Thus, the invoking method resumes its execution with its frame at the top of the Java stack.

The local variable array in a frame consists of words, each of which is called a *local variable*. The word at index $n$ in the array is called local variable $n$. The JVM uses two words in the array to store a value of type *long* or *double*. It uses the index $n$ of the first word to index the *long* or *double*. It automatically loads two words, indexed at $n$ and $n+1$, from the array to an operand stack when it is instructed to "load *long* local variable $n$."

The underlying data structure for a Java stack is implementation specific. The stack may have a fixed or varying length. The memory space for the stack of a thread may not be contiguous. A good design of the data structure for Java stack is important for space efficiency and thread speed.

A frame uses an operand stack to support the execution of a method body. Arithmetic operations and other operations take operands from the stack and place results onto the stack. A method also uses operand stack to pass arguments to invoke another method. For example, the code, extracted from Example 5.12,

```
19 aload_0
20 iload_1
21 iconst_1
22 isub
23 invokevirtual #14 <Method int valueOf(int)>
```

prepares an operand stack by pushing a reference to an object for which method *valueOf* will be invoked, loading an *int* value from local variable 1, and subtracting 1 from the *int* value. An execution of the *invokevirtual* instruction places a return value on the operand stack before the invoking method continues its computation.

### 5.3.3.3 Method Execution

The JVM uses threads of execution to run a Java program. A thread uses a program counter (*pc*) to hold the position of an instruction during the execution of a method. The JVM supports jump instructions by setting the *pc* with the position of a target instruction. Thus, the next instruction to be executed will be the target instruction.

The execution of a method may complete normally after it successfully executes a return statement or the last statement in the method body. If the return statement has an argument, the returned value is placed on the top of the operand stack owned by the invoking method. Then, the JVM restores the state of the invoking method. It also increases the *pc* of the invoking method to pass the method invocation instruction and continues the computation of the invoking method.

The execution of a statement in a method may throw an exception. The statement may throw the exception explicitly if the statement is a throw statement. It may throw the exception implicitly if the exception is thrown by the JVM or by a method invoked by the statement. If the statement throws an exception but the exception cannot be caught by a catch clause in the method, the execution of the method completes abnormally or abruptly.

If a method completes abruptly, the JVM discards the frame of the method, places the raised exception on the top of the operand stack of the invoking method, and tries to find a catch clause in the invoking method to handle the exception. If the exception cannot be caught and handled by the invoking method, the invoking method completes abruptly too; otherwise, the invoking method starts the catch clause body.

### 5.3.3.4 Exception Handling

The Java compiler compiles an exception catch clause in a method into an exception handler. It compiles all the catch clauses in a method into a list of exception handlers. The list is placed at the end of the compiled method. An exception handler records

- the range of instructions from which the catch clause can catch exceptions,
- the type of exception that the catch clause can catch, and
- the position of the compiled body of the catch clause.

When an exception is thrown from an instruction, the catch clauses for the instruction are tested from the closest one outward. The order of exception handlers in the exception handler list is important. It is possible to place all the exception handlers of a method into a list.

When an exception is thrown from an instruction of a method, the JVM tests the exception handlers of the method in sequence until either

- an exception handler is found that has a range including the instruction and that can catch the thrown exception, or
- the exception handler list is exhaustedly searched.

In the former case, the code of the exception handler is started. In the latter case, the frame of the current method is discarded, the exception object is placed on the top of the operand stack of the invoking method. In the latter case, the JVM tries to find an exception handler from the invoking method. If the search fails at a top thread, the top thread is discarded.

### 5.3.3.5 The Execution of a Recursive Method

The method *valueOf*( *int n*) presented in Example 5.12 recursively invokes *valueOf*($n$–1) and *valueOf*($n$–2) for $n \geq 2$. We now follow the instructions of the compiled code of the method to trace the frames, operand stacks and local variable arrays allocated during the execution of method invocation *valueOf*(4).

When method *valueOf* is started by expression *f.valueOf*(4), a frame is allocated, which will be referred to as *frame0*. The operand stack in *frame0* is empty, and the local variable array contains two elements:

| reference to $f$ | 4 |
|---|---|

where local variable 0 references object $f$ and local variable 1 contains argument 4.

Before method invocation instruction at offset 23 is executed, the operand stack in *frame0* is

| 3 |
|---|
| reference to $f$ |

and the local variable array remains unchanged. For the method invocation, a frame is allocated, which will be referred to as *frame1*. In *frame1*, the operand stack is empty, and the local variable array is

| reference to *f* | 3 |
|---|---|

The execution of method *valueOf* for frame *frame1* invokes method *valueOf* at offset 23. Before the method invocation, the operand stack in frame *frame1* is

| 2 |
|---|
| reference to *f* |

and the local variable array remains unchanged. A frame is allocated for the new invocation. It will be referred to as *frame2*. The operand stack in *frame2* is empty initially, and the local variable array in *frame2* is

| reference to *f* | 2 |
|---|---|

The execution of method *valueOf* for *frame2* invokes method *valueOf* at offset 23. Before the invocation, the operand stack in *frame2* is

| 1 |
|---|
| reference to *f* |

and the local variable array is unchanged. A frame is allocated for the new invocation. It will be referred to as *frame3*. The operand stack in *frame3* is empty and the local variable array in *frame3* is

| reference to *f* | 1 |
|---|---|

The execution of method *valueOf* for *frame3* returns integer 1. After it is completed, the operand stack in *frame2* is

| 1 |
|---|

The execution of method *valueOf* for *frame2* continues at offset 26. When the execution invokes method *valueOf* at offset 30, the operand stack in *frame2* looks like

| 0 |
|---|
| reference to *f* |
| 1 |

and local variable array in *frame2* has not been changed. A frame is allocated for the method invocation. It will be referred to as *frame4*. In *frame4*, the operand stack is empty and the local variable array looks like

| reference to *f* | 0 |
|---|---|

The execution of method *valueOf* for *frame4* returns integer 0. Now, the execution of method *valueOf* for *frame2* continues at offset 33 and the operand stack in *frame2* is

| 0 |
|---|
| 1 |

Then, the execution for *frame2* is completed and it returns 1. The execution of method *valueOf* for *frame1* continues at offset 26 with operand stack

| 1 |
|---|

The execution for *frame1* invokes method *valueOf* at offset 30. Before the method invocation, operand stack in *frame1* looks like

| 1 |
|---|
| reference to *f* |
| 1 |

A frame is allocated for the invocation of method *valueOf*. It will be referred to as *frame5*. In *frame5*, the operand stack is empty and the local variable array is

| reference to *f* | 1 |
|---|---|

The execution of method *valueOf* for *frame5* returns 1. After the execution is completed, the operand stack in *frame1* looks like

| 1 |
|---|
| 1 |

The execution of method *valueOf* for *frame1* continues at offset 33. It returns 2. After the execution of *valueOf* for *frame1* is completed, operand stack in *frame0* looks like

| 2 |
|---|

The execution for *frame0* continues at offset 26. It invokes method *valueOf* at offset 30. Before the invocation, the operand stack in *frame0* looks like

| 2 |
|---|
| reference to *f* |
| 2 |

As shown for *frame2*, the method invocation will pop off the top two values from the above operand stack and push 1 at the operand stack after several recursive invocations of the *valueOf* method. Thus, when execution of method *valueOf* for *frame0* continues at offset 33, the operand stack in *frame0* looks like

| 1 |
|---|
| 2 |

The continued execution of method *valueOf* for *frame0* returns 3, and the execution of expression *f.valueOf*(4) is complete.

The created frames for an execution of *f.valueOf*(4) are shown in Fig. 5.2. A node in the tree structure associates a frame with each invocation of method *valueOf*. The frame is created for the method invocation. The picture shows all the recursive invocations of method *valueOf* for the evaluation of expression *f.valueOf*(4).

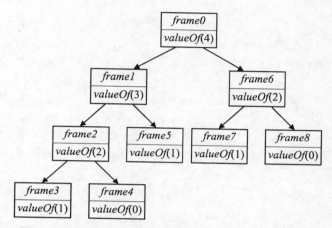

**Fig. 5.2** Recursive evaluation of expression *f.valueOf*(4)

**Exercise 5.5** We follow (trace) the evaluation of expression *f.valueOf*(4) in the above discussion. Note that object *f* is not used in the evaluation. Change the *valueOf* method in class *Fabonacci* to a static method. Trace the execution of static method invocation *Fibonacci.valueOf*(4) like the above discussion.

## 5.4 Summary

The Java compiler generates class files for classes and interfaces from compilation units. The format of class files enables the encoding of information on classes and interfaces. The information includes constants referred to in a class or interface, and descriptors of fields and methods defined in the class or interface. The compiled methods contain JVM bytecode instructions. They are included in the class file.

In this chapter, we describe various types of JVM instruction. We describe how the Java compiler compiles various types of statements. There are differences between the JVM instructions and the machine instructions of a host system. The JVM instructions represent high-level operations, which may require multiple machine instructions to implement.

We also discuss the components and mechanisms of the JVM. Java runtime systems implement the JVM to ensure portability and security. A Java runtime system may use an instruction interpreter to accept and execute compiled methods. It may also use a just-in-time execution engine to compile a compiled method to a native function and run the function.

The description of the JVM is for the purpose of understanding the computation of Java runtime systems. The understanding is necessary for analyzing data structures developed in Java and for studying programs and algorithms that are based on the data structures.

# Chapter 6
# Complexity Analysis

We often need to evaluate a software system for its efficiency in using time and memory. A simple approach to the evaluation is running the software for a benchmark problem on some platform. We can measure the time and memory space used by the execution. The quantities give us an idea about the speed and memory demand of the system when it is faced with a similar problem on a similar platform. Potential users of the software system may use the values to judge the software system.

The benchmarking approach has limitations. It depends on benchmark problems. When a project is designed for a new application, it is difficult or impossible to get benchmark problems for the application. The benchmarking approach also suffers from the drawback of platform dependency. It is difficult to convince potential users of a software system if the software system has been tested only on platforms that are different from the users' hardware. Another problem of benchmarking is the fixed size of benchmark problems. We cannot predict the performance of a software system for larger problems based on its measured performance on smaller benchmark problems.

Performance analysis for software and algorithm designs is important for software developers. In studying data structures, the evaluation of different algorithms is important for making a choice. We cannot invest precious human power and other resources to implement candidate data structures and algorithms. Benchmarking cannot be applied before an algorithm is implemented.

In this chapter, we learn the basic analysis techniques for analyzing the complexity of algorithms in the context of the JVM. The algorithms are encoded in Java methods. We discuss the fundamental concepts of time and space complexities for Java programs. We present notations for the magnitude of time and (memory) space requirement of algorithms. Specifically, we shall present

- Assumptions on time and space unit, which are used to measure the time and space needed by Java statements at runtime. The assumptions amount to the traditional uniform cost function under uniform cost criterion. They are based on the specification of the JVM, which is followed by Java runtime systems. Here, we treat the JVM like a traditional abstract computation model such as a RAM (random access machine) or a Turing machine. As we learned in Chapter 5, the JVM is object-oriented. It has a set of high-level instructions, which have no counterparts in a RAM or Turing machine. Hence, we need to propose reasonable assumptions on the time and space required by the high-level instructions.

- The notion of asymptotic analysis and its importance in judging the feasibility of an algorithm. The term *complexity analysis* usually refers to an asymptotic complexity analysis of an algorithm. It reveals the growth rate of a complexity function when the problem size increases. An asymptotic analysis is useful for predicting the performance of a software system when problem size becomes larger.
- Big-O and big-$\Omega$ notations, which describe the magnitudes of complexities of algorithms and programs. We learn how to use big-O notation as an upper bound on the magnitudes and use big-$\Omega$ notation as both an upper and a lower bound.
- The concept of dominance between complexity functions. Based on their asymptotic complexities, algorithms can be classified into categories. We discuss some complexity categories and the dominance relation between them.
- The notion of recursion. Many algorithms are recursive. They repeatedly invoke themselves directly or indirectly. We discuss how to analyze the time and space complexities of recursive methods. We use an algorithm called binary search to illustrate recursion and analysis of recursive method.

# 6.1 Execution of Java Statements

## 6.1.1 Java Virtual Machine – A Model of Computation

Quality software is robust and maintainable. Another important measure of a software system is its efficiency in the use of time and memory. The analysis of data structures and algorithms guides the selection of data structures and algorithms to ensure the performance of a software system.

Different computers may have processors of different speed and different memory size. A *platform* refers to the configuration of a hardware system and an operating system running on the hardware. It is difficult to predict the performance of a software system based on its performance on one platform. The analysis of a program should be based on an abstract model of computation so that the conclusion of an analysis of the program applies to most computers.

The general approach to estimating the time and space used by data structures, algorithms, and software systems is using an abstract model of computation, which simplifies and characterizes computers. It cuts an immense number of details of real computers from its model of computer. The abstract model captures the features of computers that are essential for estimating time and space demands of programs. There are many models of computation in the literature. The popular models of computation include the Turing machine, the random access machine (RAM), and some models of parallel computers. Different models are used to study different aspects of computation.

Here, we review the JVM as a practical model of computation for studying the performance of algorithms encoded in Java. Based on the JVM, we discuss the time and space requirements by the execution of operations and statements written in Java.

A software system written in a computer programming language like Java is designed to solve a problem. Each instance of the problem has a set of input data. The size of an instance of a problem is often referred to as a *problem size*, which is measured by the size of its input. The *time* or *space complexity* of a method measures the time or space used by the method. It is a function that maps problem sizes to integers. For a problem size, the value of the function is the number of time or space units required by the method.

## 6.1.2 Object Creation and Initialization

### 6.1.2.1 Class Instance Creation

An object of a class named *class_name* can be created with the class instance creation expression

> *new class_name(argument_list)*

in Java, where *new* is a keyword in Java and *argument_list* is a comma-separated sequence of arguments. An execution of the expression invokes a constructor of class *class_name* to initialize the fields of a newly created object with the arguments.

The Java compiler compiles the class instance creation expression into a sequence of JVM instructions, denoted with the following pseudo-bytecode:

> *new <constant_pool_index1>*
> *dup*
> *<load_instructions>*
> *invokespecial <constant_pool_index2>*

The in line operand *<constant_pool_index1>* is an index in the constant pool of the class. The indexed entry in the constant pool refers to class *class_name*. When a Java runtime system executes instruction *new <constant_pool_index1>*, it allocates memory space for an object of the class and places a reference to the created object on the top of an operand stack, which is owned by the method execution that requested for the object creation.

The bytecode instruction *dup* duplicates the reference at the top of the operand stack. The duplicate reference will be used (consumed) by an *invokespecial* instruction.

In the above pseudo-bytecode, we use symbol *<load_instructions>* to denote a sequence of instructions that load the arguments in *argument_list* onto the operand stack. Thus, when the *invokespecial* instruction is executed by the Java runtime system to invoke a constructor, a reference to the created object and the argument values for the constructor invocation are available in the operand stack.

The *invokespecial* instruction has an in line operand, denoted with *<constant_pool_index2>* in the above pseudo-bytecode. The operand refers to an entry in the constant pool, which describes the invoked instance initialization method.

We now discuss the time and space required by each of the above four steps.

The entry indexed at *<constant_pool_index1>* in the constant pool encodes a symbolic representation of class *class_name*. If the symbolic representation has not been resolved to a loaded class, the Java runtime system resolves it by searching for the class file, loading the class, and linking it.

Each class is loaded by a Java runtime system only once. We can use the class to create instances repeatedly. We assume that a class has been loaded when operator *new* is used to create an object of the class. Thus, a Java runtime system can access the class definition when it allocates memory space for the created object.

We assume that when instruction *new <constant_pool_index1>* is executed, it takes a Java runtime system one unit of time to allocate memory space for each field of the created object and initialize the field with a default value. Each field takes either one or two words of space to hold a primitive value or a reference. Therefore, we assume the space allocated for the object is equal to the number of fields in the created object.

A class may declare a private instance field, which is invisible in an object of a subclass of the class. The field exists in the object. It needs time to allocate space for the field and initialize the field with a default value when the object is created. The uniform time and space assumption applies to private fields as well.

A field in a created object may have an initialization clause such as field *orders* declared with

```
Order[] orders = new Order[20];
```

in a class. It takes time and space to create an array object and assign it to field *orders*. The time and space required by the initialization clause for a field of a created object must be added to the time and space required by the field allocation and initialization.

The instruction *dup* duplicates the top element of the operand stack. Since the instruction duplicates a reference to the created object, we assume that it takes one unit of time for a Java runtime system to execute the *dup* instruction and one unit of space in the operand stack to hold the duplicate reference.

A load instruction in sequence *<load_instructions>* loads a primitive value or a reference from a local variable onto the operand stack. The loaded value needs at most two words in the operand stack. We assume that each load instruction takes one unit of time and requires one unit of space in the operand stack.

The sequence *<load_instructions>* may include instructions other than loads. For example, when a customer object is created with expression

```
new Customer("John Smith", "Windsor, Ontario",
             "555-2341", 100f + 3f);
```

the expression *100f + 3f* will be compiled into load instructions for constants 100f and 3f and an *fadd* instruction. The cost in terms of time for the add operation must be added to the cost of the customer object creation.

When a Java runtime system executes the *invokespecial <constant_pool_index2>* instruction, it invokes the *<init>* method denoted by entry at *<constant_pool_index2>* in the constant pool. It takes one unit of time to access the compiled method in a method area. An execution of the invoked *<init>* method takes time. It may also take space if the method declares local variables and creates objects. The time and space required by the invoked instance initialization method must be added to the time and space required by the *invokespecial* instruction.

The above assumptions on the time and space requirements for object creation are based on executed JVM instructions. We now simplify the assumptions with a uniform cost criterion. The criterion assigns one unit of time to a fixed number of bytecode instructions. Specifically, the evaluation of an object creation expression

> *new class_name( <argument_list> )*

takes one unit of time and one unit of space for each instance field in the created object, one unit of time and one unit of space for invoking a constructor, one unit of time and one unit of space for each parameter declared in the constructor. The time and space required by the execution of the constructor as well as the cost of argument evaluations will be added to the cost of the object creation.

With the uniform cost criterion, expression

```
new Customer("John Smith", "Windsor, Ontario",
            "555-2341", 100f + 3f);
```

takes 5 units of time and 5 units of space for allocating and initializing the five fields in a created customer object, 1 unit for invoking a constructor of class *Customer*, 4 units for the four parameters of the constructor. In addition to the time and space required by the constructor execution, 1 unit of time must be added to the cost for evaluating the last argument.

### 6.1.2.2 Array Creation

In a Java program, we use expression

> *new primitiveType[n]*

to create an array with $n$ elements of a primitive type such as *int* or *float*. The expression is compiled to a load instruction to load integer $n$ onto an operand stack and a *newarray* instruction, which uses the primitive type *primitiveType* as an in line operand. Similarly, Java expression

> *new className[n]*

is compiled into bytecode

```
iload i
anewarray b1 b2
```

to create an array with $n$ elements, each can hold an object reference. We assume value $n$ is loaded from the $i$th local variable in the local variable array. Bytes $b1$ and $b2$ are used to index the class or interface *className* in the constant pool.

Assume an expression such as *new primitiveType[n]* or *new className[n]* that creates a one-dimensional array with $n > 0$. An evaluation of the expression allocates space for the $n$ elements and initializes the elements with a default value.

Each of the elements can be regarded as an anonymous variable. We assume that the number of units of time required by the evaluation is equal to $n$, and so is the number of units of space.

When $n = 0$, we assume that an evaluation of expression *new primitive-Type[n]* or *new className[n]* takes one unit of time and one unit of space. This assumption accounts for the time and space required for keeping information such as the *length* for the created array.

In a Java program, we may use expression

$$new\ classNameOrPrimitiveType[n_1][n_2]\ldots[n_k]$$

to create a multi-dimensional array. The first dimension defines an array with $n_1$ components. Each of the components holds a reference to an array created with expression

$$new\ classNameOrPrimitiveType[n_2]\ldots[n_k].$$

As described in Section 5.2.1.2, expression *new classNameOrPrimitiveType$[n_1][n_2]\ldots[n_k]$* is compiled to a *multianewarray* instruction, which requires three in line operands, denoted with *b1*, *b2*, and *dimension_count*. The operand *dimension_count* represents the number of dimensions of the created array. The actual sizes of the dimensions of the created array are placed onto an operand stack.

We assume that the time required by a Java runtime system to evaluate expression *new classNameOrPrimitiveType$[n_1][n_2]\ldots[n_k]$* is equal to the sum of

- the time required to create an array with $n_1$ elements, each can hold a reference,
- the time required to create $n_1$ arrays of type *classNameOrPrimitiveType$[n_2]\ldots[n_k]$*, and
- the time required to place the references to the $n_1$ arrays into the elements of the first array.

We similarly calculate the space required by expression *new classNameOrPrimitiveType$[n_1][n_2]\ldots[n_k]$* by accumulating the space requirements of the involved arrays.

We now simplify the above assumption with the uniform cost criterion by using one unit of time to perform a fixed number of instructions. We assume that the number of units of time required by expression *new classNameOrPrimitiveType$[n_1][n_2]\ldots[n_k]$* is equal to the sum of

- the time required to create an array with $n_1$ elements, and
- the time required to create $n_1$ arrays of type *classNameOrPrimitiveType$[n_2]\ldots[n_k]$*.

In a Java program, we may use expression

$$new\ classNameOrPrimitiveType[n_1][n_2]\ldots[n_k][]\ldots[]$$

to create a multi-dimensional array without creating arrays for the last several dimensions. The time and space requirements for evaluating the expression are equal to the time and space required by creating an array that has dimensions $[n_1][n_2]\ldots[n_k]$ and component type *classNameOrPrimitiveType$[]\ldots[]$*.

## 6.1.3 Arithmetic Operations

Java provides various arithmetic operators such as + (add), − (subtract and negate), * (multiply), / (divide), and % (remainder). The Java compiler compiles an arithmetic operation to one or two load instructions followed by an arithmetic instruction of the JVM. The load instructions load operands to an operand stack. The arithmetic instruction uses the operand(s) to produce a result at the top of the operand stack. For instance, expression

```
i = i + j;
```
is compiled to instructions
```
iload_1
iload_2
iadd
istore_1
```

in Section 5.2.1.3. If operands are *long* or *double*, instructions for *long* or *double* operands are used for the load and arithmetic operations.

In the uniform cost function, we charge one unit, rather than three units, of time for a Java runtime system to perform an arithmetic operation such as add (+). We stick on the uniform cost criterion even if the operands are *long* or *double* values.

A Java method may shift the bits of a numeric value leftward or rightward. Since a bit-shift operator can be applied to at most two words, we assume that a bit shift operation takes one unit of time. For a similar reason, we assume each of the logical operations supported by the Java language takes one unit of time.

## 6.1.4 Branch Statements

In Section 2.2, we describe various types of statement that transfer control. The control transfer statements include *break*, *continue*, and *return*. They may have arguments. The statements are supported with JVM instructions such as *goto*, *goto_w*, *return*, and *ireturn*. The opcode *goto* is followed by a 16-bit branch offset, and *goto_w* is followed by a 32-bit branch offset.

A control transfer statement may be compiled to a couple of bytecode instructions. The uniform cost function charges one unit of time for the execution of any of the statements *break*, *continue* and *return*.

A conditional statement

   *if* (<*boolean_expression*>) *s1*; *else s2*;

is supported by the *if*<*cond*> instructions of the JVM, where <*boolean_expression*> denotes a branching condition. For example, opcodes *ifeq* and *ifne* are associated with branching conditions that test if the top operand in the operand stack is equal to 0 or not. The JVM also has instructions *if_icmp*<*cond*> with branching conditions <*cond*> that compare the top two operands in the operand stack.

For a conditional branching statement, the comparison of the top operand with 0 or with the operand beneath the top operand takes one unit of time. This assumption is based on the observation that each operand takes either one or two words, and a comparison of two operands takes a fixed number of units of time. However, the unit of time does not include the time required by an evaluation of <*boolean_expression*>, which may invoke methods and perform logical and arithmetic operations.

The Java compiler compiles for, while, and do loops to *goto* or conditional branching instructions. For a loop statement, the uniform cost function counts logical operations required by the evaluation of the loop condition. Each logical operation takes one unit of time. The time for repeatedly executing the loop body is also added to the time required by the loop. We shall use an example, Example 6.1, to show how to analyze the time required by the execution of a for loop. Specifically, for a given problem size we count the number of repetitions each statement in the loop is executed. For each repetition, we count the number of units of time required by the statement by counting the number of operations performed by the statement.

## 6.1.5 Object Field Access

### 6.1.5.1 Instance Field Access

In a Java program, we may access or change the value in a field of an object. For example, we use statement

```
customer1.name = "John Smith";
```

to set the *name* field in customer object *customer1*. The statement can be compiled to instructions

```
aload_1
ldc #4
putfield #19
```

Here, we assume that the entry at index 4 in the constant pool encodes constant string *John Smith*, and the entry at 19 references the *name* field in the customer object, which is referenced with local variable 1. The instruction *putfield #19* places a reference to the string into the *name* field.

The JVM uses opcode *getfield* to retrieve a field from an object. The retrieved value is placed on the top of an operand stack. For example, the argument expression *customer1.name* in method invocation

```
System.out.println(customer1.name);
```

is compiled to code

```
aload_1
getfield #19
```

which loads a reference to customer object *customer1* from local variable 1 and retrieves the *name* field from the object.

We can put a value into a field such as *customer1.name* or retrieve a value held in the field. In either case, we assume the field access takes one unit of time.

### 6.1.5.2 Array Element Access

In a Java program, we can store a primitive value or a reference into an element of an array. For example, the Java code

```
Customer[] cus = new Customer[12];
Customer customer1 = new Customer();
cus[10] = customer1;
```

creates an array for variable *cus*, creates a customer object, and saves the reference to the customer object into array element *cus*[10]. The last statement accesses element *cus*[10] of the customer array. The statement can be compiled to bytecode

```
aload_1
bipush 10
aload_2
aastore
```

which loads a reference to the array *cus*, integer 10, and a customer object reference stored in local variable 2 onto the operand stack before the *aastore* instruction stores the customer object reference into the 11th element of array *cus*.

An access to an array element retrieves a primitive value or a reference to an object from the element and pushes the value or reference onto the top of an operand stack. We assume that retrieving from an array element takes one unit of time.

The assignment statement

```
cus[10] = customer1;
```

assigns array element *cus*[10] with a reference in variable *customer1*. The statement accesses variable *customer1* and array element *cus*[10]. It takes two units of time, one for accessing variable *customer1*, and one for placing the reference in variable *customer1* into array element *cus*[10].

## 6.1.6 Local Variables

As we learned in Section 5.3.3, arguments for a method invocation and local variables declared in the method body are stored in an array of local variables. The method invocation owns a frame, which contains the local variable array and an operand stack.

A Java program may use an identifier to name a local variable. A local variable access in a Java method is compiled to a load or store instruction for an indexed element of the local variable array. The load or store instruction encodes type information so that one or two consecutive words in the local variable array can be loaded or stored. Examples 5.7 and 5.8 show how the JVM uses local variable array to support arguments and local variables for method execution.

We assume that it takes one unit of time to access a local variable. This uniform cost assumption also applies when a local variable is a *long* or *double*, for which two consecutive elements in the local variable array are accessed.

With the uniform cost assumption, statement

```
j = n;
```
takes two units of time, one unit for loading *n* and one for storing the loaded value into local variable *j*.

## 6.1.7 Method Invocation

As described in Section 5.2.4.1, the JVM supports method invocation with four types of instruction – *invokevirtual, invokestatic, invokeinterface*, and *invokespecial*.

Before a method invocation instruction is executed by a Java runtime system, the invoking method loads arguments onto its operand stack. For example, statement

```
m.setName("Cheese");
```
in Example 5.9 is compiled to code
```
aload_1
ldc #1 <String "Cheese">
invokevirtual #7
            <Method void setName(java.lang.String)>
```
where local variable 1, which represents variable *m*, holds a reference to a merchandise object, the constant pool entry at index 1 encodes string *Cheese*, and the entry at index 7 refers to method *setName*. The above bytecode places a merchandise object reference and a constant string onto the top of an operand stack before the *invokevirtual* instruction is executed.

For uniform cost function, we assume a method invocation takes one unit of time for each argument and one unit of time for starting the invoked method. Note that if the invoked method is an instance method or an instance initialization method, the first argument loaded to the operand stack must be an object for which the method is invoked. This load operation takes one unit of time. After an invoked method is started, it takes time to execute the instructions of the method body. For example, method *setName* is defined by

```
void setName(String name){ this.name = name; }
```
in Example 5.1. The time required by statement

```
m.setName("Cheese");
```
is equal to 5 units of time: one unit for loading a reference from local variable *m*, one for loading reference to string *Cheese*, one for starting method *setName*, one for accessing argument *name*, and one for setting field *this.name*. Each unit corresponds to a bytecode instruction. For instance, the first unit of time is used to load a merchandise object reference from a local variable allocated for variable *m*.

**Exercise 6.1** What should be the number of units of time required by method invocation

```
"An object".equalsIgnoreCase("an Object")
```

# 6.1.8 Java Program Analysis

We now consider the analysis of Java programs. We concentrate on the time and space required by Java statements. As described in Section 5.2.3, a switch statement is compiled to a *lookupswitch* or a *tableswitch* instruction, which has a variable number of in line operands. The execution of a *lookupswitch* instruction compares the top operand in an operand stack with the in line operands. A *tableswitch* instruction uses the top operand as index in the in line offset table. Except the two types of bytecode instruction, we classify JVM instructions as either simple or complex. The complex instructions include object creation instructions, which are started with opcode *new* or an opcode for array creation. They also include method invocation instructions, which are started with opcode *invokevirtual*, *invokestatic*, *invokeinterface*, and *invokespecial*. Other JVM instructions are regarded as simple.

The uniform cost function for Java statements implies that we can ignore the length of the representation of primitive values. The ignorance is justified by the fact that Java is a strongly typed language. A primitive type such as *float* or *double* uses one or two words in the representation of its values. In Java, no one can forge an arbitrarily long integer or real number and assign it to a variable of a primitive type.

An object creation instruction allocates memory space for the created object and initializes the fields of the created object with default values. The number of time units and that of space units required by an object creation instruction depend on the class of the object. A method invocation requires a variable number of arguments. The number of arguments depends on the signature of the invoked method. The time required by a complex instruction depends on the created object or invoked method.

The number of operands required by a simple instruction is bounded by a fixed integer. For example, an addition operation requires only two operands in an operand stack. The number of constant pool accesses required by each simple instruction is also limited by an integer. Thus, the time required by a simple instruction is bounded by a constant.

We now extend the uniform cost function from bytecode instructions to Java operations and statements. We assume that an operation in Java takes one unit of time if the operation is implemented with a simple JVM instruction. For example, an evaluation of expression $3 \times 5$ takes one unit of time; expression *customer1.balance* + 5 takes two units of time, one of which is used to access the field *balance* of object *customer1*, the other performs add operation.

An element of an array is an anonymous variable. A Java runtime system maps the index of an element of an array into an address in computer memory. We assume that it takes one unit of time to access an element of an array.

In the above discussion, we focus on time complexity. A computer program needs memory space to carry out its computation. The space complexity, which is the amount of memory space needed in the execution of the program, is also an important measure of the performance of the program. The uniform cost function applies to space complexity. A primitive value is stored in an operand stack or a field in an object. An object is stored in a heap. We assume a value of a primitive type can be stored in one unit of memory space. The space occupied by an object is equal to the sum of the space occupied by its fields. The reference to an object is different from the object. It is essentially a pointer. It can be regarded as an integer. We assume a reference needs only one unit of space.

A difference between time and space is that time cannot be reused but a computer memory can. For example, if two methods are run in sequence, the space allocated for the first method invocation can be reallocated for the second. After an operation is performed, its operands are removed from the operand stack. The operand stack space can be reused for the operands of following operations.

Before a Java program is executed, its compiled code must be loaded into a method area in memory. The executable code takes space. However, we do not care about the space occupied by the executable, which is fixed and which is usually smaller than the input and intermediate data. The space complexity refers to the amount of space required by the program at runtime.

# 6.2 Asymptotic Analysis of Programs

## 6.2.1 Time and Space Functions

The time required by an execution of a method is the *time complexity* of the method. It is an integer function on problem sizes $n$. For a given integer $n$, many instances of the problem solved by the method may have their input sizes equal to $n$. For two problem instances of size $n$, the time required by the method may be different. For a non-negative integer $n$, we need to decide a value for the time complexity of the method for problem instances of size $n$.

One approach to decide a time complexity for problem instances of the same size $n$ is the *best-case analysis*, which uses the least time required by the method on an instance of size $n$ of the problem as the time complexity. The best-case analysis is too optimistic on the performance of the method. It cannot guarantee that an arbitrary instance of size $n$ of the problem can be solved by the method in the time.

The common approach to decide a time complexity for problem instances of the same size $n$ is the *worst-case analysis*. It uses the greatest amount of time required by instances of size $n$ of the problem as the time complexity for size $n$.

We use an algorithm, known as *bubble sort*, to describe the difference between the best and worst-case analyses. The algorithm sorts an array of elements by exchanging adjacent elements if the elements are not in order. The following example implements the algorithm in class *BubbleSort* to sort string arrays.

**Example 6.1** The bubble sort algorithm is implemented with static method *sort* in the following class *BubbleSort*. The method has two for loops, one embedding the other. The outer loop uses index $i$ to limit the subarray to be sorted. Specifically, the strings at indexes $i$, $i+1$, ..., *string_array.length*$-1$ in *string_array* have not been sorted. The inner loop moves index variable *j* backward from *string_array.length*–1 toward *i*+1. If it finds two adjacent elements at *j*–1 and *j* are not in order, it swaps the elements. Thus, the smallest among the strings at indexes *i*, *i*+1, ..., *string_array.length*–1 will be moved to index *i*.

Class *BubbleSort* includes a main method to test the *sort* method. The main method uses a reference to array {"*Cbc*", "*Bbc*", "*Abc*"} as argument to invoke method *sort*. After sorting the array, the main method prints strings *Abc*, *Bbc*, *Cbc* in order.

```
class BubbleSort {
    public static void main(String[] args) {
        String[] names = {"Cbc", "Bbc", "Abc"};
        BubbleSort.sort(names);
        for (int i=0; i < names.length; i++){
            System.out.print(names[i]+" ");
        }
    }
    /** Sorts a string array with bubble sort */
0.  public static void sort(
                        String[] string_array) {
1.      int i, j;
2.      String temp_string;
3.      boolean sorted = false;
4.      for (i=0; i < string_array.length-1 &&
                        !sorted; i++) {
5.          sorted = true;
6.          for (j = string_array.length-1;
                    j > i; j--) {
7.              if (string_array[j].compareTo
                        (string_array[j-1]) < 0) {
8.                  temp_string = string_array[j];
9.                  string_array[j] = string_array[j-1];
10.                 string_array[j-1] = temp_string;
11.                 sorted = false;
                }
            } // end of inner loop
        } // end of outer loop
    }
}
```

The best case for the *sort* method is that the input *string_array* is sorted. In the best case, the *sort* method runs the outer loop body only once for *i* equal to 0, but the inner loop does not swap any elements. The time required by statements in the *sort* method body is displayed in the following table. We assume the length of input *string_array* is *n*. By summing up the cost of the statements, we can derive $t_b = 7 \times n + 15$ for the total number of units of time required by method *sort* in the best case.

| Line no. | No. of repetitions | Cost (units of time) |
| --- | --- | --- |
| 3 | 1 | 1 |
| 4 | 2 | $1 + 2 \times 7 + 1 = 16$ |
| 5 | 1 | 1 |
| 6 | $n$ | $3 + n + (n-1) = 2 \times n + 2$ |
| 7 | $n-1$ | $(n-1) \times 5$ |
| 8 | 0 | 0 |
| 9 | 0 | 0 |
| 10 | 0 | 0 |
| 11 | 0 | 0 |

In the above cost estimates, each arithmetic operation in an executed statement is counted once. We do not assume any optimization. For example, each of the subtract operations in lines 4, 6, and 7 takes 1 unit of time. We assume the evaluation of expression $i < string\_array.length-1$ && !sorted takes 7 units of time, one unit for each arithmetic, relational, or logical operation and one unit for accessing variable $i$, $string\_array.length$, or sorted.

One of the worst cases for the sort method is that the values in the array are in descending order, i.e.,

$$string\_array[0] > string\_array[1] > \ldots > string\_array[n-1]$$

where $n$ is equal to $string\_array.length$. In the worst case, the outer loop body must be repeated $(n-1)$ times in order to move the values in the array to their final positions. The time required by the code of method sort in the worst case is displayed in the following table. The index variable $i$ in the following table varies from 0 to $n-2$. The total number of units required by method sort in the worst case is $t_w = 8 \times n^2 + 5 \times n - 4$.

| line no. | no. of repetitions | cost (units of time) |
| --- | --- | --- |
| 3 | 1 | 1 |
| 4 | $n$ | $1 + n \times 7 + (n-1)$ |
| 5 | $n-1$ | $n-1$ |
| 6 | $\Sigma_{0 \leq i < n-1}(n-1-i+1)$ | $\Sigma_i(3 + (n-i) + (n-i-1))$ |
| 7 | $\Sigma_i(n-1-i)$ | $\Sigma_i(n-1-i) \times 5$ |
| 8 | $\Sigma_i(n-1-i)$ | $\Sigma_i(n-1-i) \times 2$ |
| 9 | $\Sigma_i(n-1-i)$ | $\Sigma_i(n-1-i) \times 3$ |
| 10 | $\Sigma_i(n-1-i)$ | $\Sigma_i(n-1-i) \times 3$ |
| 11 | $\Sigma_i(n-1-i)$ | $\Sigma_i(n-1-i)$ |

Sometimes the time required by an execution of a method can be estimated by counting data comparisons made by the execution. In the worst case, the outer loop body in method *sort* is executed $n - 1$ times. For each execution with $0 \le i < n - 1$, the inner loop body makes $n - 1 - i$ comparisons between adjacent strings to evaluate

`string_array[j].compareTo(string_array[j-1])`

for $i < j < n$. In the worst case, the number of data comparisons made by method *sort* for a *string_array* of size $n$ is equal to

$$t_c = \Sigma_{0 \le i < n-1}(n - 1 - i) = 0.5 \times n^2 - 0.5 \times n.$$

which is another measure of the time complexity of method *sort*.

Let us summarize the above discussion for the bubble *sort* method. Suppose a problem size $n$. (The letter $n$ usually denotes a problem size in complexity analysis in the literature.) The best-case analysis of method *sort* gives a time complexity

$$t_b = 7 \times n + 15.$$

The worst-case analysis of method *sort* gives a time complexity

$$t_w = 8 \times n^2 + 5 \times n - 4.$$

If only data comparisons are counted, the worst-case analysis of method *sort* gives a time complexity

$$t_c = 0.5 \times n^2 - 0.5 \times n.$$

$\square$

**Exercise 6.2** Estimate the time complexity of method *sort* presented in Example 6.1 by counting data comparisons and data swaps. By a data swapping we mean exchanging references in adjacent elements *string_array[j]* and *string_array[j-1]*.

## 6.2.2 Dominance

To choose an algorithm for a problem, we compare the complexities of available algorithms. The comparison can be based on the dominance of a function over another. We say that function $f$ dominates function $g$ if the ratio $f(n)/g(n)$ increases without an upper bound as $n$ increases. Formally, $f$ *dominates* $g$ if for any constant $c > 0$, there is an integer $n_0$ such that $f(n)/g(n) > c$ for all integers $n > n_0$. The notation $o(f)$ is used to represent the set of all functions $g$ that are dominated by $f$, i.e.,

$$o(f) = \{g \mid f \text{ dominates } g\}.$$

Expression $g \in o(f)$ denotes that function $f$ dominates function $g$.

Let us use an example to illustrate the notion of dominance. The function $f(n) = c \times n$ for a positive real number $c$ is called a *linear function* on variable $n$. A *logarithmic function* on $n$ can be expressed in the form $c \times \log n$ for a real constant

$c > 0$. A linear function $f(n) = c \times n$ dominates a logarithmic function $g(n) = c' \times \log n$ for any constants $c, c' > 0$.

Another example of dominance is that function $f(n) = n^{k+1}$ dominates function $g(n) = n^k$ for an integer $k \geq 0$. In fact, the ratio

$$f(n)/g(n) = n$$

can be greater than any positive number as variable $n$ increases.

**Example 6.2** Let us prove that function $n^2/3$ dominates function $1000 \times n + 2000$, i.e., $1000 \times n + 2000 \in o(n^2/3)$. We assume an arbitrary constant $c > 0$. We need to find an integer $n_0$ such that for all integers $n > n_0$, we can deduce

$$(n^2/3)/(1000 \times n + 2000) > c$$

The role played by integer $n_0$ can be interpreted as a problem size such that for all problem sizes $n$ greater than $n_0$, we have the above inequality. Note that for any integer $n > 0$, we have $3000 \times n \geq 1000 \times n + 2000$. Therefore, when $n > 0$, the inequality to be deduced is implied by inequality

$$n > 9000 \times c.$$

When $n > n_0 = \lceil 9000 \times c \rceil$, the ratio $(n^2/3)/(1000 \times n + 2000) > c$. Thus, function $n^2/3$ dominates $1000 \times n + 2000$.     □

A property of the notion of dominance is transitivity: if function $f$ dominates function $g$ and $g$ dominates function $h$, then $f$ dominates $h$. We leave a proof for the property as an exercise.

**Exercise 6.3** Prove the transitivity property of function dominance.

**Exercise 6.4** Prove the following dominance relationships:
- $n + 1000 \in o(n^2)$;
- $3 \times n + 200 \in o(n^2/3)$.

## 6.2.3 Big-O and Big-$\Omega$ Notations

Notation $o(f)$ for a function $f$ denotes the set of functions $g$ that are dominated by $f$. Some complexity functions $f$ and $g$ are different but neither dominates the other. For example, neither of functions $n$ and $n + 1$ dominates the other. The notion of *order* is often used to describe some relation between functions that cannot be described with dominance. The order of a function $f$ is represented by $O(f)$, which is called "big-Oh" of $f$.

Let us define the notion big-O. Assume functions $f$ and $g$ that map positive integers $n$ to positive integers. We say that function $g$ is in the *order* of $f$, denoted with $g \in O(f)$, if there is a constant $c > 0$ such that

$$g(n) \leq c \times f(n)$$

for all but a finite number of integer values $n$. In other words, function $g$ is $O(f)$ if there is a constant $c > 0$ and an integer $n_0$ such that

$$g(n) \leq c \times f(n)$$

for all integers $n > n_0$. For a value $n \leq n_0$, we may not have the above inequality. The big-O notation ignores small problem sizes. It does not care about the magnitude of constant factor $c$ either.

**Example 6.3** Here we prove that $100 \times n + 20$ is $O(n)$. Note that when $n > 0$, we have $100 \times n + 20 \leq 120 \times n$. Therefore, when $c = 120$ and $n_0 = 1$, we have

$$100 \times n + 20 \leq c \times n$$

for all $n \geq n_0$. Thus, $100 \times n + 20 \in O(n)$. $\square$

The notion of order makes it possible to focus on the growth rate of the complexity of a program rather than constant factors. Assume linear function $f(n) = n$ and logarithmic function $g(n) = 1000 \times \log n$, where expression $\log n$ represents logarithmic function $\log_2 n$ with base 2. We have $g \in O(f)$. In fact, for all integers $n > 0$, we have

$$g(n) < 1000 \times f(n).$$

But $f$ is not $O(g)$. In fact, for any constant $c > 0$ and integer $n_0 > 0$, we can find an integer $n > n_0$ such that

$$f(n) > c \times g(n).$$

(The proof needs some property of logarithmic functions. We omit the proof here.) Therefore, $f \notin O(g)$. Because $f \notin O(g)$ but $g \in O(f)$, we prefer to use an algorithm that has complexity function $g$ than an algorithm that has complexity function $f$. In other words, comparison of algorithms can be based on the orders of their complexity functions.

The order-based comparison of complexities is not affected by a constant factor of a function. For a function $f$, we have

$$f \in O(c \times f) \text{ and } c \times f \in O(f)$$

for any constant $c > 0$. In fact, for $c > 0$, we always have

$$f \leq (1/c) \times c \times f \text{ and } c \times f \leq c \times f,$$

which can be used to establish the above two big-O claims.

Using orders to compare complexities is justified by the fact that an improvement of the complexity of a program by an order is more important than by a factor. Assume methods $f\_sort$ and $g\_sort$ that sort arrays of size $n$ in time $f(n) = n \log n$ and $g(n) = n^2/3$, respectively. The following table lists values of the functions for some integers, which are regarded as problem sizes. Function $g(n)$ grows faster than $f(n)$ when argument $n$ increases. Particularly, when problem size $n$ changes from 100 to 1000, the performance improvement of $f\_sort$ over $g\_sort$ increases from 7 to 48-fold. If the time is measured in millisecond, we have $f(100) = 0.46$ second, $g(100) = 3.33$ seconds, $f(1000) = 6.907$ seconds, and $g(1000) = 5.555$ minutes. It is obvious that a time requirement of 0.46, 3.33 or 6.9 seconds are acceptable by a user; but 5.5 minutes may not be acceptable.

| $n$ | $f(n)=n\log n$ | $g(n) = n^2/3$ | $g(n) / f(n)$ |
|------|------|------|------|
| 100 | 460 | 3333 | 7 |
| 200 | 1059 | 13333 | 12 |
| 300 | 1711 | 30000 | 17 |
| 400 | 2396 | 53333 | 22 |
| 500 | 3107 | 83333 | 26 |
| 600 | 3838 | 120000 | 31 |
| 700 | 4585 | 163333 | 35 |
| 800 | 5347 | 213333 | 39 |
| 900 | 6122 | 270000 | 44 |
| 1000 | 6907 | 333333 | 48 |

The term *asymptotic analysis* of a method refers to a study of the increase rate of the complexity of the method when problem size increases. Asymptotic analysis aims at an expression of the order of the complexity. The order is often represented with a simple expression. For example, function $n^2 + 100n + 20$ is often represented with $O(n^2)$, which is more illustrious than expression $O(n^2 + 100n + 20)$. The simplified expression is reasonable because we have

$$n^2 \in O(n^2 + 100n + 20) \text{ and } n^2 + 100n + 20 \in O(n^2).$$

We can use notion big-$\Omega$ to express the equality of the orders of two complexity functions. For functions $f(n)$ and $g(n)$, if we have $f(n) \in O(g(n))$ and $g(n) \in O(f(n))$, we say that functions $f$ and $g$ are of the same order and denote the fact with $f(n) \in \Omega(g(n))$, or simply $f \in \Omega(g)$. For example, we have $n^2 + 100n + 20 \in \Omega(n^2)$.

Based on the notion of order, we can prove that the two worst-case complexity functions $t_w$ and $t_c$ of method *sort* shown in Example 6.1 are equivalent. In fact, we have $t_w \in \Omega(n^2)$ and $t_c \in \Omega(n^2)$. We have $t_b \in o(n^2)$. We leave a formal proof of the claims as an exercise. (See Exercise 6.5.)

**Exercise 6.5** Prove $8 \times n^2 + 5 \times n - 4 \in \Omega(n^2)$, $0.5 \times n^2 - 0.5 \times n \in \Omega(n^2)$, and $7 \times n + 15 \in o(n^2)$.

**Exercise 6.6** Prove $n + 1000 \in O(n)$ and $2 \times n + 200 \in O(n)$. As a matter of fact, for any linear function $f(n)$, we have $f(n) \in \Omega(n)$.

**Exercise 6.7** Assume functions $f(n) = n$ and $g(n) = n^{1/2}$. Prove

- $g \in O(f)$;
- $g \in o(f)$;
- $f \notin O(g)$.

**Exercise 6.8** For an integer $k > 0$, prove $n^k \in O(n^{k+1})$ but $n^{k+1} \notin O(n^k)$.

**Exercise 6.9** Prove that constant function $f(n) = c > 0$ satisfies $f(n) \in \Omega(1)$.

**Exercise 6.10** Assume complexity functions $f$, $g$, and $h$, which map positive integers to positive integers. Prove

- if $f \in O(h)$ and $g \in O(h)$, then $f(n) + g(n) \in O(h)$;
- for any constant $c > 0$, if $f \in O(h)$, then $c \times f \in O(h)$;
- if $f \in O(h)$ and $g \in o(h)$, then $f + g \in O(h)$.

## 6.2.4 Complexity Categories

The notions of order and dominance can be used to classify complexity functions into categories. Let us briefly discuss the categories of exponential, polynomial, logarithmic, and constant functions. In the discussion, we apply a proposition that if functions $f$ and $g$ satisfy $f \in o(g)$, then $f \in O(g)$. To prove the proposition, assume $f \in o(g)$ and a real constant $c > 0$. According to the definition of dominance, we can find an integer $n_0$ such that

$$g(n) / f(n) > 1 / c$$

for all $n > n_0$. The above inequality is equivalent to

$$f(n) < c \times g(n),$$

which implies $f \in O(g)$.

The category of *exponential functions* include functions $2^n$, $3^n$, .... For an integer constant $k \geq 1$, we can show

$$k^n \in o((k+1)^n)$$

which implies $k^n \in O((k+1)^n)$.

A *polynomial function* is $c_k \times n^k + c_{k-1} \times n^{k-1} + \ldots + c_0$ with real constant $c_k > 0$. The given polynomial function is $O(n^k)$. A method that solves a problem in polynomial time is an *efficient* method. For an integer $k > 0$, we can prove that

$$n^k \in O(n^{k+1}) \text{ but } n^{k+1} \notin O(n^k).$$

Function $f(n) = \log_t n$ for a real number $t > 1$ is a *logarithmic function*. If the base $t$ is 2, the base is often omitted from the logarithmic function expression. If the base $t$ is the natural number $e = 2.71828\ldots$, the function is the natural logarithmic function $\ln n$. For any two different real numbers $t > 1$ and $s > 1$, we have

$$\log_t n \in \Omega(\log_s n).$$

The above claim is implied by equality

$$\log_t n = \log_s n / \log_s t,$$

where the real number $\log_s t$ is a positive constant.

Another important category of complexity functions consists of *constant functions* $f(n) = c$ for real numbers $c > 0$. All the constant functions are $O(1)$, i.e., for any real number $c > 0$, we have

$$c \in O(1).$$

An exponential function dominates any polynomial function, which in turn dominates each logarithmic function. All the constant functions are $O(1)$ and they are dominated by any logarithmic function. The four categories of complexity functions are summarized in the following table.

| Function | Category |
|---|---|
| $c$ for constant $c > 0$ | constant function |
| $\log_t n$ for base $t > 1$ | logarithmic function |
| $c_k \times n^k + c_{k-1} \times n^{k-1} + \ldots + c_0$ with integer $k \geq 1$, real $c_k > 0$ | polynomial function |
| $k^n$ for integer constant $k > 1$ | exponential function |

The above classification is not exhaustive or complete. For example, sorting algorithms will be presented in Chapter 7. Some of the sorting algorithms have time complexity $O(n \log n)$, where $n$ represents the number of elements in an array to be sorted. The function $n \log n$ is dominated by polynomial function $n^2$. It dominates linear function $n$. Another complexity function that does not belong to any of the above four categories is $\log^2 n$, which dominates $\log n$ and is dominated by $n$.

# 6.3 An Analysis of Binary Search

## 6.3.1 Linear Search

To find a value $v$ from a sequence of values, we can compare $v$ with the values in sequence. This algorithm is known as *linear search*. In the following class, class *LinearSearch*, static method *search(String[] string_array, string s)* implements linear search to find a string $s$ in a string array.

```
class LinearSearch {
    public static void main(String[] args) {
        String[] names = {"Cbc", "Bbc", "Abc"};
        System.out.print(
            LinearSearch.search(names, "Abc"));
    }

    /** Searches for a string in a string array
     *    with linear search
     */
    public static int search(
                String[] string_array, String s) {
```

```
for (int i=0; i<string_array.length; i++) {
    if (string_array[i].compareTo(s) == 0)
        return i;
    }
    return -1;
    }
}
```

We can analyze the *search* method in a worst case by counting the comparisons made by the method for problem size *n*, which is equal to *string_array.length*. One of the worst cases is that the target string *s* is not present in *string_array*. The for loop in the above method has to be repeated *n* times before the local variable *i* becomes equal to *string_array.length*. In the worst case, the total number of comparisons made by expression *string_array[i].compareTo(s)* is equal to *n*. Method *search* takes time linear in the problem size *n* to return integer −1. The worst-case time complexity of the linear *search* method is $O(n)$.

## 6.3.2 Binary Search

Let us present a common search algorithm, *binary search*. The algorithm can be applied to an array that has been sorted. The following class, class *BinarySearch*, implements binary search in static method *search*, which searches for a string *s* in a string array. It keeps two indexes in the string array with variables *low* and *high*. The two indexes delimit a search range in the array. The *search* method compares the middle element in the search range with target *s*. If they are equal, the index of the middle element is returned; otherwise, the method discards a half of the search range by setting either *high* with *mid* − 1 or *low* with *mid* + 1. The discarded search range cannot contain string *s*.

```
class BinarySearch {
    public static void main(String[] args) {
        String[] names = {"Cbc", "Bbc", "Abc"};
        BubbleSort.sort(names);
        System.out.print(BinarySearch.search
            (names, 0, names.length-1, "Cbc"));
    }

    /** Searches for a string in a string array
    *    with binary search
    */
    public static int search(String[]string_array,
                    int low, int high, String s) {
        int mid;
        while (low <= high) {
            mid = (low + high) / 2;
            int r = string_array[mid].compareTo(s);
            if (r == 0) return mid;
```

```
                    if (r > 0) high = mid - 1;
                    else low = mid + 1;
            }
            return -1;

    }

}
```

Let us analyze the binary *search* method for a worst case. One of the worst cases is that the target *s* is not in the string array. When we invoke the *search* method with

  *BinarySearch.search(string_array, 0, n − 1, s)*

where *n* is equal to *string_array.length*, the search range is [*low, high*] with *low* = 0 and *high* = *n* − 1. Each time the while loop body is executed, the size of search range [*low, high*] is reduced by at least half. Thus, the while loop body is repeated at most log *n* times. For each repetition of the loop body, the data is compared once in expression

  *string_array[mid].compareTo(s)*.

Therefore, the total number of data comparisons made by method *search* is at most log *n*. The worst-case time complexity of the *search* method is *O*(log *n*), where *n* is the size of the input *string_array*.

We now illustrate the changes of local variables *low, high*, and *mid* when the *search* method is executed for evaluating expression *BinarySearch.search(names*, 0, 6, "*Clark, A.*"), where string array *names* is

| Adams, J. | Adams, S. | Barlett, J. | Braxton, C. | Carroll, C. | Chase, S. | Clark, A. |
|-----------|-----------|-------------|-------------|-------------|-----------|-----------|

The array length *names.length* is 7. The following table lists the values of variables *low, high*, and *mid* and array element *names[mid]* in a row for each repetition of the while loop. By the last row of the table, when *mid* is equal to 6, the expression *string_array[mid].compareTo(s)* should return 0 in the body of method *search*. Thus, method *search* returns integer 6.

| *low* | *high* | *mid* | *names[mid]* |
|-------|--------|-------|--------------|
| 0     | 6      | 3     | Braxton, C.  |
| 4     | 6      | 5     | Chase, S.    |
| 6     | 6      | 6     | Clark, A.    |

**Exercise 6.11** Analyze the binary *search* method by counting all operations performed by the method in a worst case. Compare the derived time complexity with function log *n*.

## 6.3.3 Recursion

A concept or algorithm is *recursive* if the concept or algorithm applies itself in its definition. For instance, concept *superclass* is a recursive concept. A class *S* is called a superclass of class *C* if one of the following two conditions holds:

1. Class *C* extends class *S*.
2. Class *S* is a superclass of class *S'* and class *C* extends *S'*.

The second condition uses concept superclass.

In Section 6.3.2, method *search* uses index variables *low* and *high* to repeatedly reduce the search range. That method does not invoke itself. It is not a recursive method. The following method, also named *sort*, is a recursive implementation of the binary search algorithm. Specifically, if the comparison *string_array* [*mid*].*compareTo(s)* does not return 0 (equality), the method *sort* invokes itself in statement

```
        return search(string_array, low, mid-1, s);
```
or
```
        return search(string_array, mid + 1, high, s);
```
Each of the invocations reduces the search range by at least half.
```
/** Searches for a string in a string array
*    with binary search
*/
public static int search(String[] string_array,
                  int low, int high, String s) {
    if (high < low) return -1;
    int mid = (low + high) / 2;
    int r = string_array[mid].compareTo(s);
    if (r == 0) return mid;
    if (r > 0) return
            search(string_array, low, mid-1, s);
    else return
            search(string_array, mid + 1, high, s);
}
```

In the above two examples of recursion, the concept superclass and the *search* method invoke themselves directly. The definition of a recursive concept *R* may apply itself indirectly by first applying another concept *R'*, which applies the concept *R* directly or indirectly. Similarly, a recursive method may indirectly invoke itself in its computation.

## 6.3.4 Complexity of Recursive Methods

The methods that implement the bubble sort and linear search algorithms are not recursive. In the analysis of a non-recursive method, we can simply sum up the time required by statements executed by the method to derive the time complexity of the method. Method *search* defined in the above section is a recursive one, which may call itself. Its time complexity cannot be derived directly by counting the statements executed by the method. We need to establish recursive equations for the relationships between the time required by an invoking method and the time required by invoked methods. Let us analyze the worst-case time complexity $T(n)$ of the recursive binary *search* method.

Assume the problem size is $n$ with *names.length* = $n$ in method invocation

```
BinarySearch.search(names,0,names.length-1,s)
```

which assigns parameters *low* with 0 and *high* with *names.length*–1.

If *high* < *low*, the search range [*low, high*] is empty and the *search* method returns –1. The time required by method *search* for case $n = 0$ is bounded by a real number $c > 0$. We have $T(0) = c$. The quantity $c$ includes the time needed for creating and initializing the frame for the current execution of method *search*.

If $n > 0$, method *search* calculates *mid* by evaluating (*low* + *high*) / 2. Then, the method may evaluate one of the expressions

```
search(string_array, low, mid-1, s)
search(string_array, mid + 1, high, s)
```

The size of the search ranges for the above two invocations of method *search* is

$$high - mid = mid - low = n/2 - 1$$

if the size $n$ is divisible by 2. Thus, we can establish a recursive equation

$$T(n) = T(n/2 - 1) + c' \quad \text{for } n > 0 \text{ and some constant } c' > 0.$$

The constant quantity $c'$ covers the cost of comparing *low* with *high* and comparing argument $s$ with *string_array*[*mid*]. Since the value $T(n)$ is the time required by function *search* in the worst case for all string arrays of size $n$, we assume

$$T(n/2 - 1) \le T(n/2).$$

We use the recursive equation

$$T(n) = T(n/2) + c'$$

to approximate the above equation. Without loss of generality, we assume $n = 2^k$ for some integer $k \ge 0$ and $T(1) = c''$ for a constant $c'' > 0$. A solution to the system of recursive equations

$$T(n) = T(n/2) + c' \quad \text{for } n > 0,$$
$$T(0) = c$$

is

$$T(n) = k \times c' + c'' = c' \times \log n + c''$$

where $k = \log n$. Therefore, the time complexity of the recursive binary *search* method is a logarithmic function on $n$, which is $O(\log n)$.

By the above analysis, replacing the linear *search* method with the binary *search* method will improve the time complexity from a linear function to a logarithmic function. Thus, we reduce the time complexity from a function to a dominated function.

A precondition for invoking the binary *search* method is that the input array *string_array* be *sorted*. It is not required by the linear *search* method. If the input array is modified frequently, each invocation of binary *search* may require sort the array again. The combined cost of sorting and binary search is more expensive than the cost of applying linear search to the array directly. Therefore, it is judicious to apply binary search only to stable data containers such as a telephone directory, which is looked up for telephone numbers frequently but modified only annually.

## 6.3.5 Space Complexity Analysis

In the above analysis of algorithms bubble sort, linear search, and binary search, we derive only the time complexity. The space complexity of a method or algorithm is the number of storage units in memory used by the method or algorithm. It is a function from problem sizes to integers. Because of the many instances of the same size for a problem, we still distinguish the worst-case from best-case analysis of the space complexity for a method. Usually the worst case analysis is used as an indication of the space requirement of a method. Let us analyze the space complexity of binary search.

When the non-recursive method *search(string_array, 0, string_array. length–1, s)* defined in Section 6.3.2 is invoked, the size of the local variable array for the static method invocation is 6: one unit of space for each of the arguments, one for the local variable *mid*, and one for local variable *r*. The operand stack for the method invocation is required to push and pop operands. But the operand stack repeatedly uses only several elements again and again. The operand stack will never grow beyond a constant such as 4. Note that since we assume each string is a name with a limited number of letters, the space required to store a string *s* is limited by a constant. In summary, the number of storage units that the *search* method defined in Section 6.3.2 requires is a constant. That is, the space complexity of the method is $O(1)$.

An invocation of the recursive method *search* defined in Section 6.3.3 needs six elements in the local variable array to store the four arguments and local variables *mid* and *r*. Thus, six units of space are allocated for each recursive call. Assume *n* is the length of the input string array. In a worst case, the method will be recursively called for log *n* times; log *n* – 1 of the log *n* executions are halted and the last execution will be completed by returning – 1. Since each execution requires 6 units of space for local variables, the total space required by an invocation *search(string_array, 0, n – 1, s)* is 6 × log *n*. Thus, the space complexity of the binary *search* method defined in Section 6.3.3 is $O(\log n)$.

Comparing the space complexities of the non-recursive and recursive implementations of binary search, we can see a space penalty in using recursion. Since a method invocation takes time, the actual time required by the non-recursive implementation of binary search would be less than that required by the recursive implementation as well.

**Exercise 6.12** Modify the static binary *search* method defined in Section 6.3.2 to an instance method. Then, apply the method *benchmark* presented in Example 3.6 to evaluate the time required by method *search* invocation for a string array and a string. Repeat the same experiment for the *search* method defined in Section 6.3.3. Compare the evaluated time quantities.

# 6.4 Summary

Analysis of algorithms and methods should be based on an abstract model of computation so that the analysis result can be applied to most platforms. In this chapter, we discuss how to apply the JVM as an abstract model to derive a uniform cost function to measure time and space required by algorithms and methods. The uniform cost function assigns one unit of time to a JVM instruction that requires a fixed amount of time to implement. It counts the number of variables to be set to measure the time required by a complex JVM instruction such as an object creation.

The concept of asymptotic analysis is based on the notions of dominance and order. It emphasizes growth rate of the time or space complexity rather than a constant factor. The growth rate of a complexity function is an important criterion in judging an algorithm. By using order and dominance relations of complexity functions to compare algorithms, we can avoid the platform-dependence drawback of the benchmarking approach.

We present the binary search algorithm with a non-recursive and a recursive implementation in Java. We show that the time complexities of both implementations are $O(\log n)$. However, the recursive implementation takes extra time for each recursive invocation. The space complexity of the non-recursive implementation of binary search is $O(1)$, but that of the recursive one is $O(\log n)$. A recursive implementation of an algorithm that is recursively defined may be easier than a non-recursive implementation. The recursion encoded in a Java program incurs a penalty in time and space at runtime.

# Part III
# Data Structures

*- Linear data structures*
*- Trees*
*- Graphs*
*- Network flows*

# Chapter 7
# Linear Data Structures

A data structure with homogeneous elements is *linear* if it organizes its elements into a sequence. In a computer, each data structure is finite in terms of the number of its elements. A linear data structure has a first and a last element. Each of the other elements in the linear data structure has a predecessor and a successor.

There are several ways to represent the predecessor-successor relation for a linear data structure in a computer. An array is a linear data structure. An array maps its elements to contiguous words in memory. We can access the elements with their indexes in the array. The organization of an array matches the random access pattern of computer memory. The indexed access of an array element is fast. The access of each element takes a fixed amount of time. We regard the cost of array element access as constant, i.e., the time required is $O(1)$.

A vector is an instance of the Java standard class *Vector*. It is a linear data structure implemented with an array, which is replaced with a larger or smaller array dynamically as needed. Thus, a user of a vector is not concerned with errors of index out of bounds. The array replacement copies the elements of the current array in a vector to the elements of a new array. It takes time linear in the size of the current array for the data movement. It is expensive if array replacement occurs frequently for a vector.

We can link the elements of a linear data structure so that the elements may be placed in non-contiguous words in memory. In a linked linear data structure, each element maintains a link to its successor. We can follow the links to visit the elements in the data structure. A linked linear data structure is usually called a *linked list*.

The links of a linked list can be implemented with different types of value. For example, the links can be integers that are indexes of elements in an array or vector. Each element in the linked list contains a data field and a link field. It is an element of the array or vector. An array or vector may accommodate several linked lists.

The links of a linked list can be references to objects, which are called *nodes*. Each node encapsulates a data field and a link field. The reference in the link field of a node references the successor of the node. Thus, we can follow the links to visit all the nodes in the linked list.

Linear data structures store data. We often need to search for a primitive value or an object in a linear data structure. The elements of an array or vector have indexes. They can be accessed directly with their indexes. The elements of a linked list are scattered in memory. We have to follow links to access elements in the linked list.

To assist searching for values, the elements of a linear data structure may be sorted if there is a linear ordering for the values in the elements. For instance, an array of integers can be sorted in ascending order. A linked list of strings can be sorted according to the lexicographic order.

In this chapter, we discuss issues related to linear data structures. We already learned arrays and vectors in Chapter 4. Here we shall study sort and search algorithms for arrays and vectors. We also discuss linked list implementation. Specifically, we present

- Sorting methods for linear data structures. The sorting algorithms include insertion sort, selection sort, merge sort, and quick sort. The sorting methods apply for data structures that can be placed inside computer memory. The sorting algorithms are called internal sort algorithms.
- An external sort method for sorting files in secondary storage. We may have a file too large to fit in a computer memory and we need to sort the data in the file. In this case, we can apply some external sort algorithm. Here, we present an external sort algorithm based on merge sort.
- Searching algorithms. To search for a value in a linear data structure, we can apply linear search by sequentially visiting the elements of the data structure. When visiting an element, we compare it with the target value. If the linear data structure consists of indexed elements and the elements have been sorted, we can apply binary search, which was discussed in Chapter 6. Here, we present two improvements of binary search, one called Fibonaccian search, the other interpolation search.
- Linked lists. An array-based linked list uses indexes in an array as links. We can also use references to nodes to link the nodes into a linked list. We shall discuss singly and doubly linked lists.

# 7.1 Linear Data Structure Sorting

## 7.1.1 Internal Sort

In the previous chapter, we encountered bubble sort algorithm, which applies for arrays and vectors. Here, we discuss other sorting algorithms for arrays and vectors. The sorting algorithms take advantage of the random, indexed access to elements of an array or vector. Some of the algorithms can be adapted for linked lists.

Sorting applies only to data structures with elements that can be linearly ordered. For example, an array of integers can be sorted since for each pair of integers, only one of the relationships "less than", "equal to", and "greater than" applies. Two strings can be compared with method *compareTo(String s)*, which returns a negative number, 0, or a positive number when this string is less than, equal to, or greater than the argument string *s*. We shall apply sorting algorithms to sort arrays of strings. The sorting methods can be easily adapted for other types of element and for vectors.

### 7.1.1.1 Insertion Sort

An insertion sort method starts with a subarray that consists of only one element. The subarray is a sorted array. The method continuously inserts an element of the unsorted subarray into the sorted subarray. By iterating insertions, the unsorted subarray shrinks and the sorted subarray expands. Finally, the unsorted subarray becomes empty and all the elements are in the sorted array.

The following class, class *InsertionSort*, implements the insertion sort algorithm in static method *sort*. For a *string_array* with $n$ strings, the subarray that consists of the last string at index $n-1$ is a sorted subarray. The method inserts the string at index $n-2$ into the sorted subarray by comparing *string_array*$[n-2]$ and *string_array*$[n-1]$. It swaps the two elements if *string_array*$[n-2]$ is greater than *string_array*$[n-1]$. Generally speaking, when the body of the for loop

```
for (int i = n-1; i > 0; i--)
```

in the insertion *sort* method is started, the subarray *string_array*$[i]$, ..., *string_array*$[n-1]$ has been sorted and local variable *current* references *string_array*$[i-1]$. The insertion sort algorithm inserts *string_array*$[i-1]$ into subarray *string_array*$[i]$, ..., *string_array*$[n-1]$. The loop embeds a loop that uses boolean expression

```
current.compareTo(string_array[j+1]) > 0
```

to compare the *current* string with element *string_array*$[j+1]$ for $i-1 \le j < n-1$. If the *current* string is greater than *string_array*$[j+1]$, the string at position $j+1$ is moved to position $j$ and $j$ is increased by 1; otherwise, the inner loop stops. When the inner loop stops, index $j$ is the correct position for the *current* string. After inserting *current* at the position, the subarray *string_array*$[i-1]$, ..., *string_array*$[n-1]$ become sorted. When the loop variable $i$ becomes 0, the *string_array* is sorted.

```
public class InsertionSort {
    public static void main(String[] args) {
        String[] names = {"Cbc", "Bbc", "Abc"};
        InsertionSort.sort(names);
        for (int i=0; i < names.length; i++){
            System.out.print(names[i]+" ");
        }
    }

    /** Sorts string array with insertion sort */
    public static void sort(String[] string_array)
    {
        int n = string_array.length;
        for (int i = n-1; i > 0; i--) {
            String current = string_array[i-1];
            int j;
```

```
        for (j = i-1; j < n-1 &&
          current.compareTo(string_array[j+1])>0;
          j++)
            string_array[j] = string_array[j+1];
          string_array[j] = current;
      }
    }
  }
```

Given an array with $n$ strings, the body of the outer for loop will be repeated $n-1$ times with $i$ equal to $n-1$, $n-2$, ..., 1. In a worst case, for each $i$, the inner loop body is executed $n - i$ times. In the inner loop body, data comparison

```
    current.compareTo(string_array[j+1]) > 0
```

takes one unit of time for data comparison. By summing up the time for different $i$, we can derive the worst-case time complexity $\Sigma_{0<i\le n-1}(n-i) = 0.5 \times n^2 - 0.5 \times n$ for the insertion *sort* method, which is $O(n^2)$.

**Exercise 7.1** In the above description of insertion sort, we insert string *string_array*[$i-1$] into subarray *string_array*[$i$], ..., *string_array*[$n-1$]. Implement the insertion sort algorithm by inserting string stored in element *string_array*[$i$] into the subarray *string_array*[0], ..., *string_array*[$i-1$] for $i$ equal to 1, ..., $n-1$.

### 7.1.1.2 Selection Sort

Given a subarray *string_array*[$i$], ..., *string_array*[$n-1$] with $0 \le i < n-1$, we can find an index $k$ with $i \le k \le n-1$ such that *string_array*[$k$] $\le$ *string_array*[$j$] for all $j$ with $i \le j \le n-1$, i.e., $k$ indexes the minimum element in the subarray *string_array*[$i$], ..., *string_array*[$n-1$]. We can swap the elements *string_array*[$i$] and *string_array*[$k$]. Thus, the element *string_array*[$i$] contains the smallest string in subarray *string_array*[$i$], ..., *string_array*[$n-1$].

The selection sort algorithm repeats the above process for integer variable $i = 0, 1, ..., n-2$. After the repetitions,

- element *string_array*[0] contains the smallest string among *string_array*[0], ..., *string_array*[$n-1$],
- element *string_array*[1] contains the smallest string among *string_array*[1], ..., *string_array*[$n-1$],
- ...,
- element *string_array*[$n-2$] contains the smallest string among *string_array* [$n-2$], *string_array*[$n-1$],

Thus, *string_array* is sorted with the selection sort algorithm.

The following class, class *SelectionSort*, implements the selection sort algorithm in static method *sort*. The method uses two for loops, one embedding the other. The outer loop

```
      for (int i = 0; i < n-1; i++)
```

limits subarray *string_array*[*i*], *string_array*[*i*+1], ..., *string_array*[*n*−1]. The inner loop

```
for (int j = i+1; j <= n-1; j++)
```

determines the minimum element, denoted with *string_array*[*k*], in the subarray. Then, the outer loop body swaps elements *string_array*[*i*] and *string_array*[*k*].

Local variable *current* is initialized with *string_array*[*i*]. Since the inner loop compares the *current* minimum element with all the elements *string_array*[*i*+1], ..., *string_array*[*n*−1] in the worst case, the total number of data comparisons made by the *sort* method is $(n-1) + (n-2) + ... + 1 = 0.5 \times n^2 - 0.5 \times n$, which is $O(n^2)$.

```java
public class SelectionSort {
    public static void main(String[] args) {
        String[] names = {"Cbc", "Bbc", "Abc"};
        SelectionSort.sort(names);
        for (int i=0; i < names.length; i++){
            System.out.print(names[i]+" ");
        }
    }

    /** Sorts string array with selection sort */
    public static void sort(String[] string_array)
    {
        int n = string_array.length;
        for (int i = 0; i < n-1; i++) {
            String current = string_array[i];
            int k = i;
            for (int j=i+1; j <= n-1; j++){
                if (current.compareTo
                               (string_array[j]) > 0){
                    k = j;
                    current = string_array[k];
                }
            }
            string_array[k] = string_array[i];
            string_array[i] = current;
        }
    }
}
```

**Exercise 7.2** The selection sort algorithm applies to both arrays and vectors. The selection *sort* method in the above class selects the minimum element from each subarray. Implement the selection sort algorithm for a vector of strings by selecting the maximum element *string_vector*[*k*] in subarray *string_vector*[0], ..., *string_vector*[*i*] and swapping *string_vector*[*k*] and *string_vector*[*i*]. The selection repeats for integer variable $i = n-1, n-2, ..., 1$, where *n* is the size of *string_vector*.

## 7.1.1.3 MergeSort

The merge sort algorithm applies for arrays, vectors, and linked linear data structures. It can be applied to sort secondary storage files as well as data structures in memory. The following class, *MergeSort*, implements merge sort algorithm in static method *sort*. In Section 7.1.2, we shall implement the algorithm to sort files that are assumed too huge to be placed in memory for internal sort.

The following *sort* method is recursively defined. The parameters of the method represent a *string_array* and two indexes *low* and *high* in the array. The method is to sort subarray *string_array*[*low*], *string_array*[*low*+1], ..., *string_array*[*high*].

If *high* ≤ *low*, the subarray contains at most one element and is sorted.

If *high* > *low*, the *sort* method divides subarray *string_array*[*low*], *string_array*[*low*+1], ..., *string_array*[*high*] into two subarrays

> *string_array*[*low*], ..., *string_array*[*mid*]
> *string_array*[*mid*+1], ..., *string_array*[*high*]

where *mid* = (*low* + *high*)/2. The *sort* method recursively sorts the subarrays with statements

> *sort*(*string_array*, *low*, *mid*)
> *sort*(*string_array*, *mid*+1, *high*).

Then, the merge sort algorithm merges the two sorted subarrays. It uses indexes *i* and *j* to keep track of the front elements in the two sorted subarrays. The smaller one of elements *string_array*[*i*] and *string_array*[*j*] is the smallest among *string_array*[*i*], ..., *string_array*[*mid*], *string_array*[*j*], ..., *string_array*[*high*]. The smallest element is moved into an array referenced with local variable *temp*, and then index *i* or *j* is advanced by one. By repeatedly moving elements from the two sorted subarrays to the end of array *temp*, the two sorted subarrays can be merged to array *temp*, which is sorted. After copying the elements of array *temp* to subarray *string_array*[*low*], *string_array*[*low*+1], ..., *string_array*[*high*], the subarray of *string_array* becomes sorted.

```
public class MergeSort {
    public static void main(String[] args) {
        String[] names = {"Cbc", "Bbc", "Abc"};
        MergeSort.sort(names, 0, names.length-1);
        for (int i = 0; i < names.length; i++){
            System.out.print(names[i]+" ");
        }
    }


    /** Sorts a string array with merge sort.*/
    public static void sort(String[]
                string_array, int low, int high) {
        if (high <= low) return;
        int mid = (low + high)/2;
        sort(string_array, low, mid);
        sort(string_array, mid+1, high);
```

```
int i = low, j = mid+1;
String[] temp = new String[high-low+1];
int k = 0;
while (i <= mid && j <= high) {
    if (string_array[i].compareTo
                    (string_array[j])<0)
        temp[k++] = string_array[i++];
    else temp[k++] = string_array[j++];
}
while (i <= mid) {
    temp[k++] = string_array[i++];
}
while (j <= high) {
    temp[k++] = string_array[j++];
}
for (k=0, i=low; k <= high-low; k++, i++)
    string_array[i] = temp[k];
    }
}
```

**Proposition 7.1** The merge *sort* method invoked with statement

   *sort*(*string_array*, *low*, *high*)

sorts the subarray *string_array*[*low*], *string_array*[*low*+1], ...,
*string_array*[*high*].

*Proof*: By induction on size $n = high - low + 1$. If $n \leq 1$, the subarray contains at
most one element and it is sorted. If $n > 1$, statements

   *sort*(*string_array*, *low*, *mid*)
   *sort*(*string_array*, *mid*+1, *high*).

sort subarrays

   *string_array*[*low*], ..., *string_array*[*mid*]
   *string_array*[*mid*+1], ..., *string_array*[*high*].

by the induction hypothesis. The above two sorted subarrays are merged into
a sorted array referenced with *temp*, which is copied to subarray
*string_array*[*low*], *string_array*[*low*+1], ..., *string_array*[*high*]. Thus, the
*sort* method sorts the argument subarray.                                    □

We now discuss the worst-case time complexity $f(n)$ of the merge *sort*
method, where $n$ is the length of the subarray to be sorted. We use $f(n)$ to denote
the number of data comparisons made by the method for a *string_array* of length
$n$. Without loss of generality, we assume $n = high - low + 1 = 2^k$ for an integer $k \geq$
0. Note that $k = \log n$. The *sort* method makes $n - 1$ comparisons to merge the
sorted subarrays

   *string_array*[*low*], ..., *string_array*[*mid*]
   *string_array*[*mid*+1], ..., *string_array*[*high*].

Function $f(n)$ satisfies equations

$$f(n) = 2 \times f(n/2) + (n - 1) \text{ for } n > 1,$$
$$f(1) = 0,$$

The solution is $f(n) = (n-1) + 2 \times f(n/2) = (n-1) + (n-2) + 2^2 \times f(n/2^2) = \ldots = (n-1) + (n-2) + \ldots + (n - 2^k) = (k-1) \times n + 1 \in O(n \log n)$, which is better than the time complexity of insertion sort, selection sort, and bubble sort in the worst cases.

### 7.1.1.4 Quick sort

The input data for the quick sort algorithm is a subarray with elements *string_array*[*low*], *string_array*[*low*+1], ..., *string_array*[*high*]. If *low* ≥ *high*, the subarray is sorted and the sorting is done. Otherwise, the quick sort algorithm selects an element from the subarray as *pivot* and uses the pivot to divide the elements in the subarray into two parts. One part consists of elements that are less than or equal to the pivot, the other consists of elements that are greater than or equal to the pivot. The quick sort algorithm is recursively applied to sort each of the two parts.

The pivot selected by quick sort could be any element in the subarray that is to be sorted. In the following implementation of quick sort, we select the middle element of the subarray.

We now describe how the quick sort algorithm uses a pivot to separate array elements. It uses two local variables, *left_index* and *right_index*. The index variables are initialized to *low* and *high*, respectively, to point at the left-most and right-most elements in the subarray to be sorted. The quick sort algorithm repeats the following process until *left_index* > *right_index:*

- Continuously increase *left_index* by 1 until *left_index* > *high* or *string_array* [*left_index*] ≥ *pivot*. The step is implemented with Java source code
  ```
  while (left_index <= high && string_array
                  [left_index].compareTo(pivot)<0)
      left_index++;
  ```

- Continuously decrease *right_index* by 1 until *right_index* < *low* or *string_array*[*right_index*] ≤ *pivot*. The step is implemented with
  ```
  while (right_index >= low && string_array
                  [right_index].compareTo(pivot)>0)
      right_index--;
  ```

- If *left_index* ≤ *right_index*, it must be the case that *string_array*[*left_index*] ≥ *pivot* and *string_array*[*right_index*] ≤ *pivot*. The quick sort algorithm swaps elements *string_array*[*left_index*] and *string_array*[*right_index*] if the two elements are not equal. Then, it increases *left_index* by 1, and decreases *right_index* by 1.

After repetitions of the above process, the input subarray is divided into two subarrays

*string_array*[*low*], ..., *string_array*[*right_index*]
*string_array*[*left_index*], ..., *string_array*[*high*]

The elements in the first subarray are less than or equal to the pivot. The elements in the second are greater than or equal to the pivot. Note that after both subarrays are sorted, subarray *string_array*[*low*], *string_array*[*low*+1], ..., *string_array* [*high*] is sorted. We recursively apply the quick sort algorithm for each of the above two subarrays.

Several steps in an execution of the quick *sort* method for a string array are shown in Fig. 7.1. After the quick *sort* method is started with expression *sort*(*string_array*, 0, 8), the method decides *pivot Cbc*, which is shown in Fig. 7.1a. Method *sort* initializes *left_index* and *right_index* with *low* and *high*, which are equal to 0 and 8, respectively. It moves *left_index* toward right and moves *right_index* toward left. Since string *Wbc* is greater than *pivot* and *Abc* is less than *pivot*, method *sort* swaps them before it increases *left_index* by 1 and decreases *right_index* by 1. The situation is shown in Fig. 7.1b. After swapping elements *string_array*[1] and *string_array*[8], method *sort* increases *left_index* until *left_index* becomes 2 and decreases *right_index* until *right_index* becomes 4. The situation is shown in Fig. 7.1c. After swapping elements *string_array*[2] and *string_array*[4], method *sort* increases *left_index* until *left_index* is equal to 3 and decreases *right_index* until *right_index* is equal to 2, which is shown in Fig. 7.1d. We now have *left_index* > *right_index*. The quick *sort* method recursively invokes itself in statements

> *sort*(*string_array*, 0, 2)
> *sort*(*string_array*, 3, 8),

which are shown in Fig. 7.1e–f. Readers are encouraged to follow the executions of the recursive invocations of method *sort*.

```java
public class QuickSort {
    public static void main(String[] args) {
        String[] names = {"Cbc", "Bbc", "Abc"};
        QuickSort.sort(names, 0, names.length-1);
        for (int i=0; i < names.length; i++){
            System.out.print(names[i]+" ");
        }
    }

    /** Sorts a string array with quick sort */
    public static void sort(String[]
                string_array, int low, int high) {
        if (low >= high) return;

        int left_index = low;
        int right_index = high;
        String pivot = string_array[(low+high)/2];
```

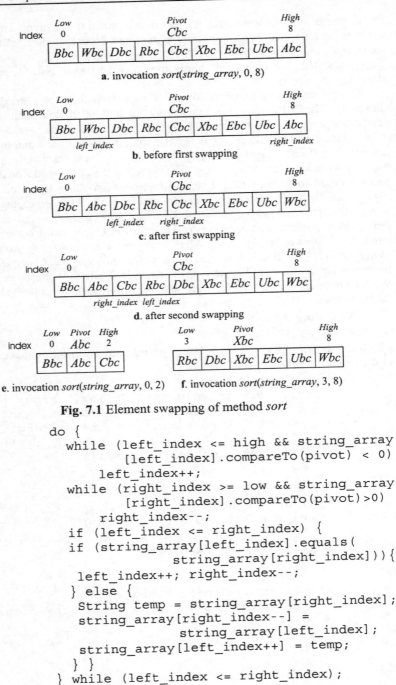

**Fig. 7.1** Element swapping of method *sort*

```
do {
  while (left_index <= high && string_array
          [left_index].compareTo(pivot) < 0)
      left_index++;
  while (right_index >= low && string_array
          [right_index].compareTo(pivot)>0)
      right_index--;
  if (left_index <= right_index) {
  if (string_array[left_index].equals(
          string_array[right_index])){
   left_index++; right_index--;
  } else {
   String temp = string_array[right_index];
   string_array[right_index--] =
          string_array[left_index];
   string_array[left_index++] = temp;
  } }
} while (left_index <= right_index);
```

```
    // recursive invocation of quick sort
    sort(string_array, low, right_index);
    sort(string_array, left_index, high);
  }
}
```

As in Proposition 7.1, we can prove the correctness of method *sort* by a simple induction on the length $n = high - low + 1$ of the array to be sorted.

One of the worst cases for method *sort* is that the selected *pivot* element is the smallest element in a subarray to be sorted. Therefore, one of the two recursive calls has an input subarray of size one and the other input subarray has one element less than the input subarray of the calling invocation. Since an execution of method *sort* compares *pivot* with each element in the subarray to be sorted, method *sort* makes

$$n + (n - 1) + \ldots + 1 = 0.5 \times n^2 + 0.5 \times n \in O(n^2)$$

comparisons. Despite its worst-case complexity $O(n^2)$, the average complexity of the quick *sort* method is $O(n \log n)$. The proof of the average complexity needs probability theory and statistics. It is omitted here. Experience of programmers has shown that quick sort algorithm is a fast, practical sorting algorithm.

**Exercise 7.3** The quick *sort* method does not require the input *string_array* consist of distinct values. In Fig. 7.1, we show how to follow (trace) the execution of the method. Trace the method for an input *string_array* with five elements, all of which hold the same string.

## 7.1.1.5 Heap Sort

The heap sort algorithm depends on a hierarchical interpretation of arrays or vectors. An element in an array has an index $i$. We regard the elements at indexes $2 \times i + 1$ and $2 \times i + 2$ as the left and right child of the element at index $i$. The interpretation is illustrated with Fig. 7.2, where a parent is connected to its children with arrowhead links. Note that the parent of an element indexed at $j$ has index $(j-1)/2$ in Java. (The Java interpreter rounds the quotient $(j-1)/2$ to an integer.)

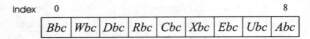

**a.** a linear representation of *string_array*

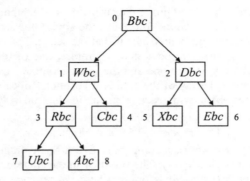

**b.** a hierarchical representation of *string_array*

**Fig. 7.2** Hierarchical representation of array

In terms of the hierarchical representation of arrays, an array is a *heap* if the value in each element is not less than the values in its child elements. The largest value in a heap is in element 0. A heap is shown in Fig. 7.3. It rearranges the values contained in the array shown in Fig. 7.2.

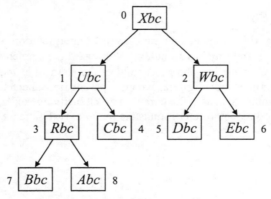

**Fig. 7.3** A heap converted from the array in Fig. 7.2

We can convert an array named *string_array* of length $n$ into a heap by building a series of heaps $H_i$ with $0 \le i \le n-1$ from the array. Each of the heaps has one more element than its predecessor. Specifically, $H_0$ consists of element *string_array*[0]. Value in element *string_array*[$i$] is added to $H_{i-1}$ by sifting the value upward in $H_{i-1}$. The sifting process is described as follows, where the sifted value *string_array*[$i$] is denoted with *current*.

1. *int j = i.*
2. If *string_array*[(*j*–1)/2] < *current*, move the value in element *string_array*[(*j*–1)/2] downward into element *string_array*[*j*] and assign *j* with (*j*–1)/2. Thus, the value in parent is moved downward by one level. Repeat the step until *j* becomes 0 or *string_array*[(*j*–1)/2] ≥ *current*.
3. Place *current* into element *string_array*[*j*].

Fig. 7.4 shows two of the heaps, $H_4$ and $H_5$. Heap $H_5$ is derived from $H_4$ by adding element *string_array*[5] to $H_4$ and sifting it upward in $H_4$.

The heap $H_{n-1}$ created by the above process for *string_array* contains all the elements of *string_array*. The largest value in *string_array* is in the top element of heap $H_{n-1}$. The heap sort algorithm swaps *string_array*[0] and *string_array*[*n*–1] so that the largest value in *string_array* is placed at index *n*–1. After swapping, the subarray *string_array*[0], ..., *string_array*[*n*–2] can be rebuilt into a heap by sifting the value in *string_array*[0] downward. Denote the value with *temp*, and the last index in the subarray with *last_index*. The heap sort algorithm performs the sift-down process as follows:

1. *int i = 0.*
2. Assume element *string_array*[*i*] has two children, which are *string_array*[2 × *i* +1] and *string_array*[2 × *i* + 2]. Find the larger value in *string_array*[2 × *i* +1] and *string_array*[2 × *i* + 2]. Assume the larger value is at index *j*, which is either 2 × *i* + 1 or 2 × *i* + 2.

    If element *string_array*[*i*] has only one child, which is *string_array*[2 × *i* +1], assign *j* with 2 × *i* +1.

    If *temp* < *string_array*[*j*], move the value in *string_array*[*j*] into element *string_array*[*i*], and assign *i* with *j*.

    Repeat the step until *string_array*[*i*] has no child in the array *string_array*[0], ..., *string_array*[*last_index*] or *temp* ≥ *string_array*[*j*].
3. Place *temp* into *string_array*[*i*].

Thus, the subarray between indexes 0 and *last_index* can be rebuilt into a heap.

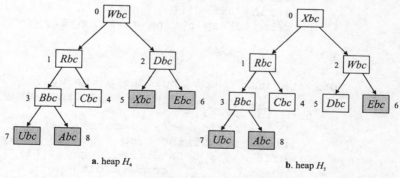

**a.** heap $H_4$          **b.** heap $H_5$

**Fig. 7.4** Heaps $H_4$ and $H_5$

With the above preparations, we can describe the heap sort algorithm as follows. We assume a *string_array* and length *n* for the array.

1. Build heaps $H_0$, $H_1$, ..., $H_{n-1}$ in sequence from the *string_array*.
2. For $i = n-1$, $n-2$, ..., 1, swap *string_array*[0] and *string_array*[*i*] and rebuild subarray *string_array*[0], ..., *string_array*[*i*–1] into a heap by sifting the value at *string_array*[0] down.

The following class, *HeapSort*, implements the heap sort algorithm in static method *sort*. The first step of the algorithm is implemented with private static method *buildHeap(String[] string_array)*, which transforms *string_array* into a heap. The second step is implemented by a loop. In the loop body, method *rebuildHeap(string_array, 0, i–1)* is invoked to rebuild the subarray *string_array*[0], ..., *string_array*[*i*–1] into a heap by sifting *string_array*[0] down. Then, the references in *string_array*[0] and *string_array*[*i*–1] are swapped.

```java
public class HeapSort {
    public static void main(String[] args) {
        String[] names = {"Cbc", "Bbc", "Abc"};
        HeapSort.sort(names);
        for (int i = 0; i < names.length; i++) {
            System.out.print(names[i]+" ");
        }
    }

    /** Sorts a string array with heap sort */
    public static void sort(String[] string_array)
    {
        buildHeap(string_array);
        String temp;
        for (int i = string_array.length - 1;
            i > 0; i--) {
            temp = string_array[0];
            string_array[0] = string_array[i];
            string_array[i] = temp;
            rebuildHeap(string_array, i-1);
        }
    }

    private static void buildHeap(String[]
                                string_array) {
        for (int i = 1;
            i < string_array.length; i++) {
            int j = i; String temp = string_array[i];
            while ( j > 0 && string_array[(j-1)/2].
                            compareTo(temp) < 0) {
                string_array[j] = string_array[(j-1)/2];
                j = (j-1)/2;
            }
```

```
            string_array[j] = temp;
        }
    }

    private static void rebuildHeap(String[]
                string_array, int last_index) {
        int i = 0, j;
        String temp = string_array[0];
        while (2 * i + 1 <= last_index) {
            if (2 * i + 2 <= last_index) {
                if (string_array[2 * i + 1].
                    compareTo(string_array[2*i+2])>=0)
                    j= 2 * i + 1;
                else j = 2 * i + 2;
            }
            else j = 2 * i + 1;
            if (temp.compareTo(string_array[j])>=0)
                break;
            else {
                string_array[i] = string_array[j];
                i = j;
            }
        }
        string_array[i] = temp;
    }
}
```

We now estimate the time complexity of the heap *sort* method, which implements the heap sort algorithm. Without loss of generality, we assume the argument *string_array* has length $n = 2^k - 1$ for some integer $k \geq 0$. The number of levels in the hierarchical representation of *string_array* is $k = \log(n+1)$.

To build each of the heaps $H_0$, $H_1$, ..., $H_{n-1}$, the while loop in the *buildHeap* method is repeated at most $k - 1$ times, and each repetition makes one data comparison in expression *string_array*$[(j-1)/2]$.*compareTo*(*temp*). The total number of data comparisons made by method *buildHeap* is at most $n \times (k - 1)$.

The *rebuildHeap*(*string_array*, *last_index*) method rebuilds subarray *string_array*[0], ..., *string_array*[*last_index*] into a heap, where *last_index* satisfies $1 \leq$ *last_index* $< n-1$. The method body uses a while loop to sift the value at *string_array*[0] downward. For each repetition of the loop body, at most two data comparisons are made with expressions *string_array*[2 * $i$ + 1].*compareTo* (*string_array*[2 * $i$ + 2]) and *temp.compareTo*(*string_array* [$j$]). Since the while loop body will be repeated at most $k - 1$ times, an invocation of method *rebuildHeap* takes at most $2 \times (k - 1)$ units of time for data comparisons.

In the heap *sort* method, method *rebuildHeap* is repeated $n-1$ times. The total number of data comparisons made by the method for a *string_array* of length $n$ is bounded by $3 \times n \times (k - 1)$, which is $O(n \log n)$.

**Exercise 7.4** Create a class that defines a static method *sort* to sort arrays of person objects based on the person names. The method implements the heap sort algorithm. Class *Person* is defined in Example 1.18. Person names are strings.

## 7.1.2 External Merge Sort

### *7.1.2.1 Reader and Writer Classes*

In the above discussion, we assume that the whole data to be sorted can be placed in a computer memory. We use a data structure such as an array or vector to hold the data in memory. The data elements are moved inside computer memory by a sorting method.

We now deal with the situation that the data to be sorted is too huge to be placed in a computer memory. We assume the data is stored in a massive secondary storage such as a disk. The file *mydata.dat* holds the data elements in sequence. To simplify the presentation of the sorting algorithm, we assume the data elements in file *mydata.dat* are strings, which are separated with blank spaces.

To sort the strings in a file, we read the strings from the file and store them in other files. Java has standard classes to support formatted data reading and writing. In the file *sort* method, we rely on classes *FileReader* and *FileWriter* to read or write strings for files.

Class *Reader* is an abstract class defined in package *java.io*. It extends class *Object*. It is designed for reading character streams. Class *FileReader* extends class *InputStreamReader*, which extends class *Reader*. An instance of class *FileReader* can be created with one of the constructors:

>      *FileReader(File)*
>      *FileReader(FileDescriptor)*
>      *FileReader(String)*.

For example, we shall use statement

```
FileReader reader = new FileReader("mydata.dat");
```

to create a file reader, which reads file *mydata.dat*.

Class *FileReader* inherits methods *read*() and *read*(*char*[], *int*, *int*) to read a character or characters from a file. It inherits methods *close* to close a file and method *ready* to test if a file is ready to be read.

In addition to subclasses *InputStreamReader* and *FileReader*, class *Reader* has subclasses *BufferedReader*, *LineNumberReader*, *CharArrayReader*, *FilterReader*, *PushbackReader*, *PipedReader*, and *StringReader*.

To read formatted data from a file reader, we can use a stream tokenizer to parse the file reader. Class *StreamTokenizer* is defined in package *java.io*. It extends class *Object*. An instance of the class can be created with constructor

>      *StreamTokenizer(Reader)*.

Assume variable *reader* references a file reader. We use statement

```
StreamTokenizer tokenizer =
                new StreamTokenizer(reader);
```

to create a stream tokenizer and assign it to variable *tokenizer*. The *tokenizer* parses the file represented by *reader*.

A stream tokenizer recognizes identifiers, numbers, quoted strings, and various comment styles. A byte read by a tokenizer is regarded as a character, which can be used to look for white space, alphabetic, numeric, string quote, and comment character.

The input mechanism supported by a tokenizer consists of instance method *nextToken()* and instance variables *nval*, *sval*, *ttype*. Method *nextToken* parses the next token. The type of the next token can be found in instance variable *ttype*. If the next token is a numeric value, instance variable *nval* holds the numeric value; otherwise, variable *sval* holds the next string token. For example, we use code

```
tokenizer.nextToken();
if (tokenizer.ttype != StreamTokenizer.TT_EOF)
   System.out.print(tokenizer.sval.toString()+" ");
```

to test if the next token denotes the end of the file stream and, if it does not, print the next string.

A reader in class *FileReader* is used to read characters from a file. A writer in class *FileWriter* can be used to write characters into a file. Class *FileWriter* is in package *java.io*. It extends class *OutputStreamWriter*, which extends class *Writer*. Class *Writer* extends class *Object*. It defines abstract methods *flush* and *close* for flushing written bytes to target storage or closing the storage. It overloads method *write* for writing characters, character arrays, integers, and strings.

Class *OutputStreamWriter* defines methods for writing characters to output streams. It also defines methods *close* and *flush*. An instance of class *OutputStreamWriter* converts written characters to bytes. It uses a buffer for the bytes. Method *flush* flushes the buffered bytes to the target output stream. The class *OutputStreamWriter* overloads the *write* method for writing character arrays, integers, and strings to an output stream.

Class *FileWriter* can be used to create output stream writers for character files. An object of the class can be created with one of the constructors

*FileWriter(File)*
*FileWriter(FileDescriptor)*
*FileWriter(String fileName)*
*FileWriter(String fileName, boolean append)*.

Class *FileWriter* inherits methods *close*, *flush*, and *write* from class *OutputStreamWriter*.

We shall use the following code to write strings from array *names* to data file *mydata.dat*.

```
FileWriter writer = new FileWriter("mydata.dat");
for (int i = 0; i < names.length; i++) {
    writer.write(names[i],0,names[i].length());
    writer.write(' ');
```

```
        }
        writer.close();
```

In the code, we invoke method *write* repeatedly to write elements of array *names* to the data file. Note that the method invocation *write(s, 0, s.length)* writes the characters in string *s* indexed at 0, ..., *s.length*–1 to a file.

In addition to subclasses *OutputStreamWriter* and *FileWriter*, the abstract class *Writer* has subclasses *BufferedWriter*, *CharArrayWriter*, *FilterWriter*, *Piped-Writer*, *PrintWriter*, and *StringWriter*.


## 7.1.2.2 Sorting Files

We now consider the problem of sorting a file with a limited memory. Data file *mydata.dat* consists of strings, which are separated with space. We apply a merge sort algorithm, which uses two auxiliary files *temp1.dat* and *temp2.dat*. The merge sort algorithm repeats the two-step process:

1.  Split the contents of file *mydata.dat* into files *temp1.dat* and *temp2.dat*.
2.  Merge files *temp1.dat* and *temp2.dat* into file *mydata.dat*.

In the first step, the algorithm reads strings one by one from file *mydata.dat* and alternately places them into files *temp1.dat* and *temp2.dat*. At the end of the step, all the strings in file *mydata.dat* are moved into files *temp1.dat* and *temp2.dat*. The difference between the numbers of strings in *temp1.dat* and *temp2.dat* is at most 1.

The second step compares the first string remaining in file *temp1.dat* with that in *temp2.dat*. Suppose the smaller one of the two strings is *string1* from *temp1.dat*. The algorithm remembers the last string that has been placed in file *mydata.dat*. Before the algorithm moves *string1* from *temp1.dat* to *mydata.dat*, it compares *string1* with the last string in *mydata.dat*. If *string1* is smaller than the last string, a boolean variable *sorted* is set with *false*.

The spilt-merge process starts by setting the variable *sorted* with *true*. It is repeated until the flag *sorted* is still *true* at the end of the second step.

The following class, *FileMergeSort*, implements the merge sort algorithm with method *sort(String fileName)*. The method sorts the strings in file *fileName*. It uses method *split* to separate the strings into files *temp1.dat* and *temp2.dat*.

When method *sort* merges files *temp1.dat* and *temp2.dat*, it uses variable *lastString* to record the last string that has been placed in file *fileName*. It uses variables *string1* and *string2* to reference the first strings remaining in *temp1.dat* and *temp2.dat*, respectively. The *merge* method places either *string1* or *string2*, whichever is smaller, into file *fileName*. If file *temp1.dat* or *temp2.dat* has been exhausted in the merge step, the *sort* method invokes either method *merge1* or *merge2* to move the remaining strings from file *temp1.dat* or *temp2.dat* to file *fileName*.

```
        import java.io.*;
        public class FileMergeSort {
            public static void main(String[] args) {
                try {
```

```java
        // prepare test data file mydata.dat
        String[] names =
            {"Cbc", "Bbc", "Xbc", "Abc", "Dbc"};
        FileWriter writer =
            new FileWriter("mydata.dat");
        for (int i = 0; i < names.length; i++) {
            writer.write(names[i], 0,
                            names[i].length());
            writer.write(' ');
        }
        writer.close();
    } catch(IOException e) { }
    (new FileMergeSort()).sort("mydata.dat");
    try { // Displays strings in mydata.dat
        FileReader reader =
                new FileReader("mydata.dat");
        StreamTokenizer tokenizer =
                new StreamTokenizer(reader);
        do {
            tokenizer.nextToken();
            if (tokenizer.ttype !=
                        StreamTokenizer.TT_EOF)
                System.out.print(tokenizer.
                        sval.toString()+" ");
        } while (tokenizer.ttype !=
                    StreamTokenizer.TT_EOF);
        reader.close();
    } catch(IOException e) { }
}

/** Sorts a file of strings with merge sort */
public void sort(String fileName) {
    try {
    while (!sorted) {

    // splits a file into two files
    reader0 = new FileReader(fileName);
    tokenizer0 = new StreamTokenizer(reader0);
    writer1 = new FileWriter("temp1.dat");
    writer2 = new FileWriter("temp2.dat");
    split();
    reader0.close();
    writer1.close();
    writer2.close();

    // merges temp1.dat and temp2.dat
    writer0 = new FileWriter(fileName);
```

```
reader1 = new FileReader("temp1.dat");
reader2 = new FileReader("temp2.dat");
tokenizer1 = new StreamTokenizer(reader1);
tokenizer2 = new StreamTokenizer(reader2);

/* Prepares for merging so that
 * 1) lastString always keeps the last string
 *    in writer0;
 * 2) int variable fromFile records from which
 *    reader the last string is from;
 * 3) if (string1 != null), string1 is the
 *    first string in file temp1.dat that has
 *    not be merged into writer0;
 * 4) if (string2 != null), string2 is the
 *    first string in file temp2.dat that has
 *    not be merged into writer0.
 */
    lastString = string1 = string2 = null;
    fromFile = 0; sorted = true;
    tokenizer1.nextToken();
    if (tokenizer1.ttype !=
                StreamTokenizer.TT_EOF)
        string1 = tokenizer1.sval.toString();
    tokenizer2.nextToken();
    if (tokenizer2.ttype !=
                StreamTokenizer.TT_EOF)
        string2 = tokenizer2.sval.toString();
    if (string1 != null && string2 != null) {
        if (string1.compareTo(string2) <= 0) {
            lastString = string1;
            writer0.write(lastString,
                        0,lastString.length());
            writer0.write(' ');
            fromFile = 1;
        } else {
            lastString = string2;
            writer0.write(lastString,
                        0, lastString.length());
            writer0.write(' ');
            fromFile = 2;
        }
    } else if (string1 != null) {
        lastString = string1;
        writer0.write(lastString,
                    0,lastString.length());
        writer0.write(' ');
        fromFile = 1; }
```

```
      else if (string2 != null) {
        lastString = string2;
        writer0.write(lastString,
                      0,lastString.length());
        writer0.write(' ');
        fromFile = 2; }

      do {
        if (fromFile == 1) {
           tokenizer1.nextToken();
           if (tokenizer1.ttype !=
                         StreamTokenizer.TT_EOF)
           string1 = tokenizer1.sval.toString();
           else string1 = null;
        }
        if (fromFile == 2) {
           tokenizer2.nextToken();
           if (tokenizer2.ttype !=
                         StreamTokenizer.TT_EOF)
           string2 = tokenizer2.sval.toString();
           else string2 = null;
        }
        if (string1 != null && string2 != null)
           // places one string to mydata.dat
           merge();
        else if (string1 != null) merge1();
            else if (string2 != null) merge2();
      } while (string1 != null
               && string2 != null);

      writer0.close();
      reader1.close();
      reader2.close();
      } } catch(Exception e) { }
}

//separates input to temp1.dat and temp2.dat
private void split() {
    int writtenFile = 1;
    for (;;) {
       try {
       tokenizer0.nextToken();
       if (tokenizer0.ttype!=
                   StreamTokenizer.TT_EOF) {
       String outString =
                   tokenizer0.sval.toString();
       if (writtenFile == 1) {
```

```
               writer1.write(outString,
                            0, outString.length());
               writer1.write(' ');
               writtenFile = 2;
               }
            else {
               writer2.write(outString,
                            0, outString.length());
               writer2.write(' ');
               writtenFile = 1;
            }
         }
         else return;
         } catch(IOException e) { }
      }
   }

   private void merge() {
      if (string1.compareTo(string2) <= 0){
         if (string1.compareTo(lastString) < 0)
            sorted = false;
         lastString = string1; fromFile = 1;
      } else {
         if (string2.compareTo(lastString) < 0)
            sorted = false;
         lastString = string2; fromFile = 2;
      }
      try {
         writer0.write(lastString,
                       0,lastString.length());
         writer0.write(' ');
      } catch(IOException e) { }
   }

   private void merge1() {
      try {
      while (string1 != null) {
         if (lastString.compareTo(string1) > 0)
            sorted = false;
         lastString = string1;
         writer0.write(lastString,
                       0, lastString.length());
         writer0.write(' ');
         tokenizer1.nextToken();
         if (tokenizer1.ttype !=
                       StreamTokenizer.TT_EOF)
            string1 = tokenizer1.sval.toString();
```

```java
        else string1 = null;
      }
    } catch(IOException e) { }
  }

  private void merge2() {
    try {
      while (string2 != null) {
        if (lastString.compareTo(string2) > 0)
          sorted = false;
        lastString = string2;
        writer0.write(lastString,
                      0, lastString.length());
        writer0.write(' ');
        tokenizer2.nextToken();
        if (tokenizer2.ttype !=
                      StreamTokenizer.TT_EOF)
          string2 = tokenizer2.sval.toString();
        else string2 = null;
      }
    } catch(IOException e) { }
  }

  private FileReader reader0;
  private StreamTokenizer tokenizer0;
  private FileWriter writer0;

  private FileReader reader1, reader2;
  private StreamTokenizer tokenizer1,tokenizer2;
  private FileWriter writer1, writer2;

  private String lastString, string1, string2;
  private int fromFile;

  private boolean sorted;
}
```

We now argue the correctness of the above file merge sort method. Assume the first pair of adjacent strings that are not in order in file *fileName* are $s_k$ and $s_{k+1}$, i.e., strings $s_i$ in file *fileName* satisfy

$s_i \leq s_{i+1}$ for $0 \leq i < k$ and $s_k > s_{k+1}$,

After file *fileName* is split into files *temp1.dat* and *temp2.dat* and then *temp1.dat* and *temp2.dat* are merged into *fileName*, file *fileName* contains

$s_0, s_1, \ldots, s_{k-1}, s_{k+1}, s'_0, \ldots, s'_i, s_k, \ldots$

where

$s_0 \leq s_1 \leq \ldots \leq s_{k-1} \leq s_k, s_{k+1} < s_k, s'_j \leq s_k$ for $i \geq 0, 0 \leq j \leq i$.

The merging mechanism moves $s_k$ behind strings $s_{k+1}$, $s'_0$, ..., $s'_i$. Thus, the order between $s_k$ and $s_{k+1}$ is corrected by the split-merge. Each execution of the split-merge process corrects the ordering for at least a pair of strings. By repeating the process, method *sort* can sort strings in the file *fileName*.

The file merge sort method may repeat the split-merge process for $n - 1$ times in the worst case, where $n$ is the number of strings in input file *fileName*.

Files *temp1.dat* and *temp2.dat* used in the above method are called buckets. We may improve the method by using more than two buckets when splitting a file. Another possible improvement for the method is using a buffer for each bucket and reading in as many strings from buckets as possible into buffers in memory. Sort a buffer before merging the strings in the buffer with strings in other buffers into file *fileName*. Buffers can also be used in method *split* to reduce the number of secondary storage accesses. We leave the improvements for the *sort* method as exercises.

**Exercise 7.5** In method *sort(String fileName)*, we use two temporary files (buckets). Overload method *sort* with signature *sort(String fileName, int number)* in class *FileMergeSort*. The new method sorts file *fileName* by using a given *number* of temporary files. (Hint: dynamically construct strings, which are used as temporary file names.)

**Exercise 7.6** Method *sort(String fileName)* reads one string from a temporary file and writes the string into file *fileName* before it reads another string from the temporary file. Improve the method by reading multiple strings from each temporary file into a buffer, which is an array. Merge the strings from the buffers into file *fileName*.

# 7.2 Searching Linear Data Structures

## 7.2.1 Searching

As described in Section 6.3.1, to find a value $v$ from a sequence of values, we can linearly search the sequence for $v$. In the worst case, searching an array or vector takes time $O(n)$, where $n$ is the size of the array or vector.

Linear search applies for any linear data structure, which allows visiting its elements in sequence. For example, in the next section we present singly and doubly linked lists. We can search a linked list for a value $v$ with linear search.

A drawback of linear search is its time complexity $O(n)$, where $n$ is the size of array or vector to be searched. Linear search is slow compared with binary search and search methods to be presented shortly. In Section 6.3.4, we learn that the time taken by binary search for a value in a sorted array is $O(\log n)$. We now present two variations of the binary search method.

## 7.2.2 Fibonaccian Search

The binary search method compares the middle element in a search range with a target value $s$. It divides the search range evenly.

Fibonacci numbers $f(i)$ map nonnegative integers $i \geq 0$ to nonnegative integers $f(i)$ with formulas

$$f(0) = 0, f(1) = 1,$$
$$f(i+2) = f(i+1) + f(i) \text{ for } i \geq 0.$$

Assume the size of a search range is $f(i+2)$. The Fibonaccian search algorithm divides the search range to two parts, one with size $f(i)$ and the other $f(i+1)$. By comparing search key $s$ with the last element of the first part or the first element of the second part, we can find $s$ or we can eliminate either the first or the second part from the search.

The following class, class *FibonaccianSearch*, implements the Fibonaccian search algorithm in static method *search*. Specifically, the method *search*(*String*[] *string_array*, *int low*, *int high*, *String s*) searches for string $s$ in subarray *string_array*[*low*], ..., *string_array*[*high*]. It uses source code

```
fib_low = 0; fib_high = 1;
while (fib_low + fib_high < high - low + 1){
    temp = fib_low;
    fib_low = fib_high;
    fib_high += temp;
}
```

to find the smallest Fibonacci number $f(i+2)$ such that $f(i+2) = fib\_low + fib\_high \geq high - low + 1$. The *search* method compares the target $s$ with element *string_array*[*low* + *fib_low*]. If the strings are equal, string $s$ is found at index *low* + *fib_low* and the method returns index *low* + *fib_low*. Otherwise, if $s$ is greater than *string_array*[*low*+*fib_low*], the method discards subarray *string_array*[*low*], ..., *string_array*[*low*+*fib_low*] from the search; if $s$ is less than *string_array* [*low*+*fib_low*], the method discards subarray *string_array*[*low*+*fib_low*], ..., *string_array*[*high*]. The method repeats the search for $s$ in the remaining subarray until either $s$ is found or the search range becomes empty with *low* > *high*.

```
class FibonaccianSearch {
    public static void main(String[] args) {
        String[] names = {"Cbc", "Bbc", "Abc"};
        InsertionSort.sort(names);
        System.out.print
            (FibonaccianSearch.search(names,
            0, names.length - 1, "Cbc"));
    }

    /** Searches for a string in a string array
    *    with Fibonaccian search
    */
    public static int search(String[]string_array,
            int low, int high, String s) {
```

```
            int fib_low, fib_high, temp;
        while (low <= high) {
            fib_low = 0; fib_high = 1;
            while (fib_low + fib_high < high-low+1)
            {
                temp = fib_low;
                fib_low = fib_high;
                fib_high += temp;
            }
            temp = string_array[low+fib_low].
                                    compareTo(s);
            if (temp == 0) return low+fib_low;
            if (temp > 0) high = low+fib_low - 1;
            else low = low + fib_low + 1;
        }
        return -1;
    }
}
```

The Fibonaccian search is preferable than binary search if an application sat-isfies a Fibonacci law. In the worst case, the time complexity of Fibonaccian search is $O(\log n)$, where $n$ is the number of elements in a sorted array in which a key is searched for.

## 7.2.3 Interpolation Search

The interpolation search algorithm assumes the values stored in an array or vector are evenly distributed in the domain of the values. When searching for a value $v$ in a sequence $v_{low}, v_{low+1}, \ldots, v_{high}$, the interpolation search algorithm assumes that if value $v$ is in the search range at position $p$, the ratios $(p - low):(high - p)$ and $(v - v_{low}):(v_{high} - v)$ are approximately equal. The interpolation position $p$ is estimated with formula $low + (high - low) \times (v - v_{low})/(v_{high} - v_{low})$.

The following class, class *InterpolationSearch*, implements interpolation search in instance method *search* to find a string $s$ in *string_array*. It uses instance method *valueOf(String s)* to evaluate the interpolation position, denoted with *inter_pos*. It compares strings $s$ and *string_array[inter_pos]*.

```
    class InterpolationSearch {
        public static void main(String[] args) {
            String[] names = {"Cbc", "Bbc", "Abc"};
            InsertionSort.sort(names);
            System.out.print(InterpolationSearch.search
                (names, 0, names.length - 1, "Cbc"));
        }
```

```
/** Searches for a string in a string array
 *   with Interpolation search
 */
public static int search(String[]string_array,
              int low, int high, String s) {
    while (low <= high) {
        if (low == high) {
            if (string_array[low].compareTo(s)==0)
                return low;
            else return -1;
        }
        int inter_pos = low +
                (high - low) * (valueOf(s)-
                 valueOf(string_array[low]))/
                (valueOf(string_array[high])-
                 valueOf(string_array[low]));
        int temp = string_array[inter_pos].
                                 compareTo(s);
        if (temp == 0) return inter_pos;
        if (temp > 0) high = inter_pos - 1;
        else low = inter_pos + 1;
    }
    return -1;
}

private static int valueOf(String s) {
    int value = 0;
    byte[] bytes = s.getBytes();
    for (int i=0; i < bytes.length; i++)
    value += (int) bytes[i] << ((3-i) * 8);
    return value;
}
}
```

In method *valueOf*(*String s*), we assume the length of argument string *s* is at most 4. The method returns a positive 32-bit integer (four bytes). When the method evaluates the integer from *s*, the first character in *s* is used to determine the first byte with code

```
value += (int) bytes[0] << (3 * 8);
```

Similarly, if *s* has other characters, the other characters will be used to evaluate other bytes for the integer with code

```
value += (int) bytes[i] << ((3-i) * 8);
```

where *i* is equal to 1, 2, or 3. Readers may modify the *valueOf*(*String s*) to deal with string *s* that has at most 8 characters or more than 8 characters.

For simplicity, we assume no two strings in *string_array* are equal. Otherwise, we need to deal with the condition *valueOf*(*string_array*[*high*]) − *valueOf* (*string_array*[*low*]) = 0 in method *search*.

The worst-case complexity of the interpolation search method is worse than that of binary search. We can find a problem such that the while loop of the method must be repeated $n$ times, where $n$ is the input size $high - low + 1$. Based on probability theory and statistics, the expected average complexity of the interpolation search method is log log $n$ plus a constant less than 1. The average performance is surprisingly good though the evaluation of *inter_pos* is complex.

# 7.3 Linked Lists

## 7.3.1 Node Links

### 7.3.1.1 Index and Reference as Link

The elements in a linked list are called *nodes*. Each node holds information regarding where to look for its successor. Specifically, it uses a field to contain a *link*. We shall present two types of link – index and reference.

Elements of an array or vector can be used as linked list nodes. They can be linked into a linked list with their indexes as links. Each element (node) contains a link field and a data field. The link field of a node contains the index of the successor, if any, of the node. The index of the first node in the linked list is maintained in a variable (header). The nodes in the linked list can be accessed through the header and the indexes contained in the link fields of the nodes.

A linked list that is embedded in an array is shown in Fig. 7.5. An element in the array contains two fields, one is a data field that references an object or *null*, the other contains an integer, which is an index in the array or integer –1. The negative integer –1 is an invalid index value. In Fig. 7.5a, we show a node, which contains index 3 in its link field.

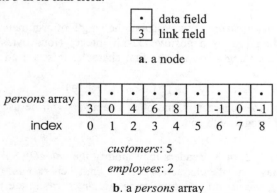

customers: 5

employees: 2

b. a *persons* array

**Fig. 7.5** An array of person objects that embeds linked lists

The *persons* array shown in Fig. 7.5b embeds two linked lists – one is named *customers* for holding references to customer objects, the other named *employees* for employee objects. The *customers* linked list is anchored at variable *customers* of type *int*. The variable contains a valid index 5. By following the index links, we can trace the nodes of the *customers* linked list as follows:

   *persons*[5], *persons*[1], *persons*[0], *persons*[3], *persons*[6].

The *employees* linked list embedded in the *persons* array in Fig. 7.5b consists of nodes

   *persons*[2], *persons*[4], *persons*[8].

Element *persons*[7] does not belong to either of lists *customers* and *employees*. It cannot be reached by either of the two linked lists.

A linked list can use references to link nodes, which may be scattered in memory. A reference references an object in the heap of a Java runtime system. A node of a reference-based linked list is shown in Fig. 7.6a. It consists of two fields. The data field contains a reference to an object or *null*, the link field contains a reference to a node or *null*.

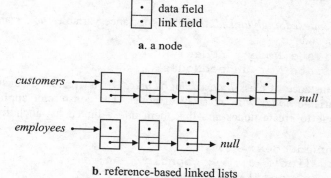

**a.** a node

**b.** reference-based linked lists

**Fig. 7.6** Singly linked lists of person objects

A variable that can reference a reference-based linked list can be declared with the class of the nodes. For example, if the class of node is named *Node*, the linked list *customers* shown in Fig. 7.6b can be declared with statement

```
Node customers = null;
```

The following statement creates a node and places the created object into the empty *customers* linked list.

```
customers = new Node();
```

Assume the link field in a node is named *next*. To create another node and link the created node, we can execute statement

```
customers.next = new Node();
```

which appends a new node to the end of the *customers* linked list.

The linked lists shown in Figs. 7.5 and 7.6 are *singly linked lists*. Each node in a singly linked list contains one link, which points to the successor of the node or which contains –1 or *null* if the node has no successor. We shall discuss doubly linked list shortly. A node in a doubly linked list contains two link fields – one referencing the predecessor of the node, the other referencing the successor.

## 7.3.1.2 Index-Based Linked List

We now discuss how to implement an index-based linked list such as the *customers* linked list shown in Fig. 7.5b. We present a class, *IndexedSinglyLinkedList*, that implements index-based singly linked list.

The class *IndexedSinglyLinkedList* has an inner class, *Node*, which is defined with code

```
class Node {
     Object data;
     int next;
}
```

As shown in Fig. 7.5a, the *data* field in a node can be used to hold a reference to an object, and the link field *next* can hold an index for another node in the same array.

Class *IndexedSinglyLinkedList* defines instance variables *nodes* and *unusedNodes* with code

```
private Node[] nodes;
private int unusedNodes;
```

When an instance of class *IndexedSinglyLinkedList* is created, a constructor initializes variable *nodes* with an array of nodes. The constructor applies the following code to create nodes and link them into a linked list anchored at index *unusedNodes*.

```
unusedNodes = 0;
for (int i=0; i < capacity - 1; i++) {
     nodes[i] = new Node();
     nodes[i].next = i+1;
}
nodes[capacity-1] = new Node();
nodes[capacity-1].next = -1;
```

where *capacity* is the length of array *nodes*. The index of the first unused node is 0, which is kept in instance variable *unusedNodes*. The last unused node has index *capacity* − 1. We use the invalid index −1 in the *next* field of the last node to indicate that the node has no successor.

We define several instance methods in class *IndexedSinglyLinkedList* to organize objects. When we need a new linked list, we invoke instance method *newList*(), which creates a header for the linked list. The method initializes the *next* field in the head with −1 since a newly created linked list is empty. The *next* field of the header node usually contains the index of the first node in the linked list.

Method *addObject*(*Object obj*) tries to find an unused node in array *nodes* and places *obj* into the node. If it cannot find an unused node, the method returns −1.

The overloaded method *addObject(Node listHead, Object obj)* adds an object into a linked list referred to with header node *listHead*. The method invokes method *findUnusedNode* to find whether the *unusedNodes* list is empty. If the *unusedNodes* list is not empty, the method *findUnusedNode* removes the first unused node from the *unusedNodes* list with code

```
int temp = unusedNodes;
unusedNodes = nodes[unusedNodes].next;
```

It returns the index *temp* of the unused node. In method *addObject*, local variable *nodeIndex* keeps the index of the unused node. Method *addObject(listHead, obj)* places *obj* into the *data* field of the unused node and adds the unused node to the linked list with code

```
nodes[nodeIndex].data = obj;
nodes[nodeIndex].next = listHead.next;
listHead.next = nodeIndex;
```

Thus, the node indexed at *nodeIndex* becomes the first node in the linked list.

```
import java.util.Enumeration;
public class IndexedSinglyLinkedList {
    public static void main(String[] args) {
        IndexedSinglyLinkedList list =
                new IndexedSinglyLinkedList();
        String[] names = {"Cbc", "Bbc", "Abc"};
        Node stringList = list.newList();
        for (int i=0; i < names.length; i++)
            list.addObject(stringList, names[i]);
        Enumeration nodes =
                    list.elements(stringList);
        while (nodes.hasMoreElements())
            System.out.print((String)
                        nodes.nextElement()+" ");
    }

    public IndexedSinglyLinkedList() {
        this(100);
    }

    public IndexedSinglyLinkedList(int capacity) {
        nodes = new Node[capacity];
        unusedNodes = 0;
        for (int i=0; i < capacity - 1; i++) {
            nodes[i] = new Node();
            nodes[i].next = i+1;
        }
        nodes[capacity-1] = new Node();
        nodes[capacity-1].next = -1;
    }
```

```
public Node newList() {
   Node tempNode = new Node();
   tempNode.next = -1;
   return tempNode;
}

public boolean addObject(Node listHead,
                                Object obj) {
   int nodeIndex = findUnusedNode();
   if (nodeIndex == -1) {
   System.out.println("Storage is full");
      return false;
   } else {
      nodes[nodeIndex].data = obj;
      nodes[nodeIndex].next = listHead.next;
      listHead.next = nodeIndex;
      return true;
   }
}

private int findUnusedNode() {
   if (unusedNodes == -1) return -1;
   int temp = unusedNodes;
   unusedNodes = nodes[unusedNodes].next;
   return temp;
}

public Enumeration elements(final Node aList){
   return (new Enumeration() {
   // anonymous inner class body
      private int index = aList.next;
      public boolean hasMoreElements() {
         return (index != -1);
      }
      public Object nextElement() {
         int tempIndex = index;
         index = nodes[index].next;
         return nodes[tempIndex].data;
      }
   });
}

class Node {
   Object data;
   int next;
}
```

```
            private Node[] nodes;
            private int unusedNodes;
    }
```

Method *addObject*(*listHead*, *obj*) moves an unused node from the *unusedNodes* list to the list referred to with argument *listHead*. It places *obj* into the unused node. In the above class, we do not define any method for deleting nodes from a linked list. A node deletion method places a deleted node into the *unusedNodes* list. We leave the development of node deletion methods as an exercise.

**Exercise 7.7** Define methods that can delete nodes from linked lists embedded in array *nodes* in class *IndexedSinglyLinkedList*. The node to be deleted may be represented by a node, an object, or an index in the array *nodes* as an argument in method invocation. It must be placed into the *unusedNodes* list for reuse.

### 7.3.1.3 Singly Linked List

The term *linked list* usually refers to a reference-based linked list. Here, we present a lightweight, reference-based singly linked list class, *SinglyLinkedList*.

The set of methods matches that of class *IndexedSinglyLinkedList*. Specifically, the method *addObject*(*Object obj*) adds *obj* to a linked list, method *elements*() returns an enumeration. By repeatedly applying methods *hasMoreElements*() and *nextElement*() for the enumeration, we can enumerate the data elements contained in a singly linked list.

Class *SinglyLinkedList* does not provide methods for data deletion. A deletion method linearly searches a singly linked list for the node or data element to be deleted. In the next section, we present a doubly linked list class, which has methods for deleting a given object or node from a doubly linked list.

```
    import java.util.Enumeration;
    public class SinglyLinkedList {
        public static void main(String[] args) {
            String[] names = {"Cbc", "Bbc", "Abc"};
            SinglyLinkedList stringList =
                            new SinglyLinkedList();
            for (int i = 0; i < names.length; i++)
               stringList.addObject(names[i]);
            Enumeration nodes = stringList.elements();
            while (nodes.hasMoreElements())
               System.out.print((String)
                            nodes.nextElement()+ " ");
        }

        public void addObject(Object obj) {
            Node tempNode = new Node();
            tempNode.data = obj;
            tempNode.next = header;
```

```
            header = tempNode;
        }

        public Enumeration elements() {
            return (new Enumeration() {
                private Node nextNode = header;

                public boolean hasMoreElements() {
                    return (nextNode != null);
                }

                public Object nextElement() {
                    Node tempNode = nextNode;
                    nextNode = nextNode.next;
                    return tempNode.data;
                }
            });
        }

        class Node {
            Object data; Node next;
        }

        private Node header;
    }
```

## 7.3.2 Doubly Linked List

A doubly linked list differs from a singly linked list in the structure of its nodes.
As shown in Fig. 7.6, a node in a singly linked list contains one link field. The
link field contains a reference to the successor of the node if the node has a successor; otherwise, the field contains *null*. A node in a doubly linked list is shown
in Fig. 7.7a. It uses a field named *data* to reference a data element for the linked
list. It has two link fields, named *prev* and *next*. The *next* field in a doubly linked
list has the same use as its counterpart in a singly linked list. Specifically, the field
*next* in a node refers to the successor of the node if the node has a successor; otherwise, it contains *null*. The link field *prev* refers to the predecessor of the node if
the node has a predecessor; otherwise, it contains *null*.

A doubly linked list named *customers* is shown in Fig. 7.7b. It uses instance
fields *first* and *last* to reference the first and last node in the list. To remove the
first node of a doubly linked list from the list, we simply assign the field *prev* in
the second node, which is referenced with *first.next*, in the list with *null* and assign the instance field *first* of the list with reference *first.next*. The following code
implements the node deletion.

```
first.next.prev = null;
first = first.next;
```

To remove the last node, we assign the field *last.prev.next* in node *last.prev* with *null* and set the instance variable *last* with *last.prev*. The following code implement the node deletion.

```
last.prev.next = null;
last = last.prev;
```

To remove a node, which is referenced with local variable *temp* and which is between the first and last nodes in the list, we execute code

```
temp.next.prev = temp.prev;
temp.prev.next = temp.next;
```

Note that to maintain the integrity of instance variable *length*, we decrease variable *length* by 1 when we remove a node from the list.

The doubly linked lists shown in Fig. 7.7b are implemented with the following class, class *DoublyLinkedList*. When a doubly linked list is created with constructor *DoublyLinkedList()*, the instance variables *length*, *first*, and *last* are initialized with 0 or *null* by default. The class defines constructor *DoublyLinked-List(Object[] input_array)* to create a non-empty list with data elements from an array.

Class *DoublyLinkedList* uses the following methods to add or remove data elements. The methods can be invoked for an object like *customers* shown in Fig. 7.7b.

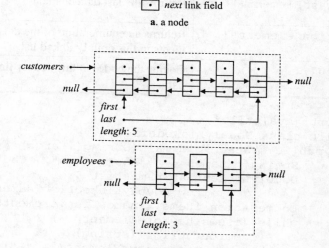

**a.** a node

**b.** reference-based doublylinked lists

**Fig. 7.7** Doubly linked lists

| Signature | Semantics |
|---|---|
| void addElement(Object obj) | Adds a new node to host *obj* at the end of this doubly linked list |
| void insertElementAt (Object obj, int index) | Inserts a new node to host *obj* at an indexed position in this doubly linked list |
| boolean removeElement (Object obj) | Removes a node that contains *obj* in data field from this doubly linked list |
| boolean removeElementAt (int index) | Removes an indexed node from the doubly linked list |

Class *DoublyLinkedList* defines the following methods for accessing the data elements and the length of a doubly linked list.

| Signature | Semantics |
|---|---|
| boolean contains(Object obj) | Tests if this doubly linked list contains *obj* |
| int indexOf(Object obj) | Determines the index of *obj* in this doubly linked list; returns −1 if the list does not contain *obj* |
| Object firstElement() | Returns the first data element from this doubly linked list |
| Object lastElement() | Returns the last data element |
| Enumeration elements() | Returns an enumeration of the data elements in this doubly linked list |
| in length() | Counts the nodes in this doubly linked list |

```java
import java.util.*;
public class DoublyLinkedList {
    public static void main(String[] args) {
        String[] names = {"Abc", "Bbc", "Cbc"};
        DoublyLinkedList namesList =
                new DoublyLinkedList(names);
        Enumeration items = namesList.elements();
        while (items.hasMoreElements()) {
            System.out.print((String)
                    items.nextElement()+ " ");
        }
    }
    private int length;
    private Node first, last;
```

```
public DoublyLinkedList(Object[] input_array){
   for (int i=0; i < input_array.length; i++)
       this.addElement(input_array[i]);
}

public final synchronized void addElement
                                (Object obj) {
   Node temp = this. new Node(obj);
   if (first == null) {
      first = last = temp;
   }
   else {
      last.next = temp; temp.prev = last;
      last = temp;
   }
   length++;
}

public final synchronized void
     insertElementAt(Object obj, int index) {
   if (index >= length)
      { addElement(obj); return; }
   int i; Node temp;
   for (i = 0, temp = first; i < index;
                     i++, temp = temp.next) {}
   Node newNode = this. new Node(obj);
   newNode.next = temp;
   newNode.prev = temp.prev;
   if (index == 0) first = newNode;
   else temp.prev.next = newNode;
   temp.prev = newNode; length++;
}

public final synchronized boolean
                 removeElement(Object obj){
   Node temp = first;
   while (temp != null) {
      if (obj.equals(temp.data)) {
         if (first == last) {
            first = last = null;
            length = 0; return true;
         }
         if (temp.next == null) {
            temp.prev.next = null;
            last = last.prev; }
         else if (temp.prev == null) {
               temp.next.prev = null;
```

```
                           first = first.next; }
              else {
                  temp.next.prev = temp.prev;
                  temp.prev.next = temp.next;
              }
              length--; return true;
          }
      }
      return false;
  }

  public final synchronized boolean
                  removeElementAt(int index){
      if (index >= length) return false;
      int i; Node temp;
      for (i = 0, temp = first; i < index;
           i++, temp = temp.next) {}
      if (temp != first && temp != last) {
          temp.prev.next = temp.next;
          temp.next.prev = temp.prev;
          length--; return true;
      }
      if (temp == first && temp != last) {
          first = first.next;
          first.prev = null;
          length--; return true;
      }
      if (temp != first && temp == last ) {
          last = last.prev;
          last.next = null;
          length--; return true;
      }
      first = last = null;
      length = 0; return true;
  }

  public final int length() {
      return length;
  }

  public final boolean contains(Object obj) {
      Node temp = first;
      while (temp != null) {
          if (obj.equals(temp.data)) {
              return true;
          }
          temp = temp.next;
```

```
    }
    return false;
}

 public final int indexOf(Object obj) {
    int i; Node temp;
    for (i=0, temp = first; temp != null;
                   i++, temp = temp.next) {
       if (obj.equals(temp.data))
          return i;
    }
    return -1;
}

public final synchronized Object
                           firstElement() {
    if (first != null) return first.data;
    return null;
}

public final synchronized Object lastElement()
{
    if (last != null) return last.data;
    return null;
}

public final synchronized Enumeration
                           elements() {
    return (new Enumeration() {
      Node current = first;

      public boolean hasMoreElements() {
         return (current != null);
      }

      public Object nextElement() {
         Object data = current.data;
         current = current.next;
         return data;
      }
    });
}

// Inner class for doubly linked list node
private class Node {
    Object data;
    Node prev, next;
```

```
Node(Object data) {
    this.data = data;
}
}
}
```

In the above class, we declare some methods with keyword *final* and *synchronized*. The synchronized methods can be used to synchronize accesses to a doubly linked list so that no two methods can access it at the same time. The *final* methods cannot be overridden in subclasses of class *DoublyLinkedList*. The public methods of class *DoublyLinkedList* have counterpart methods in class *Vector*, which was discussed in Chapter 4.


## 7.4 Summary

In this chapter, we discuss linear data structures. An array is a linear data structure in Java. It uses contiguous words in memory to store primitive values or references to objects. A linear data structure uses a node to store a data element and keep one or two links. A data field may hold a primitive value or a reference to an object. A link field may contain an index in the linear data structure or a reference to another node. It is used to point to a successor or predecessor.

We study index-based linked lists, which are embedded in node arrays. An array may host more than one linked list. A special linked list in the array is the list of unused nodes. Each time a data element is added to a list embedded in the array, a node is moved from the unused node list to the target list. When a node is removed from a list, the removed node is added to the unused node list.

Index-based linked lists can be used for the purpose of resource management. A node represents a resource. When the resource is available for allocation, the node is placed in the unused node list. When an application requires a resource, the node that represents the resource is removed from the unused node list.

We discuss linked lists that use references to link nodes. A node may encapsulate one or two node references. One of the references refers to the successor of the node. The other reference, if present, refers to the predecessor of the node. A node in a singly linked list has only one link field for referencing the next node (successor). A node in a doubly linked list uses a link field to hold a reference to the predecessor and a link field to the successor.

In this chapter, we also present various sort and search algorithms and their Java implementations. Most of the algorithms apply to linear data structures that are stored in memory. We also discuss sorting a file by using two or more external files. External file sort is important when the file is too large to fit in a computer memory. We use external files to keep data when we sort.

# Assignment

The doubly linked list class presented in Section 7.3.2 represents containers of objects. The objects are not linearly ordered. Strings are linearly ordered. For any two strings *s1* and *s2*, expression *s1.compareTo(s2)* returns 0 if *s1* and *s2* consist of the same sequence of characters, a negative value if *s1* is lexicographically less than *s2*, and a positive value if *s1* is greater than *s2*.

Create a class to represent doubly linked lists with strings as data elements. The class defines instance method *sort* that implements the insertion sort algorithm to sort doubly linked lists.

# Chapter 8
# Trees

Hierarchical structures and systems are ubiquitous in applications. File systems in computers and corporate administration systems are examples of hierarchical structures. With containment relationships, components of a hardware system can be represented with a hierarchy as well.

Hierarchical data structures are called trees. A file system is represented as a tree by an operating system. Directories and files in the file system are represented as nodes. A directory is the parent node of the files and directories that are contained in it. In Section 7.1.1.5, we discussed how to relate an element of an array with another element in the array so that they have parent-child relationship. The elements of the array and the parent-child relationships constitute a tree.

To satisfy some applications, a node in a tree may have an arbitrary number of child nodes. The tree is referred to as a general tree. For efficient representation, we may limit the number of child nodes for each node in a tree with a fixed number $m$, which is called the *arity* of the tree. The arity $m$ may be two, three, or more. A tree of arity $m$ is called a $m$-ary tree.

Some applications need a binary tree, each node in which has a left child and/or a right child. The relative positions of children of a node in a binary tree are an inherent property of the node and binary tree. For instance, we can use a binary tree to represent an arithmetic expression. A node that represents a binary operator in the expression has a left operand as its left child and a right operand as its right child.

In this chapter, we discuss various types of trees. Specifically, we shall present

- General tree, which is usually called a tree. A general tree has no limit on the number of children for a node in it. Conceptually, the order of children is immaterial for general trees. We present a recursive definition of tree. We define a data structure class named *Tree* to implement general trees.
- $m$-ary tree, which has an arity $m$. A node in a $m$-ary tree has at most $m$ children. The children are ordered from left to right. They are indexed with starting index 0.
- Binary tree, which is a 2-ary tree such that a child of a node is either the left or the right child of the node. A node in a binary tree may have no left or right child.
- Binary search tree, which is a binary tree with values stored at nodes. The value in a node of a binary search tree is greater than the values in nodes at the left of the node and less than the values at the right.

- AVL-tree, which is a balanced binary search tree. At each node in an AVL-tree, the difference between the heights of the left and right subtrees is at most 1. Search in an AVL-tree takes $O(\log n)$ time, which is better than search in binary search tree in the worst case.
- B-tree, which is a special $m$-tree. A node in a B-tree stores a sequence of keys $k_0, k_1, ..., k_l$ and a sequence of B-trees $n_0, n_1, ..., n_{l+1}$ such that the keys in a B-tree $n_i$ are greater than $k_{i-1}$ and less than $k_i$ for $0 < i \leq l$, the keys in B-tree $n_0$ are less that $k_0$, and the keys in $n_{l+1}$ are greater than $k_l$. B-trees are the de facto standard data structure for data index in a database. They have special properties to ensure a small number of disk accesses for a key retrieval and storage.

We present tree structures to store instances of class *Object*. The nodes of the data structures can be used to store any types of object. For a data structure, we may need a linear order on the stored objects. For example, the keys stored in a B-tree must have a linear order among them. When a linear order is demanded, we assume the data objects stored in a tree are strings. Readers can easily replace class *String* with another class for the objects in the tree.

# 8.1 Trees

## 8.1.1 General Trees

### 8.1.1.1 The Concept of Tree

A tree is built on a set of nodes. Each node encapsulates data and link information. One of the nodes in a tree is distinguished as the root of the tree. The concept *tree* can be recursively defined as follows.

- A single node is a tree. The node is the *root* and the only *leaf* of the tree.
- Assume a node $n$ and a set of trees $t_0, t_1, ..., t_k$ such that the trees do not share any node and node $n$ is not in any of the trees. We can build a tree $T$ such that node $n$ has the roots of trees $t_0, t_1, ..., t_k$ as its *children*. In the tree $T$, node $n$ is the *root* of $T$, and $n$ is called the *parent* of the roots of trees $t_0, t_1, ..., t_k$, which are called *subtrees* of $T$. Subtrees in the trees $t_0, t_1, ..., t_k$ are subtrees of $T$ as well.

Fig. 8.1 shows the construction of a tree by following the above definition. Fig. 8.1a is a single node tree. In Fig. 8.1b, details of subtrees $t_0, t_1, ..., t_k$ are omitted. A node encapsulates data and references to the roots of its subtrees. For example, the root node in Fig. 8.1b contains $k+1$ references.

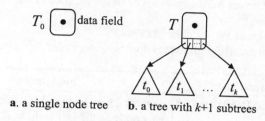

**a.** a single node tree    **b.** a tree with $k+1$ subtrees

**Fig. 8.1** Trees

Based on the definition of a tree, we can define several properties for trees. The *degree* of a node in a tree is the number of the children of the node. The *level* of a node in a tree is 0 if the node is the root of the tree; otherwise, it is equal to the level of the parent of the node plus 1. In terms of the above definition, the leaves in subtrees $t_0$, $t_1$, ..., $t_k$ of tree $T$ are the leaves of tree $T$. A *path* in a tree is a sequence of nodes $n_0$, $n_1$, ..., $n_k$ such that node $n_i$ is the parent of node $n_{i+1}$ for $0 \le i < k$. The *length* of the path is $k$. The length of a longest path in a tree is defined as the *height* of the tree. The longest path must start from the root of the tree and end at a leaf.

## 8.1.1.2 Node

A node of a tree will be implemented with a class, class *Node*. We use a field in a node to store data and use a vector named *children* to hold references to the child nodes of the node. According to the definition of tree, the order of child nodes is immaterial. Vector structure imposes an ordering on child nodes. A child of a node can be accessed with an index in the *children* vector encapsulated in the node. Class *Node* declares the two instance variables with code

```
private Object data;
private Vector children = new Vector();
```

When a node is created, the *children* field in the created node is initialized with a reference to a vector. Fig. 8.1a does not show the *children* field since the vector is empty. You can find an illustration of the *children* vector in the root of the tree in Fig. 8.1b.

Class *Node* has two constructors

```
public Node() {}
public Node(Object data) { this.data = data; }
```

The no-argument constructor does nothing. The instance variable *children* in a newly created node references a vector due to an initialization clause. The second constructor uses an argument to initialize the *data* field of a created node.

Class *Node* defines get and set methods, *getData*() and *setData(Object data)*, to access or reset the instance variable *data*. Instance method *degree*() of class *Node* returns the degree, which is equal to the size of the *children* vector, of a node. Class *Node* defines the following methods for maintaining the *children* vector for a node. The methods can be invoked for the root of a tree created in the following statement

```
Tree customers = new Tree();
```

The root can be represented with expression *customers.root*.

| Signature | Semantics |
|---|---|
| `Node addChild(Object data)` | Creates a new node to hold *data*, adds the new node as the last child of this node, and returns the new node |
| `Node addChild(Object data, int index)` | Creates a new node to hold *data*, inserts it into the *children* vector of this node at given *index*, and returns the new node |
| `Node deleteChild(int index)` | Removes an indexed child from the *children* vector of this node, and returns the removed child |

Note that the *children* field holds a vector. Method *deleteChild*(*index*) can delete an indexed child with statement

```
children.removeElementAt(index);
```

which automatically forwards the children following the deleted child in vector *children* by one position. Thus, the child at *index* + 1 before the method execution will be at *index* after the execution.

```
class Node {
    public Node() {}
    public Node(Object data) { this.data = data; }

    public void setData(Object data) {
        this.data = data;
    }

    public Object getData() { return data; }

    public Node getChild(int index) {
        if (index >= degree() || index < 0)
            return null;
        return (Node) children.elementAt(index);
    }

    public Node addChild(Object data) {
        Node tempNode = new Node(data);
        children.addElement(tempNode);
        return tempNode;
    }
```

```
        public Node addChild(Object data, int index) {
            Node tempNode = new Node(data);
            children.insertElementAt(tempNode, index);
            return tempNode;
        }

        public Node deleteChild(int index) {
            Node tempNode = (Node)
                    children.elementAt(index);
            children.removeElementAt(index);
            return tempNode;
        }

        public int degree() {
            return children.size();
        }


        private Object data;
        private Vector children = new Vector();
    }
```

The above class will be placed in class *Tree* so that it becomes a member of class *Tree*. We shall define several types of tree. Each tree class has its own *Node* class. By embedding a node class in a tree class, we can associate different node classes with different tree classes. Thus, we can avoid interference between the various node types.

### 8.1.1.3 Class Tree

Class *Tree* represents general trees. It defines only one instance variable named *root* with declaration

```
        Node root;
```

The instance field is used to hold a reference to the root node of a tree. It stores *null* if the tree has no node.

The default no-argument constructor of class *Tree* initializes the *root* instance variable with *null*.

Constructor *Tree(Object[] elements)* of class *Tree* creates a tree with data elements of an array. Each node in the created tree has at most two children. Starting from the root of the created tree, the constructor constructs the tree one level by one level, from left to right on each level. The constructor uses a queue, defined with code

```
        Vector nodeQueue = new Vector();
```

to store newly created child nodes. Thus, only after all the nodes at a level are visited, nodes at the next level can be visited. A node that is being visited is denoted with local variable *currentNode*. We add at most two children for *currentNode*. The number of children of a node is restrained with code

```
if (currentNode.degree() == 2) {
    currentNode = (Node) nodeQueue.firstElement();
    nodeQueue.removeElementAt(0);
}
```

In Fig. 8.2, we show a string array and a tree constructed with the array elements. The height of the tree is 3. The tree has five leaves, which are at levels 2 and 3. The *root* field of the tree refers to a node that contains string *Bbc*.

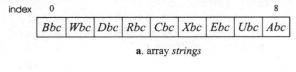

**a**. array *strings*

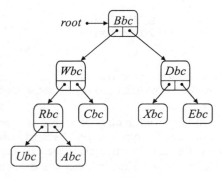

**b**. tree constructed with *Tree(strings)*

**Fig. 8.2** Constructor invocation *Tree(strings)*

Class *Tree* defines instance method *elements()* to return an enumeration of the nodes of a tree. By repeatedly invoking method *nextElement()* for the enumeration, we can visit each node of the tree. When we visit a node, we can set or get the data in the node. We can add or remove a child for a node by invoking method *addChild* or *deleteChild* for the node. Thus, we can dynamically modify the tree.

No path of a non-zero length in a tree can start from a node and end at the same node, i.e., a tree contains no cycle. The class *Tree* does not have any mechanism to prevent a cycle from its instances. It is the responsibility of the user of the class to ensure no node can reach itself by following one or more parent-child relationships in a tree.

The enumeration returned by method *elements()* is an instance of class *Traversal*. The class uses a vector called *nodes* to store the unenumerated children of enumerated nodes. It contains the *root* node initially. The *nextElement()* method uses the following code to retrieve the next node to visit. It returns the first element in vector *nodes*. It enters the children of the retrieved node into the vector *nodes*.

```
Node tempNode = (Node) nodes.elementAt(0);
nodes.removeElementAt(0);
for (int i = 0; i < tempNode.degree(); i++)
```

```
        nodes.addElement(tempNode.getChild(i));
        return tempNode;
```
The *nodes* vector is used as a queue.

Class *Node* presented in Section 8.1.1.2 is inside the following class, class *Tree*. Class *Tree* can be compiled. The main method of the class can be executed.

```
        import java.util.*;
        public class Tree {
            public static void main(String[] args) {
                String[] names = {"Cbc", "Bbc", "Abc"};
                Tree stringsTree = new Tree(names);
                Enumeration nodes = stringsTree.elements();
                while (nodes.hasMoreElements()) {
                    System.out.println(((Node)
                        nodes.nextElement()).data);
                }
            }

            /** Constructs tree with data from an array */
            public Tree(Object[] elements) {
                if (elements.length == 0) return;
                Node currentNode, tempNode;
                // create the root node
                currentNode = root = new Node(elements[0]);
                Vector nodeQueue = new Vector();
                // adds remaining elements into the tree
                for (int i=1; i < elements.length; i++){
                    if (currentNode.degree() == 2) {
                        currentNode = (Node)
                                    nodeQueue.firstElement();
                        nodeQueue.removeElementAt(0);
                    }
                    tempNode = currentNode.addChild
                                        (elements[i]);
                    nodeQueue.addElement(tempNode);
                }
            }

            public Enumeration elements() {
                return (this. new Traversal());
            }
            class Traversal implements Enumeration {
                private Vector nodes;
                public Traversal() {
                    nodes = new Vector();
                    if (root != null)
                        nodes.addElement(root);
                }
```

```java
        public boolean hasMoreElements() {
           if (nodes.size() == 0) return false;
           return true;
        }

        public Object nextElement() {
           Node tempNode = (Node)
                              nodes.elementAt(0);
           nodes.removeElementAt(0);
           for (int i=0; i<tempNode.degree(); i++)
           nodes.addElement(tempNode.getChild(i));
           return tempNode;
        }
}

class Node {
   public Node() {}

   public Node(Object data) {
      this.data = data;
   }

   public void setData(Object data) {
      this.data = data;
   }

   public Object getData() { return data; }

   public Node getChild(int index) {
      if (index > degree() || index < 0)
         return null;
      return (Node) children.elementAt(index);
   }

   public Node addChild(Object data) {
      Node tempNode = new Node(data);
      children.addElement(tempNode);
      return tempNode;
   }

   public Node addChild(Object data,int index)
   {
      Node tempNode = new Node(data);
      children.insertElementAt
                         (tempNode, index);
      return tempNode;
   }
```

```
    public Node deleteChild(int index) {
      Node tempNode = (Node)
                        children.elementAt(index);
      children.removeElementAt(index);
      return tempNode;
    }

    public int degree() {
      return children.size();
    }

    private Object data;
    private Vector children = new Vector();
  }
  Node root;
}
```

## 8.1.2 *m*-ary Trees

### 8.1.2.1 Multi-Ary Trees

In Section 8.1.1, we discuss trees whose nodes may have an arbitrary number of children. Here we focus on *multi-ary trees*, each of which has a fixed arity when it is created. If the arity of a multi-ary tree is *m*, the tree is a *m-ary* tree. A node in a *m*-ary tree has at most *m* children.

A *m*-ary tree is distinguished from a general tree by its arity. Traditionally, a *m*-ary tree and a general tree are also different in whether or not the children of a node are ordered. In a *m*-ary tree, the children of a node are ordered so that they can be indexed. As shown above, we use a vector to organize the children of a node in a general tree. The children of a node in a general tree are ordered as well. This should not be an intentional property of a general tree. The children of a node in a general tree can be organized with a data structure, which does not impose an ordering on the children.

### 8.1.2.2 Nodes with Finite Arity

An array supports faster element access than a vector. We modify class *Node* defined in class *Tree* with declaration

```
    private Node[] children;
```

for the *children* field. The field type is array rather than *Vector*. We add an instance variable called *arity*, which is declared in statement

```
    private int arity, size;
```

in class *Node*. The length of array *children* in a node is equal to value *arity* of the tree that contains the node. Field *size* in a node is used to record the number of nodes that are placed in the *children* array. That is, the number of the valid references in the *children* array is equal to *size*.

Class *Node* for *m*-ary trees has several constructors. The constructor

```
public Node(int arity) {
      this.arity = arity;
      children = new Node[arity];

}
```

sets field *arity* and creates a node array of length *arity*. Class *Node* also defines a no-argument constructor

```
public Node() { this(2); }
```

which assigns 2 to field *arity* by default. Another constructor of class *Node* has signature

```
public Node(int arity, Object data),
```

which extends the constructor *Node*(*arity*) by setting the *data* field with the *data* argument.

The class *Node* for multi-ary trees defines the same set of public methods as the class *Node* for general trees. However, the methods must adjust the *size* field when a child node is added to or deleted from the *children* array.

### 8.1.2.3 Class M_aryTree *for Multi-Ary Trees*

Class *M_aryTree* implements multi-ary trees. It uses instance variable *arity* to keep the arity *m* for a *m*-ary tree. The class defines constructor

```
public M_aryTree(int arity) {
      this.arity = arity;
}
```

which assigns a value to instance field *arity*. Constructor

```
M_aryTree(int arity, Object[] elements)
```

extends the above constructor by creating a set of nodes to store the elements of an argument array. The created nodes use the *arity* field of the created *m*-ary tree to limit the number of children for a node.

Like class *Tree*, class *M_aryTree* defines method *elements*() to return an enumeration of nodes. By repeatedly invoking methods *hasMoreElements* and *nextElement*, we can enumerate the nodes in a *m*-ary tree.

Class *M_aryTree* is defined as follows. It encloses class *Node* for creating nodes. The main method in the class can be executed.

```
import java.util.*;
public class M_aryTree {
      public static void main(String[] args) {
            String[] names = {"Cbc", "Bbc", "Abc"};
            M_aryTree stringsTree =
                              new M_aryTree(4, names);
            Enumeration nodes = stringsTree.elements();
```

```
      while (nodes.hasMoreElements()) {
         System.out.println(((Node)
                     nodes.nextElement()).data);
      }
   }

   public M_aryTree(int arity) {
      this.arity = arity;
   }

   public M_aryTree(int arity, Object[] elements)
   {
      this.arity = arity;
      if (elements.length == 0) return;
      Node currentNode, tempNode;
      // create the root node
      currentNode = root =
                  new Node(arity, elements[0]);
      Vector nodeQueue = new Vector();

      // adds remaining nodes to the tree
      for (int i=1; i < elements.length; i++){
         if (currentNode.degree() == arity){
            currentNode = (Node)
                        nodeQueue.firstElement();
            nodeQueue.removeElementAt(0);
         }
         tempNode =
            currentNode.addChild(elements[i]);
         nodeQueue.addElement(tempNode);
      }
   }

   public Enumeration elements() {
      return (this. new Traversal());
   }
   class Traversal implements Enumeration {
      private Vector nodes;

      public Traversal() {
         nodes = new Vector();
         if (root != null)
            nodes.addElement(root);
      }
      public boolean hasMoreElements() {
         if (nodes.size() == 0)
            return false;
```

```
                    return true;
                }
            public Object nextElement() {
                Node tempNode = (Node)
                                  nodes.elementAt(0);
                nodes.removeElementAt(0);
                for (int i =0; i<tempNode.degree(); i++)
                 nodes.addElement(tempNode.getChild(i));
                return tempNode;
            }
    }

    class Node {
        public Node() { this(2); }
        public Node(int arity) {
            this.arity = arity;
            children = new Node[arity];
        }
        public Node(int arity, Object data) {
            this(arity); this.data = data;
        }

        public void setData(Object data) {
            this.data = data;
        }
        public Object getData() { return data; }
        public Node getChild(int index) {
            if (index >= size || index < 0)
                return null;
            return (Node) children[index];
        }
        public Node addChild(Object data) {
            if (size == arity) return null;
            else {
                Node tempNode =new Node(arity, data);
                children[size++] = tempNode;
                return tempNode;
            }
        }

        public Node addChild(Object data,int index)
        {
            if (index < 0 || index >= size)
                return addChild(data);
            for (int i = size; i > index; i--)
                children[i] = children[i-1];
            Node tempNode = new Node(arity, data);
```

```
            children[index] = tempNode;
            size++;
            return tempNode;
        }

        public Node deleteChild(int index) {
            if (index < 0 || index >= size)
                return null;
            Node tempNode = (Node) children[index];
            for (int i = index; i < size-1; i++)
                children[i] = children[i+1];
            size--;
            return tempNode;
        }

        public int degree() { return size; }

        private Object data;
        private Node[] children;
        private int arity, size;
    }
    Node root;
    int arity;
}
```

## 8.1.3 Binary Trees

### 8.1.3.1 The Notion of Binary Tree

A *binary tree* is a 2-ary tree such that a child of a node is positioned at either the left or right of the node. A node in a binary tree may have a left but no right child. It may have a right but no left child. Positions of children of a node are an important property of a binary tree. In Fig. 8.3, we show several binary trees, which have at most three nodes. Note that the two binary trees in Fig. 8.3b–c are different. The only child of the root in Fig. 8.3b is at left, but that in Fig. 8.3c is at right.

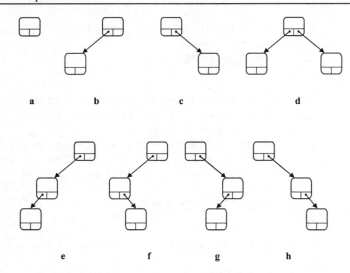

**Fig. 8.3** Binary trees with at most three nodes

### 8.1.3.2 Binary Tree Node

A node in a binary tree will be implemented with a class named *Node*. It encapsulates three instance fields, which are declared with

```
private Object data;
private Node leftChild, rightChild;
```

The *data* field holds a reference to a data object. The *leftChild* and *rightChild* fields reference the left and right child of the node, respectively. If the node has no left or right child, the field *leftChild* or *rightChild* contains *null*.

Class *Node* defines constructor

```
public Node(Object data) { this.data = data; }
```

to initialize the *data* field of a created node with given data.

As defined for a general tree, the degree of a node in a binary tree is the number of children of the node. Particularly, if the node has only a left or right child, the degree of the node is 1. Class *Node* defines instance method *degree*() to retrieve the degree of a node.

Class *Node* defines instance methods *getData*() and *setData*(*Object data*) to get or set the data field of a node. It defines get, set, and delete methods to maitain the left and right children of a node. The instance methods are described in the following table. They can be invoked for a variable *node* declared with the following statement.

```
Node node = new Node("Bbc");
```

| Signature | Semantics |
|-----------|-----------|
| `boolean hasLeftChild()` | Tests if this node has left child |
| `boolean hasRightChild()` | Tests if this node has right child |
| `Node getLeftChild()` | Retrieves the left child of this node |
| `Node getRightChild()` | Retrieves the right child of this node |
| `Node addLeftChild`<br>`(Object data)` | Creates a new node with given data, and assigns the created node as the left child of this node |
| `Node addRightChild`<br>`(Object data)` | Creates a new node with given data, and assigns the created node as the right child of this node |
| `Node deleteLeftChild()` | Deletes the left child of this node |
| `Node deleteRightChild()` | Deletes the right child of this node |

### 8.1.3.3 *Class* BinaryTree

Class *BinaryTree* represents binary trees. It defines instance variable *root* with class *Node*. The instance field references the root node of a binary tree. Starting from the root, we can use methods *getLeftChild* and *getRightChild* to access any node in the binary tree. When visiting a node, we can add or delete a child for the node.

Class *BinaryTree* has a no-argument constructor, which does nothing. Another constructor, *BinaryTree*(*Object*[] *elements*), accepts an array of data objects. Like the constructor *Tree*(*Object*[] *elements*) of class *Tree*, constructor *BinarTree* (*Object*[] *elements*) creates a binary tree to store the data elements. A difference between the two constructors is that the former uses a vector in a node to hold children for the node, the latter uses two instance fields, named *leftChild* and *rightChild*, to hold references to the left and right children of a node.

Class *BinaryTree* defines method *elements*() to return an enumeration for a binary tree. Instance method *nextElement*() of the enumeration uses a queue to store the nodes which haven not been enumerated but whose parents have been enumerated. It uses methods *getLeftChild* and *getRightChild* of class *Node* to retrieve the left or right child of a node to be enumerated. The retrieved nodes are placed into the queue. By repeatedly applying the methods *hasMoreElements*() and *nextElement*() for the enumeration, we can enumerate all the nodes in a binary tree.

Class *BinaryTree* is implemented as follows. It includes class *Node* as a member. A node object encapsulates a left and a right child field rather than an array or a vector. The fields allow direct access to a child of a node.

```
import java.util.*;
public class BinaryTree {
    public static void main(String[] args) {
```

```
            String[] names = {"Cbc", "Bbc", "Abc"};
            BinaryTree stringsTree =
                           new BinaryTree(names);
            Enumeration nodes = stringsTree.elements();
            while (nodes.hasMoreElements()) {
                System.out.println(((Node)
                    nodes.nextElement()).data);
            }
        }

    public BinaryTree() {}
    public BinaryTree(Object[] elements) {
        if (elements.length == 0) return;
        Node currentNode, tempNode;
        // create the root node
        currentNode = root = new Node(elements[0]);
        Vector nodeQueue = new Vector();

        // adds remaining nodes into the tree
        for (int i=1; i < elements.length; i++){
            if (currentNode.degree() == 2) {
                currentNode = (Node)
                           nodeQueue.firstElement();
                nodeQueue.removeElementAt(0);
            }
            if (!currentNode.hasLeftChild())
                tempNode = currentNode.
                       addLeftChild(elements[i]);
            else tempNode = currentNode.
                      addRightChild(elements[i]);
            nodeQueue.addElement(tempNode);
        }
    }

    public Enumeration elements() {
        return (this. new Traversal());
    }

    class Traversal implements Enumeration {
        private Vector nodes;
        public Traversal() {
            nodes = new Vector();
            if (root != null)
                nodes.addElement(root);
        }
        public boolean hasMoreElements() {
            if (nodes.size() == 0)
```

```
                    return false;
                 return true;
           }

      public Object nextElement() {
         Node tempNode = (Node)
                         nodes.elementAt(0);
         nodes.removeElementAt(0);
         if (tempNode.hasLeftChild())
             nodes.addElement
                 (tempNode.getLeftChild());
         if (tempNode.hasRightChild())
             nodes.addElement
                 (tempNode.getRightChild());
         return tempNode;
      }
}

class Node {
   public Node(Object data){this.data = data;}

   public void setData(Object data) {
      this.data = data;
   }

   public Object getData() { return data; }

   public boolean hasLeftChild() {
      return (leftChild != null);
   }

   public boolean hasRightChild() {
      return (rightChild != null);
   }
   public Node getLeftChild() {
      return leftChild;
   }

   public Node getRightChild() {
      return rightChild;
   }

   public Node addLeftChild(Object data) {
      Node tempNode = new Node(data);
      leftChild = tempNode;
      return tempNode;
   }
```

```
public Node addRightChild(Object data) {
    Node tempNode = new Node(data);
    rightChild = tempNode;
    return tempNode;
}

public Node deleteLeftChild() {
    Node tempNode = leftChild;
    leftChild = null;
    return tempNode;
}

public Node deleteRightChild() {
    Node tempNode = rightChild;
    rightChild = null;
    return tempNode;
}

public int degree() {
    int i = 0;
    if (leftChild != null) i++;
    if (rightChild != null) i++;
    return i;
}

    private Object data;
    private Node leftChild, rightChild;
}

Node root;
}
```

### 8.1.3.4 Binary Tree Representation of General Trees

A node in a binary tree uses two instance fields to reference its children. A node in a general tree uses a vector to keep references to children. A node in a *m*-ary tree uses an array to keep references to children. The *leftChild* and *rightChild* fields of a binary tree node are available in the node directly. Compared with the node of a general or *m*-ary tree, the representation of a binary tree node is efficient in both access speed and space use.

We now discuss how to represent a general tree with nodes that have two fields. The binary tree representation of general trees defines a node class, which has instance variables *firstChild* and *sibling*. Field *firstChild* in a node holds a reference to the first child of the node; *sibling* holds a reference to the next child of the parent of the node. Thus, the first child of a node referenced with variable *node* can be expressed with *node.firstChild*. The second and third child can be represented with expression *node.firstChild.sibling* and *node.firstChild.sibling. sibling*, respectively.

Fig. 8.4 shows the binary tree representation of a general tree. The root of the general tree in Fig. 8.4a has three children, which are linked by a *firstChild* reference followed by two *sibling* references in Fig. 8.4b.

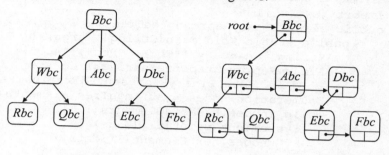

a. a general tree                    b. binary tree representation

**Fig. 8.4** The binary tree representation of a general tree

The binary tree representation of a general tree can implement indexed child access by following *firstChild* and *sibling* references. For example, the method *getChild(int index)* for accessing an indexed child of a node is defined with code

```
public Node getChild(int index) {
    if (index < 0 || index >= degree)
        return null;
    Node tempNode = firstChild;
    for (int i = 1; i <= index; i++)
        tempNode = tempNode.sibling;
    return tempNode;
}
```

When a new child is created for a node, the child is placed as the sibling of the last child. The method *addChild(Object data)* is defined as follows.

```
public Node addChild(Object data) {
    if (firstChild == null) {
        firstChild = new Node(data);
        degree++;
        return firstChild;
    }
    Node tempNode = firstChild;
    while (tempNode.sibling != null)
        tempNode = tempNode.sibling;
    tempNode.sibling = new Node(data);
    degree++;
    return tempNode;
}
```

Note that each time a child is added for a node, the degree of the node is increased by 1. When a child of a node is deleted, the degree of the node is decreased by 1.

Class *BinaryRepresentedTree* is defined as follows. It represents a general tree with a binary tree. It defines method *elements*() to return an enumeration of the nodes in a tree. It can access a child of a node in the tree with the child index. The class relates the indexes to the *firstChild* and *sibling* fields of nodes.

```java
import java.util.*;
public class BinaryRepresentedTree {
    public static void main(String[] args) {
        String[] names = {"Cbc", "Bbc", "Abc"};
        BinaryRepresentedTree stringsTree =
                new BinaryRepresentedTree(names);
        Enumeration nodes = stringsTree.elements();
        while (nodes.hasMoreElements()) {
            System.out.println(((Node)
                nodes.nextElement()).data);
        }
    }

    public BinaryRepresentedTree(Object[] elements)
    {
        if (elements.length == 0) return;
        Node currentNode, tempNode;
        // create the root node
        currentNode = root = new Node(elements[0]);
        Vector nodeQueue = new Vector();
        // adds remaining nodes into the tree
        for (int i=1; i < elements.length; i++){
            if (currentNode.degree() == 2) {
                currentNode = (Node)
                        nodeQueue.firstElement();
                nodeQueue.removeElementAt(0);
            }
            tempNode = currentNode.addChild
                                (elements[i]);
            nodeQueue.addElement(tempNode);
        }
    }

    public Enumeration elements() {
        return (this. new Traversal());
    }

    class Traversal implements Enumeration {
        private Vector nodes;
        public Traversal() {
            nodes = new Vector();
```

```
        if (root != null)
           nodes.addElement(root);
    }

    public boolean hasMoreElements() {
        if (nodes.size() == 0) return false;
        return true;
    }

    public Object nextElement() {
        Node tempNode = (Node)
                          nodes.elementAt(0);
        nodes.removeElementAt(0);
        for (int i=0; i <tempNode.degree(); i++)
           nodes.addElement
                      (tempNode.getChild(i));
        return tempNode;
    }
}

class Node {
    public Node() {}
    public Node(Object data) {this.data= data;}

    public void setData(Object data) {
        this.data = data;
    }
    public Object getData() {
        return data;
    }

    public Node getChild(int index) {
        if (index < 0 || index >= degree)
           return null;
        Node tempNode = firstChild;
        for (int i = 1; i <= index; i++)
           tempNode = tempNode.sibling;
        return tempNode;
    }

    public Node addChild(Object data) {
        if (firstChild == null) {
           firstChild = new Node(data);
           degree++;
           return firstChild;
        }
        Node tempNode = firstChild;
```

```
        while (tempNode.sibling != null)
           tempNode = tempNode.sibling;
        tempNode.sibling = new Node(data);
        degree++;
        return tempNode;
    }

    public Node addChild(Object data, int
                                    index) {
        if (index < 0 || index >= degree)
           return addChild(data);
        if (firstChild == null) {
           firstChild = new Node(data);
           degree++;
           return firstChild;
        }
        if (index == 0) {
           Node tempNode = new Node(data);
           tempNode.sibling = firstChild;
           firstChild = tempNode;
           degree++;
           return tempNode;
        }
        Node tempNode = firstChild;
        for (int i = 1; i < index; i++)
           tempNode = tempNode.sibling;
        // insert a new node after tempNode
        Node nextSibling = tempNode.sibling;
        tempNode.sibling = new Node(data);
        tempNode.sibling.sibling = nextSibling;
        degree++;
        return tempNode.sibling;
    }
    public Node deleteChild(int index) {
        if (index < 0 || index >= degree)
           return null;
        Node tempNode = firstChild;
        if (index == 0) {
           firstChild = firstChild.sibling;
           degree--;
           return tempNode;
        }
        for (int i = 1; i < index; i++)
           tempNode = tempNode.sibling;
        Node deletedNode = tempNode.sibling;
        if (index < degree-1)
           tempNode.sibling =
```

```
                        tempNode.sibling.sibling;
              else tempNode.sibling = null;
              degree--;
              return deletedNode;
          }

          public int degree() { return degree; }
          private Object data;
          private Node firstChild, sibling;
          private int degree;
      }
      Node root;
  }
```

# 8.2 Traversal of Trees

Some applications need to visit the data in each node of a tree exactly once. The process of systematically visiting nodes of a tree is called a *traversal* of the tree. For example, we can accumulate the balances of all customer objects held in a tree with a traversal of the tree. A traversal can be used to search for an object in a tree. The search will be stopped as soon as a desired object is found in a node of the tree. Let us briefly describe the different types of traversal for general trees and binary trees.

A general tree can be traversed in breadth-first order. In a *breadth-first traversal* of a tree, the nodes are visited level by level. On each level, the nodes are visited from left to right. A general tree can be traversed in depth-first order. In a *depth-first traversal* of a tree, the children of a node are visited before the siblings of the node are visited.

A node in a binary tree has a left and a right subtree. There are three strategies for traversing a binary tree, which can be described recursively. Assume a node that is the current node reached by a traversal of the binary tree. The *preorder* traversal visits the node first, visits the left subtree of the node in preorder, and then visits the right subtree. The *inorder* traversal visits the left subtree of the node in inorder, visits the node, and finally visits the right subtree in inorder. The *postorder* traversal visits the left and right subtrees of the node in postorder before the node is visited.

In the following, we present Java implementation of the traversal strategies for general and binary trees. The strategies are implemented in method *elements()*, which returns an enumeration of the nodes in a tree. By repeatedly invoking the *hasMoreElements* and *nextElement* methods for the enumeration, the tree can be traversed. The various *elements* methods can be easily adapted to search for an object in a tree.

A *m*-ary tree can be regarded as a special type of general tree. The breadth-first and depth-first traversal strategies apply to *m*-ary trees. The preorder and postorder traversal strategies can be applied for both general and *m*-ary trees. We implement a postorder traversal for general trees.

## 8.2.1 Traversal of General Trees

### 8.2.1.1 Breadth-First Traversal

The breadth-first traversal of a general tree is supported with a queue, which stores the children of a node before the node is visited. The front of the queue references the next node to be visited. The queue named *nodes* is an object of class *Vector*. After method *nextElement*() retrieves a node from the queue, it places the children of the node into the queue with statements

```
Node tempNode = (Node) nodes.elementAt(0);
nodes.removeElementAt(0);
for (int i = 0; i < tempNode.degree(); i++)
    nodes.addElement(tempNode.getChild(i));
```

The *nextElement* method is defined in an adapter class named *Traversal* of class *Tree* presented in Section 8.1.1.3. It can be applied repeatedly to enumerate the nodes of a tree in breadth-first order. The inner class *Traversal*, extracted from class *Tree*, can be found in the following code.

```
public Enumeration elements() {
    return (this. new Traversal());
}
class Traversal implements Enumeration {
    private Vector nodes;
    public Traversal() {
        nodes = new Vector();
        if (root != null)
            nodes.addElement(root);
    }
    public boolean hasMoreElements() {
        if (nodes.size() == 0) return false;
        return true;
    }
    public Object nextElement() {
        Node tempNode =(Node)nodes.elementAt(0);
        nodes.removeElementAt(0);
        for (int i =0; i<tempNode.degree(); i++)
            nodes.addElement
                    (tempNode.getChild(i));
        return tempNode;
    }
}
```

## 8.2.1.2 Depth-First Traversal

A depth-first traversal of a tree is supported with a stack of nodes, which is referenced with variable *nodes*. Before visiting a node, we place the first child of the node onto the stack. After all the children of a node have been visited, the node is popped out of the stack.

We couple a node and the number of its children that have been visited with an object of class *Child*, which is defined as

```
class Child {
    Child(Node node) { this.node = node; }
    Node node;
    int childIndex;
}
```

The variable *childIndex* associated with a *node* in an object of class *Child* denotes the number of children of the *node* that have been visited. The value of the variable is the index of the next child to be visited.

During a depth-first traversal, we use local variable *currentNode* to reference the current node, which is on the top of stack *nodes*. If the value, denoted with *index*, of the field *childIndex* associated with *currentNode* is less than *currentNode.degree*(), *currentNode.getChild*(*index*) is the next child to be visited in depth-first traversal; otherwise, all the children of *currentNode* have been visited and *currentNode* is popped out of the stack.

The method *hasMoreElements*() uses boolean variable *started* to decide whether a depth-first traversal has been started. If the root of the tree references *null*, there is no node to visit and the method returns *false*. If the traversal has started but the stack is empty, there are no more nodes to visit and the method returns *false*. In other cases, the method returns *true*.

Method *nextElement* pushes a node onto the stack *nodes* if the node has at least one more child to visit. The method uses the following code to pop the top node out of stack *nodes*, where *index* denotes the value of *childIndex* associated with *currentNode* in the stack.

```
while (index == currentNode.degree()) {
    nodes.pop();
    if (!nodes.isEmpty()) {
        index = ((Child) nodes.peek()).childIndex;
        currentNode = ((Child)nodes.peek()).node;
    } else break;
}
```

Thus, the top element in stack *nodes* always holds a node whose child indexed with *childIndex* has not been visited.

Class *DepthFirstTraversal* implements depth-first traversal for trees. An implementation of method *elements* for class *Tree* is shown as follows. Method *elements* invoked for a tree returns an object of class *DepthFirstTraversal*, which is an enumeration. By applying method *nextElement* repeatedly for the enumeration, we can enumerate the nodes in the tree in depth-first order.

```
public Enumeration elements() {
```

```java
            return (this. new DepthFirstTraversal());
    }
    class DepthFirstTraversal implements Enumeration {
        private Stack nodes = new Stack();
        private boolean started;

        public boolean hasMoreElements() {
            if (root == null) return false;
            if (started && nodes.size()==0)
                return false;
            return true;
        }

        public Object nextElement() {
            if (!started) {
                started = true;
                if (root.degree() >= 1)
                    nodes.push(new Child(root));
                return root;
            }
            Node tempNode =((Child) nodes.peek()).node;
            int index =
                    ((Child) nodes.peek()).childIndex;
            ((Child) nodes.peek()).childIndex++;
            tempNode = tempNode.getChild(index);
            nodes.push(new Child(tempNode));
            index = 0;
            Node currentNode = tempNode;
            while (index == currentNode.degree()) {
                nodes.pop();
                if (!nodes.isEmpty()) {
                    index = ((Child)
                            nodes.peek()).childIndex;
                    currentNode = ((Child)
                            nodes.peek()).node;
                } else break;
            }
            return tempNode;
        }

        class Child {
            Child(Node node) { this.node = node; }
            Node node;
            int childIndex;
        }
    }
```

### 8.2.1.3 Postorder Traversal

As in a depth-first traversal, we encapsulate a node and the number of children of the node that have been enumerated with an object of class *Child* for postorder traversal of a tree. The traversal is supported with a stack, named *nodes*, of child objects. In a postorder traversal, method *nextElement*() uses the value of field *childIndex* associated with the top node in stack *nodes* to determine whether all the children of the top node have been visited. After all the children have been visited, the top node is visited and it is popped out of the stack. After method *nextElement* pushes a node onto the stack, it pushes the first child of the node onto the stack immediately.

The method *elements* and inner class *PostorderTraversal* for class *Tree* are shown as follows. One can place them in class *Tree* and invoke method *elements* for a tree to return an enumeration. By repeatedly applying method *nextElement* for the enumeration, the nodes of the tree are enumerated in postorder.

```
public Enumeration elements() {
    return (this. new PostorderTraversal());
}

class PostorderTraversal
                implements Enumeration {
    private Stack nodes;

    public PostorderTraversal() {
        nodes = new Stack();
        if (root != null)
            nodes.push(new Child(root));
    }

    public boolean hasMoreElements() {
        if (nodes.size() == 0)
            return false;
        return true;
    }

    public Object nextElement() {
        Node tempNode =
                ((Child) nodes.peek()).node;
        int index = ((Child) nodes.
                        peek()).childIndex;
        while (index < tempNode.degree()) {
            ((Child) nodes.peek()).childIndex++;
            tempNode = tempNode.getChild(index);
            nodes.push(new Child(tempNode));
            index = 0;
        }
        nodes.pop(); return tempNode;
    }
```

```
class Child {
    Child(Node node) { this.node = node; }
    Node node; int childIndex;
    }
}
```

## 8.2.2 Traversal of Binary Trees

We now present several traversal strategies implemented in Java for binary trees. The strategies can be described recursively. Assume that a traversal has reached a node *n* in a binary tree.

- The preorder traversal of the binary tree visits the data object in *n*, traverses the left subtree of *n* in preorder, and traverses the right subtree of *n* in preorder.

- The inorder traversal of the binary tree traverses the left subtree of *n* in inorder, visits the data in *n*, and traverses the right subtree of *n* in inorder.

- The postorder traversal of the binary tree traverses the left subtree of *n* in postorder, traverses the right subtree of *n* in postorder, and visits the data in *n*.

The traversal strategies for binary tree can be implemented with recursive methods. We implement the traversal strategies with non-recursive methods. The traversals are represented with enumerations, which are instances of adapter classes *PreorderTraversal*, *InorderTraversal*, and *PostorderTraversal* for class *BinaryTree*. The *elements* method of class *BinaryTree* can return an enumeration object in an adapter class. By repeatedly applying method *nextElement* for the enumeration, we can traverse a binary tree with a traversal strategy.

### 8.2.2.1 Preorder Traversal

Class *PreorderTraversal* implements the preorder traversal strategy for binary trees. It keeps a stack, named *nodes*, of nodes whose parents have been visited but which themselves have not been visited. In the *nextElement* method, after a node is popped out from the stack, the right and left child of the node are pushed onto the stack. Thus, after the node is visited, the left subtree can be visited in preorder, and then the right subtree. The following statements maintain the *nodes* stack when traversing a binary tree in preorder.

```
Node currentNode = (Node) nodes.peek();
nodes.pop();
if (currentNode.hasRightChild())
    nodes.push(currentNode.rightChild);
if (currentNode.hasLeftChild())
    nodes.push(currentNode.leftChild);
```

The following class, class *PreorderTraversal*, implements the preorder traversal strategy for binary trees. An instance of the class is an enumeration of the nodes in a binary tree. It can be created and returned by method *elements*() in class *BinaryTree*.

```
class PreorderTraversal implements Enumeration{
    private Stack nodes;
    public PreorderTraversal() {
        nodes = new Stack();
        if (root != null) nodes.push(root);
    }
    public boolean hasMoreElements() {
        if (nodes.size() == 0) return false;
        return true;
    }
    public Object nextElement() {
        Node currentNode = (Node) nodes.peek();
        nodes.pop();
        if (currentNode.hasRightChild())
            nodes.push(currentNode.rightChild);
        if (currentNode.hasLeftChild())
            nodes.push(currentNode.leftChild);
        return currentNode;
    }
}
```

### 8.2.2.2 Inorder Traversal

We use an enumeration class, class *InorderTraversal*, to implement the inorder traversal strategy for binary trees. The class uses a stack named *nodes* to keep nodes. In method *nextElement* of class *InorderTraversal*, when a node is at the top of the *nodes* stack, all of the nodes in its left subtree must have been visited. Before the method returns the node, it pushes the right child of the node onto the *nodes* stack and continuously uses the *leftChild* reference in the top node to find the left child of the top node and pushes it onto the *nodes* stack. Thus, the top node on the stack is the next node to be returned by the *nextElement* method.

We use Fig. 8.5 to illustrate the use of stack *nodes* in inorder traversal. For the binary tree shown in Fig. 8.5a, expression *new InorderTraversal*() creates an *InorderTraversal* object and initializes the *nodes* stack with nodes *Bbc* and *Wbc*. The invocation of method *nextElement* returns node *Wbc* and pushes its right child *Qbc* onto the stack. Another invocation of method *nextElement* returns node *Qbc* from the *nodes* stack and exposes node *Bbc*. Before *Bbc* is returned by method *nextElement*, the method pushes nodes *Dbc*, *Ebc* and *Fbc* onto the stack. An inorder traversal of the tree shown in Fig. 8.5a visits the nodes in order

*Wbc*, *Qbc*, *Bbc*, *Fbc*, *Ebc*, *Dbc*.

Class *InorderTraversal* is defined as follows. It can be used by the *elements* method of class *BinaryTree* to create an enumeration. By repeatedly applying method *nextElement* for the enumeration, the nodes in a binary tree can be traversed in inorder.

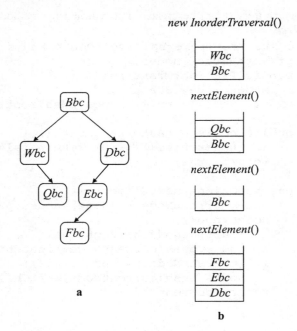

**Fig. 8.5** A binary tree for inorder traversal

```java
class InorderTraversal implements Enumeration {
    private Stack nodes;
    public InorderTraversal() {
        nodes = new Stack();
        if (root != null) {
            Node tempNode = root;
            do {
                nodes.push(tempNode);
                tempNode = tempNode.leftChild;
            } while (tempNode != null);
        }
    }

    public boolean hasMoreElements() {
        if (nodes.size() == 0) return false;
        return true;
    }

    public Object nextElement() {
        Node currentNode = (Node) nodes.pop();
        if (currentNode.hasRightChild()) {
            Node tempNode = currentNode.rightChild;
            do {
```

```
                nodes.push(tempNode);
                tempNode = tempNode.leftChild;
            } while (tempNode != null);
        }
        return currentNode;
    }
}
```

### 8.2.2.3 Postorder Traversal

Class *PostorderTraversal* implements the postorder traversal for binary trees. It uses a stack referenced with variable *nodes* to store objects of the class *Child*, which encapsulates a node and an integer variable named *childIndex*. After a node is wrapped in a child object and the child object is pushed onto the *node* stack, the left child of the node is wrapped and pushed onto the stack on the top of the node immediately. Thus, for each node in the stack, its left child is in the stack or has been enumerated.

When a node is popped out from the *nodes* stack, the method tests if the popped node has a right sibling. If the popped node has a right sibling, the method sets the *childIndex* variable of the top object in the stack with integer 1, wrapps the right child into a new child object, and pushes the child object onto the *nodes* stack. We can use the variable *childIndex* of a node in the *nodes* stack to decide whether all the children of the node have been enumerated.

The following code is used by the *nextElement* method to determine whether all the children of a node referenced with local variable *currentNode* have been enumerated. If all the children have been enumerated, *currentNode* is enumerated by the method.

```
Node currentNode =((Child) nodes.peek()).node;
    int childIndex =
                ((Child) nodes.peek()).childIndex;
    if (childIndex == 1) {
        nodes.pop();
        return currentNode;
}
```

Class *PostorderTraversal* can be placed in class *BinaryTree*. The method *nextElement* can be applied repeatedly for a *PostorderTraversal* object to enumerate the nodes of a binary tree in postorder.

```
class PostorderTraversal implements Enumeration {
    private Stack nodes;
    public PostorderTraversal() {
        nodes = new Stack();
        if (root == null) return;
        Node tempNode = root;
        while (tempNode != null) {
            nodes.push(new Child(tempNode));
```

```
                tempNode = tempNode.leftChild;
        }
        Node currentNode =
                ((Child) nodes.peek()).node;
        while (currentNode.hasRightChild()) {
            ((Child) nodes.peek()).childIndex++;
            tempNode = currentNode.rightChild;
            nodes.push(new Child(tempNode));
            for (tempNode = tempNode.leftChild;
                    tempNode != null;
                    tempNode = tempNode.leftChild)
                nodes.push(new Child(tempNode));
            currentNode =
                    ((Child) nodes.peek()).node;
        }
    }
}
public boolean hasMoreElements() {
    if (nodes.size() == 0) return false;
    return true;
}

public Object nextElement() {
    Node currentNode =
                ((Child) nodes.peek()).node;
    int childIndex =
                ((Child) nodes.peek()).childIndex;
    if (childIndex == 1) {
        nodes.pop();
        return currentNode;
    }
    Node tempNode;
    while (currentNode.hasRightChild()) {
        ((Child) nodes.peek()).childIndex++;
        tempNode = currentNode.rightChild;
        nodes.push(new Child(tempNode));
        for (tempNode = tempNode.leftChild;
                tempNode != null;
                tempNode = tempNode.leftChild)
            nodes.push(new Child(tempNode));
        currentNode =
                ((Child) nodes.peek()).node;
    }
    nodes.pop();
    return currentNode;
}
```

```
class Child {
    Child(Node node) { this.node = node; }
    Node node;
    int childIndex;
}
}
```

# 8.3 Binary Search Trees

## 8.3.1 The Notion of Binary Search Tree

A *binary search tree* is a binary tree for storing data objects that have a linear order. In a binary search tree, the data object in a node is greater than each of the data objects in the left subtree of the node and less than the data objects in the right subtree. Strings can be compared for a less-than, equal-to, or greater-than relationship. We shall store strings in a binary search tree.

Searching for a data object in a binary search tree is based on comparing the object with data objects in nodes. The search starts from the root of the binary search tree by identifying the root as the current node. If the data object in the current node is equal to the target, the search is done. If the data object is greater than the target, the target data object cannot be in the right subtree of the current node, and we search the left subtree of the current node by using the root of the left subtree as the current node. We can similarly cut the left subtree from the search when the target is greater than the data object stored in the current node.

Here we discuss how to build a binary search tree from a sequence of data objects and how to sort the data objects.

### 8.3.1.1 Construction of Binary Search Tree

Assume a sequence of data objects for which there is a linear order. We construct a binary search tree to store the data objects by inserting the data objects into an initially empty binary search tree. To insert a data object into a binary search tree, we compare the data object with the data at the root. If it is less than the data at the root, we insert the data object into the left subtree of the root; otherwise, we insert it into the right subtree. The comparison continues with the root of the left or right subtree until one of three situations happens:

1. The object to be inserted and the object at the root of a subtree are equal. In this case, we do not store the data object in the tree.
2. The object to be inserted is less than the object in the root of a subtree but the root has no left subtree. In this case, we create a node, store the data object in the node, and assign the new node as the left child of the root.

3. The object to be inserted is greater than the object in the root of a subtree but the root has no right subtree. As in Case 2, we create a node to store the data object and assign the new node as the right child of the root.

A binary search tree with strings as data can be constructed with method *addData*(*Node currentNode, String s*), which inserts a data object *s* into the binary search tree rooted at *currentNode*. The method compares the data in *currentNode* with *s* to decide whether to insert *s* into the left or right subtree of *currentNode*. It is shown as follows.

```
private void addData(Node currentNode, String s){
    int c = ((String) currentNode.
                    getData()).compareTo(s);
    if (c == 0) return;
    else if (c > 0) {
        if (currentNode.hasLeftChild())
            addData(currentNode.getLeftChild(),s);
        else currentNode.addLeftChild(s);
    }
    else {
        if (currentNode.hasRightChild())
            addData(currentNode.getRightChild(),s);
        else currentNode.addRightChild(s);
    }
}
```

The following class named *BinarySearchTree* can be used to create a binary search tree to store strings. It extends class *BinaryTree* with the *addChild* method. By invoking method *addData*(*root, s*), the string *s* is inserted into a binary search tree that is rooted at node *root*. By repeatedly invoking method *addData*(*String s*) for an initially empty binary search tree, one can build the binary search tree with a sequence of strings.

```
import java.util.*;
public class BinarySearchTree extends BinaryTree {
    public static void main(String[] args) {
        String[] names = {"Cbc", "Bbc", "Abc"};
        BinarySearchTree stringsTree =
                        new BinarySearchTree();
        for (int i = 0; i < names.length; i++)
            stringsTree.addData(names[i]);
        Enumeration nodes = stringsTree.elements();
        while (nodes.hasMoreElements()) {
            System.out.println(((Node)
                    nodes.nextElement()).getData());
        }
    }
    public BinarySearchTree() { }
    public void addData(String s) {
        if (root == null) root = new Node(s);
```

```
        else addData(root, s);
}

private void addData(Node currentNode,
                                   String s) {
    int c = ((String) currentNode.
                getData()).compareTo(s);
    if (c == 0) return;
    else if (c > 0) {
        if (currentNode.hasLeftChild())
        addData(currentNode.getLeftChild(),s);
        else currentNode.addLeftChild(s);
    }
    else {
        if (currentNode.hasRightChild())
        addData(currentNode.getRightChild(),s);
        else currentNode.addRightChild(s);
    }
}
}
```

**Exercise 8.1** Class *BinarySearchTree* inherits methods *deleteLeftChild* and *deleteRightChild* from the *BinaryTree* class. The methods simply remove the left or right subtree of a node. Override the inherited methods in class *BinarySearchTree* so that the *deleteLeftChild* and *deleteRightChild* methods delete only the left or right child but no other nodes in the left or right subtree.

### 8.3.1.2 Tree Sort

Binary search trees can be used to sort data objects. We can construct a binary search tree by inserting the data objects into an initially empty binary search tree. Then, enumerate the nodes of the binary search tree in an inorder traversal. The enumeration is demonstrated with the following code, which is similar with the main method of class *BinarySearchTree* presented in Section 8.3.1.1. It sorts a string array called *names*.

In the following code, method *elements* returns an inorder enumeration called *nodes* for binary search tree *stringsTree*. (Inorder traversal was discussed in Section 8.2.2.2). The code repeatedly applies methods *hasMoreElements* and *nextElement* for enumeration *nodes* and inserts the data objects into array *names*. Thus, the *names* array is sorted.

```
BinarySearchTree stringsTree =
                    new BinarySearchTree();
for (int i = 0; i < names.length; i++)
    stringsTree.addData(names[i]);
Enumeration nodes = stringsTree.elements();
```

```
int i = 0;
while (nodes.hasMoreElements())
    names[i++] = (String) (((Node)
                    nodes.nextElement()).getData());
```

## 8.3.2 AVL-Tree

### 8.3.2.1 AVL-Tree as Improved Binary Search Tree

The height of a binary search tree may be $n - 1$, where $n$ is the number of data objects stored in the binary tree. Assume the main method of class *BinarySearchTree* creates a binary search tree from a sequence of strings and the sequence is in ascending order. Each non-leaf node in the tree has only one child, which is the right child. The path from the root of the binary search tree to the only leaf of the tree includes all the nodes of the tree. To search for the string stored in the leaf, we have to make $n - 1$ data comparisons. The performance of the binary search tree is retrograded to that of a linked list.

Unbalanced subtrees in a binary search tree cause a performance problem for the tree. Particularly, the difference between the heights of the left and right subtrees of a node can be as high as $O(n)$, where $n$ is the number of nodes in the binary search tree.

Approaches to balancing binary search trees have been proposed in the literature. Here, we look at a type of balanced binary search tree, which is called an *AVL-tree*. The difference between the heights of the left and right subtrees at a node in an AVL-tree is at most 1.

We now define left and right height to measure the left and right subtrees of a node. For a node denoted with *node* in a binary tree, we use expression *node. height* to denote the height of the subtree rooted at *node*. The *left height* of *node*, denoted with *node.leftHeight*, is equal to 0 if *node* has no left child, and equal to 1 + *node.leftChild.height* otherwise. Similarly, the *right height* of *node*, denoted with *node.rightHeight*, is equal to 0 if *node* has no right child, and equal to 1 + *node.rightChild.height* otherwise. The *balance* of *node*, denoted as *node.balance*, is the difference between the left and right height of *node*, i.e.,

$$node.balance = node.leftHeight - node.rightHeight.$$

An *AVL-tree* is a binary search tree such that the balance of each node in the tree is equal to -1, 0, or 1. Fig. 8.6 presents several AVL-trees. The two AVL-trees in Figs. 8.6b and c are different. The balances of their roots are equal to 1 and -1, respectively.

The balancing condition of an AVL-tree improves a binary search tree. It is maintained automatically by an AVL-tree when a node is inserted to or deleted from the AVL-tree.

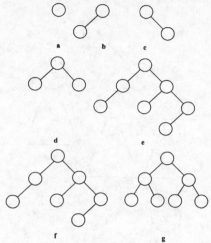

**Fig. 8.6** AVL-trees

## 8.3.2.2 Balancing AVL-Trees

In Section 8.3.1.1, we present method *addData* for adding a data object to a binary search tree. The resulting tree is a binary search tree. An AVL-tree restores the balances of nodes after a node is added to or deleted from it. Node addition and deletion methods of an AVL-tree are responsible to rebalance the resulting binary search tree into an AVL-tree. We now describe techniques to balance each node in a binary search tree resulting from a node addition.

Suppose we insert a node into an AVL-tree shown in Fig. 8.7. In the following figures, we use capital letters $A$, $B$, ..., $Z$ to label nodes in AVL-trees. The labels are not the actual data objects stored in the nodes. Let us assume the balance of the root of the tree in Fig. 8.7 is 1; the height of the left subtree of the root is $h$, and the height of the right subtree is $h-1$.

For the AVL-tree in Fig. 8.7, inserting a node into the right subtree of node $A$ may increase the right height of node $A$ by at most one. Therefore, the insertion will not affect the balance of the AVL-tree rooted at node $A$.

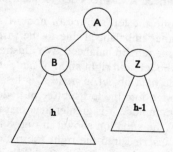

**Fig. 8.7** An AVL-tree with balance 1 at its root

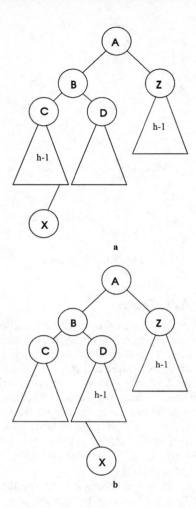

**Fig. 8.8** Unbalanced AVL-trees due to insertion of node $X$

Let us insert node $X$ into the left subtree of node $A$ in the AVL-tree in Fig. 8.7. Assume node $A$ becomes unbalanced due to the insertion. We also assume that all other nodes in the tree remain balanced. We illustrate the unbalance in Fig. 8.8. Node $B$ and $Z$ denote the left and right child of node $A$, respectively. Fig. 8.8a shows the situation that the data object in node $X$ is less than the data object in node $B$, and node $X$ is inserted into the left subtree of node $B$. Fig. 8.8b shows the situation that the data object in node $X$ is greater than that in node $B$.

We can further clarify the situation shown in Fig. 8.8b with the two trees in Fig. 8.9. When node $X$ is inserted into the right subtree of node $B$, it is inserted into either the left or the right subtree of node $D$, which is the right child of node $B$. The two subtrees of node $D$ are rooted at node $E$ and $F$, respectively.

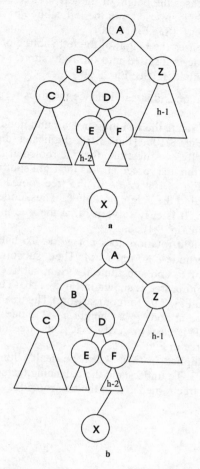

**Fig. 8.9** Unbalanced AVL-trees due to insertion of node $X$

By our assumption, node $D$ is balanced but node $A$ is unbalanced after node $X$ is inserted. Therefore, in the tree of Fig. 8.9a, the height of node $E$ is $h - 1$, the height of $E$ with node $X$ removed is $h - 2$, and the height of node $F$ is $h - 2$.

Similarly, node $F$ in the tree of Fig. 8.9b has height $h - 1$, it has height $h - 2$ if node $X$ is deleted from the tree, and node $E$ has height $h - 2$.

In summary, when inserting node $X$ into the left subtree of node $A$ in the AVL-tree shown in Fig. 8.7, we have the following four cases to deal with:

1.  The insertion does not increase the height of the left subtree of node $A$. The balance of node $A$ remains 1, and node $A$ is balanced.
2.  The insertion increases the height of the left subtree of node $A$ by 1. Furthermore, the new node is inserted into the left subtree of the left child $B$ of node $A$. (See Fig. 8.8a.) The balance of node $A$ becomes 2.

3.  The insertion increases the height of the left subtree of node $A$ by 1. Further-more, the new node is inserted into the left subtree of the right child $D$ of the left child $B$ of node $A$. (See Fig. 8.9a.)
4.  The insertion increases the height of the left subtree of node $A$ by 1. Further-more, the new node is inserted into the right subtree of the right child $D$ of the left child $B$ of node $A$. (See Fig. 8.9b.)

We now describe techniques that can balance the trees resulting from Cases 2, 3, and 4.

In Case 2, we can rotate the resulting tree around node $A$ to the right. The ro-tation is depicted in Fig. 8.10b. (Fig. 8.10a duplicates the tree of Fig. 8.8a for comparison.) Specifically, we substitute the tree rooted at $D$ for the left subtree of node $A$. Then, we add the tree rooted at $A$ as the right subtree of node $B$. Since the height of node $D$ in Fig. 8.10a is $h - 1$, the tree rooted at $A$ in Fig. 8.10b has height $h$, which is equal to the height of node $C$. Thus, nodes $A$ and $B$ are balanced with the right rotation. It is easy to verify that the tree in Fig. 8.10b is a binary search tree if the tree in Fig. 8.10a is.

For Case 3, the right rotation does not work. To balance the binary tree in Fig. 8.9a, we promote node $D$ to replace $A$. Then, substitute the left subtree of $D$ for the right subtree of $B$, and substitute the right subtree of node $D$ for the left subtree of $A$. The resulting tree is shown in Fig. 8.11b. (The tree in Fig. 8.11a is a duplicate of the tree in Fig. 8.9a for comparison.) The tree rooted at $E$ has height $h - 1$, and the tree rooted at node $F$ has height $h - 2$. Node $A$, $B$, and $D$ are all bal-anced in Fig. 8.11b. It is easy to verify that if the tree in Fig. 8.11a is a binary search tree, so is the tree in Fig. 8.11b.

The unbalance implied in Case 4 can be dealt with by the same balancing technique as for Case 3. To understand the balancing technique for Case 4, simply move leaf $X$ from the tree rooted at $E$ to the tree rooted at $F$ in Fig. 8.11.

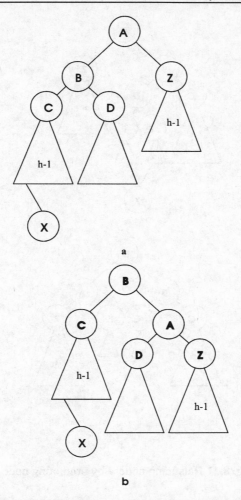

**Fig. 8.10** Balancing AVL-tree with right rotation

In the above discussion, we focus on inserting node $X$ into the left subtree of node $A$. The discussion can be extended to the situation that a node $X$ is inserted into the right subtree of node $A$. The balancing techniques work by "mirroring" left to right and right to left.

In the above discussion, we assume node $A$ is the root of an AVL-tree. The balancing techniques work well when $A$ is a child of a node in an AVL-tree. When we adjust the subtree rooted at node $A$, we need to adjust the parent-child relation. For example, in Case 3, after promoting node $D$ to replace $A$, node $D$ should be the child of the former parent of node $A$. The adjustment of parent-child relation is straightforward. The details can be found in class *AVL_Tree*.

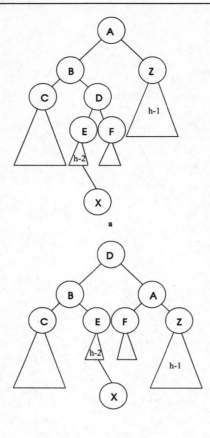

**Fig. 8.11** Balancing node *A* by promoting node *D*

### 8.3.2.3 *Class* Node *for AVL-Trees*

Nodes in an AVL-tree are represented with class *Node*, which defines instance variables with code

```
private Object data;
private Node parent, leftChild, rightChild;
int height;
```

The *Node* class uses instance field *parent* to reference the parent of a node. The height of a node in an AVL-tree is recorded in field *height*. Class *Node* defines instance method *setHeight* to set variable *height* of a node by accessing the heights of the children of the node. The *setHeight* method is defined as follows.

```
public void setHeight() {
    if (hasLeftChild() && hasRightChild())
```

```
        height = 1 + Math.max(leftChild.height,
                                rightChild.height);
    else if (hasLeftChild())
        height = 1 + leftChild.height;
      else if (hasRightChild())
          height = 1 + rightChild.height;
          else height = 0;
}
```

Class *Node* supports the addition of a child for a node with methods *addLeft* (*Object data*) and *addRight*(*Object data*), which simply create a node with given *data* object, assign the left or right child field of the node with the created node, and assign the *parent* field of the new node with the node. It supports the addition of a left or right child with methods *addLeftChild*(*Node node*) and *addRightChild* (*Node node*), which assign the left or right child field of the receiving node with the argument *node* and assign the parent field of the argument *node* with the receiving node. Thus, the receiving node and argument *node* are related with a parent-child relationship.

### 8.3.2.4 Class AVL_Tree

We now present class *AVL_Tree*. The class uses the data insertion algorithm of binary search tree to insert a data object into an AVL-tree *T*. This fact implies that after a new node, denoted with *node*, is added into an AVL-tree *T*, *T* is a binary search tree. The added *node* is a leaf of *T*. Some nodes in the resulting tree may no longer be balanced due to the node addition. For any node that is not an ancestor of *node*, the subtree of *T* rooted at the node is not affected by the addition of *node* and the balance of the node is not changed. To rebalance *T* into an AVL-tree, we adjust the ancestors of *node* bottom-up until we find an ancestor whose balance has not been affected by the addition of *node*.

The following Java code traces a path from the parent of the added *node* toward the root of *T*. The local variables *currentNode* and *currentParent* are initialized with *node* and the parent of *node*, respectively. The method balances *currentParent* if *currentParent* is unbalanced. The balancing details will be explained shortly.

```
while (currentNode != root) {
    int h = currentParent.height;
    currentParent.setHeight();
    if (h == currentParent.height)
        return; // Case 1
    if (currentParent.balanced()) {
        currentNode = currentParent;
        currentParent = currentNode.parent;
        continue;
    }
    if (currentParent.leftHeight() -
            currentParent.rightHeight() == 2) {
```

```
        ... // balancing currentParent
     }
     if (currentParent.leftHeight() -
             currentParent.rightHeight() == -2) {
        ... // balancing currentParent
     }
   }
```

When *currentNode* references the root of the resulting tree, all nodes in the resulting tree are balanced. Thus, *T* becomes an AVL-tree again. The above code is included in method *balance(Node node)* of class *AVL_Tree*.

The first case discussed in Section 8.3.2.2 is detected in the above code by comparing the height of *currentParent* before the node addition and the height after the node addition. It is indicated with comment *Case 1* in the above code.

The above code invokes boolean method *balanced()* in expression *current-Parent.balanced()* to detect the situation that the node *currentParent* is balanced though its height has been changed. In this case, the while loop is repeated for the parent of *currentParent*.

The above code deals with the two situations represented with Fig. 8.8 when the following condition is true.

```
     currentParent.leftHeight() -
             currentParent.rightHeight() == 2
```

The last if statement in the above code deals with the situation that the balance of *currentParent* is equal to –2.

We now explain method *balance(Node node)*. In the following code, *currentParent* corresponds to node *A* in Fig. 8.10. The code implements right rotation shown in Fig. 8.10.

```
   Node nodeA = currentParent,
           nodeB = nodeA.getLeftChild(),
           nodeC = nodeB.getLeftChild(),
           nodeD = nodeB.getRightChild();
   if (nodeB.leftHeight() > nodeB.rightHeight()){
       // right rotation for Case 2
       nodeA.addLeftChild(nodeD);
       if (nodeA != root) {
           if (nodeA.isLeftChild())
               nodeA.parent.addLeftChild(nodeB);
           else nodeA.parent.addRightChild(nodeB);
       }
       else { root = nodeB; };
       nodeB.addRightChild(nodeA);
       nodeA.setHeight();
       nodeB.setHeight();
       currentNode = nodeB;
       currentParent = currentNode.parent;
       continue;
   }
```

The *balance(Node node)* method implements the promotion technique shown in Fig. 8.11 with the following code.

```
// Cases 3 and 4
Node nodeE = null, nodeF = null;
if (nodeD.hasLeftChild()) {
    nodeE = nodeD.getLeftChild();
    nodeB.addRightChild(nodeE);
} else nodeB.removeRightChild();
if (nodeD.hasRightChild()) {
    nodeF = nodeD.getRightChild();
    nodeA.addLeftChild(nodeF);
} else nodeA.removeLeftChild();

if (currentParent != root) {
    if (nodeA.isLeftChild())
        nodeA.parent.addLeftChild(nodeD);
    else nodeA.parent.addRightChild(nodeD);
} else root = nodeD;
nodeD.addLeftChild(nodeB);
nodeD.addRightChild(nodeA);
nodeB.setHeight();
nodeA.setHeight();
nodeD.setHeight();
currentNode = nodeD;
currentParent = currentNode.parent;
continue;
```

In the above code, we use local variables *nodeE* and *nodeF* to denote nodes *E* and *F* in Fig. 8.11.

When the balance of *currentParent* is −2, the *balance* method uses code similar to the code dealing with Cases 2, 3, and 4 for balance 2. It simply mirrors the left to right and right to left.

Method *addData(String s)* of class *AVL_Tree* creates a node, denoted with *newNode*, to hold string *s* as data. The *newNode* is added as a leaf to the AVL-tree. As we said earlier, the tree resulting from the node insertion is a binary search tree. The method invokes method *balance(newNode)* to balance the tree into an AVL-tree.

Class *AVL_Tree* is defined as follows. It includes class *Node* as an inner class for storing data objects and maintaining parent-child relation. Its main method can be executed for unit testing.

```
import java.util.*;
public class AVL_Tree {
    public static void main(String[] args) {
        String[] names = {"Cbc", "Bbc", "Abc"};
        AVL_Tree stringsTree = new AVL_Tree();
        for (int i=0; i < names.length; i++)
            stringsTree.addData(names[i]);
```

```java
        Enumeration nodes = stringsTree.elements();
        int i = 0;
        while (nodes.hasMoreElements()) {
            names[i] = (String) (((Node)
                    nodes.nextElement()).getData());
            System.out.print(names[i]+" ");
            i++;
        }
    }

    public AVL_Tree() { }

    /** Retrieves a node that holds the minimum
     *    value in this AVL-tree
     */
    public Node getMinNode() {
        if (root == null) return null;
        Node tempNode = root;
        while (tempNode.hasLeftChild())
            tempNode = tempNode.getLeftChild();
        return tempNode;
    }

    public Node getMaxNode() {
        if (root == null) return null;
        Node tempNode = root;
        while (tempNode.hasRightChild())
            tempNode = tempNode.getRightChild();
        return tempNode;
    }

    /** Inserts string s as data into this AVL-
     *    tree
     */
    public Node addData(String s) {
        if (root == null) {
            root = new Node(s);
            return root;
        }
        Node tempNode = root;
        while (true) {
            int c = ((String) tempNode.
                        getData()).compareTo(s);
            if ( c == 0) return null;
            if (c > 0) {
                // inserts s into left subtree.
                if (tempNode.hasLeftChild()){
```

```
                    tempNode= tempNode.getLeftChild();
                    continue;
                }
                else {
                    Node newNode = tempNode.addLeft(s);
                    balance(newNode);
                    return newNode;
                }
            }
            else {
                // inserts s to right subtree
                if (tempNode.hasRightChild()) {
                    tempNode=tempNode.getRightChild();
                    continue;
                }
                else {
                    Node newNode=tempNode.addRight(s);
                    balance(newNode);
                    return newNode;
                }
            }
        }
    }

    private void balance(Node node) {
        Node currentNode, currentParent;
        currentNode = node;
        currentParent = node.parent;
        while (currentNode != root) {
            int h = currentParent.height;
            currentParent.setHeight();
            if (h == currentParent.height)
                return; // Case 1
            if (currentParent.balanced()) {
                currentNode = currentParent;
                currentParent = currentNode.parent;
                continue;
            }
            if (currentParent.leftHeight()-
                    currentParent.rightHeight() == 2)
            {
                Node nodeA = currentParent,
                    nodeB = nodeA.getLeftChild(),
                    nodeC = nodeB.getLeftChild(),
                    nodeD = nodeB.getRightChild();
                if (nodeB.leftHeight() >
                            nodeB.rightHeight())
```

```
        { // right rotation for Case 2
        nodeA.addLeftChild(nodeD);
        if (nodeA != root) {
        if (nodeA.isLeftChild())
        nodeA.parent.addLeftChild(nodeB);
        else nodeA.parent.
                        addRightChild(nodeB);
        }
        else root = nodeB;
        nodeB.addRightChild(nodeA);
        nodeA.setHeight();
        nodeB.setHeight();
        currentNode = nodeB;
        currentParent =currentNode.parent;
        continue;
        }
    // Cases 3 and 4
    Node nodeE = null, nodeF = null;
    if (nodeD.hasLeftChild()) {
        nodeE = nodeD.getLeftChild();
        nodeB.addRightChild(nodeE);
    } else nodeB.removeRightChild();
    if (nodeD.hasRightChild()) {
        nodeF = nodeD.getRightChild();
        nodeA.addLeftChild(nodeF);
    } else nodeA.removeLeftChild();

    if (currentParent != root) {
     if (nodeA.isLeftChild())
        nodeA.parent.addLeftChild(nodeD);
     else nodeA.parent.addRightChild(nodeD);
    } else root = nodeD;
    nodeD.addLeftChild(nodeB);
    nodeD.addRightChild(nodeA);
    nodeB.setHeight();
    nodeA.setHeight();
    nodeD.setHeight();
    currentNode = nodeD;
    currentParent = currentNode.parent;
    continue;
    }
if (currentParent.leftHeight() -
        currentParent.rightHeight() == -2) {
    Node nodeA = currentParent,
        nodeB = nodeA.getRightChild(),
        nodeC = nodeB.getLeftChild(),
        nodeD = nodeB.getRightChild();
```

```
            if (nodeB.leftHeight() <
                        nodeB.rightHeight()) {
                // left rotation for Case 2
                nodeA.addRightChild(nodeC);
                if (nodeA != root){
                if (nodeA.isLeftChild())
                    nodeA.parent.addLeftChild(nodeB);
                else
                    nodeA.parent.addRightChild(nodeB);
                }
                else root = nodeB;
                nodeB.addLeftChild(nodeA);
                nodeA.setHeight();
                nodeB.setHeight();
                currentNode = nodeB;
                currentParent = currentNode.parent;
                continue;
            }
            // Cases 3 and 4
            Node nodeE = null, nodeF = null;
            if (nodeC.hasLeftChild()){
                nodeE = nodeC.getLeftChild();
                nodeA.addRightChild(nodeE);
            } else nodeA.removeRightChild();
            if (nodeC.hasRightChild()) {
                nodeF = nodeC.getRightChild();
                nodeB.addLeftChild(nodeF);
            } else nodeB.removeLeftChild();
            if (nodeA != root) {
             if (nodeA.isLeftChild())
                 nodeA.parent.addLeftChild(nodeC);
             else nodeA.parent.addRightChild(nodeC);
            } else root = nodeC;
            nodeC.addLeftChild(nodeA);
            nodeC.addRightChild(nodeB);
            nodeB.setHeight();
            nodeA.setHeight();
            nodeC.setHeight();
            currentNode = nodeC;
            currentParent = currentNode.parent;
            continue;
        }
    }
}
public Enumeration elements() {
    return (this. new InorderTraversal());
}
```

```
class InorderTraversal
               implements Enumeration {
    private Stack nodes;

    public InorderTraversal() {
        nodes = new Stack();
        if (root != null) {
            Node tempNode = root;
            do {
                nodes.push(tempNode);
                tempNode = tempNode.leftChild;
            } while (tempNode != null);
        }
    }

    public boolean hasMoreElements() {
        if (nodes.size() == 0) return false;
        return true;
    }

    public Object nextElement() {
        Node currentNode = (Node) nodes.peek();
        nodes.pop();
        if (currentNode.hasRightChild()) {
         Node tempNode = currentNode.rightChild;
         do { nodes.push(tempNode);
                tempNode = tempNode.leftChild;
         } while (tempNode != null);
        }
        return currentNode;
    }
}

class Node {
    public Node(Object data) {
        this.data = data;
    }

    public void setData(Object data) {
        this.data = data;
    }

    public Object getData() { return data; }

    public boolean hasLeftChild() {
        return (leftChild != null);
    }
```

```java
public boolean hasRightChild() {
   return (rightChild != null);
}

public Node getLeftChild() {
   return leftChild;
}

public Node getRightChild() {
   return rightChild;
}

public boolean balanced() {
   return (Math.abs(leftHeight() -
                    rightHeight()) <= 1);
}

public Node addLeft(Object data) {
   Node tempNode = new Node(data);
   leftChild = tempNode;
   tempNode.parent = this;
   return tempNode;
}

public Node addLeftChild(Node node) {
   leftChild = node;
   if (node != null)
      node.parent = this;
   return node;
}

public Node addRight(Object data) {
   Node tempNode = new Node(data);
   rightChild = tempNode;
   tempNode.parent = this;
   return tempNode;
}

public Node addRightChild(Node node){
   rightChild = node;
   if (node != null)
      node.parent = this;
   return node;
}

public Node removeLeftChild() {
   Node tempNode = leftChild;
```

```
                leftChild = null; return tempNode;
        }

        public Node removeRightChild() {
            Node tempNode = rightChild;
            rightChild = null; return tempNode;
        }

        public int degree() {
            int i = 0;
            if (leftChild != null) i++;
            if (rightChild != null) i++;
            return i;
        }

        public void setHeight() {
            height = Math.max(leftHeight(),
                              rightHeight());
        }

        public boolean isLeftChild() {
            return (this == parent.leftChild);
        }

        public boolean isRightChild() {
            return (this == parent.rightChild);
        }

        public int leftHeight() {
            if (hasLeftChild())
                return (1+leftChild.height);
            return 0;
        }
        public int rightHeight() {
            if(hasRightChild())
                return(1+rightChild.height);
            return 0;
        }
        public int height() { return height; }
        private Object data;
        private Node parent, leftChild, rightChild;
        int height;
    }
    Node root;
}
```

## 8.3.2.5 Data Deletion

In Section 8.2.2.2, we describe an inorder listing of the nodes of a binary tree. For a non-leaf node in an AVL-tree, we can find the inorder predecessor or successor that is at a lower level than the node. To remove the non-leaf node from an AVL-tree, we use the data object in the inorder predecessor or successor to replace the data object in the node. Then, the method tries to delete the inorder predecessor or successor from the lower level.

For a non-leaf node, the inorder predecessor of the node is in the left subtree of the node if the node has left child; the inorder successor is in the right subtree otherwise. The *removeNode(Node node)* method removes argument *node* from an AVL-tree. It uses the following code to find an inorder predecessor or successor of *node*. The predecessor or successor of *node* will be denoted with local variable *tempNode*, which is initialized with the argument *node* before the code is executed.

```
if (tempNode.hasLeftChild()) {
    tempNode = tempNode.getLeftChild();
    while (tempNode.hasRightChild())
        tempNode = tempNode.getRightChild();
} else {
    tempNode = tempNode.getRightChild();
    while (tempNode.hasLeftChild())
        tempNode = tempNode.getLeftChild();
}
```

The first while loop in the above code finds the inorder predecessor of *node* in the left subtree of *node*, and the second finds the inorder successor in the right subtree. The following statements replace the data object in *node* with the data object in *tempNode*.

```
tempData = (String) tempNode.getData();
node.setData(tempData);
node = tempNode;
```

The last statement assigns variable *node* with the node to be removed. Thus, parameter variable *node* holds a node to be removed from the AVL-tree.

The above process repeats until *node* has neither a left nor a right child, i.e., until *node* becomes a leaf.

After removing *node*, we need to balance its ancestors. We apply the *balance* method of class *AVL_Tree* to balance the ancestors of the deleted node.

The following method *searchData(String s)* can be invoked to find a node that stores string *s* in an AVL-tree. It searches the AVL-tree as a binary search tree. It returns a node that contains the data. Then, we can apply the *removeNode (Node node)* method to remove the node from the AVL-tree. For instance, after adding the methods *searchData* and *removeNode* into the class *AVL_Tree* presented in the above section, we can add the following statements into the main method of class *AVL_Tree*.

```
Node node = stringsTree.searchData("Abc");
if (node != null) stringsTree.removeNode(node);
```

The statements remove data *Abc* from AVL-tree *stringsTree*.

```java
public Node searchData(String s) {
    if (root == null) return null;
    Node tempNode = root;
    while (tempNode != null) {
        int c = ((String)
            tempNode.getData()).compareTo(s);
        if (c == 0) return tempNode;
        if (c < 0) tempNode =
            tempNode.getRightChild();
        else tempNode = tempNode.getLeftChild();
    }
    return null;
}
public void removeNode(Node node) {
    Node tempNode = node;
    while (tempNode.hasLeftChild() ||
                tempNode.hasRightChild()) {
        if (tempNode.hasLeftChild()) {
            tempNode = tempNode.getLeftChild();
            while (tempNode.hasRightChild())
                tempNode = tempNode.getRightChild();
        } else {
                tempNode = tempNode.getRightChild();
                while (tempNode.hasLeftChild())
                    tempNode = tempNode.getLeftChild();
        }
        node.setData(tempNode.getData());
    }
    if (tempNode == root) {
        root = null; return;
    }
    if (tempNode.isLeftChild()) {
        node = tempNode.parent;
        node.removeLeftChild();
        if (node.hasRightChild())
            balance(node.getRightChild());
        else balance(node);
    } else {
        node = tempNode.parent;
        node.removeRightChild();
        if (node.hasLeftChild())
            balance(node.getLeftChild());
        else balance(node);
    }
}
```

## 8.3.2.6 Analysis of AVL-Trees

Assume that an instance of class *Node* can be created in constant time, and a data comparison can be done in constant time. The assumptions may not be valid for complex object creation and complex data object comparison. A time complexity based on the assumptions for methods of AVL-trees can be adjusted to accommodate complex object creations and comparisons.

We show that the time complexity of methods *addData(String s)*, *balance (Node node)*, and *removeNode(Node node)* in class *AVL_Tree* is $\Omega(\log n)$, where $n$ is the number of nodes in an AVL-tree, for which the methods are invoked. The complexity is implied by the following two propositions.

**Proposition 8.1** *The height of an AVL-tree with n nodes is* $\Omega(\log n)$.

*Proof:* We can prove two conclusions:

1.  An AVL-tree of height $h$ has at most $2^{h+1} - 1$ nodes.
2.  An AVL-tree of height $h$ has at least $((5+2\sqrt{5})/5)\times((1+\sqrt{5})/2)^h + ((5-2\sqrt{5})/5)\times((1-\sqrt{5})/2)^h - 1$ nodes.

The number of nodes in a *complete binary tree* implies the first conclusion. A complete binary tree of height $h$ has $h+1$ levels of nodes. Each node in the last level is a leaf. All the nodes in other levels have both a left and a right child. It has the maximum number of nodes among all AVL-trees of height $h$. A complete binary tree has $2^{h+1} - 1$ nodes, which can be proved by a simple induction on the number of levels in a complete binary tree.

Assume an AVL-tree of height $h$. The tree has the minimum number of nodes if

*   the left subtree of the root is of height $h - 1$ and it has the minimum number of nodes among all AVL-trees of height $h - 1$, and
*   the right subtree of the root is of height $h - 2$ and it has the minimum number of nodes among all AVL-trees of height $h - 2$.

By a simple induction on the height $h$ of an AVL-tree that satisfies the above two conditions, we can prove that the number of nodes in the AVL-tree is $((5+2\sqrt{5})/5)\times((1+\sqrt{5})/2)^h + ((5-2\sqrt{5})/5)\times((1-\sqrt{5})/2)^h - 1$.

By the above two conclusions, we can see that the height of an AVL-tree with $n$ nodes is at most $c \times \log n$ and is at least $c' \times \log n$ for some real constants $c, c' > 0$. Therefore, the height of an AVL-tree with $n$ nodes is $\Omega(\log n)$. $\square$

**Proposition 8.2** *The time required by a left or right rotation to balance node A shown in Fig. 8.10 is* $O(1)$, *so is the time required by the promotion technique shown in Fig. 8.11.*

*Proof:* The proposition can be proved by counting the number of statements in the implementation of the rotation or promotion in class *AVL_Tree*. The number is bounded by a constant integer. Each of the statements exchanges node references, which can be performed in constant time. $\square$

**Proposition 8.3** *The time required by each of the methods addData(String s), balance(Node node), searchData(String s), and removeNode(Node node) for an AVL-tree with n nodes is O(log n).*

*Proof:* Let us assume an AVL-tree of height $h$ with $n$ nodes. As shown in Proposition 8.1, the height $h$ is $\Omega(\log n)$.

Method *addData(String s)* of class *AVL_Tree* repeatedly compares $s$ with the data object in *tempNode* and executes one of the two statements

```
tempNode = tempNode.getLeftChild();
tempNode = tempNode.getRightChild();
```

until *tempNode* has no left or right subtree that should contain $s$. Then, a new node is created by *tempNode.addLeft(s)* or *tempNode.addRight(s)*, and the *balance* method is invoked with the new node.

Method *addData* makes at most $h+1$ comparisons between $s$ and the data object in *tempNode*. The invoked *getLeftChild* and *getRightChild* methods directly access instance fields of *tempNode*. Each access takes one unit of time. The invoked methods are repeated at most $h+1$ times. Shortly we shall show that an invocation of the *balance* method takes at most $c \times h$ units of time for some constant $c > 0$. Therefore, the total time required by method *addData* is $c' \times h$ for some $c' > 0$. By Proposition 8.1, the time is $\Omega(\log n)$.

The method *balance(Node node)* initializes local variable *currentNode* with argument *node*. It executes statement

```
currentParent = currentNode.parent;
```

to advance to the upper level. For each execution of the above statement, method *balance* compares the left and right height of *currentParent*. According to the comparison result, the method may rotate a subtree or promote a node. By Proposition 8.2, a rotation or promotion takes constant time. There are at most $h + 2$ levels in the tree being balanced. For each level, the method spends time limited by a constant $c > 0$. The total time required by method *balance* is at most $c \times (h + 2)$. By Proposition 8.1, the time complexity of method *balance* is $O(\log n)$.

The method *searchData(String s)* starts by initializing local variable *tempNode* with the root of an AVL-tree. It compares $s$ with the data object in *tempNode*, and moves to either the left or right child of *tempNode* by assigning *tempNode* with the left or right child. The process of comparison and movement can be finished in a constant time $c$. It repeats until either a data object equal to $s$ is found or *tempNode* becomes *null*. Since the height of the AVL-tree is $h$, the process is repeated at most $h+1$ times. Therefore, the time complexity of method *searchData* is $c \times h$, which is $O(\log n)$ by Proposition 8.1.

The method *removeNode(Node node)* uses the data object in the inorder leaf predecessor or successor of *node* to replace the data object in *node*. The total number of movements made with statements

```
tempNode = tempNode.getRightChild();
tempNode = tempNode.getLeftChild();
```

to find inorder predecessors and successors is $h$. Each movement takes constant time. It takes constant time to remove a left or right child for a node. Therefore, the total time required by method *removeNode* is at least $c \times h$ and at most $c' \times h$ for constants $c, c' > 0$. By Proposition 8.1, the time complexity of method *removeNode* is $\Omega(\log n)$.     □

By the above analysis, the efficiency of an AVL-tree for data object insertion or deletion is $\Omega(\log n)$, better than the worst-case complexity of a binary search tree for data object insertion and deletion, which is $O(n)$.

# 8.4 B-Trees

## 8.4.1 B-Tree as *m*-ary Tree

The B-tree is the de facto standard data structure for indexing data in secondary storage for database systems. A B-tree can be designed to minimize the number of secondary storage accesses. It is a special type of $m$-ary tree. It extends a binary search tree by allowing more than two ways to switch.

In the following definition, we use the ceiling notation $\lceil r \rceil$ for a real number $r$ to denote the smallest integer that is greater than or equal to r. For an integer $k$, the Java expression $(k+1)/2$ returns an integer that is equal to ceiling $\lceil k/2 \rceil$. For example, we have $(3+1)/2 = \lceil 3/2 \rceil = 2$.

A *B-tree* of arity $m$ with $m \geq 3$ is a $m$-ary tree such that

1. The root has at least two children if it is not a leaf.
2. Each non-leaf node, except the root, has at least $\lceil m/2 \rceil$ children.
3. Each node that is not the root of the B-tree contains at least $\lceil m/2 \rceil - 1$ and at most $m - 1$ data objects.
4. If a non-leaf node has $k+1$ child nodes $t_0, t_1, \ldots, t_k$ with $\lceil m/2 \rceil - 1 \leq k \leq m - 1$, it contains $k$ data objects $s_0, s_1, \ldots, s_{k-1}$ such that

    - $s_0 < s_1 < \ldots < s_{k-1}$,
    - data objects in subtree rooted at $t_0$ are less than $s_0$,
    - data objects stored in subtree rooted at node $t_i$ with $0 < i < k$ are greater than $s_{i-1}$ and less than $s_i$, and
    - data objects in subtree rooted at $t_k$ are greater than $s_{k-1}$.

5. All the leaf nodes are at the same level in the tree.

Non-leaf nodes in a B-tree may have various numbers of children. A node in a B-tree of arity $m$ has at most $m$ children. Condition 2 ensures a minimum number of children for each non-leaf node. Thus, a B-tree is balanced and has a better performance than a linearly linked list. Condition 4 extends the 2-way switch supported by binary search tree with a $k+1$-way switch. The value of $k$ varies at nodes with $\lceil m/2 \rceil \leq k+1 \leq m$. Condition 5 is a balancing condition. It ensures that no node can have a leaf child and a non-leaf child.

By the above definition, a non-leaf node in a B-tree of arity 3 has at least two children and at most 3 children. Fig. 8.12 shows a B-tree of arity 3. Its root contains one data object. The root provides two ways to switch after comparing a target data object with the data object in the root. Since $m = 3$, we have $\lceil m/2 \rceil - 1 = 1$, $m-1 = 2$, and a node in the B-tree contains at least one data object and at most two data objects.

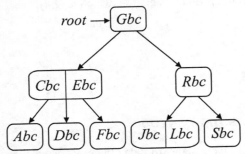

**Fig. 8.12** A B-tree with arity 3

## 8.4.2 Class *B_Tree*

We now implement B-trees with Java class *B_Tree*, which extends class *M_aryTree*. The inner class *Node* in class *M_aryTree* is available for class *B_Tree*. A node in a B-tree needs to keep a sequence of data objects, which are called keys and have a linear order. We can compare keys for less-than, equal-to, and greater-than relationships.

### 8.4.2.1 A Structure for Keys

We define an inner class named *Struct* in class *B_Tree* to organize the keys in nodes. We use the class *Node* defined in class *M_aryTree*, and the data in a node of a B-tree is a struct of keys.

Class *Struct* defines instance variables with declarations

```
int arity, size;
Object[] keys;
```

The integer variable *arity* denotes the maximum number of keys a struct may contain. The value of variable *size* is the number of keys stored in a struct.

As described in the definition of B-tree, the number of keys in a non-leaf node is one less than the number of children of the node. In other words, the *size* of a struct in a node is one less than the degree of the node, which is at most equal to the *arity* of the B-tree.

Assume a B-tree with arity *m*. For the convenience of implementation of node addition and merge operations, we allow a node to have *m*+1 children temporarily. Half of the *m*+1 children will be shifted into a new node in the B-tree. Similarly, we allow a struct to hold *m* keys temporarily. Except for the middle key in the struct, all the remaining *m*−1 keys will be separated into two structs in two nodes, one of which is a new node. The middle key will be stored in the common parent of the two nodes.

Class *Struct* defines two constructors. The no-argument constructor

```
public Struct() { }
```

does nothing. The constructor *Struct(int arity)* initializes the *arity* instance field and creates an array of length *arity* to hold keys.

Class *Struct* defines instance methods *keyAt(int index)*, *search(Object key)*, *addKey(Object key)*, and *deleteKey(Object key)* to retrieve a key at a given index, search for the index of a given key, add a key into or delete a key from a struct. The *addKey* method inserts a key into the array encapsulated in a struct. It maintains the array in ascending order.

## 8.4.2.2 Class B_Tree

Class *B_Tree* defines constructor

```
public B_Tree(int arity) { super(arity); }
```

to initialize the *arity* field, inherited from class *M_aryTree*. Methods of class *B_Tree* apply expression *new Node(arity + 1)* to create nodes. Thus, each node can hold *arity*+1 children. Similarly, a struct is created with expression *new Struct(arity)*. Thus, a struct may temporarily hold one more key than allowed.

Class *B_Tree* defines method *addKey(Object key)* to add a key into a B-tree. If the B-tree is empty, i.e., if field *root* in the B-tree has value *null*, the method creates a node as root, creates a struct to hold the key, and assigns the data field of the node with the struct.

For a non-empty B-tree, method *addKey(Object key)* finds a leaf node to host the key. It follows an approach similar to that of a binary search tree to find the leaf. A node in a B-tree may have a multi-way switch rather than a 2-way switch. The *addKey* method uses variables *currentNode* and *currentKeys* to hold a node and the struct in the node. It uses the expression *currentKeys.search(key)* to find an index in the struct. If the target *key* is not in *currentKeys*, the index value identifies a subtree that should contain *key*; otherwise, the expression evaluates to −1 and the *addKey* method returns. Variables *currentNode* and *currentKeys* are updated with statements

```
currentNode = currentNode.getChild(index);
currentKeys = (Struct) currentNode.getData();
```

The search process repeats until the *currentNode* variable references a leaf node, into which we add the argument *key*.

After method *addKey(Object key)* adds *key* into the struct in the *currentNode*, the struct may contain an *arity* number of keys, which is one more than allowed. Then, the method moves the middle key from struct *currentKeys* into the parent node of *currentNode*, and separates the remaining keys in *currentNode* into two nodes. Assume the middle key has index $k$ in the parent struct. A new node is created to host the first $(arity+1)/2 - 1$ keys in the struct *currentKeys*. It is inserted at index $k$ in the *children* array in the parent node.

Class *B_Tree* is defined as follows. It can be compiled and its main method can run.

```java
import java.util.*;
public class B_Tree extends M_aryTree {
    public static void main(String[] args) {
        String[] names = {"Cbc", "Bbc", "Abc"};
        B_Tree stringsTree = new B_Tree(3);
        for (int i = 0; i < names.length; i++)
            stringsTree.addKey(names[i]);
        stringsTree.deleteKey("Abc");
        Enumeration nodes = stringsTree.elements();
        while (nodes.hasMoreElements()) {
            Node tempNode =
                    (Node) nodes.nextElement();
            Struct struct =
                    (Struct) tempNode.getData();
            for (int i = 0; i < struct.size; i++)
                System.out.print
                    ((String) struct.keyAt(i) + " ");
            System.out.println(" ");
        }
    }

    public B_Tree(int arity) { super(arity); }

    public void addKey(Object key) {
        if (root == null) {
            Node newNode = new Node(arity+1);
            Struct keys = new Struct(arity);
            keys.addKey(key);
            newNode.setData(keys);
            root = newNode;
            return;
        }

        /* Finds a leaf to insert key. The leaf
         * will be referenced by currentNode.
         */
        Node currentNode = root;
        Struct currentKeys =
                    (Struct) root.getData();
        int index;
        Stack nodes = new Stack();
        while (currentNode.degree() > 0) {
```

```
            index = currentKeys.search(key);
            if (index == -1) return;
            nodes.push(currentNode);
            currentNode =
                    currentNode.getChild(index);
            currentKeys = (Struct)
                    currentNode.getData();
        }

        index = currentKeys.search(key);
        if (index == -1) return;

        // insert key into currentNode
        currentKeys.addKey(key);

        /* If a node contains arity number of keys,
         * split the node to two nodes.
         * Repeat the step for its parent
         * and other ancesters if necessary.
         */
        while (currentKeys.size == arity) {
            int mid = (arity+1)/2 - 1;
            key = currentKeys.keyAt(mid);
            currentKeys.deleteKey(key);
            Node newNode = new Node(arity+1);
            Struct newStruct = new Struct(arity);
            newNode.setData(newStruct);

            // move keys from currentNode to newNode
            for (int i= 0; i < (arity+1)/2-1; i++) {
                Object tempKey= currentKeys.keyAt(0);
                newStruct.addKey(tempKey);
                currentKeys.deleteKey(tempKey);
            }

            // move children
            if (currentNode.degree() > 0)
            for (int i=0; i <= (arity+1)/2 - 1;i++){
                Node child = currentNode.getChild(0);
                newNode.addChild(child, i);
                currentNode.deleteChild(0);
            }

            if (currentNode == root) {
                root = new Node(arity+1);
                Struct tempStruct =new Struct(arity);
                tempStruct.addKey(key);
```

```
            root.setData(tempStruct);
            root.addChild(newNode, 0);
            root.addChild(currentNode, 1);
            return;
        }

        // add key and newNode into parent
        currentNode = (Node) nodes.peek();
        nodes.pop();
        currentKeys = (Struct)
                        currentNode.getData();
        index = currentKeys.addKey(key);
        currentNode.addChild(newNode, index);
    }
}

class Struct {
    public Struct() { this(3); }
    public Struct(int arity) {
        this.arity = arity;
        keys = new Object[arity];
    }
    public Object keyAt(int index) {
        if (index < 0 || index >= size)
            return null;
        return keys[index];
    }
    public int search(Object key) {
        for (int i = 0; i < size; i++) {
            int c = ((String) key).
                    compareTo((String) keys[i]);
            if (c < 0) return i;
            if (c == 0) return -1;
        }
        return size;
    }
    public int addKey(Object key) {
        int index = search(key);
        if (index == -1) return -1;
        for (int k = size; k > index; k--)
            keys[k] = keys[k-1];
        keys[index] = key;
        size++;
        return index;
    }
```

```
public boolean deleteKey(Object key) {
    int index = -1;
    for (int i = 0; i < size; i++) {
        int c = ((String) key).
                compareTo((String) keys[i]);
        if (c < 0) return false;
        if (c == 0) {
            index = i; break;
        }
    }
    if (index == -1) return false;
    for (int j = index+1; j < size; j++)
        keys[j-1] = keys[j];
    size--;
    return true;
}
int arity, size;
Object[] keys;
}
}
```

## 8.4.2.3 Key Deletions

We now consider the problem of deleting a key from a B-tree. The keys in the B-tree can be enumerated in ascending order. The enumeration extends the notion of inorder traversal of a binary tree for a B-tree. For a node $n$ that has children $n_0$, $n_1$, ..., $n_k$ and that contains keys $s_0, s_1, ..., s_{k-1}$ in the B-tree, the extended inorder traversal of the B-tree rooted at $n$ can be recursively described as

- traversing the B-tree rooted at $n_0$ in inorder,
- visiting key $s_0$,
- traversing the B-tree rooted at $n_1$ in inorder,
- visiting key $s_1$,
- ...,
- traversing the B-tree rooted at $n_k$ in inorder.

To delete a key from a B-tree, if the key is in a leaf, we delete it from the leaf. Otherwise, we use its inorder predecessor or successor that is in a leaf node of the B-tree to replace the key and delete the predecessor or successor from the leaf node. Thus, we can delete a key, a copy of which may have been placed into a higher-level node, from a leaf of the B-tree. With the B-tree in Fig. 8.12 as example, to delete string *Ebc*, we can replace the string with *Dbc* and delete *Dbc* from the lowest level. Another solution is to replace *Ebc* with *Fbc* and delete *Fbc* from the leaf that contains *Fbc*.

Assume a struct referenced with variable *currentKeys* and a *key* in the struct. The index of *key* in the struct can be found in variable *index* after executing statements

```
currentKeys.deleteKey(key);
index = currentKeys.search(key);
```

The code also deletes *key* from *currentKeys*.

We use the following code to replace a key that is to be deleted with its inorder predecessor or successor in a leaf. After the code is executed, variable *key* references a key that should be deleted, struct *currentKeys* contains the key, and *currentNode* is a leaf node that contains the struct. The local variable *currentNode* is initialized with the root of the B-tree, and *currentKeys* with the struct in the root. Integer variable *index* is set with –1 if *key* is in *currentKeys*; otherwise, it is set with the index of a subtree that should contain *key*. We use a stack referenced with local variable *nodes* to store nodes encountered during the key replacement.

```
// search for key in the B_Tree
while (currentNode.degree() > 0) {
    if (index == -1) break;
    nodes.push(currentNode);
    currentNode = currentNode.getChild(index);
    currentKeys = (Struct)
                         currentNode.getData();
    index = currentKeys.search(key);
}

if (index == -1 && currentNode.degree() > 0){
    // key is in a non-leaf node
    currentKeys.deleteKey(key);
    index = currentKeys.search(key);
    nodes.push(currentNode);

    Struct tempStruct;
    if (index < currentNode.degree()-1) {
        // finds inorder successor
        currentNode=currentNode.
                         getChild(index+1);
        while (currentNode.degree()>0){
            nodes.push(currentNode);
            currentNode=currentNode.getChild(0);
        }
        tempStruct = (Struct)
                         currentNode.getData();
        key = tempStruct.keyAt(0);
    } else {
        // finds inorder predecessor
        currentNode=currentNode.getChild(index);
        while (currentNode.degree()>0){
            nodes.push(currentNode);
            currentNode = currentNode.getChild(
                         currentNode.degree()-1);
        }
```

```
        tempStruct = (Struct)
                            currentNode.getData();
        key=tempStruct.keyAt(tempStruct.size-1);
    }


    currentKeys.addKey(key);
    tempStruct.deleteKey(key);
    currentKeys = tempStruct;
} else {
    if (index == -1)
        // key to be deleted is in a leaf
        currentKeys.deleteKey(key);
    else // key is not in the B-tree
        return false;
}
```

After the above code is run, *key* is deleted from the B-tree, local variable *currentNode* references a leaf that lost a key, and *currentKeys* references the struct in the leaf.

After a *key* is deleted from struct *currentKeys*, the number of keys in the struct may be less than the required minimum number $\lceil m/2 \rceil - 1$, where *m* is equal to the *arity* of the B-tree. In order to rebuild the B-tree, we can either

- remove a key from an adjacent sibling of *currentNode*, add the key into the parent of *currentNode*, and move a key from the parent into *currentNode*, or
- merge *currentNode* with an adjacent sibling.

The first technique moves keys. The second merges nodes. We now describe how to implement the key movement and node merge.

The key movement applies when the number of keys in an adjacent sibling of *currentNode* is at least $\lceil m/2 \rceil$. If the sibling is the left sibling of *currentNode* and it is at *index* in the *children* array of the parent node of *currentNode*, we move the key at *index* in the parent into *currentKeys*, move the last key from the sibling to the parent. This process is called a right rotation in method *deleteKey*. We can similarly implement a left rotation, which removes a key from the right sibling of *currentNode*.

The node merge applies when the number of keys in a sibling of *currentNode* is equal to $\lceil m/2 \rceil - 1$. If the sibling is the left sibling of *currentNode* and it is at *index* in the *children* array of the parent of *currentNode*, we add the key at *index* in the parent and all the keys in *currentNode* into the left sibling. Then we delete the *currentNode* from the *children* array of the parent node. Thus, *currentNode* is merged into its left sibling. If the sibling is the right sibling of *currentNode*, we merge the sibling into *currentNode*.

We may apply the key movement and node merge operations for ancestors of the leaf from which a key is deleted.

The following method, *deleteKey(Object key)*, applies the techniques of key replacement, key movement, and node merge to delete *key* from a B-tree and re-

build the resulting tree into a B-tree. The method can be added into class *B_Tree*.
It can be invoked with statements

```
stringsTree.deleteKey("Abc");
stringsTree.deleteKey("Cbc");
```

in the main method of class *B_Tree*, which is presented in the above section.

```
public boolean deleteKey(Object key) {
    if (root == null) return false;

    Node currentNode = root;
    Struct currentKeys = (Struct) root.getData();
    int index = currentKeys.search(key);

    Stack nodes = new Stack();
    // searches for key in the B_Tree
    while (currentNode.degree() > 0) {
        if (index == -1) break; // key is found
        nodes.push(currentNode);
        currentNode = currentNode.getChild(index);
        currentKeys = (Struct)
                             currentNode.getData();
        index = currentKeys.search(key);
    }

    if (index == -1 && currentNode.degree() > 0) {
        // key is in a non-leaf node
        currentKeys.deleteKey(key);
        index = currentKeys.search(key);
        nodes.push(currentNode);

        Struct tempStruct;
        if (index < currentNode.degree() - 1) {
            // finds inorder successor
            currentNode =
                    currentNode.getChild(index+1);
            while (currentNode.degree() > 0) {
                nodes.push(currentNode);
                currentNode =
                        currentNode.getChild(0);
            }
            tempStruct = (Struct)
                    currentNode.getData();
            key = tempStruct.keyAt(0);
        } else {
            // finds inorder predecessor
            currentNode =
                    currentNode.getChild(index);
            while (currentNode.degree() > 0) {
```

```
                    nodes.push(currentNode);
                    currentNode =
                            currentNode.getChild(
                                currentNode.degree()-1);
                }
                tempStruct = (Struct)
                            currentNode.getData();
                key = tempStruct.keyAt(
                                    tempStruct.size-1);
            }

        currentKeys.addKey(key);
        tempStruct.deleteKey(key);
        currentKeys = tempStruct;
    } else {
        if (index == -1)
            currentKeys.deleteKey(key);
        else return false; // key is not in B-tree
    }
    while (currentNode != root &&
            currentKeys.size < (arity+1)/2 -1) {
    Node parent = (Node) nodes.peek();
    nodes.pop();
    Struct parentKeys = (Struct)
                                parent.getData();

    /* finds the index of currentNode in the
     * children array of parentNode
     */
    for (int i = 0; i < parent.degree(); i++)
        if (currentNode == parent.getChild(i)) {
            index = i;
            break;
        }
    if (index > 0) {
    // currentNode has left sibling
        Node leftSibling =
                    parent.getChild(index-1);
        Struct leftKeys = (Struct)
                    leftSibling.getData();
        Object tempKey =
                    parentKeys.keyAt(index-1);
        parentKeys.deleteKey(tempKey);

        if (leftKeys.size >= (arity+1)/2) {
            // right rotation
            Object movedKey =
```

```
            leftKeys.keyAt(leftKeys.size-1);
        leftKeys.deleteKey(movedKey);
        parentKeys.addKey(movedKey);
        currentKeys.addKey(tempKey);

        if (currentNode.degree() > 0) {
            Node movedNode =
                leftSibling.getChild(
                    leftSibling.degree()-1);
            leftSibling.
                    removeChild(movedNode);
            currentNode.addChild(movedNode,0);
        }
        return true;
    } else {
        // node merge
        leftKeys.addKey(tempKey);
        for (int i=0;i<currentKeys.size;i++){
            leftKeys.addKey(
                        currentKeys.keyAt(i));
            if (currentNode.degree() > 0) {
                Node tempNode =
                    currentNode.getChild(i);
                leftSibling.addChild(
                tempNode,leftSibling.degree());
            }
        }
        if (currentNode.degree() > 0)
        leftSibling.addChild(
            currentNode.getChild
                (currentNode.degree()-1));
        parent.deleteChild(index);
        currentNode = parent;
        currentKeys = parentKeys;
        continue;
    }
} else {
// currentNode has right sibling
    Node rightSibling =
                    parent.getChild(index+1);
    Struct rightKeys = (Struct)
                    rightSibling.getData();
    Object tempKey =
                    parentKeys.keyAt(index);
    parentKeys.deleteKey(tempKey);

    if (rightKeys.size >= (arity+1)/2) {
```

```
        // left rotation
        Object movedKey = rightKeys.keyAt(0);
        rightKeys.deleteKey(movedKey);
        parentKeys.addKey(movedKey);
        currentKeys.addKey(tempKey);
        if (currentNode.degree() > 0){
            Node movedNode =
                    rightSibling.getChild(0);
            rightSibling.removeChild
                            (movedNode);
            currentNode.addChild(movedNode,
                    currentNode.degree());
        }
        return true;
    } else {
        currentKeys.addKey(tempKey);
        for (int i=0; i<rightKeys.size;i++) {
            currentKeys.addKey(
                    rightKeys.keyAt(i));
            if (currentNode.degree() > 0) {
                Node tempNode =
                    rightSibling.getChild(i);
                currentNode.addChild(tempNode);
            }
        }
        if (currentNode.degree() > 0)
            currentNode.addChild(rightSibling.
            getChild(rightSibling.degree()-1));
        parent.deleteChild(index+1);
        currentNode = parent;
        currentKeys = parentKeys;
        continue;
    }
  }
 }
 if (currentNode == root)
    if (((Struct) root.getData()).size == 0)
        if (root.degree() > 0)
            root = root.getChild(0);
        else root = null;
 return true;
}
```

**Exercise 8.2** When *currentNode* contains less than $\lceil m/2 \rceil - 1$ keys, the *deleteKey* method considers its left sibling for key movement or node merge. If *currentNode* has no left sibling, the method considers its right sibling for key movement or node merge. Modify method *deleteKey(Object key)* that considers both the left and right siblings for node merge and, if node merge is impossible, the method considers key movement from an adjacent sibling. The resulting tree may be "shorter" than that produced with the above *deleteKey* method.

## 8.4.3 Analysis of Class *B_Tree*

### 8.4.3.1 B-Tree Sizes

Assume a B-tree of arity $m$ and height $h$. A node in the tree has at most $m$ children. The maximum number of nodes in the tree is equal to

$$1 + m + m^2 + \ldots + m^h = (m^{h+1} - 1) / (m - 1).$$

When the B-tree has the maximum number of nodes, each node inside the tree has $m - 1$ keys. A leaf in the tree has at most $m - 1$ keys. The maximum number of keys in the B-tree is $m^{h+1} - 1$.

The root of the B-tree may have only two children. Other nodes in the B-tree must have at least $\lceil m/2 \rceil$ children. The minimum number of nodes in the B-tree is

$$1 + 2 + 2 \times \lceil m/2 \rceil + 2 \times \lceil m/2 \rceil^2 + \ldots + 2 \times \lceil m/2 \rceil^{h-1}$$
$$= 2 \times (\lceil m/2 \rceil^h - 1) / (\lceil m/2 \rceil - 1) + 1.$$

When the B-tree has the minimum number of keys, its root node has only one key, and each of the other nodes has $\lceil m/2 \rceil - 1$ keys. Therefore, the minimum number of keys in the B-tree is $2 \times \lceil m/2 \rceil^h - 1$.

If we regard arity $m$ as a constant, the above two quantities can be used to establish the claims

- $h < c \times \log n$, and
- $h > c' \times \log n$,

for real constants $c', c > 0$, where $n$ is the number of nodes in a B-tree and $h$ is the height of the B-tree. We have $h \in \Omega(\log n)$.

### 8.4.3.2 Insertion Cost

As described in Section 8.4.2.2, the method *addKey(Object key)* finds a leaf in a B-tree to host the argument *key*. To find the leaf, denoted with *currentNode*, it takes time in $\Omega(\log n)$.

If *currentNode* contains fewer than *arity* keys, the method *addKey* returns; otherwise, the methods moves a key from *currentNode* to the parent of *currentNode* and separates the remaining keys in *currentNode* into two nodes. Then, the *addKey* method treats the parent of *currentNode* as *currentNode* and tests if *currentNode* contains more than *arity* − 1 keys. If *currentNode* does, *currentNode* will be split by the method again.

The splitting operation may be applied for all the ancestors of the leaf that hosts the added key. An application of the operation takes constant time. The number of ancestors of a leaf node is equal to $h$, the height of the B-tree. Therefore, the total cost of the splitting operations is $O(\log n)$.

By summing up the costs, we can see that the time complexity of method *addKey* is $\Omega(\log n)$.

### 8.4.3.3 Search Cost

To search for a key in a B-tree, we start with the root as *currentNode*. We compare the key with the keys in *currentNode*. If the key is equal to a key in *currentNode*, the search is done; otherwise, we can find a child of *currentNode* such that if the target key is in the B-tree, it must be in the subtree rooted at the child. Thus, we can use the child as *currentNode* and repeat the above process. Since each comparison takes one unit of time and we need to make at most $m \times h$ comparisons, the worst-case cost of finding a key in a B-tree of height $h$ is proportional to $h$. By the conclusion of Section 8.4.3.1, the cost of searching a B-tree for a key is $O(\log n)$.

### 8.4.3.4 Deletion Cost

The *deleteKey*(*Object key*) method takes two steps:

1.  Find the inorder predecessor or successor key in a leaf for the *key* to be deleted, replace *key* with the predecessor or successor in the leaf, and delete the predecessor or successor from the leaf.
2.  Correct the deficiency in the number of keys in a node. Initially, the current node is the leaf that lost a key. The correction may take the form of either key movement or node merge. It takes a constant time for a key movement or node merge. The correction may be repeated for the leaf and all the ancestors of the leaf.

The first step takes time proportional to $h$, the height of the B-tree. Since $h$ is $\Omega(\log n)$, the time required by Step 1 is $\Omega(\log n)$. The time required by the second step is proportional to the number of key movements and node merges, which is $O(\log n)$. Therefore, the time complexity of method *deleteKey* is $\Omega(\log n)$.

# 8.5 Summary

In this chapter, we discuss an important type of data structure – tree. Some applications can be naturally represented with trees. For example, the administration hierarchy of a company can be easily modeled with a tree. The components of a computer can be described with a tree. Trees are extensively used to organize data and information in computer programs. A tree representation can have a better performance than a linear data structure.

The first part of the chapter describes various types of tree. We present general trees, each node in which can have an arbitrary number of children. We also present $m$-ary trees, each of which has a fixed arity $m$. A node in a $m$-ary tree can have at most $m$ children. The children of a node in a $m$-ary tree are ordered. We discuss binary trees. Each node in a binary tree has a left and/or a right child.

Some applications involve systematically enumerating the nodes of a tree. The second part of the chapter discusses the various traversal strategies for trees. Specifically, we present the breadth-first and depth-first traversals for general trees and the preorder, inorder, and postorder traversals for binary trees.

We present binary search trees, which separate data into left and right subtrees. For a node in a binary search tree, all the data objects in the left subtree of the node are less than the data object in the node, all the data objects in the right subtree are greater than the data object. Each subtree in a binary search tree is a binary search tree. A node in a binary search tree provides a two-way switch. If a data object is less than the data in the node, it can be found only in the left subtree; if it is greater than the data, it can be found only in the right subtree.

A special type of binary search tree is an AVL-tree, which is a balanced tree. A node is balanced if the difference between its left and right heights is at most 1. A binary search tree is an AVL-tree if all nodes in it are balanced. In this chapter, we discuss how to insert data objects into an AVL-tree and how to delete data objects from an AVL-tree. An AVL-tree can be built from a sequence of data objects by inserting the data objects into an initially empty AVL-tree. By enumerating the data objects of the AVL-tree in inorder, we get a sorted sequence of the data objects.

A B-tree is the de facto standard indexing data structure for database systems. All the leafs in a B-tree are at the same level. A B-tree extends a $m$-ary tree. For a B-tree of arity $m$, a node contains at least $\lceil m/2 \rceil - 1$ and at most $m - 1$ keys. B-trees are balanced. It takes time $O(\log n)$ for key access, insertion, and deletion operations, where $n$ is the number of nodes in a B-tree.

# Chapter 9
# Graphs

An application may keep a set of objects and a binary relation between the objects. For example, in order to plan a tour we need the information on a set of cities and the roads between the cities. Another example is a club. We may represent the members of the club and the acquaintance relation between the members in a computer. A set of objects and a binary relation between the objects can be represented with a graph. A *graph* is a data structure that consists of a set of vertices and a set of edges between the vertices. Vertices can represent cities, club members, or other types of object. Edges represent binary relationships between the objects such as roads between cities or acquaintances between club members.

In mathematics, a graph denoted with $G = (V, E)$ consists of a set $V$ of vertices and a set $E$ of edges. Each edge represents a binary relationship between a pair of vertices in $V$. From the perspective of object-oriented programming, we can implement vertices and edges with objects, which contain information on individual vertices and on relationships between the vertices. We define operations for the vertex and edge objects. The operations can be invoked to access and process the information. We can define a class for vertices, a class for edges, and a class for graphs, which enclose vertices and edges.

In this chapter, we study graphs and define several classes in Java to represent graphs. A graph may be *undirected* if the direction of its edges does not matter. In our daily life, a relationship between two entities may have an orientation. Reversing the relationship may not have any sense for the entities. For example, the relationship *contains* between a directory $d$ and a file $f$ in a file system can be represented with predicate *contain*($d$, $f$), but predicate *contain*($f$, $d$) is senseless. Accordingly, the edges in a graph may be *directed*, and the graph is called a directed graph. We shall discuss how to implement both undirected and directed graph classes.

The edges of a graph may be associated with weights. The weight of an edge may represent the length or capacity of a road, or other type of measure on the edge. For simplicity, we assume weights are positive integers. We shall discuss how to represent the integer weights of edges in graphs, which are called weighted graphs.

An application may need to visit each vertex in a graph once and apply some method to process the vertex being visited. In this case, we need an algorithm to traverse the graph. We present two traversal methods – one implementing the *depth-first traversal*, the other *breadth-first*.

We can regard the weight of an edge as a measure of the length of the edge in an assumed unit. Based on implementations of weighted graphs, we present two algorithms for evaluating distances between vertices in a weighted graph. One algorithm calculates the shortest distances from a single vertex to other vertices in a graph. Another algorithm evaluates the shortest distance between each pair of vertices in a graph.

This chapter discusses the following topics on graphs.

- The notion graph and its variants. A graph may be directed or undirected based on whether the orientation of edges matters. In mathematics, a directed graph is treated as a special type of undirected graph by imposing directions on edges. In a computer program, an undirected graph is often treated as a special type of directed graph. Specifically, an edge in an undirected graph can be represented with a pair of directed edges that connect the same pair of vertices and have opposite orientations. We discuss how to use a matrix to represent the edges in a graph and how to use vectors to organize the edges.

- The traversal of a graph. We implement breadth-first traversal with a method for an undirected graph the edges of which are organized with a matrix and a method for an undirected graph the edges of which are structured with vectors. We also implement depth-first traversal for the two types of graph representation.

- The shortest distances from a single vertex to all vertices in a graph. They will be evaluated with a method named *distances*, which returns an array of integers to denote the distances. The shortest distances between all pairs of vertices in a graph are calculated with a method named *allDistances* that returns a 2-dimensional array of integers. The distance between a pair of vertices can be found in an entry of the array.

# 9.1 Graphs

## 9.1.1 The Notion of Graph

### 9.1.1.1 Vertex and Edge

A graph uses vertices to represent real-world entities, which are abstract or concrete. When the graph is drawn on paper, the vertices are presented as nodes. To represent the real-world entities with a graph in a computer program, we can use a class to represent the vertices of the graph. The instance fields and methods of the vertex class depend on the application of the program. For example, if we use a graph to describe employees and leaderships between employees, we need instance fields for employee name, position, address, and salary in the vertex class. We can define methods in the vertex class to access and process employee information. For simplicity, we shall not implement a particular vertex class. Instead, we use class *Object* as the vertex class. Readers can define specific vertex classes for different applications.

A graph stores data in vertices and represents a binary relation between the vertices. For example, a road between a pair of cities can be represented with an edge that joins the two vertices in a graph. The edge has attributes such as the length of the road. It can be regarded as an object, which has attribute *length*.

We shall describe various types of edge representation. The representations include boolean matrix, integer matrix, and vectors to satisfy particular applications. The representations encode various types of information.

A graph $G$ is modeled with a pair $(V, E)$, where $V$ is a set of vertex objects and $E$ a set of binary relationships between the vertices. The graph is *undirected* if for each pair of vertices $v_1, v_2 \in V$, edge $\langle v_1, v_2 \rangle \in E$ implies edge $\langle v_2, v_1 \rangle \in E$ in the graph. For a *directed* graph, an edge $\langle v_1, v_2 \rangle$ in the graph may not imply the existence of edge $\langle v_2, v_1 \rangle$. For example, the undirected graph shown in Fig. 9.1 has set $V = \{Quebec, Montreal, Ottawa, Toronto, London, Windsor\}$ of some Canadian city names as vertices and undirected edge set $E = \{\langle Quebec, Montreal \rangle, \langle Montreal, Ottawa \rangle, \langle Montreal, Toronto \rangle, \langle Ottawa, Toronto \rangle, \langle Toronto, London \rangle, \langle London, Windsor \rangle\}$. The edges joining cities represent highways.

**Exercise 9.1** Define a vertex class in Java to represent the various types of information on cities. For example, name, population, and area can be represented with instance variables in the class. In the main methods of the following graph classes, one can replace a city name, which is a string, with an instance of the class.

## 9.1.1.2 Path and Connectivity

We can navigate a graph to retrieve information from the graph. The navigation is based on the notion of path. Given a graph, a *path* is a sequence of vertices $v_0, v_1, \ldots, v_k$ such that $\langle v_i, v_{i+1} \rangle$ is an edge in the graph for $i = 0, 1, \ldots, k - 1$. The length of the path is the number $k$ of edges in the path. If the starting and ending vertices $v_0$ and $v_k$ of the path are the same vertex, the path is a *cycle*. A cycle of length 1 is called a *self-loop*. In the graph of Fig. 9.1, The sequence of vertices *Quebec, Montreal, Ottawa, Toronto, London, Windsor* denotes a path, which visits each vertex once in the graph. The graph has a cycle, which is *Montreal, Ottawa, Toronto, Montreal*. The cycle is a *simple* one since it visits each vertex in the cycle only once. The cycle *Montreal, Ottawa, Toronto, London, Toronto, Montreal* is not simple since it visits *Toronto* twice.

A graph is *disconnected* if the graph contains a pair of vertices such that there is no path between them; otherwise, the graph is *connected*. For example, the graph in Fig. 9.1 is connected. If a graph is not connected, we cannot reach all the vertices in the graph from a given vertex by following the edges of the graph.

A tree can be regarded as a special type of directed graph. There is a path from the root to each node in the tree. A tree has no cycle.

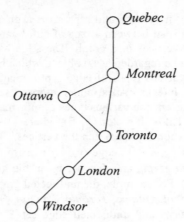

**Fig. 9.1** A graph with 6 vertices and 6 edges

### 9.1.1.3 Adjacency Set

If an edge joins vertices $v_1$ and $v_2$ in a graph, we say that $v_2$ is adjacent to $v_1$, and the edge is incident with the vertices. For a vertex $v$ in a graph, we can keep the vertices adjacent to $v$ in a set, which is called the *adjacency set* of vertex $v$. For example, the adjacency set of vertex *Montreal* in the undirected graph of Fig. 9.1 is {*Quebec, Ottawa, Toronto*}.

The adjacency set of a vertex can be equivalently represented with a set of edges that are incident with the vertex. That is, we can use a set of edges that have the vertex as starting vertex to represent the adjacency set.

We shall assume that there is at most one edge between each pair of vertices in a graph. One way to represent a graph in a computer is to associate each vertex in the graph with an adjacency set, which can be implemented with a linked list. In one of the graph implementations to be presented, we use a vector to represent an adjacency set. The vector is called an adjacency vector. For example, we can use an adjacency vector to hold vertices *Quebec, Ottawa, Toronto* for vertex *Montreal*.

### 9.1.1.4 Graph as ADT

Here, we describe graphs as an abstract data type (ADT) named *Graph*, which specifies the publicly available methods for graphs. The ADT can be used as a type to declare variables and create objects that represent graphs. The methods can be invoked for the graph objects. In software development, an ADT is the design of a class. A user can use the ADT to understand the class.

We assume the maximum number of vertices in a graph is fixed after the graph object is created. We leave an implementation of graph that can dynamically add and delete vertices as an assignment. The constructors of ADT *Graph* can accept an integer parameter that specifies the number of vertices for a created graph object. The ADT has the following three constructors:

```
Graph()
Graph(int vertexNumber)
Graph(Object[] vertices)
```

The no-argument constructor actually does nothing. The second constructor uses argument *vertexNumber* to indicate the number of vertices to be accommodated by the created graph. The third constructor has an object array as parameter. The elements of the array are used as the vertices of the created graph object.

We assume the vertices in a graph are indexed. We can use the index of a vertex to access the vertex. ADT *Graph* provides the following methods to access or set a vertex.

```
Object getVertex(int index)
void setVertex(Object vertex, int index)
```

Given two vertices or their indexes, a graph can decide whether the two vertices are connected with an edge. ADT *Graph* defines the following methods to test edges.

```
boolean isAdjacent(Object vertex1, Object vertex2)
boolean isAdjacent(int index1, int index2)
```

The edges (connections) between vertices can be dynamically added to and removed from a graph. ADT *Graph* provides the following methods for updating the edge set of a graph.

```
void addEdge(Object vertex1, Object vertex2)
void addEdge(int index1, int index2)
void removeEdge(Object vertex1,Object vertex2)
void removeEdge(int index1, int index2)
```

Removing an edge does not remove any vertex.

By using ADT *Graph* and its public methods, the following code creates a graph with strings as vertices. The code adds an edge between vertices *Ottawa* and *Quebec*. It uses the *getVertex* method to retrieve the stored strings.

```
String[] names = {"Ottawa", "Montreal", "Quebec"};
Graph stringsGraph = new Graph(names);
stringsGraph.addEdge("Ottawa", "Quebec");
for (int i = 0; i < names.length; i++)
    System.out.println((String)
                    stringsGraph.getVertex(i));
```

**Exercise 9.2** Create objects of the city class developed in Exercise 9.1 and replace the city names with the objects in the above code.

## 9.1.2 Graphs with Adjacency Matrix

The data stored in a graph includes the vertices and edges of the graph. We use an array to store the vertices. Readers may use different data structures to organize the vertices. For example, a linear data structure such as a vector or a linked list can be used to store the vertices. If vertices in a graph represent linearly ordered objects, we may use a binary search tree to organize the vertices of the graph. The graph creates an instance of class *BinarySearchTree* to host its vertices.

As with the storage of vertices, different data structures can be used to store the edges of a graph. Here, we present two representations for the edge set of a graph. The first representation uses a 2-dimensional array of integers or booleans. Note that the vertices in a graph are indexed. The indexes of vertices are used to index the entries in the matrix. Particularly, an element at position $(i, j)$ in the matrix is greater than 0 or *true* only if there is an edge from the vertex indexed at $i$ to the vertex indexed at $j$ in the vertex array.

Another representation of the edge set for a graph uses an adjacency vector for each vertex and an array to hold references to the vectors. Readers may choose a different data structure to organize the adjacency vectors. For example, a vector can be used to keep the adjacency vectors. A tree structure can store the references to the adjacency vectors if the vertices are organized with a tree.

We present three classes for graphs in this section. All the classes use an adjacency matrix to keep the edges of a graph. We shall use adjacency vectors in the next section for graphs. The classes to be presented are shown in Fig. 9.2. The class *Graph* implements the methods of the ADT *Graph* specified in Section 9.1.1.4. It represents undirected graphs. In its subclass *Digraph*, we modify some of the methods for directed graphs. Subclass *WeightedGraph* of class *Graph* represents undirected graphs the edges of which are weighted. As an exercise, readers can implement a class named *WeightedDigraph* that represents weighted, directed graphs. The class can extend class *WeightedGraph* like class *Digraph* extending *Graph*.

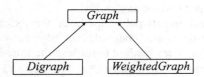

**Fig. 9.2** Graph classes

### 9.1.2.1 Class Graph for Undirected, Unweighted Graphs

The following class, class *Graph*, implements ADT *Graph*. It declares instance variables with statements

```
protected boolean[][] adjacencyMatrix;
protected Object[] vertices;
protected int vertexNumber;
```

Object array *vertices* is used to hold references to vertices. The 2-dimensional matrix *adjacencyMatrix* of booleans uses its element *adjacencyMatrix*[$i$][$j$] to indicate whether vertices indexed at $i$ and $j$ in the *vertices* array are connected with an edge. The length of the *vertices* array is equal to *vertexNumber*. The length of each dimension in the 2-dimensional array *adjacencyMatrix* is also equal to *vertexNumber*.

Fig. 9.3 illustrates the use of instance fields *vertices* and *adjacencyMatrix* in a graph object. It describes the graph shown in Fig. 9.1. The length of array *vertices* is 6, which is the value of *vertexNumber*. Matrix *adjacencyMatrix* is a 6 × 6 matrix of booleans. In Fig. 9.3, we use value 1 to denote boolean value *true*, and 0 to indicate *false*. From the matrix, we can see that the vertex *Montreal* is connected with vertices *Quebec*, *Ottawa*, and *Toronto*.

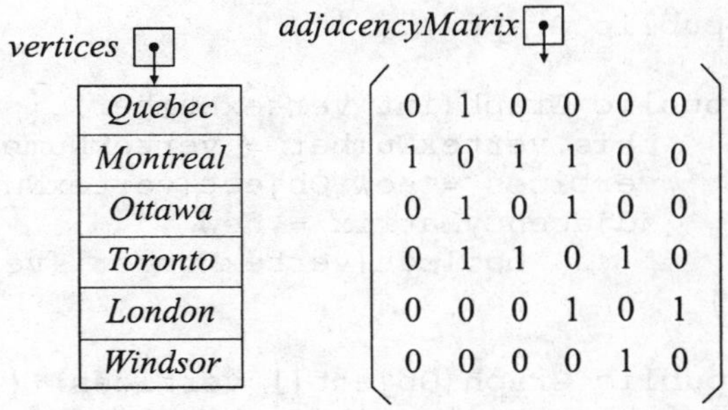

$$vertices \;\Box \qquad adjacencyMatrix\;\Box$$

| | | | | | | |
|---------|---|---|---|---|---|---|
| Quebec  | 0 | 1 | 0 | 0 | 0 | 0 |
| Montreal| 1 | 0 | 1 | 1 | 0 | 0 |
| Ottawa  | 0 | 1 | 0 | 1 | 0 | 0 |
| Toronto | 0 | 1 | 1 | 0 | 1 | 0 |
| London  | 0 | 0 | 0 | 1 | 0 | 1 |
| Windsor | 0 | 0 | 0 | 0 | 1 | 0 |

**Fig. 9.3** A matrix-based representation of a graph

Class *Graph* defines three constructors. The no-argument constructor *Graph()* does nothing. The constructor *Graph(int vertexNumber)* initializes the three instance fields for the created graph object. Specifically, the *vertexNumber* field of the created graph object is initialized with the argument; an array of length *vertexNumber* is created and assigned to variable *vertices*; and a 2-dimensional boolean array is created and assigned to variable *adjacencyMatrix*. The constructor *Graph(Object[] vertices)* invokes the above constructor to initialize the three instance variables. It initializes the elements of the *vertices* array in a created graph object with the elements of argument array *vertices*.

Class *Graph* implements methods *getVertex*, *setVertex*, *isAdjacent*, *addEdge*, and *removeEdge* to access and modify the information stored in a graph object. The semantics and signatures of the methods are explained in Section 9.1.1.4.

Class *Graph* includes a main method for testing the class. The main method uses a string array as argument to create a graph. It adds an edge between a pair of the strings (vertices). Then, it uses methods *getVertex* and *isAdjacent* to access the information stored in the graph object.

```
/** Class Graph for undirected, unweighted
 *    graphs. Vertex indexes are 0, ...,
 *    vertexNumber-1. Edges are represented in a
 *    2-dimensional boolean array.
 */
public class Graph {
    public static void main(String[] args) {
        String[] names =
```

```
                    {"Ottawa", "Montreal", "Quebec"};
      Graph stringsGraph = new Graph(names);
      stringsGraph.addEdge("Ottawa", "Quebec");
      for (int i= 0; i < names.length; i++)
         System.out.println((String)
                        stringsGraph.getVertex(i));
      if (stringsGraph.isAdjacent
                        ("Quebec", "Ottawa"))
         System.out.println("an edge");
   }

   public Graph() { }

   public Graph(int vertexNumber) {
      this.vertexNumber = vertexNumber;
      vertices = new Object[vertexNumber];
      adjacencyMatrix = new
            boolean[vertexNumber][vertexNumber];
   }

   public Graph(Object[] vertices) {
      this(vertices.length);
      for (int i=0; i < vertexNumber; i++)
         this.vertices[i] = vertices[i];
   }

   public Object getVertex(int index) {
      return vertices[index];
   }

   public void setVertex(Object vertex, int index)
   {
      vertices[index] = vertex;
   }

   public boolean isAdjacent(Object vertex1,
                             Object vertex2)
   {
      int index1 = indexOf(vertex1),
          index2 = indexOf(vertex2);
      return isAdjacent(index1, index2);
   }

   public boolean isAdjacent(int index1,
                             int index2) {
      if (index1 < 0 || index1 >= vertexNumber
         || index2 < 0 || index2 >= vertexNumber)
```

```
                    return false;
            return adjacencyMatrix[index1][index2];
    }

    public void addEdge(Object vertex1,
                        Object vertex2) {
        int index1 = indexOf(vertex1),
            index2 = indexOf(vertex2);
        addEdge(index1, index2);
    }

    public void addEdge(int index1, int index2) {
        if (index1 < 0 || index1 >= vertexNumber
            || index2 < 0 || index2 >= vertexNumber)
              return;
        adjacencyMatrix[index1][index2] =
        adjacencyMatrix[index2][index1] = true;
    }

    public void removeEdge(Object vertex1,
                           Object vertex2) {
        int index1 = indexOf(vertex1),
                index2 = indexOf(vertex2);
        removeEdge(index1, index2);
    }

    public void removeEdge(int index1, int index2)
    {
        if (index1 < 0 || index1 >= vertexNumber
            || index2 < 0 || index2 >= vertexNumber)
              return;
        adjacencyMatrix[index1][index2] =
        adjacencyMatrix[index2][index1] = false;
    }

    protected int indexOf(Object vertex) {
        for (int i= 0; i < vertexNumber; i++)
          if (vertex == vertices[i]) return i;
        return -1;
    }

    protected boolean[][] adjacencyMatrix;
    protected Object[] vertices;
    protected int vertexNumber;
}
```

## 9.1.2.2 *Class* Digraph *for Directed, Unweighted Graphs*

The class *Graph* presented in the above section represents undirected graphs. Here, we present a class for directed graphs. The class *Digraph* extends class *Graph*. Its constructors invoke constructors of class *Graph* to initialize the instance fields of a created directed graph.

Class *Digraph* overrides the inherited methods

```
public void addEdge(int index1, int index2)
public void removeEdge(int index1, int index2)
```

In class *Graph*, method *addEdge(int index1, int index2)* executes statement

```
adjacencyMatrix[index1][index2] =
adjacencyMatrix[index2][index1] = true;
```

Class *Digraph* implements the method with statement

```
adjacencyMatrix[index1][index2] = true;
```

In an object of class *Graph*, the edge between vertices indexed at *index1* and *index2* implies the opposite edge between *index2* and *index1*. The implication does not hold for a directed graph.

Similarly, when the *removeEdge* method is executed for an instance of class *Graph*, two symmetric entries in the *adjacencyMatrix* are set with *false* simultaneously. When the method is executed for a directed graph, only one entry in the matrix is changed to *false*.

The following class can be compiled. Its main method can be executed after the compilation.

```
/** Class Digraph for directed, unweighted
 *  graphs. The nodes are indexed with int 0,
 *  ..., vertexNumber-1. The edges are
 *  represented in 2-dimensional boolean array.
 */
public class Digraph extends Graph {
    public static void main(String[] args) {
        String[] names =
                {"Ottawa", "Montreal", "Quebec"};
        Digraph stringsGraph = new Digraph(names);
        stringsGraph.addEdge("Ottawa", "Quebec");
        for (int i= 0; i < names.length; i++)
            System.out.println((String)
                        stringsGraph.getVertex(i));
        if (stringsGraph.isAdjacent
                        ("Ottawa", "Quebec"))
            System.out.println("an edge");
    }

    public Digraph(int vertexNumber) {
        super(vertexNumber);
    }
```

```
       public Digraph(Object[] vertices) {
           super(vertices);
       }

       public void addEdge(int index1, int index2) {
           if (index1 < 0 || index1 >= vertexNumber
              || index2 < 0 || index2 >= vertexNumber)
               return;
           adjacencyMatrix[index1][index2] = true;
       }

       public void removeEdge(int index1, int index2)
       {
           if (index1 < 0 || index1 >= vertexNumber
              || index2 < 0 || index2 >= vertexNumber)
               return;
           adjacencyMatrix[index1][index2] = false;
       }
   }
```

### 9.1.2.3 Class WeightedGraph *for Undirected, Weighted Graphs*

We now extend class *Graph* to introduce weights for edges. The extended class, class *WeightedGraph*, redeclares variable *adjacencyMatrix* with the type *int*[][] in declaration

```
       protected int[][] adjacencyMatrix;
```

The integers in the 2-dimensional array are weights of edges. Since the element type of the array is changed from *boolean* to *int* in the subclass *WeightedGraph*, we have to override inherited methods that depend on the boolean array *adjacencyMatrix*. The redefined methods include

```
       public boolean isAdjacent(int index1, int index2)
       public void addEdge(int index1, int index2)
       public void removeEdge(int index1, int index2)
```

The *addEdge* methods use integer 1 as the default weight of edges. They can accept a *weight* argument to initialize an entry in *adjacencyMatrix*. Specifically, class *WeightedGraph* defines the following methods for weighted edge additions.

```
       public void addEdge(Object vertex1,
                           Object vertex2, int weight)
       public void addEdge(int index1, int index2,
                           int weight)
```

The method *isAdjacent* in class *WeightedGraph* uses the comparison

```
       adjacencyMatrix[index1][index2] > 0
```

to decide if the vertices indexed at *index1* and *index2* in array *vertices* are adjacent.

The following class can be compiled. The main method can be executed to test the class.

```java
/** Class WeightedGraph for undirected, weighted
 *  graphs. Vertices are indexed with int 0,
 *  ..., vertexNumber-1. Edge weights are stored
 *  in a 2-dimensional integer array.
 */
public class WeightedGraph extends Graph {
    public static void main(String[] args) {
        String[] names =
                {"Ottawa", "Montreal", "Quebec"};
        WeightedGraph stringsGraph = new
                            WeightedGraph(names);
        stringsGraph.addEdge("Ottawa","Quebec",12);
        for (int i= 0; i < names.length; i++)
            System.out.println((String)
                        stringsGraph.getVertex(i));
        if (stringsGraph.isAdjacent
                        ("Quebec", "Ottawa"))
            System.out.println("an edge");
    }

    public WeightedGraph(int vertexNumber) {
        this.vertexNumber = vertexNumber;
        vertices = new Object[vertexNumber];
        adjacencyMatrix = new
                    int[vertexNumber][vertexNumber];
    }

    public WeightedGraph(Object[] vertices) {
        this(vertices.length);
        for (int i=0; i < vertexNumber; i++)
            this.vertices[i] = vertices[i];
    }

    public boolean isAdjacent(int index1,
                              int index2) {
        if (index1 < 0 || index1 >= vertexNumber
        || index2 < 0 || index2 >= vertexNumber)
            return false;
        return (adjacencyMatrix[index1][index2]>0);
    }

    public void addEdge(Object vertex1,
                        Object vertex2) {
        int index1 = indexOf(vertex1),
            index2 = indexOf(vertex2);
```

```
            addEdge(index1, index2, 1);
        }

        public void addEdge(Object vertex1,
                    Object vertex2, int weight) {
            int index1 = indexOf(vertex1),
                index2 = indexOf(vertex2);
            addEdge(index1, index2, weight);
        }

        public void addEdge(int index1, int index2) {
            addEdge(index1, index2, 1);
        }

        public void addEdge(int index1, int index2,
                                   int weight) {
            if (index1 < 0 || index1 >= vertexNumber
                || index2 < 0 || index2 >= vertexNumber)
                return;
            adjacencyMatrix[index1][index2] =
            adjacencyMatrix[index2][index1] = weight;
        }

        public void removeEdge(int index1, int index2)
        {
            if (index1 < 0 || index1 >= vertexNumber
                || index2 < 0 || index2 >= vertexNumber)
                return;
            adjacencyMatrix[index1][index2] =
            adjacencyMatrix[index2][index1] = 0;
        }

        protected int[][] adjacencyMatrix;
    }
```

**Exercise 9.3** Store objects of the class developed for Exercise 9.1 in an instance of class *WeightedGraph*. Use the weight of an edge to denote the distance between a pair of cities.

**Exercise 9.4** Extend class *WeightedGraph* so that the edges of an instance of the extended class are directed. The extended class can be called *WeightedDigraph*.

## 9.1.3 Graphs with Adjacency Vectors

In the above section, we use a 2-dimensional matrix of booleans or integers to represent the edges of a graph. Here, we present graph classes that use adjacency vectors to keep edges of graphs. We still use the object array *vertices* to store vertices. In the graph classes, each vertex is associated with an adjacency vector. For an unweighted graph, the elements in the vector are vertices that are adjacent to the vertex. For a weighted graph, we use an edge object to encapsulate both a vertex and a weight. The edge objects are stored in adjacency vectors. Thus, if $\langle v_1, v_2 \rangle$ is an edge with weight $w$ in a weighted graph, the adjacency vector for vertex $v_1$ will contain an edge that encapsulates a reference to vertex $v_2$ and the integer value $w$. Thus, the edge along with its weight is stored in an adjacency vector.

Fig. 9.4 illustrates the use of adjacency vector to store the adjacent vertices for a vertex. It represents the undirected, unweighted graph shown in Fig. 9.1. The adjacency vector referenced with *adjacencies*[3] is associated with vertex *Toronto*. It contains vertices *Montreal*, *Ottawa*, and *London*, which are adjacent to *Toronto* in the graph.

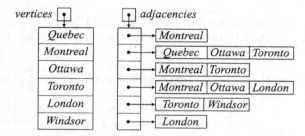

**Fig. 9.4** Vector representation of adjacencies of a graph

The following classes implement the classes shown in Fig. 9.2. Specifically, classes *Graph*, *Digraph*, and *WeightedGraph* support the same public methods as their counterparts presented in Section 9.1.2. But the classes use adjacency vectors to represent edges of graphs.

### 9.1.3.1 Class Graph for Undirected, Unweighted Graphs

The following class named *Graph* uses integer instance field *vertexNumber* to keep the number of vertices of a graph and defines object array *vertices* to hold references to vertex objects. It declares instance field *adjacencies* with an array of vectors

```
protected Vector[] adjacencies;
```

Class *Graph* defines three constructors. The no-argument constructor does nothing. The constructor *Graph(int vertexNumber)* initializes the instance field *vertexNumber*, creates an object array for variable *vertices*, and creates an array of vectors for variable *adjacencies*. Particularly, it uses the following statement to initialize the *adjacencies* field with an array of vectors.

```
adjacencies = new Vector[vertexNumber];
```

Each vertex of a graph has the same index in arrays *vertices* and *adjacencies*. The constructor *Graph(Object[] vertices)* invokes the above constructor to initialize the instance variables. It uses the elements of the argument array to initialize the *vertices* instance field.

Class *Graph* implements method *isAdjacent(Object vertex1, Object vertex2)* by checking whether *vertex2* is stored in the adjacency vector of *vertex1*. Specifically, the method finds the index, denoted with *index1*, of *vertex1* in the *vertices* array and tests whether *vertex2* is contained in vector *adjacencies[index1]* with code

```
index2 = adjacencies[index1].indexOf(vertex2);
return (index2 >= 0);
```

The integer value *index2* is equal to −1 if *vertex2* is not in vector *adjacencies[index1]*; otherwise, it is the index of *vertex2* in the vector.

Method *addEdge(Object vertex1, Object vertex2)* adds an edge between *vertex1* and *vertex2* into a graph. It finds the index of *vertex1*, denoted as *index1*, in the array *vertices* and then inserts *vertex2* into vector *adjacencies[index1]* with code

```
if (adjacencies[index1] == null)
    adjacencies[index1] = new Vector();
adjacencies[index1].addElement(vertex2);
```

Since class *Graph* represents undirected graphs, the method also adds *vertex1* into the adjacency vector associated with *vertex2*.

Method *removeEdge(Object vertex1, Object vertex2)* removes an edge ⟨*vertex1, vertex2*⟩ from a graph. The method removes *vertex2* from the adjacency vector associated with *vertex1* and removes *vertex1* from the adjacency vector associated with *vertex2* with code

```
adjacencies[index1].removeElement(vertex2);
adjacencies[index2].removeElement(vertex1);
```

The class *Graph* can be compiled. The main method of the class can be executed to test the class.

```
/** Class Graph for undirected, unweighted
 *  graphs. Vertices are stored in array
 *  vertices. Edges are organized into
 *  adjacency vectors.
 */
import java.util.*;
public class Graph {
    public static void main(String[] args) {
        String[] names =
                {"Ottawa", "Montreal", "Quebec"};
        Graph stringsGraph = new Graph(names);
        stringsGraph.addEdge("Ottawa", "Quebec");
        for (int i= 0; i < names.length; i++)
            System.out.println((String)
```

```
                          stringsGraph.getVertex(i));
        if (stringsGraph.isAdjacent
                              ("Quebec", "Ottawa"))
            System.out.println("an edge");
    }
    public Graph() { }
    public Graph(int vertexNumber) {
        this.vertexNumber = vertexNumber;
        vertices = new Object[vertexNumber];
        adjacencies = new Vector[vertexNumber];
    }
    public Graph(Object[] vertices) {
        this(vertices.length);
        for (int i=0; i < vertexNumber; i++)
            this.vertices[i] = vertices[i];
    }

    public Object getVertex(int index) {
        return vertices[index];
    }

    public void setVertex(Object vertex,
                          int index) {
        vertices[index] = vertex;
    }

    public boolean isAdjacent(Object vertex1,
                              Object vertex2) {
        int index1 = indexOf(vertex1);
        if (index1 < 0) return false;
        if (adjacencies[index1] == null)
            return false;
        int index2 =
            adjacencies[index1].indexOf(vertex2);
        return (index2 >= 0);
    }

    public boolean isAdjacent(int index1,
                              int index2) {
        if (index1 < 0 || index1 >= vertexNumber
          || index2 < 0 || index2 >= vertexNumber)
            return false;
        return isAdjacent(vertices[index1],
                          vertices[index2]);
    }

    public void addEdge(Object vertex1,
```

```
                       Object vertex2) {
    int index1 = indexOf(vertex1);
    if (index1 < 0) return;
    int index2 = indexOf(vertex2);
    if (index2 < 0) return;
    if (adjacencies[index1] == null)
        adjacencies[index1] = new Vector();
    adjacencies[index1].addElement(vertex2);
    if (adjacencies[index2] == null)
        adjacencies[index2] = new Vector();
    adjacencies[index2].addElement(vertex1);
}

public void addEdge(int index1, int index2) {
    if (index1 < 0 || index1 >= vertexNumber
       || index2 < 0 || index2 >= vertexNumber)
          return;
    addEdge(vertices[index1],vertices[index2]);
}
public void removeEdge(Object vertex1,
                      Object vertex2) {
    int index1 = indexOf(vertex1);
    if (index1 < 0) return;
    int index2 = indexOf(vertex2);
    if (index2 < 0) return;
    adjacencies[index1].removeElement(vertex2);
    adjacencies[index2].removeElement(vertex1);
}
public void removeEdge(int index1, int index2)
{
    if (index1 < 0 || index1 >= vertexNumber
       || index2 < 0 || index2 >= vertexNumber)
          return;
    removeEdge(vertices[index1],
                 vertices[index2]);
}

protected int indexOf(Object vertex) {
    for (int i= 0; i < vertexNumber; i++)
       if (vertex == vertices[i])
          return i;
    return -1;
}
protected Vector[] adjacencies;
protected Object[] vertices;
protected int vertexNumber;
}
```

### 9.1.3.2 *Class* Digraph *for Directed, Unweighted Graphs*

We now extend class *Graph* with class *Digraph* for directed classes. The constructors of class *Digraph* invoke the constructors of class *Graph* to initialize instance fields. Class *Digraph* overrides the inherited methods

```
public void addEdge(Object vertex1,
                              Object vertex2)
public void removeEdge(Object vertex1,
                              Object vertex2)
```

In class Graph, method *addEdge(Object vertex1, Object vertex2)* executes the following statements to modify both vectors *adjacencies[index1]* and *adjacencies[index2]*.

```
if (adjacencies[index1] == null)
    adjacencies[index1] = new Vector();
adjacencies[index1].addElement(vertex2);
if (adjacencies[index2] == null)
    adjacencies[index2] = new Vector();
adjacencies[index2].addElement(vertex1);
```

In class *Digraph*, the method *addEdge* executes only the statements

```
if (adjacencies[index1] == null)
    adjacencies[index1] = new Vector();
adjacencies[index1].addElement(vertex2);
```

Thus, the edge between vertices at *index1* and *index2* in array *vertices* will not imply the opposite edge.

When method *removeEdge(Object vertex1, Object vertex2)* is executed for an undirected graph, the adjacency vectors associated *vertex1* and *vertex2* are changed simultaneously. When the method is executed for a directed graph, only one vector, which is *adjacencies [index1]*, is changed by removing *vertex2* from the vector, where we assume *vertices[index1]* == *vertex1*.

```
/** Class Digraph for directed, unweighted
 *  graphs. Vertices are referenced by elements
 *  of array vertices. Directed edges are
 *  organized into adjacency vectors.
 */
import java.util.*;
public class Digraph extends Graph {
    public static void main(String[] args) {
        String[] names =
                {"Ottawa", "Montreal", "Quebec"};
        Digraph stringsGraph = new Digraph(names);
        stringsGraph.addEdge("Ottawa", "Quebec");
        for (int i= 0; i < names.length; i++)
           System.out.println((String)
                       stringsGraph.getVertex(i));
        if (stringsGraph.isAdjacent
                   ("Ottawa", "Quebec"))
```

```
                System.out.println("an edge");
            }

        public Digraph(int vertexNumber) {
            super(vertexNumber);
        }
        public Digraph(Object[] vertices) {
            super(vertices);
        }

        public void addEdge(Object vertex1,
                            Object vertex2) {
            int index1 = indexOf(vertex1);
            if (index1 < 0) return;
            if (adjacencies[index1] == null)
                adjacencies[index1] = new Vector();
            adjacencies[index1].addElement(vertex2);
        }

        public void removeEdge(Object vertex1,
                              Object vertex2) {
            int index1 = indexOf(vertex1);
            if (index1 < 0) return;
            adjacencies[index1].removeElement(vertex2);
        }
    }
```

## 9.1.3.3 Class WeightedGraph for Undirected, Weighted Graphs

We now extend class *Graph* with class *WeightedGraph* to introduce weights for edges. The subclass *WeightedGraph* represents undirected, weighted graphs. Edge weights are nonnegative integers. The class defines an inner class, *Edge*, to encapsulate a vertex and an integer weight. Default weight for edges is 1. The edges of a weighted graph are stored in vectors *adjacencies[index]* with $0 \leq index <$ *vertexNumber*. For instance, if an edge object that encapsulates vertex $v$ and weight $w$ is stored in *adjacencies[5]* and the vertex in array element *vertices[5]* is $v_0$, there is an edge between $v_0$ and $v$ with weight $w$.

In the classes *Graph* and *Digraph*, the element type of vectors *adjacencies[i]* is *Object*. In class *WeightedGraph*, the element type is *Edge*. In class *Weighted-Graph*, we define the following methods to access or manage the adjacency vectors.

```
    public boolean isAdjacent(int index1, int index2)
    public void addEdge(Object vertex1,Object vertex2)
    public void addEdge(Object vertex1,
                        Object vertex2, int weight)
    public void addEdge(int index1, int index2)
```

```
        public void addEdge(int index1, int index2,
                                    int weight)
        public void removeEdge(int index1, int index2)
```

The *isAdjacent* method uses statements

```
        index2 = indexOf(index1, vertex2);
        return (index2 >= 0);
```

to decide if the vertex at *index1* in array *vertices* and *vertex2* are adjacent. The overloaded *addEdge* methods use integer 1 as default weight. Some of them can accept a *weight* argument to initialize the weight of a new edge.

```
    /** Class WeightedGraph for undirected weighted
     *  graphs. Vertices are referenced by elements
     *  of array vertices. Weighted edges are
     *  organized into adjacency vectors.
     */
    import java.util.*;
    public class WeightedGraph extends Graph {
        public static void main(String[] args) {
            String[] names =
                    {"Ottawa", "Montreal", "Quebec"};
            WeightedGraph stringsGraph = new
                            WeightedGraph(names);
            stringsGraph.addEdge("Ottawa","Quebec",12);
            stringsGraph.removeEdge("Quebec","Ottawa");
            for (int i= 0; i < names.length; i++)
                System.out.println((String)
                            stringsGraph.getVertex(i));
            if (stringsGraph.isAdjacent
                            ("Quebec", "Ottawa"))
                System.out.println("an edge");
        }

        public WeightedGraph() { }
        public WeightedGraph(int vertexNumber) {
            super(vertexNumber);
        }
        public WeightedGraph(Object[] vertices) {
            super(vertices);
        }

        public boolean isAdjacent(Object vertex1,
                            Object vertex2) {
            int index1 = indexOf(vertex1);
            if (index1 < 0) return false;
            if (adjacencies[index1] == null)
                return false;
            int index2 = indexOf(index1, vertex2);
```

```
        return (index2 >= 0);
    }

    public void addEdge(int index1, int index2) {
        addEdge(vertices[index1],
                vertices[index2], 1);
    }

    public void addEdge(int index1, int index2,
                                    int weight) {
        addEdge(vertices[index1],
                vertices[index2], weight);
    }

    public void addEdge(Object vertex1,
                               Object vertex2) {
        addEdge(vertex1, vertex2, 1);
    }

    public void addEdge(Object vertex1,
                    Object vertex2, int weight) {
        int index1 = indexOf(vertex1);
        if (index1 < 0) return;
        int index2 = indexOf(vertex2);
        if (index2 < 0) return;
        if (adjacencies[index1] == null)
            adjacencies[index1] = new Vector();
        adjacencies[index1].addElement
                    (new Edge(vertex2, weight));
        if (adjacencies[index2] == null)
            adjacencies[index2] = new Vector();
        adjacencies[index2].addElement
                    (new Edge(vertex1, weight));
    }

    public void removeEdge(Object vertex1,
                               Object vertex2) {
        int index1 = indexOf(vertex1);
        if (index1 < 0) return;
        int index2 = indexOf(index1, vertex2);
        if (index2 < 0) return;
        adjacencies[index1].
                        removeElementAt(index2);
        index2 = indexOf(vertex2);
        if (index2 < 0) return;
        index1 = indexOf(index2, vertex1);
        if (index1 < 0) return;
```

```
            adjacencies[index2].removeElementAt(index1);
        }

        int indexOf(int index, Object vertex) {
            if (adjacencies[index] == null) return -1;
            return adjacencies[index].
                            indexOf(new Edge(vertex));
        }
    class Edge {
        Object vertex;
        int weight = 1;

        Edge(Object vertex) {
            this.vertex = vertex;
        }
        Edge(Object vertex, int weight) {
            this.vertex = vertex;
            this.weight = weight;
        }

        boolean equals(Edge edge) {
            return (vertex == edge.vertex);
        }
    }
}
```

**Exercise 9.5** Define a class named *WeightedDigraph* to represent weighted, directed graphs. The class uses adjacency vectors to organize directed edges and their weights.

**Exercise 9.6** Modify the class *WeightedGraph* so that when method *addEdge(vertex1, vertex2)* is invoked with *vertex1* $\notin V$ or *vertex2* $\notin V$ for a graph $G = (V, E)$, *vertex1* or *vertex2* as well as the edge $\langle vertex1, vertex2 \rangle$ is added to the graph.

# 9.2 Traversals of Graphs

## 9.2.1 The Traversal Problem

A graph contains information with vertices and edges. We may need to apply some operation for each vertex or search for a vertex in a graph. For example, when a graph represents roads between cities, we may want to know the cities reachable from a given city. We can start from a given vertex and follow the

edges of the graph to collect the reachable vertices. A difficulty in graph traversing is implied by cycles in graph. We need to avoid falling into a cycle.

Assume we are traversing a graph. When we reach a vertex *n*, we call the
vertices that are adjacent to *n* the *children* of vertex *n*. The vertices are *siblings* of
each other with respect to their parent *n*.

We can use one of three algorithms to traverse all the vertices reachable from
a given vertex in a graph. In a *depth-first traversal* of a graph, when we reach a
vertex *v*, we visit the data in *v* and traverse the children of *v* in depth-first order
before we visit the siblings of vertex *v*. A *postorder traversal* visits the children of
a reachable vertex *v* in postorder before it visits the data of *v* and its siblings. A
*breadth-first traversal* visits the data in a reached vertex *v* and then the data in the
siblings of *v* and the children of other visited vertices before visiting the children
of *v* in the graph.

We present the traversal algorithms with enumerations. Method *elements* invoked for a graph returns an enumeration. By repeatedly applying the *nextElement* for the enumeration, we can enumerate the vertices of the graph in depth-
first order, postorder, or breadth-first order.

A graph can be regarded as a generalization of a tree. It allows cycles. In a
traversal of a graph, we may reach a node several times before we complete the
traversal. A traversal algorithm must use a mechanism to remember which vertices have been visited so that the data in them will not be accessed repeatedly.

The traversal algorithms can be adapted for the searching problem. In a
search for a vertex, we stop traversing as soon as we find the vertex.

## 9.2.2 Traversing Graph with Adjacency Matrix

### 9.2.2.1 Depth-First Traversal

When a depth-first traversal reaches a vertex *v*, it visits the data in *v* and then
accesses each of the children of vertex *v* before it accesses the siblings of *v*. With
the graph shown in Fig. 9.1 as example, starting from vertex *Quebec*, a depth-first
traversal may generate the sequence

> *Quebec, Montreal, Toronto, London, Windsor, Ottawa.*

The following code implements depth-first traversal. It uses a stack named
vertexStack to keep vertices the parents of which have been visited. We use a
boolean array *visited* to indicate whether a vertex has been placed in the stack.

The code can be added to class *Graph* presented in Section 9.1.2.1. Each of
the two *elements* methods can be invoked for a graph to enumerate the vertices of
the graph in depth-first order. The first *elements*() method has no argument. It
uses vertex *vertices*[0] to start a depth-first traversal. The second *elements* method
specifies a starting vertex as argument for a depth-first traversal.

```
public Enumeration elements() {
```

```
            return new DPFEnumerator();
        }

        public Enumeration elements(Object startingVertex)
        {
            return new DPFEnumerator(startingVertex);
        }

        class DPFEnumerator implements Enumeration {
            DPFEnumerator() {
                visited = new boolean[vertexNumber];
                vertexStack = new Stack();
                vertexStack.push(vertices[0]);
                visited[0] = true;
            }
            DPFEnumerator(Object startingVertex) {
                visited = new boolean[vertexNumber];
                vertexStack = new Stack();
                vertexStack.push(startingVertex);
                visited[indexOf(startingVertex)] = true;
            }

            public boolean hasMoreElements() {
                if (vertexStack.isEmpty())
                    return false;
                else return true;
            }

            public Object nextElement() {
                Object currentVertex = vertexStack.pop();
                int index = indexOf(currentVertex);
                for (int i=vertexNumber-1; i>=0; i--)
                    if (adjacencyMatrix[index][i]
                            && !visited[i]) {
                        vertexStack.push(vertices[i]);
                        visited[i] = true;
                    }
                return currentVertex;
            }

            boolean[] visited;
            Stack vertexStack;
        }
```

**Exercise 9.7** In class *DPFEnumerator*, when a vertex is pushed onto the *vertexStack*, the vertex is regarded as having been enumerated and marked as *vis-*

*ited.* Modify the class so that only when a vertex is returned by the *nextElement* method, it is regarded as enumerated and marked as *visited*.

**Exercise 9.8** Use an array of city objects to construct a weighted graph in the main method of class *WeightedGraph*. Add some edges in the graph. Add code into the class for traversing the graph in a depth-first order.

### 9.2.2.2 Postorder Traversal

A postorder traversal of a graph is supported with a vertex stack called *vertexStack*. The stack is initialized with a vertex, from which we start the postorder traversal. After a vertex is placed into the stack, it is marked as *visited*. Assume vertex *v* is in the top element of the stack. If *v* has a child that has not been placed onto the stack, i.e., if the child has not been marked as *visited*, the child is pushed onto the stack. The data in the top vertex in the stack is accessed only after all the children of the vertex have been visited. With the graph shown in Fig. 9.1 as example, a postorder traversal starting from vertex *Quebec* may generate the following sequence

*Windsor, London, Toronto, Ottawa, Montreal, Quebec.*

When the graph being traversed in postorder is a tree and the starting vertex for the traversal is the root of the tree, the postorder traversal of the graph is a postorder traversal of the tree.

The following code implements postorder traversal for graphs. A difference between depth-first and postorder traversals is when to visit the data in the top vertex in *vertexStack*. In a depth-first traversal, the data in the top vertex is visited before the data in its children are accessed; in a postorder traversal, the data in the top vertex will be accessed only after the data in its children are accessed.

The following code can be included in the class *Graph* presented in Section 9.1.2.1. The *elements* methods can be invoked for a graph to enumerate vertices reachable from a starting vertex in a postorder traversal.

```
public Enumeration elements() {
    return new PSEnumerator();
}
public Enumeration elements(Object startingVertex)
{
    return new PSEnumerator(startingVertex);
}
class PSEnumerator implements Enumeration {
    PSEnumerator() {
        visited = new boolean[vertexNumber];
        vertexStack = new Stack();
        vertexStack.push(vertices[0]);
        visited[0] = true;
    }
```

```
PSEnumerator(Object startingVertex) {
    visited = new boolean[vertexNumber];
    vertexStack = new Stack();
    vertexStack.push(startingVertex);
    int index = indexOf(startingVertex);
    visited[index] = true;
}

public boolean hasMoreElements() {
    if (vertexStack.isEmpty())
        return false;
    return true;
}

public Object nextElement() {
    Object currentVertex = vertexStack.peek();
    int index = indexOf(currentVertex);
    l: while (true) {
        for (int i = 0; i < vertexNumber; i++)
        if (adjacencyMatrix[index][i]
                        && !visited[i]) {
            vertexStack.push(vertices[i]);
            visited[i] = true;
            index = i;
            continue l;
        }
        break;
    }
    return vertexStack.pop();
}

boolean[] visited;
Stack vertexStack;
}
```

### 9.2.2.3 Breadth-First Traversal

A breadth-first traversal is supported with a vertex queue named *vertexQueue*. The queue is initialized with the starting vertex of the breadth-first traversal. After a vertex is placed at the end of the queue, it is marked as *visited*. Assume vertex $v$ is at the front of the queue, i.e., $v$ has index 0 in the queue. Each child of $v$ that has not been marked as *visited* is placed at the end of the queue. Then the front vertex $v$ in the queue is accessed and it is removed from the queue. Starting from vertex *Quebec* of the graph in Fig. 9.1, a breadth-first traversal may generate the following sequence

> *Quebec, Montreal, Ottawa, Toronto, London, Windsor.*

The following code implements breadth-first traversal. It uses a vector to implement *vertexQueue*. In a breadth-first traversal, the front vertex in the queue will be accessed after the unvisited children of the front vertex are placed at the end of the queue.

The code can be included in class *Graph* presented in Section 9.1.2.1. The *elements* methods can be invoked for a graph to return an enumeration, which enumerates vertices in breadth-first order.

```
public Enumeration elements() {
    return new BDFEnumerator();
}
public Enumeration elements(Object startingVertex)
{
    return new BDFEnumerator(startingVertex);
}

class BDFEnumerator implements Enumeration {
    BDFEnumerator() {
        visited = new boolean[vertexNumber];
        vertexQueue = new Vector();
        vertexQueue.addElement(vertices[0]);
        visited[0] = true;
    }
    BDFEnumerator(Object startingVertex) {
        visited = new boolean[vertexNumber];
        vertexQueue = new Vector();
        vertexQueue.addElement(startingVertex);
        visited[indexOf(startingVertex)] = true;
    }

    public boolean hasMoreElements() {
        if (vertexQueue.isEmpty()) return false;
        return true;
    }

    public Object nextElement() {
        Object currentVertex =
                        vertexQueue.elementAt(0);
        vertexQueue.removeElementAt(0);
        int index = indexOf(currentVertex);
        for (int i=0; i < vertexNumber; i++)
            if (adjacencyMatrix[index][i]
                            && !visited[i]) {
                vertexQueue.addElement(vertices[i]);
                visited[i] = true;
            }
        return currentVertex;
    }
```

```
        boolean[] visited;
        Vector vertexQueue;
}
```

## 9.2.3 Traversing Graph with Adjacency Vectors

The edges of a graph can be represented with an adjacency matrix or organized with an array of adjacency vectors. In the above section, we discuss how to implement the various traversal strategies for graphs with adjacency matrices. Here, we implement the traversal strategies for graphs that use adjacency vectors to organize edges. We extend the class *Graph* presented in Section 9.1.3.1 with traversing methods.

The traversing methods use the same stack or queue as in the above section to keep vertices. But they access the adjacency vectors instead of adjacency matrix of a graph for edges.

### 9.2.3.1 Depth-First Traversal

The following code is similar to the code in Section 9.2.2.1, where an adjacency matrix is used to determine whether there is an edge between vertices. It enumerates the vertices reachable from a vertex in depth-first order. An example of depth-first traversal for a graph is shown in Section 9.2.2.1.

The following code uses the expression

```
adjacencies[index].elementAt(i) == vertices[j]
```

to access an element indexed at $i$ in adjacency vector *adjacencies[index]*. The expression decides whether the vertex *vertices[index]* is connected with the vertex *vertices[j]*.

The code can be added to the class *Graph* presented in Section 9.1.3.1. The *elements* methods shown below can be invoked for a graph to return an enumeration that enumerates vertices of the graph in depth-first order.

```
        public Enumeration elements() {
            return new DPFEnumerator();
        }
        public Enumeration elements(Object startingVertex)
        {
            return new DPFEnumerator(startingVertex);
        }

        class DPFEnumerator implements Enumeration {
            DPFEnumerator() {
                visited = new boolean[vertexNumber];
                vertexStack = new Stack();
                vertexStack.push(vertices[0]);
```

```
            visited[0] = true;
        }
        DPFEnumerator(Object startingVertex) {
            visited = new boolean[vertexNumber];
            vertexStack = new Stack();
            vertexStack.push(startingVertex);
            visited[indexOf(startingVertex)] = true;
        }

        public boolean hasMoreElements() {
            if (vertexStack.isEmpty())
                return false;
            return true;
        }

        public Object nextElement() {
            Object currentVertex = vertexStack.pop();
            int index = indexOf(currentVertex);
            if (adjacencies[index] != null)
            /* push adjacent, unvisited vertices onto
               vertexStack. */
            for (int i = adjacencies[index].size()-1;
                 i >= 0; i--)
                for (int j = 0; j < vertexNumber; j++)
                    if (adjacencies[index].elementAt(i)
                        == vertices[j] && !visited[j]) {
                        vertexStack.push(vertices[j]);
                        visited[j] = true; }
            return currentVertex;
        }
        boolean[] visited;
        Stack vertexStack;
    }
```

## 9.2.3.2 Postorder Traversal

The following code is similar to the code in Section 9.2.2.2, where an adjacency matrix is used to keep edges for a graph. An instance of class *PSEnumerator* can enumerate the vertices of the graph in a postorder. Here, the expression

```
    adjacencies[index].elementAt(i) == vertices[j]
```

accesses adjacency vector *adjacencies[index]* to decide whether the vertex *vertices[index]* is connected to vertex *vertices[j]* with an edge.

```
    public Enumeration elements() {
        return new PSEnumerator();
    }
```

```
public Enumeration elements(Object startingVertex)
{
    return new PSEnumerator(startingVertex);
}

class PSEnumerator implements Enumeration {
    PSEnumerator() {
        visited = new boolean[vertexNumber];
        vertexStack = new Stack();
        vertexStack.push(vertices[0]);
        visited[0] = true;
    }

    PSEnumerator(Object startingVertex) {
        visited = new boolean[vertexNumber];
        vertexStack = new Stack();
        vertexStack.push(startingVertex);
        int index = indexOf(startingVertex);
        visited[index] = true;
    }

    public boolean hasMoreElements() {
        if (vertexStack.isEmpty())
            return false;
        return true;
    }

    public Object nextElement() {
        Object currentVertex = vertexStack.peek();
        int index = indexOf(currentVertex);
        l: while (true) {
            if (adjacencies[index] != null)
            /* push adjacent, unvisited vertices
               onto vertexStack. */
            for (int i = 0;
                 i < adjacencies[index].size(); i++)
                for (int j= 0; j < vertexNumber; j++)
                if (adjacencies[index].elementAt(i)
                        == vertices[j] && !visited[j])
                { vertexStack.push(vertices[j]);
                    visited[j] = true;
                    currentVertex = vertices[j];
                    index = j;
                    continue l;
                }
            break;
        }
```

```
        vertexStack.pop();
        return currentVertex;
    }
    boolean[] visited;
    Stack vertexStack;
}
```

### 9.2.3.3 Breadth-First Traversal

Like the breadth-first traversal implementation in Section 9.2.2.3 for graphs with adjacency matrices, the following code uses a queue named *vertexQueue* to maintain unvisited vertices the parents of which have been visited in a breadth-first traversal. Vertices are placed at the end of the queue and retrieved from the front. The method *nextElement()* uses the expression

```
        adjacencies[index].elementAt(i) == vertices[j]
```

to access a vertex at index *i* in vector *adjacencies[index]* and tests whether there is an edge between *vertices[index]* and *vertices[j]*.

The following code can be added to the *Graph* class presented in Section 9.1.3.1. The *elements* methods can be invoked for traversing a graph in breadth-first order.

```
    public Enumeration elements() {
        return new BDFEnumerator();
    }
    public Enumeration elements(Object startingVertex)
    {
        return new BDFEnumerator(startingVertex);
    }

    class BDFEnumerator implements Enumeration {
        BDFEnumerator() {
            visited = new boolean[vertexNumber];
            vertexQueue = new Vector();
            vertexQueue.addElement(vertices[0]);
            visited[0] = true;
        }
        BDFEnumerator(Object startingVertex) {
            visited = new boolean[vertexNumber];
            vertexQueue = new Vector();
            vertexQueue.addElement(startingVertex);
            int index = indexOf(startingVertex);
            visited[index] = true;
        }

        public boolean hasMoreElements() {
            if (vertexQueue.isEmpty())
                return false;
```

```
            return true;
        }

    public Object nextElement() {
        Object currentVertex =
                    vertexQueue.elementAt(0);
        vertexQueue.removeElementAt(0);
        int index = indexOf(currentVertex);
        if (adjacencies[index] != null)
        /* appends adjacent, unvisited vertices
            to vertexQueue. */
        for (int i=0;
            i < adjacencies[index].size(); i++)
            for (int j = 0; j < vertexNumber; j++)
                if (adjacencies[index].
                        elementAt(i) == vertices[j]
                        && !visited[j]) {
                    vertexQueue.addElement(vertices[j]);
                    visited[j] = true;
                }
        return currentVertex;
    }
    boolean[] visited;
    Vector vertexQueue;
}
```

# 9.3 Computing Distances between Vertices

## 9.3.1 Single-Source Distances

### 9.3.1.1 Shortest Distances

If edges in a graph represent roads, they have lengths. A problem is computing the (shortest) distance between a pair of vertices. To solve the problem, we may need to compute the distances between a given vertex and other vertices. For example, assume edge $\langle v_1, v_2 \rangle$ has length 12, but the length of path $v_1, v_3, v_2$ is 11. After we determine the distance between $v_1$ and $v_3$, we can find that the distance between $v_1$ and $v_2$ is at most 11. The problem of computing the distances between a vertex and other vertices in a graph is the *single-source distances* problem.

An approximate solution to the single-source distances problem is to apply a breadth or depth-first traversal to the graph. When we reach a new vertex $v$ from vertex $v'$, a path from the source vertex to the parent $v'$ of $v$ has been determined. We can use the sum of the length of the path and the length of edge $\langle v', v \rangle$ as the distance between the source vertex and $v$.

The approximate solution may be good enough for most graphs. But it may not calculate the shortest distance. For example, we can assume a depth-first traversal accesses vertices $v_1$, $v_2$, $v_3$ in order, and the lengths of the edges $\langle v_1, v_2 \rangle$, $\langle v_1, v_3 \rangle$, and $\langle v_3, v_2 \rangle$ are 12, 9, and 2, respectively. The depth-first traversal may determine a distance 12 between vertices $v_1$ and $v_2$, which is not the shortest one. A breadth-first traversal of the vertices in the same order still fails to deduce the shortest distance between vertices $v_1$ and $v_2$.

## 9.3.1.2 Computing Single-Source Distances

Assume graph $G = (V, E)$ and vertex $v_0 \in V$. In class *Graph*, we use array *vertices* to keep vertices. To compute the distances between vertex $v_0$ and other vertices, we keep a vertex set $S \subseteq V$ such that for any vertex $v \in V$, we have $v \in S$ if and only if the shortest distance between $v_0$ and $v$ in the graph $G$ has been computed. We use element *found*[*index*] of boolean array *found* to indicate whether $v \in S$, where *index* is the index of vertex $v$ in array *vertices*. When *found*[*index*] is *true*, the shortest distance between $v_0$ and $v$ is in element *distances*[*index*] of integer array *distances*. We use negative integer $-1$ in an element *distances*[*i*] to indicate that no distance between $v_0$ and *vertices*[*i*] has been decided.

Set $S$ is initialized with $\{v_0\}$. The shortest distance between $v_0$ and itself is 0. If *index* is the index of vertex $v_0$ in array *vertices*, we initialize boolean variable *found*[*index*] with *true*, integer element *distances*[*index*] with 0, and local variable *currentVertex* with $v_0$. We use local variable *currentDistance* to keep the shortest distance from $v_0$ to *currentVertex*.

The algorithm moves vertices from set $V - S$ to set $S$. It terminates when no more vertex in $V - S$ can be added to $S$. The algorithm repeats the following pseudo-code until boolean variable *updated* remains *false*, which means no more vertex in $V - S$ can be added to $S$. It uses *minimumIndex* to keep the index of a vertex in $V - S$ that has the minimum distance from $v_0$ to vertices in $V - S$. The minimum distance is kept in variable *minimumDistance*.

1.  *minimumDistance* = $-1$; *minimumIndex* = $-1$; *updated* = *false*;
2.  For each vertex $v \in V - S$, perform the following two steps. We assume $v$ is vertex *vertices*[*i*].

    - If there is no edge between *currentVertex* and $v$, skip the step. If *distances*[*i*] = $-1$ (the distance between $v_0$ and $v$ has not been decided), assign *distances*[*i*] with the sum of *currentDistance* and the length of edge $\langle currentVertex, v \rangle$; otherwise, if the sum is less than *distances*[*i*], assign *distances*[*i*] with the sum.
    - If *distances*[*i*] != $-1$, then if *minimumDistance* = $-1$ or *distances*[*i*] < *minimumDistance*, update *minimumDistance* with *distances*[*i*] and assign *minimumIndex* with *i*.

3.  If *minimumDistance* != −1, assign boolean variables *found*[*minimumIndex*] and *updated* with *true*, assign *currentVertex* and *currentDistance* with *vertices*[*minimumIndex*] and *minimumDistance*, respectively.
4.  If *update* = *true*, go to step1; otherwise, terminate.

When the above pseudo-code terminates, the value *distances*[*i*] for vertex *vertices*[*i*] with *found*[*i*] = *true* is equal to the shortest distance between $v_0$ and *vertices*[*i*].

We now argue the correctness of the algorithm. By a simple induction on the number of vertices in a shortest path between $v_0$ and a vertex $v$ = *vertices*[*i*], we can prove that after the second last vertex in the shortest path is assigned to local variable *currentVertex*, the second step in the above pseudo-code assigns array element *distances*[*i*] with the shortest distance between source $v_0$ and $v$. The assumption that each edge has a positive length implies the correctness of the above algorithm.

### 9.3.1.3 Shortest Distances in a Graph with Adjency Matrix

The above algorithm is implemented with method *distances*(*Object sourceVertex*). The method uses integer array *distances* to record distances between the source vertex and vertices in the graph. Boolean variable *found*[*i*] indicates whether the value in variable *distances*[*i*] is the shortest distance between the source vertex and *vertices*[*i*]. If the variable is *true*, vertex *vertices*[*i*] is in the set *S*, which is described in the above algorithm.

The method *distances* accesses the adjacency matrix of the graph to determine if vertices *vertices*[*index*] and *vertices*[*i*] are connected by using expression

```
adjacencyMatrix[index][i] > 0.
```

It uses the edge weight *adjacencyMatrix*[*index*][*i*] in the statement

```
distances[i] = currentDistance +
                    adjacencyMatrix[index][i];
```

to calculate a distance between the source vertex and vertex *vertices*[*i*]. The local variable *currentDistance* denotes the shortest distance between the source vertex and the last vertex added to set *S*.

We use a while statement with loop condition *updated* to continuously add vertices into set *S*. Each time when a vertex, denoted with local variable *currentVertex*, is added to *S*, the shortest distance between the source and the vertex can be found in *distances*[*index*].

Upon the return of the method, if variable *distances*[*i*] equals −1, vertex *vertices*[*i*] is not reachable from the source vertex. Otherwise, the array element *distances*[*i*] holds the shortest distance between the source vertex and vertex *vertices*[*i*].

The method can be added to the *Graph* class defined in Section 9.1.2.3. By invoking the method for a graph object with a vertex as argument, the method evaluates the shortest *distances* from the *sourceVertex* to all other vertices.

```
public int[] distances(Object sourceVertex) {
```

```
int[] distances = new int[vertexNumber];
boolean[] found = new boolean[vertexNumber];
for (int i=0; i < vertexNumber; i++)
   distances[i] = -1;
int index = indexOf(sourceVertex);
distances[index] = 0;

// distance from source to itself was found
found[index] = true;
Object currentVertex = sourceVertex;
int currentDistance = 0;

int minimumIndex = -1, minimumDistance;
boolean updated = true;
while (updated) {
   minimumDistance = -1; updated = false;
   // updates distances
   for (int i = 0; i < vertexNumber; i++)
      if (!found[i]) {
         if (adjacencyMatrix[index][i] > 0) {
         /* currentVertex and vertices[i]
          * are adjacent */
            int d = currentDistance +
               adjacencyMatrix[index][i];
            if ((distances[i] == -1) ||
                  (d < distances[i]))
               distances[i] = d;
         }
         if (distances[i] != -1)
            if (minimumDistance < 0 ||
              minimumDistance > distances[i]){
              minimumDistance = distances[i];
              minimumIndex = i;
            }
      }
   if (minimumDistance > -1) {
      //add vertices[minimumIndex] to set S
      index = minimumIndex;
      found[index] = true;
      updated = true;
   }
}
return distances;
}
```

## 9.3.1.4 Shortest Distances in a Graph with Adjacency Vectors

The following method named *distances* applies the same algorithm as the above method. It depends on an undirected, weighted graph the edges of which are encoded in adjacency vectors. For example, it uses expressions

```
adjacencies[index].elementAt(i).vertex
adjacencies[index].elementAt(i).weight
```

to access the vertex and weight encapsulated in the (*i*+1)st edge in adjacency vector *adjacencies[index]*. The other end of the edge is vertex *vertices[index]*.

Method *distances* can be added to the *Graph* class defined in Section 9.1.3.3. Applying the method for an undirected, weighted graph with a source vertex as argument returns an integer array, which contains the distances between the source vertex and vertices in the graph.

```
public int[] distances(Object sourceVertex) {
    int[] distances = new int[vertexNumber];
    boolean[] found = new boolean[vertexNumber];
    for (int i = 0; i < vertexNumber; i++)
        distances[i] = -1;
    int index = indexOf(sourceVertex);
    distances[index] = 0;
    found[index] = true;

    Object currentVertex = sourceVertex;
    int currentDistance = 0;
    int minimumIndex = -1, minimumDistance;
    boolean updated = true;
    while (updated) {
        minimumDistance = -1; updated = false;
        // updates distances
        for (int i=0; i < vertexNumber; i++) {
        if (!found[i]) {
            int j = indexOf(index, vertices[i]);
            if (j >= 0) {
                int w = ((Edge) adjacencies[index].
                               elementAt(j)).weight;
                int d = currentDistance + w;
                if ((distances[i] == -1) ||
                                (d < distances[i]))
                    distances[i]= d;
                if (distances[i] > -1)
                    if (minimumDistance < 0 ||
                        minimumDistance > distances[i])
                    {
                        minimumDistance = distances[i];
                        minimumIndex = i;
                    }
                }
            }
        }
```

```
        }
    }
    if (minimumDistance > -1) {
        index = minimumIndex;
        found[index] = true;
        updated = true;
    }
}
return distances;
}
```

### 9.3.1.5 Analysis of Method distances

We now analyze the *distances* method presented in Section 9.3.1.3. Assume the number of vertices in a graph is $n$. For each execution of the body of the while loop in the method, the body of the for loop inside the while loop body is repeated $n$ times. An execution of each of the statements in the for loop body takes constant time. Therefore, an execution of the for loop takes time proportional to $n$, which is $O(n)$. The if statement in the while loop adds a vertex to set $S$. Since the size of $S$ is at most $n$, the body of the while loop is repeated at most $n$ times. Therefore, the time complexity of the *distances* method is $O(n^2)$.

We now discuss the *distances* method presented in Section 9.1.3.4 for weighted graphs that use adjacency vectors to keep edges. A careful reader may notice that the *indexOf* method uses a linear search to find the index of a vertex in an adjacency vector. The index of a vertex *vertices*[$i$] in an adjacency vector *adjacencies*[$j$] can be organized in a 2-dimensional array with entry at $(i, j)$ to denote the index. By using the auxiliary array, an access to the index takes constant time. This implementation guarantees time complexity $O(n^2)$ for the *distances* method presented in Section 9.3.1.4.

## 9.3.2 All Distances in a Graph

### 9.3.2.1 All Distances Problem

Method *distances*(*sourceVertex*) computes the distances from *sourceVertex* to other vertices in a graph. Here we study the *all distances* problem, which requests for the distance between each pair of vertices in a graph.

The following discussion involves the notion of subgraph. Given a graph $G = (V, E)$ and a vertex set $V' \subseteq V$, the *subgraph* on $V'$, denoted with $G_{V'} = (V', E')$, of graph $G$ is a graph such that for any vertices $v, v' \in V'$, edge $\langle v, v' \rangle \in E'$ if and only if $\langle v, v' \rangle \in E$. The edge set $E'$ of the subgraph can be denoted with $E_{V'}$.

To compute all the distances between vertices in a graph $G = (V, E)$, we maintain a set of vertices $S \subseteq V$ such that for each pair of vertices $v_1, v_2 \in V$, the distance between the two vertices in subgraph $G_{S \cup \{v_1, v_2\}} = (S \cup \{v_1, v_2\}, E_{S \cup \{v_1, v_2\}})$ has been computed. The vertices $v_1$ and $v_2$ may not be in set $S$.

The set $S$ is initially empty. When $S$ is empty, the distance between vertices $v_1$, $v_2$ in subgraph $G_{S \cup \{v_1, v_2\}} = (\{v_1, v_2\}, E_{\{v_1, v_2\}})$ is equal to the length of edge $\langle v_1, v_2 \rangle$ if $\langle v_1, v_2 \rangle \in E$; otherwise, the distance is denoted with the negative integer $-1$.

We move vertices from set $V - S$ to $S$. After we add a vertex, denoted with *vertices*[$i$], to $S$, we recalculate the distances between each pair of vertices *vertices*[$j$] and *vertices*[$k$] in the subgraph $G_{S \cup \{vertices[i], vertices[j], vertices[k]\}}$ with code

```
if (allDistances[j][i] != -1
        && allDistances[i][k] != -1)
{
    int d = allDistances[j][i]+allDistances[i][k];
    if ((allDistances[j][k] == -1) ||
        (allDistances[j][k] > d))
    allDistances[j][k] = d;
}
```

A shortest path connecting *vertices*[$j$] and *vertices*[$k$] in subgraph $G_{S \cup \{vertices[i], vertices[j], vertices[k]\}}$ either passes vertext *vertices*[$i$] or does not contain *vertices*[$i$]. For the former case, the above code uses the sum of the length of a path connecting *vertices*[$j$] and *vertices*[$i$] and that of a path connecting *vertices*[$i$] and *vertices*[$k$] to improve variable *allDistances*[$j$][$k$]. In the above code, if the value in variable *allDistances*[$j$][$i$] is not equal to $-1$, it represents the distance between *vertices*[$j$] and *vertices*[$i$] in subgraph $G_{S \cup \{vertices[j], vertices[i]\}}$. The value in variable *allDistances*[$i$][$k$] has a similar interpretation. Therefore, if both variables *allDistances*[$j$][$i$] and *allDistances*[$i$][$k$] are not equal to $-1$, their sum is the length of the shortest path that connects *vertices*[$j$] and *vertices*[$k$] and that goes through vertex *vertices*[$i$] in the subgraph $G_{S \cup \{vertices[i], vertices[j], vertices[k]\}}$.

We now assume that the edge weights of a graph are encoded in *adjacencyMatrix*. When vertex set $S$ is empty, paths that go through vertices in $S$ are the edges in the graph. Therefore, we initialize the elements of array *allDistances* with edge lengths in code

```
for (int i=0; i < vertexNumber; i++)
    for (int j=0; j < vertexNumber; j++)
        if (adjacencyMatrix[i][j] != 0)
            allDistances[i][j] = adjacencyMatrix[i][j];
        else allDistances[i][j] = -1;
```

The shortest distance between a vertex and itself is 0, which is assigned to variable *allDistances*[$i$][$i$] with statement

```
for (int i=0; i < vertexNumber; i++)
    allDistances[i][i] = 0;
```

## 9.3.2.2 All Distances in a Graph with Adjacency Matrix

The above algorithm is implemented with method *allDistances*, which returns a 2-dimensional array referenced with local variable *allDistances*. An element *allDistances[i][j]* in the array may be $-1$, which indicates that there is no path from vertex *vertices[i]* to *vertices[j]* in the graph. If there is a path between two vertices, the element contains the shortest distance between them.

The following method can be included in the *WeightedGraph* class presented in Section 9.1.2.3.

```
public int[][] allDistances() {
    // initializes matrix allDistances
    int[][] allDistances = new
                   int[vertexNumber][vertexNumber];
    for (int i=0; i < vertexNumber; i++)
        for (int j=0; j < vertexNumber; j++)
            if (adjacencyMatrix[i][j] != 0)
                allDistances[i][j] =
                adjacencyMatrix[i][j];
            else allDistances[i][j] = -1;
    for (int i=0; i < vertexNumber; i++)
        allDistances[i][i] = 0;

    for (int i=0; i < vertexNumber; i++)
        for (int j=0; j < vertexNumber; j++)
            for (int k = 0; k < vertexNumber;k++)
                if (allDistances[j][i] != -1
                    && allDistances[i][k] != -1) {
                    int d = allDistances[j][i] +
                        allDistances[i][k];
                    if ((allDistances[j][k] == -1) ||
                        (allDistances[j][k] > d))
                        allDistances[j][k] = d;
                }
    return allDistances;
}
```

## 9.3.2.3 All Distances in a Graph with Adjacency Vectors

The above method can be adapted for class *WeightedGraph* defined in Section 9.1.3.3, which encodes connected vertices and edge weights in adjacency vectors *adjacencies[i]* for $0 \leq i < vertextNumber$. The adapted *allDistances* method initializes array elements *allDistances[i][j]* with edge weight

((*Edge*) *adjacencies[i].elementAt[index]).weight*,

where vertex *vertices[j]* is stored at *index* in the adjacency vector *adjacencies[i]*.

The following method can be added to the *WeightedGraph* class presented in Section 9.1.3.3. It returns a 2-dimensional integer array with element *allDis-*

*tances*[*i*][*j*] equal to the shortest distance between vertices *vertices*[*i*] and *vertices*[*j*].

```
public int[][] allDistances() {
    // initialize matrix allDistances
    int[][] allDistances = new
                int[vertexNumber][vertexNumber];
    for (int i=0; i < vertexNumber; i++)
        for (int j=0; j < vertexNumber; j++){
            int index = indexOf(i, vertices[j]);
            if ( index >= 0)
                allDistances[i][j] = (int)
                        ((Edge) adjacencies[i].
                        elementAt(index)).weight;
            else allDistances[i][j] = -1;
        }
    for (int i=0; i < vertexNumber; i++)
        allDistances[i][i] = 0;

    for (int i=0; i < vertexNumber; i++)
        for (int j=0; j < vertexNumber; j++)
            for (int k=0; k < vertexNumber; k++)
                if (allDistances[j][i] != -1
                        && allDistances[i][k] != -1) {
                    int d = allDistances[j][i] +
                            allDistances[i][k];
                    if ((allDistances[j][k] == -1) ||
                            (allDistances[j][k] > d))
                        allDistances[j][k] = d;
                }
    return allDistances;
}
```

### 9.3.2.4 Analysis of Method allDistances

To evaluate the 2-dimensional array *allDistances* in method *allDistances*, we use three loops – the first enclosing the second, which encloses the third. Each loop varies an integer variable from 0 to $n-1$, where $n$ is the number of vertices in a graph. Therefore, the body of the third loop will be repeated $n^3$ times. The third loop body takes constant time to access array elements. Therefore, the time complexity of the *allDistances* method is $O(n^3)$.

# 9.4 Summary

This chapter presents a notion of a graph and variants of the notion. We discuss undirected and directed, weighted and unweighted graphs. A graph stores data in vertices and edges. Some applications such as maps can be represented with graphs. Trees discussed in Chapter 8 can be regarded as a special type of graph. A tree does not allow cycle. It has a distinctive vertex as root. From the root of a tree, we can reach all the vertices in the tree by following edges. From a vertex in a graph, we may not be able to reach some vertex of the graph and the graph may not be connected.

We present two approaches to representing graphs in a computer. One approach uses a 2-dimensional array to encode the adjacency relationships between vertices. The element type of the array may be *boolean* for unweighted graphs. It is *int* to encode edge weights in a weighted graph. We implement the approach in several classes – class *Graph* for undirected, unweighted graphs, *Digraph* for directed, unweighted graphs, and *WeightedGraph* for undirected, weighted graphs.

Another approach to representing a graph in a computer uses adjacency vectors to store edges. Each vertex is associated with an adjacency vector. If the edges incident with the vertex are not weighted, we store vertices adjacent to the vertex in the adjacency vector of the vertex. Otherwise, we use an edge object to encapsulate the incident vertex and the weight of an edge. We store edge objects in an adjacency vector.

We implement the adjacency vector approach in several classes. Class *Graph* uses an adjacency vector to store adjacent vertices for each vertex in an undirected, unweighted graph. We also present classes *Digraph* and *WeightedGraph* for directed, unweighted graphs and for undirected, weighted graphs, respectively.

In an application, we may need to visit the data in the vertices of a graph. We present three traversal strategies for traversing a graph. A depth-first traversal accesses the data in a reached vertex and then visits the children of the vertex before visiting the siblings of the vertex. A postorder traversal visits the data in children of a vertex before visiting the vertex and its siblings. In a breadth-first traversal, we visit a reached vertex and its siblings before visiting the children of the reached vertex.

We can calculate distances between vertices in a graph. Here, we implement an algorithm for calculating the distances from a source vertex to all other vertices in a graph. We also present methods to evaluate the distances between pairs of vertices in a graph. The graph is assumed to be an undirected, weighted graph. Edge weights are assumed to be positive integers.

# Assignment

In the above implementations of graph, we assume that no vertex will be added to or removed from a graph after the graph object is created. Modify the classes *Graph* presented in Sections 9.1.2.1 and 9.1.3.1 with functions to add and remove vertices for a graph at runtime. When a vertex is removed from a graph, the edges incident to the vertex are removed as well.

# Chapter 10
# Network Flows

A directed, weighted graph $N = (V, E)$ can be used to represent a network. The weight of an edge in $E$ represents the flow capacity of the edge. Two of the vertices in $V$ are distinguished as the source and sink of the network. Here, we are interested in finding a maximum flow between the source and sink in the network.

The maximum flow problem for networks has various applications. It has elegant solutions. In this chapter, we discuss how to represent networks in Java, and how to solve the maximum flow problem.

For a network, we can find a minimum cut, which is a set of edges. The edges in a minimum cut are saturated by maximum flow. A minimum cut represents the bottleneck of a network; i.e., to increase the maximum flow of the network, we have to either add edges into the cut or increase the capacities of the edges in the cut.

A network is a special type of directed, weighted graph. This chapter extends Chapter 9. We modify a graph class defined in Chapter 9 slightly to facilitate the computation of maximum flow. In the computation, we need special networks. We also discuss how to find a minimum cut for a network.

In this chapter, we shall present

- The notion of network, which is a type of data structure representing transportation networks and other types of network. Each edge in a network has a limited capacity to restrict the flow through it. The capacity may be expressed with a floating-point number. We assume integer values for capacities of edges and for flows over edges in a network.
- The residual network of a network for a flow. It represents the remaining capacities of edges for the flow. It allows rerouting flow by reducing the flow of some edges and increasing the flow of other edges.
- The leveled network of a residual network, which uses a topological list of vertices determined with a breadth-first traversal of the residual network to decide its edges. The leveled network includes only edges from a vertex in the list to an after vertex in the list. Other edges in the residual network are omitted from the leveled network. Leveled networks will be used to evaluate a flow increment for a network.
- Two algorithms for finding maximum flow in a network – the path augment and wave algorithms. The path augment algorithm tries to find a path that can be used to pass more flow from source to sink. The wave algorithm tries to saturate the edges emitting from vertices and then balance the flow at vertices. The flow saturating step pushes as much flow as possible through vertices toward the sink. Then, the wave algorithm applies a flow decreasing step

to balance vertices by reducing the flow into vertices. The flow increasing
and decreasing steps are repeated as long as the flow can be increased. The
two algorithms are implemented with Java methods.

- An algorithm for finding a minimum cut for a network. The algorithm is implemented in a network class.


# 10.1 Network and Network Flows

## 10.1.1 Networks

A *network* is a directed, weighted graph $N = (V, E)$ that has two distinctive vertices $s, t \in V$, which are called the *source* and *sink* of the network. The weight $w(v,$
$v')$ of an edge $\langle v, v' \rangle \in E$ is called the *capacity* of the edge. We assume that each
edge has a nonnegative, integer capacity. If there is no edge between a pair of
vertices $v, v'$, we regard the capacity $w(v, v')$ as equal to 0.

In Fig. 10.1a, we show a network and the capacities of its edges. Vertices $A$
and $F$ are the source and sink of the network. A network is a directed graph. Edge
$\langle B, C \rangle$ in Fig. 10.1a is different from edge $\langle C, B \rangle$. The two edges have capacities 6
and 2, respectively. We shall use an array named *vertices* to organize the vertices
in a network. For example, the vertices in Fig. 10.1a are organized in the *vertices*
array shown in Fig. 10.1b. The vertices of a network have indices in the *vertices*
array. For example, the vertices $A, B, C, D, E$ and $F$ have indices 0, 1, 2, 3, 4, and
5, respectively. With the vertex indices, we organize the capacities of edges into a
2-dimensional array. An entry indexed at $(i, j)$ in the array is equal to the capacity
of edge $\langle vertices[i], vertices[j] \rangle$. The capacity matrix for the network in Fig. 10.1a
is shown in Fig. 10.1c.

In the study of networks, we often separate the vertices in a network $N = (V,$
$E)$ into two disjoint sets, say $V_0$ and $V_1$, such that source $s$ of the network is contained in $V_0$ and sink $t$ in $V_1$. We call such a partition $\langle V_0, V_1 \rangle$ a *cut* of the network.
A cut of a network represents a set of edges $\langle v_0, v_1 \rangle$ that connect vertices $V_0$ with
vertices in $V_1$. For example, the cut $\langle \{A, C, D\}, \{B, E, F\} \rangle$ for the network shown
in Fig. 10.1 consists of edges $\langle A, B \rangle, \langle C, B \rangle, \langle C, E \rangle, \langle C, F \rangle$, and $\langle D, E \rangle$.

A cut $\langle V_0, V_1 \rangle$ has a *capacity*, denoted with $w(V_0, V_1)$. The capacity is equal to
the sum of the capacities of the edges that connect vertices in $V_0$ with vertices in
$V_1$. For example, the cut $\langle \{A, C, D\}, \{B, E, F\} \rangle$ in Fig. 10.1a has a capacity 19.

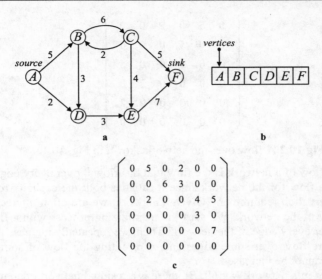

Fig. 10.1 A network and its capacity matrix

## 10.1.2 Flows in Networks

A *flow* in a network $N = (V, E)$ assigns a flow to each edge in $E$. It is represented with a function from edges to integers $f: E \to Z$, where $Z$ denotes the set of nonnegative integers. A flow satisfies the following conditions:

- *capacity restraint*: The flow $f(v, v')$ over an edge $\langle v, v' \rangle$ is less than or equal to the capacity $w(v, v')$ of the edge for each pair of vertices $v, v' \in V$; i.e., $f(v, v') \leq w(v, v')$.
- *flow conservation*: For any vertex $v \in V$ that is not the source $s$ or sink $t$, we have $\Sigma_{v'} f(v', v) = \Sigma_{v'} f(v, v')$; i.e., the sum of incoming flows to vertex $v$ is equal to the sum of outgoing flows from $v$.

The network shown in Fig. 10.1a admits a flow $f$ with $f(A, B) = 5, f(A, D) = 2, f(B, C) = 5, f(C, F) = 5, f(D, E) = 2, f(E, F) = 2$, and flow 0 for other edges. We shall use a 2-dimensional matrix of integers, named *flowMatrix*, in Java programs to represent flows. For example, the flow $f$ can be represented with the matrix shown in Fig. 10.2.

For a network $N = (V, E)$ and a flow $f$ in $N$, the value of flow $f$, denoted with $|f|$, is the difference between the sum of flows leaving source $s$ and the sum of flows going into source $s$, i.e., $|f| = \Sigma_{v'} f(s, v') - \Sigma_v f(v, s)$. Due to the flow conservation requirement, the value of a flow $f$ is also equal to the difference between the sum of flows going to sink $t$ and the sum of flows leaving sink $t$, i.e., $|f| = \Sigma_v f(v, t) - \Sigma_{v'} f(t, v')$.

$$\begin{pmatrix} 0 & 5 & 0 & 2 & 0 & 0 \\ 0 & 0 & 5 & 0 & 0 & 0 \\ 0 & 0 & 0 & 0 & 0 & 5 \\ 0 & 0 & 0 & 0 & 2 & 0 \\ 0 & 0 & 0 & 0 & 0 & 2 \\ 0 & 0 & 0 & 0 & 0 & 0 \end{pmatrix}$$

**Fig 10.2** A flow over the network shown in Fig. 10.1a

A special flow of a network is the flow that has flow 0 over every edge of the network. It is a flow for the network since it satisfies both the capacity restraints and flow conservation requirement. Given a network, we are often interested in a maximum flow in the network. We start the maximizing process with a flow that has value 0 over every edge of the network. Then, we repeatedly increase the flow by passing more flow over some edges and/or rerouting the flow of some edges until the flow cannot be increased.

For a flow $f$ in a network $N = (V, E)$, there is a residual network, denoted with $R = (V, E^-)$, which has the same vertex set $V$ as network $N$. The residual $R$ has an edge $\langle v, v' \rangle$ between two vertices $v, v' \in V$ if and only if we can increase the flow $f(v, v')$ without violating the capacity restraint $w(v, v')$ or decrease the flow $f(v', v)$. Given capacity $w(v, v')$ and flow $f(v, v')$ for an edge $\langle v, v' \rangle$, we can increase the flow by at most $w(v, v') - f(v, v')$ and decrease it by at most $f(v, v')$. The capacity of an edge $\langle v, v' \rangle$ in the residual network is equal to the sum of the maximum increment possible for $f(v, v')$ and flow $f(v', v)$. For the network in Fig. 10.1a and the flow in Fig. 10.2, the capacity of edge $\langle A, B \rangle$ in the residual network is 0, that of edge $\langle B, A \rangle$ is 5, that of edge $\langle B, C \rangle$ is 1, and that of edge $\langle C, B \rangle$ is 7. Note that there is no edge from vertex $B$ to $A$ in the network in Fig. 10.1a. We use edge $\langle B, A \rangle$ with capacity 5 to indicate that we can reduce 5 units of flow over the opposite edge $\langle A, B \rangle$. The capacity of edge $\langle C, B \rangle$ in the network in Fig. 10.1a is 2. Since we can decrease the flow $f(B, C)$ by 5 and increase the flow over edge $\langle C, B \rangle$ by 2, the capacity of edge $\langle C, B \rangle$ is 7 in the residual network.

The residual of a network that has a flow is a network. It has the same set of vertices as the network. We can use the same representation of a network to represent the residual network. Specifically, we use the *vertices* array to organize the vertices of the residual network and a 2-dimensional array of integers to represent the capacities. For example, for the network in Fig. 10.1a and the flow in Fig. 10.2, the residual network can be represented with Fig. 10.3a. The capacities of edges in the residual are organized in a matrix shown in Fig. 10.3b.

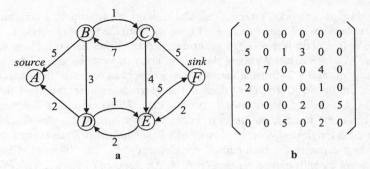

**Fig. 10.3** Residual of the network in Fig. 10.1a with flow in Fig. 10.2

Given a residual network $R = (V, E^-)$, we can generate a leveled network $L(R)$ $= (V', E')$ with $V' \subseteq V$ and $E' \subseteq E^-$ as follows. Starting from the source vertex, we traverse the vertices in $R$ level by level in breadth-first order. The first level consists of the source vertex only. The traversal introduces a list of vertices. Only those edges in $E^-$ that connect a vertex with a late vertex in the list will be included in the edge set $E'$. The breadth-first traversal stops as soon as the sink is reached. Therefore, the last level of a leveled network contains the sink vertex. A leveled network will be used to deduce flows between the source and sink for the residual network. A breadth-first traversal starting from the source cannot reach the sink if the flow in the residual network is a maximum one.

For the residual network shown in Fig. 10.3, the leveled network consists of the only vertex $A$ and no edge. The breadth-first traversal cannot go to any level beyond the first level $\{A\}$.

**Exercise 10.1** In Fig. 10.2, we assume flow $f(A, B)$ over edge $\langle A, B \rangle$ is 5. Change the flow over each of the edges $\langle A, B \rangle$, $\langle B, C \rangle$, and $\langle C, F \rangle$ to 4. Describe the residual and leveled networks for the network shown in Fig. 10.1a and the modified flow.

# 10.2 Maximum Flow in Networks

Here, we present four classes for networks. Class *Network* represents networks that have capacities for edges but no flows. Class *PreflowedNetwork* represents networks that have capacities and flows for edges. The flow over an edge in a *PreflowedNetwork* object satisfies the capacity constraint of the edge. But the flows in the preflowed network may not satisfy the flow conservation requirement for some vertices. The user of a *PreflowedNetwork* is responsible for maintaining flow conservation when she sets or changes a flow. Class *ResidualNetwork* describes the residual network of a preflowed network. One of its constructors creates a residual network for a given preflowed network. Class *LeveledNetwork* represents leveled networks. Given a residual network as argument, a constructor of class *LeveledNetwork* creates a leveled network from the residual network.

We define class *Network* for generic networks. Other network classes inherit the class *Network*. Class *Network* defines an array of vertices to hold the vertices for a network and a 2-dimensional array of integers to organize the capacities of edges in the network. The class does not support the representation of flows for networks. Class *PreflowedNetwork* extends class *Network* with a 2-dimensional array of integers to organize flows of edges in a network. Class *ResidualNetwork* inherits class *PreflowedNetwork*. Thus, each *ResidualNetwork* can maintain a flow as well as a capacity for each pair of vertices in the *ResidualNetwork*. Class *LeveledNetwork* extends class *ResidualNetwork*. An instance of class *LeveledNetwork* represents the leveled network of a residual network. The class inheritance relationships are shown in Fig. 10.4.

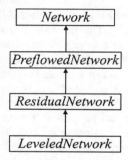

**Fig. 10.4** Network classes

## 10.2.1 Network Representations

### 10.2.1.1 Representing Networks in Java

We now discuss how to implement networks in Java. In the following class named *Network*, we use array *vertices* to keep vertices of a network. The vertices are instances of class *Vertex*, which is an inner class of class *Network*. The class *Vertex* encapsulates instance variables *data* and *index*. The data in a vertex is an object, the index is the position (index) of the vertex in the *vertices* array. When we place a vertex into the *vertices* array, we set the *index* field of the vertex with the index of the vertex in the *vertices* array. The *index* field in a vertex is used to support operations for networks. It should be hidden from users of a network. The length of the *vertices* array, which is the number of vertices of the network, is kept in instance field *size*.

Class *Network* uses a 2-dimensional array *capacityMatrix* to organize edge capacities for a network. The matrix is declared with code

```
protected int[][] capacityMatrix;
```

Entries in the matrix are nonnegative. We use integer 0 in the matrix to indicate that no edge connects a pair of vertices or the capacity of the edge is 0.

Class *Network* defines constructors

```
Network()
Network(int size)
Network(Object[] vertices)
```

to initialize a created network object. The no-argument constructor does nothing. The second constructor uses the *size* argument to create array *vertices* with length equal to *size*. It also creates a 2-dimensional array for instance variable *capacityMatrix*. The class *Network* uses instance variable *vertexNumber* to denote the number of vertices that a network object accommodates. The last constructor needs an array of objects as argument. It uses the objects to create vertices for the created network.

Class *Network* defines the following methods for accessing and setting source and sink for a network object. The methods can be applied for a local variable *roads* declared with statement

```
Network roads = new Network(25);
```

| Signature | Semantics |
|---|---|
| `Object getSource()` | Returns the data object encapsulated in the source vertex of this network |
| `void setSource (Object source)` | Sets the source with a vertex that encapsulates the *source* object |
| `void setSource(int sourceIndex)` | Sets the source with the vertex at *sourceIndex* in the *vertices* array |
| `Object getSink()` | Returns the data object encapsulated in the sink vertex of this network |
| `void setSink (Object sink)` | Sets the sink with the vertex that encapsulates object *sink* |
| `void setSink(int sinkIndex)` | Sets the sink with the vertex at *sinkIndex* in the *vertices* array |

Class *Network* defines the following instance methods for accessing and setting edge capacities. We use integer matrix *capacityMatrix* to store capacities of edges in a network. If there is no edge between a pair of vertices, the entry in the matrix is 0. An entry with value 0 can be interpreted as an edge with capacity 0. The capacity managing methods are overloaded with different parameter types. Some of the *setCapacity* methods are described as follows. They can be invoked for the local variable *roads*.

| Signature | Semantics |
|---|---|
| `void setCapacity (Vertex vertex1, Vertex vertex2, int capacity)` | Sets the capacity of the edge that connects *vertex1* and *vertex2* in this network with a given *capacity* |
| `void setCapacity (Object data1, Object data2, int capacity)` | Sets the capacity of the edge between vertices that encapsulate *data1* and *data2* in this network |
| `void setCapacity (int index1, int index2, int capacity)` | Sets the capacity of the edge that connects *vertices[index1]* and *vertices[index2]* in this network |

Class *Network* also defines *setCapacity* methods that have no *capacity* parameter. We regard the default capacity of an edge as 1.

We can test whether two vertices are adjacent with method *isAdjacent (Vertex vertex1, Vertex vertex2)*. The method checks if the entry in the capacity matrix is nonzero. Similarly, the class overloades methods *isAdjacent(Object data1, Object data2)* and *isAdjacent(int index1, int index2)*, which identify a vertex with a data object or an index in the *vertices* array.

Class *Network* defines methods *capacity(Vertex vertex1, Vertex vertex2)*, *capacity(Object data1, Object data2)*, and *capacity(int index1, int index2)* to retrieve the capacity of an edge.

### 10.2.1.2 Class Network

We shall use class *Vertex* to represent vertices in a network. Each instance of the class encapsulates data and the index of the vertex in array *vertices*.

The following class named *Network* defines the basic data structure and operations for networks. It can be compiled. The main method of the class can be executed to test the class. Instance method *elements()* in class *Network* returns an enumeration of vertices of a network. By repeatedly invoking the *nextElement()* method for the enumeration, we can traverse the vertices in the network in breadth-first order.

```
/** Class Network for directed, weighted
 *   networks. Vertices are indexed with 0, 1,
 *   ..., vertexNumber-1 in array vertices.
 *   Edges are represented with 2-dimensional
 *   array capacityMatrix.
 */
import java.util.*;
public class Network {
    public static void main(String[] args) {
```

```
    String[] names = {"Cbc", "Abc", "Bbc"};
    Network stringsNetwork = new
                                Network(names);
    stringsNetwork.setCapacity("Bbc","Cbc",12);
    stringsNetwork.setCapacity("Cbc", "Abc");
    if (stringsNetwork.isAdjacent("Bbc","Cbc"))
        System.out.println("an edge");
    Enumeration enumeration =
                stringsNetwork.elements("Bbc");
    while (enumeration.hasMoreElements()) {
        System.out.println
                (enumeration.nextElement());
    }
}

// Constructors of class Network
public Network() { }

public Network(int size) {
    vertexNumber = size;
    vertices = new Vertex[vertexNumber];
    capacityMatrix = new
            int[vertexNumber][vertexNumber];
}

public Network(Object[] vertices) {
    this(vertices.length);
    for (int i=0; i < vertexNumber; i++)
        this.vertices[i] = new
                    Vertex(vertices[i], i);
}

// Source and sink maintenance
public Object getSource() {
    if (vertices[sourceIndex] == null)
        return null;
    else return vertices[sourceIndex].data;
}

public void setSource(Object source) {
    int index = indexOf(source);
    if (index == -1) {
        addVertex(source);
        sourceIndex = indexOf(source);
    } else sourceIndex = index;
}
```

```java
public void setSource(int sourceIndex) {
   this.sourceIndex = sourceIndex;
}

public Object getSink() {
   if (vertices[sinkIndex] == null)
      return null;
   else return vertices[sinkIndex].data;
}

public void setSink(Object sink) {
   int index = indexOf(sink);
   if (index == -1) {
      addVertex(sink);
      sinkIndex = indexOf(sink);
   } else sinkIndex = index;
}

public void setSink(int sinkIndex) {
   this.sinkIndex = sinkIndex;
}

// Vertex maintenance
public Object getData(int index) {
   return vertices[index].data;
}

public Vertex getVertex(int index) {
   return vertices[index];
}

public void addVertex(Object data) {
   vertices[vertexNumber] = new
                   Vertex(data, vertexNumber);
   vertexNumber++;
}
public void setVertex(Object data, int index){
   vertices[index] = new Vertex(data, index);
}

// Edge access
public boolean isAdjacent(Object data1,
                          Object data2) {
   int index1 = indexOf(data1),
       index2 = indexOf(data2);
   return isAdjacent(index1, index2);
}
```

```java
    public boolean isAdjacent(Vertex vertex1,
                              Vertex vertex2) {
       int index1 = vertex1.index,
           index2 = vertex2.index;
       return isAdjacent(index1, index2);
    }

    public boolean isAdjacent(int index1,
                              int index2) {
       if (index1 < 0 || index1 >= vertexNumber
          || index2 < 0 || index2 >= vertexNumber)
             return false;
       return (capacityMatrix[index1][index2]>0);
    }

    public int capacity(int index1, int index2) {
       if (index1 < 0 || index1 >= vertexNumber
          || index2 < 0 || index2 >= vertexNumber)
             return 0;
       return capacityMatrix[index1][index2];
    }

    public int capacity(Object data1,
                        Object data2) {
       int index1 = indexOf(data1),
           index2 = indexOf(data2);
       return capacity(index1, index2);
    }

    public int capacity(Vertex vertex1,
                        Vertex vertex2) {
       int index1 = vertex1.index,
           index2 = vertex2.index;
       return capacity(index1, index2);
    }

    // Capacity maintenance
    public void setCapacity(Object data1,
                  Object data2, int capacity) {
       int index1 = indexOf(data1);
       int index2 = indexOf(data2);
       setCapacity(index1, index2, capacity);
    }
    public void setCapacity(Object data1,
                            Object data2) {
       setCapacity(data1, data2, 1);
    }
```

```
public void setCapacity(Vertex vertex1,
              Vertex vertex2, int capacity) {
  capacityMatrix[vertex1.index]
               [vertex2.index] = capacity;
}

public void setCapacity(Vertex vertex1,
                     Vertex vertex2) {
  setCapacity(vertex1, vertex2, 1);
}

public void setCapacity(int index1,
              int index2, int capacity) {
  if (index1 < 0 || index1 >= vertexNumber
     || index2 < 0 || index2 >= vertexNumber)
        return;
  capacityMatrix[index1][index2] = capacity;
}

public void setCapacity(int index1,
                     int index2) {
  setCapacity(index1, index2, 1);
}

public void removeEdge(Vertex vertex1,
                    Vertex vertex2) {
  int index1 = vertex1.index,
      index2 = vertex2.index;
  removeEdge(index1, index2);
}

public void removeEdge(int index1,int index2){
  if (index1 < 0 || index1 >= vertexNumber
     || index2 < 0 || index2 >= vertexNumber)
        return;
  capacityMatrix[index1][index2] = 0;
}

int indexOf(Object data) {
  for (int i = 0; i < vertexNumber; i++)
     if (data.equals.(((Vertex)
                       vertices[i]).data))
        return i;
  return -1;
}
```

```
public Enumeration elements() {
   return new BDFEnumerator();
}
public Enumeration elements(Object
                        startingVertexData) {
 return new BDFEnumerator(startingVertexData);
}

class BDFEnumerator implements Enumeration {
   BDFEnumerator() {
       visited = new boolean[vertexNumber];
       vertexQueue = new Vector();
       vertexQueue.addElement
                      (vertices[sourceIndex]);
       visited[sourceIndex] = true;
   }
   BDFEnumerator(Object vertexData) {
       visited = new boolean[vertexNumber];
       vertexQueue = new Vector();
       int index = indexOf(vertexData);
       vertexQueue.addElement(vertices[index]);
       visited[index] = true;
   }

   public boolean hasMoreElements() {
       if (vertexQueue.isEmpty())
          return false;
       return true;
   }

   public Object nextElement() {
       int index = ((Vertex)
            vertexQueue.elementAt(0)).index;
       vertexQueue.removeElementAt(0);
       for (int i=0; i < vertexNumber; i++)
          if (capacityMatrix[index][i] > 0 &&
                             !visited[i]) {
          vertexQueue.addElement(vertices[i]);
          visited[i] = true;
          }
       return ((Vertex) vertices[index]).data;
   }

   boolean[] visited;
   Vector vertexQueue;
}
protected int[][] capacityMatrix;
```

```
protected Vertex[] vertices;
protected int vertexNumber;
protected int sourceIndex, sinkIndex;

class Vertex {
   Object data;
   int index;
   Vertex(Object data) {
      this.data = data;
   }
   Vertex(Object data, int index) {
      this.data = data;
      this.index = index;
   }
}
}
```

## 10.2.2 Preflowed Networks

### 10.2.2.1 Networks with Preflows

Class *Network* has no instance field to hold flow for networks. The following class, *PreflowedNetwork*, extends class *Network* with instance variable *flowMatrix* declared as

```
protected int[][] flowMatrix;
```

When an instance of class *PreflowedNetwork* is created, the constructors *PreflowedNetwork*(*int size*) and *PreflowedNetwork*(*Object[] vertices*) use the following statement to initialize the instance field with a 2-dimensional array.

```
flowMatrix = new int[size][size];
```

Class *PreflowedNetwork* provides the following instance methods for managing the *flowMatrix*. It does not guarantee *flowMatrix* represents a valid flow that satisfies both the capacity constraints and flow conservation. In fact, the methods ensure the capacity constraints but not flow conservation. When method *setFlow*(*vertex1*, *vertex2*, *flow*) is invoked with a *flow* greater than the capacity of edge ⟨*vertex1*, *vertex2*⟩, the method will not change the *flowMatrix*.

| Signature | Semantics |
|---|---|
| void setFlow(Vertex vertex1, Vertex vertex2, int flow) | Sets the flow of the edge that connects *vertex1* and *vertex2* in this network with given *flow* |
| void setFlow(Object data1, Object data2, int flow) | Sets the flow of the edge between vertices that encapsulate *data1* and *data2* in this network |
| void setFlow (int index1, int index2, int flow) | Sets the flow of the edge that connects *vertices[index1]* and *vertices[index2]* in this network |

When a *PreflowedNetwork* removes a flow between a pair of vertices, it actually sets the entry in *flowMatrix* with 0.

We can retrieve the flow of an edge in a preflowed network with the overloaded *flow* methods. The no-argument method *flow()* applied for an instance of class *PreflowedNetwork* returns the *flowMatrix* of the preflowed network.

### 10.2.2.2 Class PreflowedNetwork

```
/** Class PreflowedNetwork for network with flow.
 *   Edges are represented with 2-dimensional array
 *   capacityMatrix. Flows over edges are
 *   represented in array flowMatrix.
 */
import java.util.*;
public class PreflowedNetwork extends Network {
    public static void main(String[] args) {
        String[] names = {"Cbc", "Abc", "Bbc"};
        PreflowedNetwork stringsNetwork = new
                        PreflowedNetwork(names);
        stringsNetwork.setCapacity("Bbc","Cbc",12);
        stringsNetwork.setCapacity("Cbc","Abc");
        stringsNetwork.setSource("Cbc");
        stringsNetwork.setSink("Bbc");
        if (stringsNetwork.isAdjacent("Bbc","Cbc"))
           System.out.println("an edge");
        Enumeration enumeration =
                   stringsNetwork.elements();
        while (enumeration.hasMoreElements()) {
          System.out.println
                   (enumeration.nextElement());
        }
    }
```

```
public PreflowedNetwork() { }
public PreflowedNetwork(int size) {
    super(size);
    flowMatrix = new
            int[vertexNumber][vertexNumber];
}
public PreflowedNetwork(Object[] vertices) {
    super(vertices);
    flowMatrix = new
            int[vertexNumber][vertexNumber];
}

// Flow access
public int flow(int index1, int index2) {
    if (index1 < 0 || index1 >= vertexNumber
        || index2 < 0 || index2 >= vertexNumber)
        return 0;
    else return flowMatrix[index1][index2];
}

public int flow(Object data1, Object data2) {
    int index1 = indexOf(data1),
        index2 = indexOf(data2);
    return flow(index1, index2);
}

public int flow(Vertex vertex1,
                Vertex vertex2) {
    int index1 = vertex1.index,
        index2 = vertex2.index;
    return flow(index1, index2);
}

// Flow maintenance
public void setFlow(Object data1,
            Object data2, int flow) {
    int index1 = indexOf(data1);
    int index2 = indexOf(data2);
    setFlow(index1, index2, flow);
}

public void setFlow(Object data1,
                    Object data2) {
    setFlow(data1, data2, 1);
}

public void setFlow(Vertex vertex1,
```

```
                          Vertex vertex2, int flow) {
         setFlow(vertex1.index, vertex2.index,flow);
   }

   public void setFlow(Vertex vertex1,
                       Vertex vertex2) {
       setFlow(vertex1, vertex2, 1);
   }

   public void setFlow(int index1,
                    int index2, int flow) {
       if (index1 < 0 || index1 >= vertexNumber
         || index2 < 0 || index2 >= vertexNumber)
          return;
       if (flow <= capacityMatrix[index1][index2])
          flowMatrix[index1][index2] = flow;
   }

   public void setFlow(int index1, int index2) {
       setFlow(index1, index2, 1);
   }

   public void removeFlow(Vertex vertex1,
                          Vertex vertex2) {
       int index1 = vertex1.index,
           index2 = vertex2.index;
       removeFlow(index1, index2);
   }

   public void removeFlow(int index1,int index2){
       if (index1 < 0 || index1 >= vertexNumber
         || index2 < 0 || index2 >= vertexNumber)
         return;
       flowMatrix[index1][index2] = 0;
   }

   public int[][] flow() { return flowMatrix; }

   protected int[][] flowMatrix;
}
```

## 10.2.3 Residual Networks

### 10.2.3.1 Capacities in Residual Networks

The following class, class *ResidualNetwork*, can create a residual network from a preflowed network. Its constructor *ResidualNetwork(PreflowedNetwork original)* derives a residual network from the *original* preflowed network. Particularly, the constructor uses statement

```
for (int i = 0; i < size; i++)
    for (int j = 0; j < size; j++) {
        int increment =
            original.capacityMatrix[i][j] -
            original.flowMatrix[i][j];
        capacityMatrix[i][j] = increment +
                    original.flowMatrix[j][i];

    }
```

to initialize entries of *capacityMatrix* for the created residual network. The above code uses formula $(w(v, v') - f(v, v')) + f(v', v)$ to calculate a capacity for the edge $\langle v, v' \rangle$ in the residual network. The capacity includes the amount of flow that can be added to the flow over the edge and the amount of flow that can be reduced from the opposite edge $\langle v', v \rangle$.

When we maximize the flow in a preflowed network, we derive a residual network from the preflowed network. The newly created residual network has zero flow over every edge. Class *ResidualNetwork* uses instance field *originalPreflowed* to reference the preflowed network from which the residual network is derived. Thus, the residual network can access and update the flow of the preflowed network.

### 10.2.3.2 Class ResidualNetwork

The following class, class *ResidualNetwork*, represents residual networks. The main method in the class uses a breadth-first traversal to list the vertices in a residual network named *stringsNetwork*. The reader can add code to the main method to list the capacity matrix of the residual network. We leave the code as an exercise.

```
/** Class ResidualNetwork represents residual
 *   networks of preflowed networks. Vertices
 *   are indexed with 0, 1, ..., vertexNumber-1
 *   in array vertices. Edge capacities of a
 *   residual network are represented with
 *   2-dimensional array capacityMatrix.
 *   Variable originalPreflowed in a residual
 *   network references a PreflowedNetwork.
 */
```

```java
import java.util.*;
public class ResidualNetwork
                extends PreflowedNetwork {
    public static void main(String[] args) {
        String[] names = {"Cbc", "Abc", "Bbc"};
        PreflowedNetwork stringsNetwork = new
                        PreflowedNetwork(names);
        stringsNetwork.setSource("Cbc");
        stringsNetwork.setSink("Bbc");
        stringsNetwork.setCapacity("Cbc","Bbc",12);
        stringsNetwork.setCapacity("Cbc","Abc",13);
        stringsNetwork.setCapacity("Abc","Bbc",13);
        stringsNetwork.setFlow("Abc", "Bbc", 5);
        stringsNetwork = new
                    ResidualNetwork(stringsNetwork);
        if (stringsNetwork.isAdjacent("Bbc","Cbc"))
            System.out.println("an edge");
        Enumeration enumeration =
                        stringsNetwork.elements();
        while (enumeration.hasMoreElements()) {
            System.out.println
                        (enumeration.nextElement());
        }
    }

    public ResidualNetwork() { }
    public ResidualNetwork(int size) {
        super(size);
    }
    public ResidualNetwork(PreflowedNetwork
                            original) {
        super(original.vertexNumber);
        vertices = original.vertices;
        sourceIndex = original.sourceIndex;
        sinkIndex = original.sinkIndex;
        originalPreflowed = original;
        for (int i = 0; i < vertexNumber; i++)
            for (int j = 0; j < vertexNumber; j++) {
                int increment =
                    original.capacityMatrix[i][j] -
                    original.flowMatrix[i][j];
                capacityMatrix[i][j] = increment +
                    original.flowMatrix[j][i];
            }
    }
    protected PreflowedNetwork originalPreflowed;
}
```

**Exercise 10.2** Add Java statements in the main method of the above class to display the entries of *capacityMatrix* encapsulated in the residual network referenced by local variable *stringsNetwork*.

## 10.2.4 Maximizing Flows

### 10.2.4.1 Leveled Networks

We use class *LeveledNetwork* to represent leveled networks, which are derived from residual networks. For a leveled network, instance variable *capacityMatrix* references a matrix that holds capacities of edges in the leveled network. The capacities are the same as the capacities of the edges in the residual network from which the leveled network is derived.

Let us assume a residual network $R$ derived from preflowed network $N$ with flow $f_N$. One of the constructors of class *LeveledNetwork* constructs a leveled network $L$ from $R$ and defines a topological order for vertices. The *topological order* is a partial order for vertices such that a vertex is before (less than) another if an edge in $L$ connects the former vertex to the latter.

Instance methods *pathSaturate* and *vertexSaturate* in class *LeveledNetwork* can be applied to find a maximum flow $f_L$ in a leveled network $L$. The flow $f_L$ will be added to the flow $f_N$ of the original preflowed network $N$. The *pathSaturate* method repeatedly finds an augment path in a leveled network. The *vertexSaturate* method saturates vertices by forwarding as much flow as possible from the source to the sink in the leveled network and then balances the resulting flow.

### 10.2.4.2 Maximizing Network Flows

In the main method of class *LeveledNetwork*, we show how to deduce a maximum flow for a preflowed network called *stringsNetwork*. The initial flow of *stringsNetwork* is 0 over every edge. The deduction repeatedly creates a residual network from the preflowed network and current flow, derives a leveled network from the residual network, and deduces a maximum flow for the leveled network. The flow in the leveled network is added to that of *stringsNetwork*. The repetition is implemented with the following code. It continues until the flow over the original network cannot be increased.

```
while (updated) {
    ResidualNetwork residualNetwork = new
            ResidualNetwork(stringsNetwork);
    LeveledNetwork leveledNetwork = new
            LeveledNetwork(residualNetwork);
    updated = leveledNetwork.vertexSaturate();
}
```

The following class, *LeveledNetwork*, includes both methods *pathSaturate* and *vertexSaturate*. Method *pathSaturate* tries to find an augment path, which starts from the source and ends at the sink. It uses a depth-first search to find an augment path. The current flow over each edge in the path is less than the residual capacity of the edge. We can increase the current flow of the *LeveledNetwork* by pushing more flow through the path.

The *vertexSaturate* method traverses the topological list of the vertices in a leveled network forth and back. When it traverses the vertex list from source to sink, it tries to push as much flow forward as possible by following the topological list and edges. When it traverses backward from sink to source, it tries to balance vertices by reducing the incoming flow to a vertex. A vertex is labeled as *blocked* if every path from the vertex to the sink contains an edge saturated by the current flow in the leveled network. When the method traverses the topological list backward, it detects blocked vertices and labels them as blocked.

### 10.2.4.3 *Class* LeveledNetwork

The main method of the following class, class *LeveledNetwork*, applies the *vertexSaturate* method to evaluate a maximum flow for the *leveledNetwork* deduced from *stringsNetwork*. One can replace method *vertexSaturate* with *pathSaturate* to deduce a maximum flow for the *leveledNetwork*.

Constructor *LeveledNetwork(ResidualNetwork original)* creates a leveled network from a residual network. It traverses the residual network in breadth-first order and collects visited vertices into a queue referenced by variable *topologicalList*. It initializes only the *capacityMatrix* entries for the edges in the leveled network.

Method *pathSaturate* invokes method *augmentPath* to find an augment path in a leveled network. It uses a stack named *augmentPath* to keep a path starting from the source vertex. It pushes a vertex onto the stack when the path can be extended to the vertex by an unsaturated edge. We use an integer array named *nextIndex* to avoid repeatedly testing a vertex for the path extension. Specifically, if the top vertex in the *augmentPath* stack is *vertices[i]*, all the vertices *vertices[0]*, ..., *vertices[nextIndex[i]–1]* have been tested for extending from vertex *vertices[i]*. We consider to extend the path with vertex *vertices[nextIndex[i]]*.

Method *vertexSaturate* uses boolean array *blocked* to indicate whether or not a vertex can be used to forward more flow toward the sink. We set *blocked[i]* with *true* if all the paths from vertex *vertices[i]* to the sink in the leveled network are saturated.

```
/** Class LeveledNetwork represents leveled
 *  networks derived from residual networks.
 *  It uses instance variables originalPreflow
 *  and originalResidual to reference the
 *  preflowed and residual networks from which
 *  a leveled network is derived. Vertices are
 *  indexed with 0, 1, ..., vertexNumber-1 in
```

```
 *   array vertices. Edge capacities and flows
 *   are represented with 2-dimensional arrays
 *   capacityMatrix and flowMatrix in a leveled
 *   network.
 */
import java.util.*;
public class LeveledNetwork
                      extends ResidualNetwork {
    public static void main(String[] args) {
        String[] names = {"Cbc", "Abc", "Bbc"};
        PreflowedNetwork stringsNetwork = new
                      PreflowedNetwork(names);
        stringsNetwork.setCapacity("Cbc","Bbc",12);
        stringsNetwork.setCapacity("Cbc","Abc",13);
        stringsNetwork.setCapacity("Abc","Bbc",15);
        stringsNetwork.setSource("Cbc");
        stringsNetwork.setSink("Bbc");
        boolean updated = true;
        // computes maximum flow for stringsNetwork
        while (updated) {
            ResidualNetwork residualNetwork = new
                  ResidualNetwork(stringsNetwork);
            LeveledNetwork leveledNetwork = new
                  LeveledNetwork(residualNetwork);
            updated =
                  leveledNetwork.vertexSaturate();
        }
        // prints the maximum flow
        for (int i=0;
            i<stringsNetwork.vertexNumber; i++) {
            for (int j=0;
                j<stringsNetwork.vertexNumber; j++)
                System.out.print(stringsNetwork.
                          flowMatrix[i][j] + " ");
            System.out.println(" ");
        }
        Enumeration enumeration =
                    stringsNetwork.elements();
        while (enumeration.hasMoreElements()) {
            System.out.println
                    (enumeration.nextElement());
        }
    }

    public LeveledNetwork() { }
    public LeveledNetwork(ResidualNetwork
                          original) {
```

```
        super(original.vertexNumber);
        vertices = original.vertices;
        sourceIndex = original.sourceIndex;
        sinkIndex = original.sinkIndex;
        originalPreflowed =
                    original.originalPreflowed;
        originalResidual = original;

        // breadth-first traversal
        topologicalList = new Vector();
        boolean[] visited = new
                        boolean[vertexNumber];

        topologicalList.addElement
                    (vertices[sourceIndex]);
        visited[sourceIndex] = true;
        for (int i=0;i<topologicalList.size();i++){
            int index = ((Vertex)
                topologicalList.elementAt(i)).index;
            if (index == sinkIndex) return;
            if (!visited[sinkIndex])
            /* adds unvisited vertices to the
                topological list */
            for (int j = 0; j < vertexNumber; j++)
                if (!visited[j] && originalResidual.
                        capacityMatrix[index][j]>0){
                    topologicalList.addElement
                                    (vertices[j]);
                    visited[j] = true;
                }
            // adds edges to this leveled network
            for (int k = i+1;
                    k < topologicalList.size(); k++) {
                int j = ((Vertex)
                topologicalList.elementAt(k)).index;
                capacityMatrix[index][j] =
                    originalResidual.
                            capacityMatrix[index][j];
            }
        }
        if (!visited[sinkIndex])
            topologicalList.removeAllElements();
    }

    private boolean pathAugment() {
        Stack augmentPath = new Stack();
        boolean[] visited = new
```

```
                        boolean[vertexNumber];
        int[] nextIndex = new int[vertexNumber];
        augmentPath.addElement
                        (vertices[sourceIndex]);
        visited[sourceIndex] = true;

        while (!augmentPath.isEmpty()) {
           int index = ((Vertex)
                        augmentPath.peek()).index;
           if (index == sinkIndex) break;
           boolean extended = false;
           for (int j = nextIndex[index];
                        j < vertexNumber; j++) {
              nextIndex[index]++;
              if (!visited[j] &&
                 capacityMatrix[index][j] >
                        flowMatrix[index][j]) {
                 augmentPath.push(vertices[j]);
                 visited[j] = true;
                 extended = true;
                 break;
              }
           }
           if (!extended) augmentPath.pop();
        }

        if (!augmentPath.isEmpty()) {
           int delta = 0;
           for (int i=0;i<augmentPath.size()-1;i++)
           {
              int index1 = ((Vertex)
                 augmentPath.elementAt(i)).index;
              int index2 = ((Vertex)
                 augmentPath.elementAt(i+1)).index;
              if (delta == 0) delta =
              capacityMatrix[index1][index2] -
                    flowMatrix[index1][index2];
              else if (delta >
                    capacityMatrix[index1][index2]-
                    flowMatrix[index1][index2])
                 delta =
                    capacityMatrix[index1][index2]-
                    flowMatrix[index1][index2];
           }
           for (int i=0;i<augmentPath.size()-1;i++)
           {
              int index1 = ((Vertex)
```

```
                augmentPath.elementAt(i)).index;
            int index2 = ((Vertex)
                augmentPath.elementAt(i+1)).index;
            flowMatrix[index1][index2] += delta;
        }
        return true;
    } else return false;
}

public boolean pathSaturate() {
    boolean improved;
    do {
        improved = pathAugment();
    } while (improved);
    return updateOriginal();
}

private boolean vertexSaturate() {
    boolean[] blocked = new
                boolean[vertexNumber];
    flowMatrix = new
                int[vertexNumber][vertexNumber];

    for (int i = 1;
            i < topologicalList.size(); i++){
        int k = ((Vertex)
            topologicalList.elementAt(i)).index;
        flowMatrix[sourceIndex][k] =
            capacityMatrix[sourceIndex][k];
    }

    boolean updated = true;
    while(updated) { updated = false;
    // forwards wave
    for (int i = 1;
            i < topologicalList.size()-1; i++) {
        int index = ((Vertex)
            topologicalList.elementAt(i)).index;
        if (!blocked[index]){
            // evaluates total income flow
            int incomeFlow = 0;
            for (int j = 0; j < i; j++) {
                int k = ((Vertex) topologicalList.
                            elementAt(j)).index;
                incomeFlow +=flowMatrix[k][index];
            }
            // evaluates total outgoing flow
```

```
int outgoFlow = 0;
for (int j = i+1;
    j<topologicalList.size(); j++) {
    int k = ((Vertex) topologicalList.
                elementAt(j)).index;
    outgoFlow +=flowMatrix[index][k];
}
int netFlow = incomeFlow - outgoFlow;

if (netFlow > 0) {
// forwards flow
for (int j = i+1;
    j<topologicalList.size(); j++) {
    int k = ((Vertex) topologicalList.
                elementAt(j)).index;
    if (!blocked[k] &&
        flowMatrix[index][k] <
        capacityMatrix[index][k]) {
        int remCapacity =
        capacityMatrix[index][k] -
        flowMatrix[index][k];
        if (remCapacity >= netFlow) {
        flowMatrix[index][k] +=
                            netFlow;
        break;
        }
        else {
        flowMatrix[index][k] =
            capacityMatrix[index][k];
        netFlow -= remCapacity;
        }
        updated = true;
    }
    }
}
}
}

// backward balancing
for (int i = topologicalList.size()-2;
    i > 0; i--){
    int index = ((Vertex)
    topologicalList.elementAt(i)).index;
    if (blocked[index]) continue;
    // evaluates total income flow
    int incomeFlow = 0;
    for (int j = 0; j < i; j++) {
```

```
        int k = ((Vertex) topologicalList.
                    elementAt(j)).index;
        incomeFlow +=flowMatrix[k][index];
}
// evaluates total outgoing flow
int outgoFlow = 0;
for (int j = i+1;
        j<topologicalList.size(); j++) {
    int k = ((Vertex) topologicalList.
                    elementAt(j)).index;
    outgoFlow +=flowMatrix[index][k];
}
int netFlow = incomeFlow - outgoFlow;

// detects if vertices[index] is blocked
boolean blocking = true;
for (int j = i+1;
        j<topologicalList.size(); j++) {
    int k = ((Vertex) topologicalList.
                    elementAt(j)).index;
    if (flowMatrix[index][k] <
        capacityMatrix[index][k]
        && !blocked[k]) {
        blocking = false;
        break;
    }
}
blocked[index] = blocking;

// balances flow for vertices[index]
if (netFlow > 0)
    for (int j = i-1; j >= 0; j--) {
        int k = ((Vertex) topologicalList.
                    elementAt(j)).index;
        if (flowMatrix[k][index] > 0) {
        if (flowMatrix[k][index] >=
                            netFlow) {
            flowMatrix[k][index] -=
                            netFlow;
            break;
        }
        else {
            netFlow -=
                flowMatrix[k][index];
            flowMatrix[k][index] = 0;
        }
    }
```

```
                    }
                }
            } // end while(updated)
            return updateOriginal();
        }

        private boolean updateOriginal() {
            boolean updated = false;
            for (int i=0; i < vertexNumber; i++)
              for (int j=0; j < vertexNumber; j++)
              if (flowMatrix[i][j] > 0) {
                  updated = true;
                  int remCapacity = originalPreflowed.
                                   capacityMatrix[i][j] -
                     originalPreflowed.flowMatrix[i][j];
                  if (flowMatrix[i][j] <= remCapacity)
                     originalPreflowed.flowMatrix[i][j]
                                   += flowMatrix[i][j];
                  else {
                     originalPreflowed.flowMatrix[i][j]
                        = originalPreflowed.
                                   capacityMatrix[i][j];
                     flowMatrix[i][j] -= remCapacity;
                     originalPreflowed.flowMatrix[j][i]
                                   -= flowMatrix[i][j];
                  }
              }
            return updated;
        }

        private Vector topologicalList;
        private ResidualNetwork originalResidual;
    }
```

**Exercise 10.3** (Continuation of Exercise 10.1) Modify the main method of class *LeveledNetwork* so that the *stringsNetwork* represents the network described in Fig. 10.1a with the flow described in Exercise 10.1. After compiling the class, run the method to find a maximum flow for the *stringsNetwork* by applying the *vertexSaturate* method.

**Exercise 10.4** (Continuation of Exercise 10.2) Repeat the above exercise by replacing the *vertexSaturate* method with the *pathSaturate* method in the main method of class *LeveledNetwork*.

# 10.3 Minimum Cuts

## 10.3.1 The Notion of Minimum Cut

Assume a network $N = (V, E)$. A *cut* for the network is a partition $\langle V_0, V_1 \rangle$ of $V$ such that $V_0 \cap V_1 = \varnothing$, $V = V_0 \cup V_1$, the source of $N$ is in $V_0$, and the sink is in $V_1$. The *capacity* of cut $\langle V_0, V_1 \rangle$, denoted with $w(V_0, V_1)$, is the sum of the capacities of edges that connect vertices in $V_0$ with vertices in $V_1$:

$$w(V_0, V_1) = \Sigma_{v \in V_0, v' \in V_1} w(v, v').$$

For a flow $f: E \to Z$ in network $N$ and a cut $\langle V_0, V_1 \rangle$, the flow of the cut, denoted with $f(V_0, V_1)$, is the sum of the flows of edges that connect vertices in $V_0$ with vertices in $V_1$:

$$f(V_0, V_1) = \Sigma_{v \in V_0, v' \in V_1} f(v, v').$$

Given a flow and a cut in a network, the cut is saturated by the flow if the capacity of the cut is equal to the flow of the cut.

For a maximum flow $f$ in a network $N$, we can find a cut saturated by $f$. In fact, if no cut in $N$ is saturated by $f$, we can find a sequence of cuts $C_i = (V_i, V'_i)$ with $0 \le i \le k$ such that

1. $C_0 = \langle \{source\}, V - \{source\} \rangle$;
2. cut $C_{i+1} = \langle V_i \cup \{v'\}, V'_i - \{v'\} \rangle$ for $0 \le i < k$, $v \in V_i$, $v' \in V'_i$, edge $\langle v, v' \rangle$ is not saturated by $f$; and
3. a vertex $v \in V_k$ such that edge $\langle v, sink \rangle$ is not saturated by $f$.

By a simple induction on $i$, we can prove that for each vertex $v \in V_i$ with $0 < i \le k$, there is a path from *source* to $v$ in $N$ and no edge in the path is saturated by flow $f$. By condition 3, we can find a path from *source* to *sink* such that each edge in the path is not saturated by the flow $f$. The path implies that flow $f$ is not a maximum one.

We can also show that a flow $f$ in a network $N$ is maximum if a cut $\langle V_0, V_1 \rangle$ in $N$ is saturated by the flow $f$, i.e., if $f(V_0, V_1) = w(V_0, V_1)$. To prove the proposition, let us assume a cut $\langle V_0, V_1 \rangle$ saturated by flow $f$ in $N$. The proof depends on the proposition that $|f| \le w(V_0, V_1)$ for any flow $f$ and cut $\langle V_0, V_1 \rangle$. We leave proving the proposition as an exercise. Therefore, if we have $f(V_0, V_1) = w(V_0, V_1)$ for a cut $\langle V_0, V_1 \rangle$, $f$ is maximum.

A cut $\langle V_0, V_1 \rangle$ that has the minimum capacity in a network is called a *minimum cut* of the network. A minimum cut represents a bottleneck for maximum flows. By reducing the capacity of any edge between $V_0$ and $V_1$ for a minimum cut $\langle V_0, V_1 \rangle$, the maximum flow of the network will be reduced as well.

**Exercise 10.5** By applying induction on the size of vertex set $V_0$, prove $|f| \le w(V_0, V_1)$ for any flow $f$ and cut $\langle V_0, V_1 \rangle$. (Hint: A flow satisfies capacity conservation at any vertex $v$ that is not the source or sink. For a cut $\langle V, V' \rangle$, moving vertex $v$ from set $V'$ to $V$ amounts to removing edges between vertices in $V$

and $v$ from the cut and adding edges between $v$ and vertices in $V' - \{v\}$ into the cut.)

## 10.3.2 Computing Minimum Cuts

We now discuss how to find a minimum cut for a network $N = (V, E)$. The discussion in the above section implies that minimum cuts are saturated by any maximum flow. We now describe an approach that uses the network classes to find a minimum cut for a network $N$.

Constructor *LeveledNetwork(ResidualNetwork original)* of class *LeveledNetwork* accepts a residual network *original*. Assume network *original* is deduced from a preflowed network $N$. The constructor produces a leveled network in a breadth-first traversal of the *original* residual network. It collects vertices encountered in the traversal into vector *topologicalList*. If no more vertices can be placed into the vector and the sink vertex is not in the vector, we know that all the edges from vertices in *topologicalList* to other vertices have capacity 0 in the residual network. Thus, all the edges from vertices in *topologicalList* to other vertices in network $N$ are saturated by the flow in $N$. Let $V_0$ consist of vertices in vector *topologicalList*, and $V_1 = V - V_0$. Cut $\langle V_0, V_1 \rangle$ is a minimum one.

The following code can be used to print the vertex set $V_0$ for a minimum cut $\langle V_0, V_1 \rangle$ in a preflowed *network*. We assume the entries in the *flowMatrix* in *network* are equal to 0 initially.

```
ResidualNetwork residualNetwork;
LeveledNetwork leveledNetwork;
while (updated) {
    residualNetwork = new
               ResidualNetwork(network);
    leveledNetwork = new
               LeveledNetwork(residualNetwork);
    updated = leveledNetwork.vertexSaturate();
}
residualNetwork = new ResidualNetwork(network));
Enumeration V0 = residualNetwork.elements();
while (V0.hasMoreElements()) {
    System.out.println(((Vertex)
               V0.nextElement()).data);
}
```

When the evaluation of expression *leveledNetwork.vertexSaturate()* returns *false*, all and only the vertices reachable from the source in *residualNetwork* can be enumerated with the *elements()* method. The cut $\langle V_0, V-V_0 \rangle$ is saturated by the maximum flow in *network*. This fact implies a minimum cut $\langle V_0, V-V_0 \rangle$ for *network*, where $V$ is the vertex set of *network*.

# 10.4 Summary

A network is a special type of directed, weighted graph. It designates a source and a sink vertex. The weight of an edge in a network is treated as a flow capacity of the edge. We define the notion of flow for networks and discuss the maximum flow problem.

We present several network classes. Class *Network* represents generic networks, which have capacities but no flow for edges. Class *PreflowedNetwork* extends class *Network* with a flow matrix. It maintains the capacity constraints automatically when flows over edges change. Users of the class are responsible for keeping flow conservation. Class *ResidualNetwork* extends class *Preflowed-Network*. One of its constructors creates the residual network for a preflowed network. Class *LeveledNetwork* extends class *ResidualNetwork*. It represents leveled networks for residual networks. Given a residual network, a constructor of class *LeveledNetwork* creates a leveled network for the residual network.

This chapter presents two Java methods in class *LeveledNetwork* to compute maximum flows for networks. Method *pathSaturate* finds paths that can be used to augment a flow. Method *vertexSaturate* saturates vertices by increasing their outgoing flows and balances them by decreasing the incoming flows of the vertices. It tries to find a flow that can be added to the flow of a network.

In this chapter, we also discuss the notion of minimum cut for a network. We describe how to apply the *pathSaturate* or *vertexSaturate* method to find a minimum cut for a network.

# Part IV
# Data Persistence

*- Object serialization*
*- Data structure serialization*

# Chapter 11
# Object Serialization

Applications, except those dealing with only transient data, need to store data in secondary storage. Some applications also transport objects through Internet or intranet. Both secondary storage and network are serial devices. They can accept series of bytes only. The objects to be stored in a secondary storage or transferred through a network must be serialized. Java provides serializability for programs to serialize objects into byte arrays or files.

The Java serialization mechanism provides serialization and deserialization functions. *Serialization* is the process of creating a serial representation of objects. The serialized objects can be stored in a file or transferred through a network. *Deserialization* is the process of creating the replicas of the serialized objects in the same or a remote machine based on the serial representation. The replicas have the same states as the original objects.

The Java serialization mechanism is based on a structure for storing serialized objects in a file or byte array. It records various attributes of a serialized object in the structure so that a replica of the object can be created from the representation. The attributes include class descriptions, field descriptions, and field values. If an object is referred to in a serialization process more than once, a back reference will be used to represent the object in the serial representation so that each object is serialized only once. The back reference is an integer handle, which is assigned to the object when the object is serialized for the first time.

The Java serialization mechanism represents different types of object differently. Specifically, it uses different representations for class, new object, null reference, array, string, and back reference. A serial representation is compact and structured. The representation allows efficient deserialization.

The Java serialization mechanism provides flexibility for users to control serialization of objects. Serializable objects are classified as either serializable or externalizable. A serializable class depends on the default serialization mechanism for serialization and deserialization. A programmer has no control over the default process of serialization and deserialization. He may add more data into the serial representation of a serialized object. The programmer of an externalizable class is totally responsible for serializing the fields in objects of the class and for deserializing the serial representations. Externalizability provides data structure programmers with flexibility in serializing data structures. It offers an opportunity for efficient serial representation of large data structures.

This chapter focuses on the Java serialization mechanism. We shall discuss:

- The structure of serial representations of objects. We focus on the representation of objects that refer to other objects. Both the referring and referenced objects are serialized automatically by the Java serialization mechanism. The class of a serialized object is encoded in the serial representation of the object. We also discuss the representation of other types of data such as string, array, and primitive type values.

- The architecture of the Java object serialization mechanism. It is founded on object output and input stream classes. Each of the streams encapsulates a byte array or a file. They provide methods for writing (serializing) objects or reading (deserializing) objects. We discuss serialization interfaces, which must be implemented by serializable classes.

- The externalizability of the Java serialization mechanism. The programmer of an externalizable class is responsible for defining methods that serialize and deserialize objects of the class. The methods are invoked automatically by the serialization mechanism of Java. We discuss the flexibility and efficiency introduced by the externalizability of Java.

We use hexadecimal representations of serialized objects to reveal the serialization mechanism. The representations are used to compare serializability and externalizability. They are produced from binary serial representations by invoking the *dumpfile* program, which can be found in Appendix A.

# 11.1 Serial Representation of Objects

## 11.1.1 Object Stream Format

### 11.1.1.1 Elements of Object Stream

The serial representation of an object stores object graphs. The *graph* of an object in a computer memory consists of the object and the objects referenced, directly or indirectly, by the object. An object may reference itself. The referenced objects are an important part of the data in the object. When the object is serialized, other objects involved in the object graph are serialized as well.

We show the graph of a customer object in Fig. 11.1a. The customer object contains a reference to an order object, which has an *owner* field. The *owner* field refers to the customer object. Thus, when the customer object is serialized, the order object are serialized as well. The references between the objects must be maintained in the serial representation of the customer object. As shown in Fig. 11.1b, the graph of object *order* includes the customer object.

The following example illustrates how a program creates object graph. The customer and order objects shown in the example will be used in the following examples of serialization.

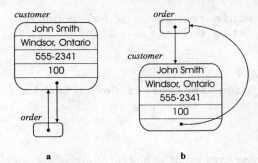

**Fig. 11.1** Object graphs

**Example 11.1** The following is a compilation unit with three classes –*Person*, *Customer*, and *Order*. The main method of class *Person* creates a customer and an order object. The *order* field of the customer references the order object, the *owner* field of the order object references the customer object. Thus, the graph of the customer object includes the order object, as shown in Fig. 11.1a. The graph of the order object includes the customer objects, as shown in Fig. 11.1b.

```
import java.io.*;
class Person {
    String name, address, telephone;
    public static void main(String[] args) {
        try {
            Customer customer = new Customer
                    ("John Smith", "Windsor, Ontario",
                    "555-2341", 100f);
            Order order = new Order();
            order.owner = customer;
            customer.order = order;
        } catch (Exception e) {
            e.printStackTrace();
        }
    }
}

class Customer extends Person
                    implements Serializable {
    float balance;
    Order order;
    Customer() { }
    Customer(String name, String address,
            String telephone, float balance) {
        this.name = name;
        this.address = address;
```

```
                    this.telephone = telephone;
                    this.balance = balance;
            }
    }

    class Order implements Serializable {
            Customer owner;
    }
```

□

The serial representation of an object consists of various elements, written by the Java serialization mechanism. It is used by the Java deserialization to create a replica of the serialized object graph in a runtime system, which may be different from the runtime system that generated the representation. We call the serial representation an object stream or a serialization stream.

The basic unit of data in an object stream is either a serialized object or a primitive value. The structure of a serialized object starts with a description of the class of the object. In addition to the class name and a serial version UID for the class description, a class description describes the number, names, and types of the instance fields of the serialized object. The class description is followed by the field values of the object. A field value may be a serialized object. Thus, the object stream may include another serialized object. The whole graph of the object is stored in the object stream.

A serialization stream may contain several serialized object graphs, which may be independent of each other. Some of the serialized object graphs may reference objects in different object graphs. An object may be referenced more than once in an object graph or in a stream. In a serialization stream, a *back reference* refers to an object that was already stored in the stream. An object reference in memory is essentially a memory address. It has no meaning for a replica of the referenced object created in the same or a different computer. The Java serialization mechanism associates an object with an integer handle when the object is serialized in an object stream. When an object is serialized, if the object references another object that has not been serialized, the referenced object graph will be serialized as a field value in the serial representation of the referencing object. If an object being serialized references a stored object in the same stream, the reference is replaced with the handle to the stored object. Thus, references to an object are replaced with either the serial representation of the object or an integer handle of the serialized object.

We use the following example to illustrate the basic structure of a serialization stream, which includes two object graphs, two class descriptions, and two object handles.

**Example 11.2** (Continuation of Example 11.1) As shown in Example 11.1, the main method of class *Person* creates two objects, which are denoted with local variables *customer* and *order*. It relates them by mutual referencing. We now extend the main method with serialization shown as follows. The extended main method creates a file output stream, which is encapsulated within an object output stream. It invokes method *writeObject* to place the serialized graphs of the two objects into the object output stream.

```
public static void main(String[] args) {
    try {
        Customer customer = new Customer
                ("John Smith", "Windsor, Ontario",
                 "555-2341", 100f);
        Order order = new Order();
        order.owner = customer;
        customer.order = order;

        FileOutputStream fout = new
                FileOutputStream("customer.dat");
        ObjectOutputStream out = new
                ObjectOutputStream(fout);
        out.writeObject(customer);
        out.writeObject(order);
        fout.close();
    } catch (Exception e) {
        e.printStackTrace();
    }
}
```

The above main method creates file *customer.dat*, shown as follows. We separate the bytes in the file into lines, 16 bytes per line. Each byte is coded with a two-digit hexadecimal integer.

| *Offset* | *Hexadecimal code* |
|---|---|
| 0x0000 | AC ED 00 05 73 72 00 08 43 75 73 74 6F 6D 65 72 |
| 0x0010 | DD 1F 2D 10 41 4B 00 74 02 00 02 46 00 07 62 61 |
| 0x0020 | 6C 61 6E 63 65 4C 00 05 6F 72 64 65 72 74 00 07 |
| 0x0030 | 4C 4F 72 64 65 72 3B 78 70 42 C8 00 00 73 72 00 |
| 0x0040 | 05 4F 72 64 65 72 9E 7B A0 F0 DD DD 59 E7 02 00 |
| 0x0050 | 01 4C 00 05 6F 77 6E 65 72 74 00 0A 4C 43 75 73 |
| 0x0060 | 74 6F 6D 65 72 3B 78 70 71 00 7E 00 02 71 00 7E |
| 0x0070 | 00 05 |

The data file *customer.dat* starts with a magic number and a version number. The constructor *ObjectOutputStream(OutputStream fout)* of class *ObjectOutputStream* writes a magic number and a version number to an object output stream when the stream is created. As shown in the above file, the magic number is *AC ED*, and version number is 00 05.

Class *ObjectOutputStream* defines method *writeObject(Object obj)* for serializing an object *obj* into a series of bytes. The serial representation of the object includes a description of the class of the object and the values of non-transient instance fields of the object. It starts with constant *TC_OBJECT* = 0x73 defined in interface *ObjectStreamConstants*. The constant denotes the start of a serialized object. In the above data file, the constant starts the graph of object *customer* at position 0x0004 and starts the graph of object *order* at position 0x003d.

Following constant *TC_OBJECT* in a serialized object stream, integer constant *TC_CLASSDESC* = 0x72 specified in interface *ObjectStreamConstants* is used to start the description of the class of the object. In the above data file, the constant starts the description of class *Customer* at position 0x0005 and that of class *Order* at 0x003e.

A class name, which is a string, follows the constant *TC_CLASSDESC* in an object output stream. It is encoded in a Utf8 string, which uses two bytes (a short) to specify the number of bytes in the Utf8 encoding. For example, in the above data file, integer 0x0008 at position 0x0006 indicates that the eight bytes at positions 0x0008, ..., 0x000f encode a class name, which is *Customer*.

In a class description in an object output stream, a serial version UID follows the class name. The UID is used to uniquely identify the class throughout the stream. If the class has a static field named *serialVersionUID*, the value in the field is used as the serial version UID for the class in object output streams. Otherwise, Java generates the UID from the class definition. In the above data file, the serial version UID of class *Customer* starts at position 0x0010 and ends at 0x0017. It is DD 1F 2D 10 41 4B 00 74.

Following the UID, a byte is used to encode the *flags* of the class. The *flags* byte indicates whether the class has a customized *writeObject* method, whether it implements interface *Serializable* or *Externalizable*. (Interface *Externalizable* extends interface *Serializable*.) The above file uses value 0x02 to record that class *Customer* implements only the interface *Serializable*, but the class does not define a *writeObject* method.

Following the *flags* byte in a class description, a description of the fields defined in the class specifies the number of fields with a short (two bytes) and the list of field descriptions. If a field is a primitive type field, its description consists of the type code and the field name. A primitive type code is a character. A field name is encoded in Utf8. If a field is an object type field, its description starts with character *[* for an array type and *L* for a class type.

The example data file contains the field count 0x0002 for class *Customer* at position 0x0019. It presents descriptions for field *balance* and *order* at positions 0x001b and 0x0025, respectively. The description of field *balance* starts with *float* type code *F* = 0x46 at position 0x001b. The field name is encoded at positions 0x001c, ..., 0x0024. The Utf8 encoding is

```
00 07 62 61 6C 61 6E 63 65
```

which uses seven bytes to encode string *balance*. The description of field *order* starts with character *L*, which is followed by Utf8 encoding of string *order*. It ends by constant *TC_STRING* = 0x74 at position 0x002d. The constant *TC_STRING* starts a Utf8 encoding of the class type of field *order*. The encoding is

```
00 07 4C 4F 72 64 65 72 3B
```

which represents *LOrder;*. This completes the *order* field description.

A class description in an object output stream contains a class annotation, which may include additional data for the class and which is ended with constant *TC_ENDBLOCKDATA* = 0x78. The description of class *Customer* in the above data file does not have any specific data in its annotation. The class annotation ends with constant *TC_ENDBLOCKDATA* at position 0x0037.

A class description may also include superclass descriptions for the class. The superclasses to be included in a serializable stream must be serializable; i.e., they must implement interface *Serializable*. Since class *Customer* has no serializable superclass, the superclass description for class *Customer* in the above file is denoted with the constant *TC_NULL* = 0x70 at position 0x0038.

The class *Customer* description is complete at position 0x0038. Following the class description for the customer object, the field values of the object are stored in the object output stream. Specifically, the *balance* field value 100f is stored at position 0x0039 with the four bytes

    42  C8  00  00

The value of filed *order* is a serialized object of class *Order*. Like the serialized customer object, the serialized order object has a class description and a field value for the object. We now go through the serialized order object, which is included in the serialized customer object as a field value. It is assigned with an integer handle, which will be used as reference to the order object in the same object stream.

Constants *TC_OBJECT* = 0x73 and *TC_CLASSDESC* = 0x72 at positions 0x003d and 0x003e start the object graph and class description, respectively, for the order object. The class description encodes class name *Order* in Utf8 with bytes

    00  05  4F  72  64  65  72

at position 0x003f. The class name is followed by an eight-byte serial version UID

    9E  7B  A0  F0  DD  DD  59  E7

which is started at position 0x0046 in the data file. The UID is followed by a *flags* byte 0x02, which indicates that class *Order* implements interface *Serializable*. Field count 0x0001 is displayed at positions 0x004f and 0x0050. The only field description starts with class type code $L$ = 0x4C at position 0x0051. The field name is encoded in Utf8 as

    00  05  6F  77  6E  65  72

which represents string *owner*. The type of the field is encoded with

    74  00  0A  4C  43  75  73  74  6F  6D  65  72  3B

The constant character *TC_STRING* = 0x74 introduces a Utf8 string *Lcustomer;* with length 0x000A = 10. The string describes the type of the *owner* field. The class annotation part of class *Order* contains nothing but constant *TC_ENDBLOCKDATA* = 0x78. Since class *Order* has no serializable superclass, its superclass descriptions list consists of the only constant *TC_NULL* = 0x70. Thus, the description of class *Order* is complete. The field value for the only field of object *order* is encoded with

    71  00  7E  00  02

where constant *TC_REFERENCE* = 0x71 is used to introduce the handle of the object *customer*. The handle is followed by another handle

        71 00 7E 00 05

which references the graph of object *order* and which was included in the graph of object *customer*. Its handle is added to the object output stream due to the expression *out.writeObject(order)*, which serializes the *order* object, in the main method. Thus, the serial representation of object *order* is a back reference handle.                                                                            □

The above example shows the structure of a serialized object, which is simple and efficient. An object output stream uses constant *TC_OBJECT* to start a serialized object. The constant is followed immediately by constant *TC_CLASSDESC*, which indicates the start of a class description for the serialized object.

In a class description, the class name is encoded in Utf8. A serial version UID is used to identify the class in the object output stream. The UID is followed by a *flags* byte, which indicates whether the class has a customized *writeObject* method, whether the class implements interface *Serializable* or *Externalizable*. The *flags* byte is followed by a field description, which includes a field count and the individual field descriptions. After the field description for the class, the class description has an annotation, which can be arbitrarily long and which is terminated with constant *TC_ENDBLOCKDATA*. Serializable superclass descriptions are listed at the end of the class description. If there is no serializable superclass, the superclass list is represented with constant *TC_NULL*.

In the serial representation of a serializable object, the field values follow the class description of the object. A field value may be a primitive value, a Utf8 string, an array, another serializable object, or a back reference.

### 11.1.1.2 Array Serialization

When the Java serialization mechanism serializes an array, it uses constant *TC_ARRAY* = 0x75 in an object stream to start the serialized array. The constant is followed by constant *TC_CLASSDESC* = 0x72 to introduce the class description for the serialized array. An array class description is similar to that of an object class such as class *Customer*. The field count in an array class description is 0x0000 = 0. Following the array class description, an integer is used to denote the number of elements of the array, and the elements are serialized in sequence.

The following example uses an array of customer objects to describe array serialization. The array class description describes the type of elements. The serial representation of each element must include a class description due to the polymorphism of Java. An element may be an instance of a subclass of the declared class of the array element.

**Example 11.3** The following class, class *ArraySerialization*, is used to test array serialization. The main method of the class creates two customer objects, creates an array, and places the customer objects into the array. Then, an object output stream applies the *writeObject* method to serialize the array. The serialized object is stored in file *customer.dat*.

```java
import java.io.*;
class ArraySerialization {
    public static void main(String[] args) {
        try {
            Customer customer1 = new Customer
                    ("John Smith", "Windsor, Ontario",
                     "555-2341", 100f),
            customer2 = new Customer( "Tom David",
                    "London, Ontario", "555-1234", 0f);
            Customer[] customers = new Customer[2];
            customers[0] = customer1;
            customers[1] = customer2;
            FileOutputStream fout = new
                    FileOutputStream("customer.dat");
            ObjectOutputStream out = new
                    ObjectOutputStream(fout);
            out.writeObject(customers);
            fout.close();
        } catch (Exception e) {
            e.printStackTrace();
        }
    }
}
```

The *customer.dat* file is shown in the following. It starts with a magic number and a version number. It uses constant *TC_ARRAY* = 0x75 to introduce the serialized array. Then it uses constant *TC_CLASSDESC* = 0x72 to introduce the class description for the serialized array. The array class name starts at position 0x0006. It is *[LCustomer;*. The encoding of the class name is followed by an eight-byte serial version UID. The *flags* byte of the class description is 0x02, which indicates that the array class implements only *Serializable* interface. A field count at position 0x001C is equal to 0x0000. An array class description has no field description. The class annotation is empty. It is represented with constant *TC_ENDBLOCK-DATA* = 0x78 at position 0x001e. The superclass description of the array class is represented with *TC_NULL* = 0x70 at position 0x001f. This completes the class description for the serialized array.

| *Offset* | | | | | | *Hexadecimal code* | | | | | | | | | | |
|---|---|---|---|---|---|---|---|---|---|---|---|---|---|---|---|---|
| 0x0000 | AC | ED | 00 | 05 | 75 | 72 | 00 | 0B | 5B | 4C | 43 | 75 | 73 | 74 | 6F | 6D |
| 0x0010 | 65 | 72 | 3B | 08 | E2 | 51 | 8D | DE | 26 | 57 | 9E | 02 | 00 | 00 | 78 | 70 |
| 0x0020 | 00 | 00 | 00 | 02 | 73 | 72 | 00 | 08 | 43 | 75 | 73 | 74 | 6F | 6D | 65 | 72 |
| 0x0030 | DD | 1F | 2D | 10 | 41 | 4B | 00 | 74 | 02 | 00 | 02 | 46 | 00 | 07 | 62 | 61 |
| 0x0040 | 6C | 61 | 6E | 63 | 65 | 4C | 00 | 05 | 6F | 72 | 64 | 65 | 72 | 74 | 00 | 07 |
| 0x0050 | 4C | 4F | 72 | 64 | 65 | 72 | 3B | 78 | 70 | 42 | C8 | 00 | 00 | 70 | 73 | 71 |
| 0x0060 | 00 | 7E | 00 | 02 | 00 | 00 | 00 | 00 | 70 | | | | | | | |

An integer value for the element count of the serialized array can be found after the class description. It is equal to 0x00000002. The two serialized elements of the serialized array follow the element count.

The first serialized element represents a customer object. It starts at position 0x0024 with constant *TC_OBJECT* = 0x73. The *Customer* class description starts at position 0x0025 and ends at position 0x0058. It includes the class name, serial version UID, a *flags* byte, two field descriptions for the *balance* and *order* fields, an empty annotation, and a null serializable superclass list.

Following the description of class *Customer* in the *customer.dat* file, we can find values of the two fields of the first customer object. The values 100f and *null* are represented with 42 C8 00 00 and 0x70, respectively. The second serialized customer is described at position 0x005e with constant *TC_OBJECT* = 0x73, which is followed by constant *TC_REFERENCE* = 0x71. The integer handle is equal to 00 7E 00 02, which represents the *Customer* class description for the first serialized customer object. The field values 0f and *null* of the second customer are represented with 00 00 00 00 and 0x70.                                                                    □

### 11.1.1.3 Vector Serialization

Class *Vector* is a standard Java class. Like other serializable objects, a serialized vector includes a description of class *Vector* and the field values of the vector. Class *Vector* defines three instance variables, which are called *capacityIncrement*, *elementCount*, and *elementData*. The first two instance variables are integers, the last one is an array. The serial representation of a vector encodes two integers for the first two fields and an array for the last field. We use the following example to show the contents of a serialized vector.

**Example 11.4** The following class, *VectorSerialization*, is used to test vector serialization. The main method of the class creates two customer objects, creates a vector, and places the customer objects into the vector. Then, an object output stream uses method *writeObject* to serialize the vector. The serialized object is stored in file *customer.dat*.

```
import java.io.*;
import java.util.Vector;
class VectorSerialization {
    public static void main(String[] args) {
        try {
            Customer customer1 = new Customer
                    ("John Smith", "Windsor, Ontario",
                    "555-2341", 100f),
                customer2 = new Customer("Tom David",
                    "London, Ontario", "555-1234", 0f);
            Vector customers = new Vector(2);
            customers.addElement(customer1);
            customers.addElement(customer2);
```

```
                  FileOutputStream fout = new
                          FileOutputStream("customer.dat");
                  ObjectOutputStream out = new
                          ObjectOutputStream(fout);
                  out.writeObject(customers);
                  fout.close();
              } catch (Exception e) {
                  e.printStackTrace();
              }
          }
      }
```

The contents of file *customer.dat* are shown as follows. After the magic number and version number, constant *TC_OBJECT* = 0x73 starts the serialized vector. Then, constant *TC_CLASSDESC* = 0x72 starts a class description for the vector. The class name *java.util.Vector* is 0x0010 = 16 bytes long. It is followed by an eight-byte serial version UID. The *flags* byte 0x02 at position 0x0020 records that class *Vector* implements the *Serialization* interface.

| *Offset* | *Hexadecimal code* |
|----------|--------------------|
| 0x0000 | AC ED 00 05 73 72 00 10 6A 61 76 61 2E 75 74 69 |
| 0x0010 | 6C 2E 56 65 63 74 6F 72 D9 97 7D 5B 80 3B AF 01 |
| 0x0020 | 02 00 03 49 00 11 63 61 70 61 63 69 74 79 49 6E |
| 0x0030 | 63 72 65 6D 65 6E 74 49 00 0C 65 6C 65 6D 65 6E |
| 0x0040 | 74 43 6F 75 6E 74 5B 00 0B 65 6C 65 6D 65 6E 74 |
| 0x0050 | 44 61 74 61 74 00 13 5B 4C 6A 61 76 61 2F 6C 61 |
| 0x0060 | 6E 67 2F 4F 62 6A 65 63 74 3B 78 70 00 00 00 00 |
| 0x0070 | 00 00 00 02 75 72 00 13 5B 4C 6A 61 76 61 2E 6C |
| 0x0080 | 61 6E 67 2E 4F 62 6A 65 63 74 3B 90 CE 58 9F 10 |
| 0x0090 | 73 29 6C 02 00 00 78 70 00 00 00 02 73 72 00 08 |
| 0x00a0 | 43 75 73 74 6F 6D 65 72 DD 1F 2D 10 41 4B 00 74 |
| 0x00b0 | 02 00 02 46 00 07 62 61 6C 61 6E 63 65 4C 00 05 |
| 0x00c0 | 6F 72 64 65 72 74 00 07 4C 4F 72 64 65 72 3B 78 |
| 0x00d0 | 70 42 C8 00 00 70 73 71 00 7E 00 05 00 00 00 00 |
| 0x00e0 | 70 |

Class *Vector* has three fields. The first field has type code 0x49 = *I* for *int*. The field name starts at position 0x0024. It is *capacityIncrement*. The second field starts at position 0x0037. Its type is *int*. Its name is *element-Count*. The third field starts at position 0x0046 with a type code 0x5B = *[*, which denotes an array type. The name of the field is *elementData* stored at position 0x0047. The type of the field is encoded in Utf8 string at position 0x0055, which is *[Ljava/lang/Object;*.

The class description has an empty annotation data block, which is ended at position 0x006a with constant *TC_ENDBLOCKDATA* = 0x78. The superclass list is empty. It is represented with constant *TC_NULL* at position 0x006b. Thus, the class description for class *Vector* is complete.

The field values of the serialized vector follow the class description. The value for the *capacityIncrement* field is equal to 0x00000000 = 0. The value for field *elementCount* is equal to 0x00000002 = 2. The value of field *elementData* is stored at position 0x0074. It is started with constant *TC_ARRAY* = 0x75, which is followed by constant *TC_CLASSDESC* = 0x72 and an array class description. The array class is *[Ljava/lang/Object;*. Its description starts at position 0x0075 and ends at 0x0097. The array class description is followed by an element count 0x00000002. Then, the two serialized elements of the array follow. They are similar to the serialized elements of the customers array shown in Example 11.3. The only difference is in an integer handle value. Since the data file contains more serialized objects and classes than the data file in Example 11.3, the description of class *Customer* has handle 00 7E 00 05 here. It has handle 00 7E 00 02 in Example 11.3.                    □

## 11.1.2 Object Output Streams

We use object output streams to create data files in the above examples. For instance, Example 11.2 uses code

```
FileOutputStream fout = new
            FileOutputStream("customer.dat");
ObjectOutputStream out = new
            ObjectOutputStream(fout);
out.writeObject(customer);
```

to write a serial representation of object *customer* to data file *customer.dat*. An object output stream encapsulates a file or a byte array onto which serialized objects are written. They provide methods such as *writeObject* to serialize objects.

We now explain how object output streams create the data files shown in the above examples. An object output stream uses an instance of class *ObjectStreamClass* to represent a class.

### 11.1.2.1 Class ObjectStreamClass

The serial representation of an object contains a class description for the objet. Class *ObjectStreamClass* is responsible for providing information on serializable classes. An instance of the class encapsulates a class name and a *serialVersionUID*. It also contains information on the immediate superclass and fields of the class and on whether the class is serializable or externalizable.

Class *ObjectStreamClass* defines static method *lookup(Class class)* to return an *ObjectStreamClass* object that describes the argument *class*. Given an object, we can retrieve an instance of class *Class* by invoking the instance method *getClass* for the object. With the *Class* object *class* as argument, method *lookup* (*Class class*) returns an instance of class *ObjectStreamClass*, which encapsulates information on argument *class*.

The class name and *serialVersionUID* encapsulated in an *ObjectStreamClass* object can be retrieved with instance methods *getName()* and *getSerialVersion-*

*UID*(). The instance method *write(ObjectOutputStream outputStream)* defined in class *ObjectStreamClass* composes and writes *flags* into the class descriptor in an object output stream. It also writes the field count and attributes of the class onto the stream. In the above examples, we directly invoke method *writeObject(Object obj)* of class *ObjectOutputStream* to serialize an object. The *writeObject* method invokes the *write* method of an *ObjectStreamClass* object to serialize the field count and attributes for the class of the object.

The *ObjectStreamClass* object for a class uses a field to reference the *ObjectStreamClass* of the superclass of the class. It does not encode any information for the superclass. For instance, the *ObjectStreamClass* object describes only the fields defined locally in the class.

## 11.1.2.2 *Class* ObjectOutputStream

An object output stream, which is an instance of class *ObjectOutputStream*, encapsulates an output stream, which represents a file or a byte array. It can write primitive type values and objects onto the file or byte array. When an object output stream writes an object, it writes information on the class of the object and the serializable superclasses of the class onto the output stream. If the written object references other objects, the referenced objects will be written transitively to the output stream as well.

Class *ObjectOutputStream* extends class *OutputStream*. It implements interfaces *ObjectOutput* and *ObjectStreamConstants*. Interface *ObjectOutput* extends interface *DataOutput*, which defines methods for writing primitive type values such as bytes, integers, floats, Utf8 strings, etc.

Class *ObjectOutputStream* defines instance method *writeObject(Object obj)* to write an object to an output stream. Strings and arrays are objects. They can be serialized with the *writeObject* method. Values of primitive types are written to an output stream with methods from the *DataOutput* interface, which is implemented by class *ObjectOutputStream*.

The Java serialization mechanism supported by the *ObjectOutputStream* class serializes graphs of objects. As shown in the main methods of the above examples, the *writeObject(Object obj)* method is invoked with an object to be serialized as argument. The method automatically traces the object graph to serialize each new object that is encountered. The basic use of class *ObjectOutputStream* can be shown with code

```
FileOutputStream fout = new
            FileOutputStream("customer.dat");
ObjectOutputStream out = new
            ObjectOutputStream(fout);
out.writeInt(2);
out.writeObject(" customers ");
out.writeObject(customers);
fout.close();
```

which stores integer 2, string *customers* , and a serialized graph of an object referenced with variable *customers* to file *customer.dat*.

### 11.1.2.3 Object Serialization

The *writeObject(Object obj)* method of class *ObjectOutputStream* is recursively invoked by Java to serialize the state of an object *obj*. If the class of *obj* is not serializable, the method simply throws a *NotSerializableException*. When the method serializes *obj*, it serializes the fields defined in the serializable superclasses of the class of *obj* before it serializes the fields defined locally in the class of *obj*. If the superclass is not serializable, the fields defined in the superclass will not be included in the serial representation of *obj*. A class is not serializable if the class does not implement interface *Serializable* or *Externalizable*.

We use the following example to illustrate the effect of a non-serializable object. It is compared with the serial representation shown in Example 11.2.

**Example 11.5** The following compilation unit defines the same classes as the compilation unit shown in Example 11.1 except that we add clause *implements Serializable* for class *Person*, which is the superclass of class *Customer*. The main method is the same as the main method described in Example 11.2.

```
import java.io.*;
class Person implements Serializable {
    String name, address, telephone;

    public static void main(String[] args) {
    try {
        Customer customer = new Customer
                ("John Smith", "Windsor, Ontario",
                 "555-2341", 100f);
        Order order = new Order();
        order.owner = customer;
        customer.order = order;

        FileOutputStream fout = new
                FileOutputStream("customer.dat");
        ObjectOutputStream out = new
                ObjectOutputStream(fout);
        out.writeObject(customer);
        out.writeObject(order);
        fout.close();
    } catch (Exception e) {
        e.printStackTrace();
    }
    }
}
```

```
class Customer extends Person
                    implements Serializable {
    float balance;
    Order order;
    Customer() { }
    Customer(String name, String address,
                  String telephone, float balance) {
        this.name = name;
        this.address = address;
        this.telephone = telephone;
        this.balance = balance;
    }
}

class Order implements Serializable {
    Customer owner;
}
```

The main method of class *Person* creates the following data file. Compared with the *customer.dat* file created in Example 11.2, the method invocation *writeObject(customer)* adds the bytes between positions 0x0038 and 0x00a9 to describe the superclass *Person* of class *Customer*. It also adds the bytes between positions 0x00aa and 0x00d4 to encode the values of fields *name*, *address*, and *telephone*, which are declared in superclass *Person*. Thus, the complete state of the *customer* object is serialized in the *customer.dat* file.

| *Offset* | *Hexadecimal code* |
|----------|--------------------|
| 0x0000 | AC ED 00 05 73 72 00 08 43 75 73 74 6F 6D 65 72 |
| 0x0010 | DD 1F 2D 10 41 4B 00 74 02 00 02 46 00 07 62 61 |
| 0x0020 | 6C 61 6E 63 65 4C 00 05 6F 72 64 65 72 74 00 07 |
| 0x0030 | 4C 4F 72 64 65 72 3B 78 72 00 06 50 65 72 73 6F |
| 0x0040 | 6E 6D 9F C8 2D EC 66 82 34 02 00 03 4C 00 07 61 |
| 0x0050 | 64 64 72 65 73 73 74 00 12 4C 6A 61 76 61 2F 6C |
| 0x0060 | 61 6E 67 2F 53 74 72 69 6E 67 3B 4C 00 04 6E 61 |
| 0x0070 | 6D 65 74 00 12 4C 6A 61 76 61 2F 6C 61 6E 67 2F |
| 0x0080 | 53 74 72 69 6E 67 3B 4C 00 09 74 65 6C 65 70 68 |
| 0x0090 | 6F 6E 65 74 00 12 4C 6A 61 76 61 2F 6C 61 6E 67 |
| 0x00a0 | 2F 53 74 72 69 6E 67 3B 78 70 74 00 10 57 69 6E |
| 0x00b0 | 64 73 6F 72 2C 20 4F 6E 74 61 72 69 6F 74 00 0A |
| 0x00c0 | 4A 6F 68 6E 20 53 6D 69 74 68 74 00 08 35 35 35 |
| 0x00d0 | 2D 32 33 34 31 42 C8 00 00 73 72 00 05 4F 72 64 |
| 0x00e0 | 65 72 9E 7B A0 F0 DD DD 59 E7 02 00 01 4C 00 05 |
| 0x00f0 | 6F 77 6E 65 72 74 00 0A 4C 43 75 73 74 6F 6D 65 |
| 0x0100 | 72 3B 78 70 71 00 7E 00 06 71 00 7E 00 0C |

The data file is also different from the data file shown in Example 11.2 at position 0x0104, where two object handles are displayed in sequence. Since the *writeObject* method adds the description for class *Person*, the handles of the *customer* and *order* objects are not equal to their counterparts in Example 11.2.                                                                            □

As shown in the above example, the default serialization mechanism of Java does not serialize the fields of an object that are inherited from non-serializable superclasses. The non-serializable superclasses must have no-argument constructor to allow their fields to be initialized. It is the responsibility of the class of the serialized object to save and restore the values of non-serializable fields. We now explain a technique for saving the inherited non-serializable fields of a serialized object.

A serializable class may implement a *writeObject(ObjectOutputStream out)* method. When the *writeObject(Object obj)* method is invoked for an *ObjectOutputStream* object *out*, if the class of *obj* defines the *writeObject* method, the *writeObject* method in the class of *obj* is invoked with statement

```
obj.writeObject(out);
```

Thus, the programmer of the class of *obj* may customize the serialization of *obj* with the *writeObject* method.

The *writeObject* method defined in a serializable class *C* should invoke the *defaultWriteObject* method of class *ObjectOutputStream* first. The *defaultWriteObject* method serializes the fields inherited by class *C* from serializable superclasses and the fields defined in class *C* locally. Then, the *writeObject* method of class *C* can serialize the fields inherited by *C* from non-serializable superclasses of class *C*. Thus, the complete state of an instance of class *C* can be serialized with the *writeObject* method.

We use the following example to illustrate how to define a customized *writeObject* method for the serializable class *Customer*. The method serializes the fields inherited from the non-serializable superclass *Person*.

**Example 11.6** The following compilation unit defines the same classes as the compilation unit presented in Example 11.1. It adds a *writeObject(ObjectOutputStream out)* method into class *Customer*. The method is defined with code

```
private void writeObject(ObjectOutputStream out)
                throws IOException {
    out.defaultWriteObject();
    out.writeObject(name);
    out.writeObject(address);
    out.writeObject(telephone);
}
```

which first invokes the *defaultWriteObject* method of class *ObjectOutputStream*. The *defaultWriteObject* method serializes any fields inherited from serializable superclasses and the fields defined locally in class *Customer*. Since the superclass *Person* is not serializable, the *defaultWriteObject* method serializes only the local fields *balance* and *order*. The *writeObject* method invokes *writeObject* method to serialize the non-serializable fields *name*, *address*, and *telephone*.

The following compilation unit can be compiled and the main method of class *Person* can be executed.

```
import java.io.*;
class Person {
    String name, address, telephone;

    public static void main(String[] args) {
    try {
        Customer customer = new Customer
                ("John Smith", "Windsor, Ontario",
                 "555-2341", 100f);
        Order order = new Order();
        order.owner = customer;
        customer.order = order;

        FileOutputStream fout = new
                FileOutputStream("customer.dat");
        ObjectOutputStream out = new
                ObjectOutputStream(fout);
        out.writeObject(customer);
        out.writeObject(order);
        fout.close();
    } catch (Exception e) {
        e.printStackTrace();
    }
    }
}

class Customer extends Person
                    implements Serializable {
    float balance;
    Order order;
    Customer() { }
    Customer(String name, String address, String
            telephone, float balance) {
        this.name = name;
        this.address = address;
        this.telephone = telephone;
        this.balance = balance;
    }

    private void writeObject(ObjectOutputStream
                out) throws IOException {
        out.defaultWriteObject();
        out.writeObject(name);
        out.writeObject(address);
        out.writeObject(telephone);
    }
}
```

```
class Order implements Serializable {
    Customer owner;
}
```

The *customer.dat* file created by the main method of class *Person* is shown as follows. Compared with the *customer.dat* file displayed in Example 11.2, the data file changes the byte at position 0x0018 from 0x02 to 0x03. The added flag 0x01 indicates that class *Customer* implements the *writeObject* method. The file includes the Utf8 coding of the three strings *John Smith*, *Windsor, Ontario*, and *555-2341*, which are added by the *writeObject* method of class *Customer*. Thus, this completes the state of the *customer* object in file *customer.dat*.

| *Offset* | *Hexadecimal code* |
|---|---|
| 0x0000 | AC ED 00 05 73 72 00 08 43 75 73 74 6F 6D 65 72 |
| 0x0010 | DD 1F 2D 10 41 4B 00 74 03 00 02 46 00 07 62 61 |
| 0x0020 | 6C 61 6E 63 65 4C 00 05 6F 72 64 65 72 74 00 07 |
| 0x0030 | 4C 4F 72 64 65 72 3B 78 70 42 C8 00 00 73 72 00 |
| 0x0040 | 05 4F 72 64 65 72 9E 7B A0 F0 DD DD 59 E7 02 00 |
| 0x0050 | 01 4C 00 05 6F 77 6E 65 72 74 00 0A 4C 43 75 73 |
| 0x0060 | 74 6F 6D 65 72 3B 78 70 70 71 00 7E 00 02 74 00 0A |
| 0x0070 | 4A 6F 68 6E 20 53 6D 69 74 68 74 00 10 57 69 6E |
| 0x0080 | 64 73 6F 72 2C 20 4F 6E 74 61 72 69 6F 74 00 08 |
| 0x0090 | 35 35 35 2D 32 33 34 31 78 71 00 7E 00 05 |

☐

# 11.2 Java Serialization Mechanism

## 11.2.1 Overview of Java Serialization

In the above section, we look at how to serialize objects so that the object graphs can be stored in an output stream. The serialization process is only one part of the Java serialization mechanism. The other part is the deserialization process, which deserializes serialized objects to create a replica of a serialized object in the same or a different computer. We now describe the architecture of the Java serialization.

A serializable class is also deserializable. If it defines a *writeObject* method to serialize some fields, the class must define a *readObject(ObjectInputStream in)* to deserialize the fields. Otherwise, a serializable class relies on the default *readObject* method of an object input stream to create a replica of a serialized object. The following example describes how to apply the default *readObject* method.

**Example 11.7** (Continuation of Example 11.6) We modify the compilation unit shown in Example 11.6 with object input in the main method of class *Person* and in the class *Customer*. As shown in the following compilation unit, the main method uses code

```
FileInputStream fin = new
                FileInputStream("customer.dat");
ObjectInputStream in = new
                ObjectInputStream(fin);
Customer customer1 = (Customer) in.readObject();
Order order1 = (Order) in.readObject();
fin.close();
```

to create a file input stream, which encapsulates file *customer.dat*, and create an object input stream *in*, which is built on the file input stream. The above code reads in a customer and an order object stored in the *customer.dat* file with method invocations *in.readObject()*. The recreated customer and order objects are assigned to local variables *customer1* and *order1*, respectively. To verify whether the created objects are the replicas of objects referenced with variables *customer* and *order*, we test the condition

```
customer.name.equals(customer1.name) &&
customer.address.equals(customer1.address)&&
customer.telephone.equals(customer1.telephone)
&& customer.balance == customer1.balance
&& order1.owner == customer1
```

which is true after the main method is run. The condition also indicates that the recreated order object refers to the recreated customer object with variable *owner*. Thus, the serialized object graph is recreated with the *readObject* method invocations.

```
import java.io.*;
class Person {
    String name, address, telephone;
    public Person() {}

    public static void main(String[] args) {
    try {
    Customer customer = new Customer("John Smith",
        "Windsor, Ontario", "555-2341", 100f);
    Order order = new Order();
    order.owner = customer;
    customer.order = order;

    FileOutputStream fout = new
        FileOutputStream("customer.dat");
    ObjectOutputStream out = new
        ObjectOutputStream(fout);
    out.writeObject(customer);
    out.writeObject(order);
    fout.close();
```

```
            FileInputStream fin = new
                FileInputStream("customer.dat");
            ObjectInputStream in = new
                ObjectInputStream(fin);
            Customer customer1 =(Customer)in.readObject();
            Order order1 = (Order) in.readObject();
            fin.close();

            if (customer.name.equals(customer1.name) &&
                customer.address.equals(customer1.address)
                && customer.telephone.equals
                                    (customer1.telephone)
                && customer.balance == customer1.balance
                && order1.owner == customer1)
                System.out.println("The replicas of " +
                            "customer and order " +
                            "objects are created.");

        } catch (Exception e) {
            e.printStackTrace();
        }}
    }

class Customer extends Person
                    implements Serializable {
        float balance;
        Order order;

        Customer() { }
        Customer(String name, String address,
                    String telephone, float balance) {
            this.name = name;
            this.address = address;
            this.telephone = telephone;
            this.balance = balance;
        }

        private void writeObject(ObjectOutputStream
                    out) throws IOException {
            out.defaultWriteObject();
            out.writeObject(name);
            out.writeObject(address);
            out.writeObject(telephone);
        }

        private void readObject(ObjectInputStream in)
            throws IOException, ClassNotFoundException
```

```
    {
        in.defaultReadObject();
        name = (String) in.readObject();
        address = (String) in.readObject();
        telephone = (String) in.readObject();
    }
}

class Order implements Serializable {
    Customer owner;
}
```

□

We now summarize the above discussions of the Java serialization. The Java serialization mechanism supports the serialization of objects into a file or byte array, which can be deserialized with the Java serialization mechanism. The serialization and deserialization processes may take place in different computers.

The serialization process tests whether an object to be serialized has a *writeObject* method. If the object does, the *writeObject* method of the object output stream invokes the *writeObject* method of the object being serialized. The *writeObject* method of the object being serialized should invoke the *default-WriteObject* method for the object output stream. The invocation serializes all the serializable fields, which are defined locally or inherited from serializable superclasses. The *writeObject* method of the object being serialized can serialize the fields that are inherited from non-serializable superclasses.

The deserialization process of the Java serialization mechanism reverses the serialization process. It is started with the creation of an object input stream, which opens a file or a byte array that stores serialized objects. To create replicas of the stored objects, we invoke the *readObject* method for the object input stream. The method reads a stored object state from the medium, invokes the no-argument constructors of the stored object for a created object, and uses the input data to initialize the created object. Thus, the created object will have the same state as the stored object.

The *readObject* method of an object input stream detects whether a deserialized object has a *readObject* method by reading byte *flags*. If the object does, its *readObject* method is invoked to deserialize the stored object. The *readObject* method should read what the *writeObject* method of the object writes. In this way, some non-serialized fields of the object can be retrieved by the *readObject* method. The *readObject* method first invokes the *defaultReadObject* method of the object input stream so that the serializable fields can be retrieved from the storage. Then, the *readObject* method of the deserialized object can retrieve the stored non-serializable fields.

## 11.2.2 Java Serialization Classes and Interfaces

### 11.2.2.1 *Interface* Serializable

A class represents serializable objects if the class implements the *Serializable* interface. Otherwise, the instances of the class are not serializable. The interface does not specify any method or constant. Arrays are serializable by nature. Class *Vector* implements the interface. A vector can be serialized. Class *String* also implements the *Serializable* interface. A subclass of a serializable class is serializable. Hence, the implements clause in class *Customer* in Example 11.5 is redundant.

Instances of classes that do not implement interface *Serializable* are not serializable. During serialization, if a non-serializable object is encountered by the default serialization mechanism, a *NotSerializableException* will be thrown.

### 11.2.2.2 *Class* ObjectOutputStream

Class *ObjectOutputStream* supports the serialization process. An instance of the class encapsulates a file, a byte array, or a network socket stream to support data persistency and object transportation.

Class *ObjectOutputStream* defines only one constructor

*ObjectOutputStream(OutputStream out)*

which accepts an output stream as argument. The serial representation of objects produced by the *ObjectOutputStream* is delegated to the encapsulated output stream.

The instance methods of class *ObjectOutputStream* include methods *writeObject(Object obj)* and *defaultWriteObject()*. The *defaultWriteObject* method can be invoked only in a *writeObject* method for an object that is being serialized. It serializes the serializable fields of an object being serialized. An example of invoking the method can be found in Example 11.7. The *writeObject* method detects if an object being serialized has a *writeObject* method. If the object has, its *writeObject* method is invoked. Otherwise, the default serialization process is started for the object.

In addition to the *writeObject* method, class *ObjectOutputStream* defines methods to serialize primitive type values such as float and integer.

### 11.2.2.3 *Class ObjectInputStream*

Class *ObjectInputStream* plays a reverse role compared with class *ObjectOutputStream*. It uses constructor

*ObjectInputStream(InputStream in)*

to create an object input stream for deserializing data stored in input stream *in*. The source stream may represent a file, a byte array, or a network socket stream.

Class *ObjectInputStream* defines method *readObject* to deserialize the stored state of an object. If the deserialized object class has a *readObject* method, the customized *readObject* method is invoked to deserialize the field values for a created object. The *readObject* method of the object should invoke the *defaultRead-Object* method for the object input stream to deserialize the serializable fields. It may also deserialize the values for non-serializable fields. An example of application of the serialized *readObject* and *defaultReadObject* methods can be found in Example 11.7.

## 11.2.2.4 Serializable and Non-Serializable Fields

A class variable of a class cannot be serialized by the Java serialization mechanism because the *writeObject* methods can be applied to objects only. The value of a class variable is either a primitive value or an object. The *writeObject* methods may store the value of the class variable into an object output stream. But the Java serialization mechanism cannot relate the serialized value with the class variable. It is the responsibility of a user-defined class to deserialize a static variable value and assign the value to the static variable.

A *transient* field in an object will not be serialized by the Java serialization. A sensitive instance field can be declared as *private transient*. In this way, the field cannot be accessed outside the object or serialized into a stream.

A *transient* field of an object can be assigned to the field in a replica of the object by the *readObject* method. Particularly, we may encrypt the value of a transient field when the object that contains the field is serialized with the *writeObject* method. The encrypted value can be decrypted and assigned to the field in a replica of the serialized object when the replica is created with the *readObject* method. This approach, without invoking decryption, is demonstrated in the following example.

**Example 11.8** (Continuation of Example 11.7) The following compilation unit is the same as that presented in Example 11.7 except

- the instance variable *balance* declared in class *Customer* is modified with keyword *transient* so that the field will not be automatically serialized when a customer object is serialized;
- the *writeObject* method of class *Customer* is extended with statement
  ```
  out.writeFloat(balance);
  ```
  so that the value of field *balance* will be serialized into an output stream encapsulated by object output stream *out*;
- the *readObject* method of class *Customer* is extended with statement
  ```
  balance = in.readFloat();
  ```
  so that the *balance* field of a created customer object can be initialized with a value from object input stream *in*.

The main method in the following compilation unit does essentially the same thing as the main method presented in Example 11.7. Here, the transient field *balance* is "manually" serialized and deserialized by methods *writeObject* and *readObject* of class *Customer*.

```java
import java.io.*;
class Person {
    String name, address, telephone;
    public Person() {}

    public static void main(String[] args) {
    try {
    Customer customer = new Customer("John Smith",
            "Windsor, Ontario", "555-2341", 100f);
    Order order = new Order();
    order.owner = customer;
    customer.order = order;

    FileOutputStream fout = new
            FileOutputStream("customer.dat");
    ObjectOutputStream out = new
            ObjectOutputStream(fout);
    out.writeObject(customer);
    out.writeObject(order);
    fout.close();

    FileInputStream fin = new
            FileInputStream("customer.dat");
    ObjectInputStream in = new
            ObjectInputStream(fin);
    Customer customer1 =(Customer)in.readObject();
    Order order1 = (Order) in.readObject();
    fin.close();

    if (customer.name.equals(customer1.name) &&
       customer.address.equals(customer1.address)
       && customer.telephone.equals
                        (customer1.telephone)
       && customer.balance == customer1.balance
       && order1.owner == customer1)
        System.out.println("The replicas of " +
                "customer and order " +
                "objects are recreated.");

    } catch (Exception e) {
      e.printStackTrace();
    }}
}
```

```
    class Customer extends Person
                    implements Serializable {
        transient float balance;
        Order order;
        Customer() { }
        Customer(String name, String address,
                String telephone, float balance) {
            this.name = name;
            this.address = address;
            this.telephone = telephone;
            this.balance = balance;
        }
        private void writeObject
                    (java.io.ObjectOutputStream out)
            throws IOException {
        out.defaultWriteObject();
        out.writeFloat(balance);
        out.writeObject(name);
        out.writeObject(address);
        out.writeObject(telephone);
        }
        private void readObject
                    (java.io.ObjectInputStream in)
            throws IOException,ClassNotFoundException{
            in.defaultReadObject();
            balance = in.readFloat();
            name = (String) in.readObject();
            address = (String) in.readObject();
            telephone = (String) in.readObject();
        }
    }

    class Order implements Serializable {
        Customer owner;
    }
```

□

# 11.3 Externalizable Classes

## 11.3.1 Interface *Externalizable*

Interface *Externalizable* extends interface *Serializable*. It specifies two methods
for an externalizable object to write its state to an output stream and read the

stored state from an input stream. The externalizable class controls the format and contents of the output stream. It may invoke the Java serialization mechanism to serialize an instance field. The externalizable class is aware of the specific format of its instances in a storage. It is responsible for reading the stored fields of the instances when the Java serialization mechanism creates replicas of stored objects.

The interface *Externalizable* specifies methods

> *public abstract void writeExternal(ObjectOutput out)*
> *throws IOException*
> *public abstract void readExternal(ObjectInput in)*
> *throws IOException, ClassNotFoundException*

The *writeExternal(ObjectOutput out)* method defined in an externalizable class may serialize any fields of an instance of the class into the object output *out*. The *readExternal(ObjectInput in)* method deserializes the fields and assigns the retrieved values to the fields of a created object of the class. The Java serialization mechanism creates an instance of an externalizable class when an object input stream applies the method *readObject* to read in an externalized object. It invokes the no-argument constructor of the class to create the object with default initial field values. The *readExternal* method is invoked to deserialize values and assign the values to the fields.

We use the following example to illustrate the *Externalizable* interface. The support of Java for interface *Externalizable* is demonstrated with the classes presented in Example 11.8. The class *Customer* implements the interface. It defines methods for serializing the fields of a customer object, deserializing the fields, and rebuilding the state in a customer object.

**Example 11.9** We now introduce externalizability into the class *Customer* presented in Example 11.8. We implement the *writeExternal* and *readExternal* methods of interface *Externalizable* in class *Customer*. To enable the Java serialization classes to locate class *Customer*, we place class *Customer* into file *Customer.java*.

The following class, *Person*, is the same as class *Person* defined in Example 11.8. Place the class into a file named *Person.java*.

```
import java.io.*;
class Person {
    String name, address, telephone;
    public Person() {}

    public static void main(String[] args) {
    try {
    Customer customer = new Customer("John Smith",
        "Windsor, Ontario", "555-2341", 100f);
    Order order = new Order();
    order.owner = customer;
    customer.order = order;
    FileOutputStream fout = new
        FileOutputStream("customer.dat");
```

```
ObjectOutputStream out = new
      ObjectOutputStream(fout);
out.writeObject(customer);
out.writeObject(order);
fout.close();

FileInputStream fin = new
      FileInputStream("customer.dat");
ObjectInputStream in = new
      ObjectInputStream(fin);
Customer customer1= (Customer)in.readObject();
Order order1 = (Order) in.readObject();
fin.close();

if (customer.name.equals(customer1.name) &&
   customer.address.equals(customer1.address)
   && customer.telephone.equals
                  (customer1.telephone)
   && customer.balance == customer1.balance
   && order1.owner == customer1)
System.out.println("The replicas of " +
            "customer and order " +
            "objects are recreated.");
} catch (Exception e) {
   e.printStackTrace();
}}
}
```

The following class, class *Customer*, is different from the *Customer* class presented in Example 11.8 in several aspects. Since the no-argument constructor of the *Customer* class will be used by the Java serialization to create an object, we change the access mode of the class and its no-argument constructor to public. The class implements interface *Externalizable* rather than *Serializable*. It implements methods *writeExternal* and *readExternal* but not *writeObject* or *readObject*. Note that the methods *writeExternal* and *readExternal* are public methods. In the *writeExternal* method, we serialize all the fields, inherited and local, into an object output stream. In *readExternal*, we deserialize all the field values from an object input stream and assign the values to the fields in a created customer object.

```
import java.io.*;
class Customer extends Person
                  implements Externalizable {
   transient float balance;
   Order order;
   public Customer() { }
   Customer(String name, String address,
         String telephone, float balance) {
```

```
            this.name = name;
            this.address = address;
            this.telephone = telephone;
            this.balance = balance;
        }

        public void writeExternal(ObjectOutput out)
                        throws IOException {
            out.writeFloat(balance);
            out.writeObject(name);
            out.writeObject(address);
            out.writeObject(telephone);
            out.writeObject(order);
        }

        public void readExternal(ObjectInput in)
            throws IOException, ClassNotFoundException {
            balance = in.readFloat();
            name = (String) in.readObject();
            address = (String) in.readObject();
            telephone = (String) in.readObject();
            order = (Order) in.readObject();
        }
    }
```

The following class, class *Order*, is the same as the class *Order* presented in Example 11.8. The class will be used by Java serialization. We place the class in a separate file named *Order.java*.

```
import java.io.*;
class Order implements Serializable {
    Customer owner;
}
```

When the main method of class *Person* is run, the statement

```
out.writeObject(customer);
```

invokes the *writeObject* method of class *ObjectOutputStream*. The *writeObject* method detects that the class of the *customer* object is *Customer*, which implements interface *Externalizable* and defines the *writeExternal* method. After the *writeObject* method of class *ObjectOutputStream* serializes the descriptor of class *Customer*, it invokes the *writeExternal* method of class *Customer* for the customer object. The *writeExternal* method serializes the fields of the customer object.

When the statement

```
Customer customer1 = (Customer) in.readObject();
```

in the main method of class *Person* is executed, the *readObject* method of the object input stream *in* reads the descriptor of class *Customer* and discovers that the class of the deserialized object, which is *Customer*, is externalizable. Then, the *readObject* method invokes the *readExternal* method for a created

*Customer* object. The *readExternal* method deserializes stored field values and assigns the values to instance variables of the created *Customer* object. Thus, a replica of the externalized object is created with the *readObject* method.

When the main method of class *Person* is executed, it prints

>*The replicas of customer and order objects are recreated.*

on the standard output. □

## 11.3.2 Externalizing Vectors

Class *Vector* is a standard data structure of Java. In Section 11.1.1.3, we serialize a vector with the default Java serialization mechanism. As shown in Example 11.4, the serialization of a vector includes an array serialization for the *elementData* field. We now show that a vector can be serialized with the *writeExternal* method specified in interface *Externalizable*. The serial representation of the vector will not include the array for data elements. The *writeExternal* method serializes the data elements directly. Thus, we can reduce the size of the serial representation, which is crucial for reducing secondary storage accesses, lowering transporting cost, and speeding up network transportation.

The inheritance mechanism of Java makes it possible to serialize objects of a class without having to implement interface *Serializable* or *Externalizable* in the class. We can extend the class and let the subclass implement interface *Externalizable*. Although the inherited fields in the subclass are not serializable, the externalizable subclass can control the externlization of the inherited fields in the *writeExternal* method. Similarly, the *readExternal* method of the subclass can assign deexternalized values to the inherited non-serializable fields.

The following example shows how to externalize a subclass of the Java standard class *Vector*. The subclass implements the *Externalizable* interface. It shows the advantages of externalizing a vector rather than applying the default serialization of Java for the vector.

**Example 11.10** The following class, *ExternalizableVector*, extends class *Vector* and implements interface *Externalizable*. The *writeExternal* method of the class uses code

```
out.writeInt(size());
for (int i=0; i < size(); i++)
    out.writeObject(elementAt(i));
```

to write the size of the vector into an object output stream named *out* and serialize each of the elements of the vector. The *readExternal* method of class *ExternalizableVector* uses code

```
int size = in.readInt();
for (int i=0; i < size; i++)
    addElement(in.readObject());
```

to find the size of a serialized vector and populate a created vector with the
deserialized elements.

```java
import java.util.*;
import java.io.*;
class ExternalizableVector extends Vector
                    implements Externalizable {
    public static void main(String[] args) {
        try {
            Customer customer1 = new Customer
                    ("John Smith", "Windsor, Ontario",
                    "555-2341", 100f),
            customer2 = new Customer("Tom David",
                    "London, Ontario","555-1234", 0f);
            ExternalizableVector customers
                    = new ExternalizableVector();
            customers.addElement(customer1);
            customers.addElement(customer2);
            FileOutputStream fout = new
                    FileOutputStream("customer.dat");
            ObjectOutputStream out = new
                    ObjectOutputStream(fout);
            out.writeObject(customers);
            fout.close();
        } catch (Exception e) {
            e.printStackTrace();
        }
    }

    public ExternalizableVector() { }

    public void writeExternal(ObjectOutput out)
                    throws IOException {
        out.writeInt(size());
        for (int i=0; i<size(); i++)
            out.writeObject(elementAt(i));
    }

    public void readExternal(ObjectInput in)
            throws IOException,ClassNotFoundException{
        int size = in.readInt();
        for (int i=0; i < size; i++)
            addElement(in.readObject());
    }
}
```

The data file *customer.dat* generated by the main method of class *Externalizable Vector* is shown as follows. The description of class *Externalizable Vector* starts at position 0x0005 and ends at 0x0028. Since the class implements interface *Externalizable*, the *flags* byte at position 0x0024 is 0x04 and the field count is 0x0000 at position 0x0025. Following the class description are integer 2 and two serialized customer objects. The first customer object has a description of class *Customer* at positions 0x002e through 0x0045. The second uses the  handle of the class description at position 0x0078.

Compared with the data file shown in Example 11.4, the following data file does not keep array class description. Its size is 170 bytes. The size of the data file in Example 11.4 is 225 bytes. The size reduction is due to the elimination of the serialization of the auxiliary array and two other fields.

| *Offset* | *Hexadecimal code* |
|----------|--------------------|
| 0x0000 | AC ED 00 05 73 72 00 14 45 78 74 65 72 6E 61 6C |
| 0x0010 | 69 7A 61 62 6C 65 56 65 63 74 6F 72 71 42 8E 53 |
| 0x0020 | BE AB E7 0F 04 00 00 78 70 00 00 00 02 73 72 00 |
| 0x0030 | 08 43 75 73 74 6F 6D 65 72 8E 52 30 05 43 29 61 |
| 0x0040 | 46 04 00 00 78 70 42 C8 00 00 74 00 0A 4A 6F 68 |
| 0x0050 | 6E 20 53 6D 69 74 68 74 00 10 57 69 6E 64 73 6F |
| 0x0060 | 72 2C 20 4F 6E 74 61 72 69 6F 74 00 08 35 35 35 |
| 0x0070 | 2D 32 33 34 31 70 73 71 00 7E 00 02 00 00 00 00 |
| 0x0080 | 74 00 09 54 6F 6D 20 44 61 76 69 64 74 00 0F 4C |
| 0x0090 | 6F 6E 64 6F 6E 2C 20 4F 6E 74 61 72 69 6F 74 00 |
| 0x00a0 | 08 35 35 35 2D 31 32 33 34 70 |

□

The class *ExternalizableVector* inherits a serializable but not externalizable class, class *Vector*. The above technique of storing data structures with an externalizable subclass can be applied to a non-serializable data structure class. When we need to serializable data structures in the class, we extend the class with an externalizable subclass, which implements interface *Externalizable*. In the next chapter, we discuss how to externalize linear data structures, trees, and graphs.

# 11.4 Summary

This chapter discusses serialization of object graphs. It enables a serial medium such as a file or a network socket stream to be used to store or transfer serialized objects. The Java serialization mechanism consists of several interfaces and classes. The most important interfaces are *Serializable* and *Externalizable*. The most important classes are *ObjectOutputStream* and *ObjectInputStream*.

If a class implements interface *Serializable*, the objects can be serialized by an object output stream. The serialized objects can be stored in files or byte arrays, which are used to create objects with the same state. The serializable class may define a *writeObject* and a *readObject* method, which can serialize and deserialize non-serializable fields. The methods can be used to complement the default serialization of Java.

If a class implements interface *Externalizable*, the class must implement the *writeExternal* and *readExternal* methods, which control the serialization and deserialization of the instances of the class. The *writeExternal* method is responsible for serializing fields, *readExternal* for deserializing the field values and assigning the values to a created object of the externalizable class.

When implementing interface *Externalizable* in a class, we can intentionally reduce the size of a serial representation for the objects of the class and use secondary storage more efficiently. The smaller size of a serial representation also means fast delivery through a network and fewer secondary storage accesses.

# Chapter 12
# Data Structure Serialization

Applications may need to store data structures in secondary storage or transport them through a network. Thus, the data structures survive after the execution of a program that created them. The living-on capability of data structures and the information in the data structures is called *data persistence*, or simply persistence.

As we learn in Part III, we need auxiliary structures such as nodes or vertices in a data structure to organize the elements of the data structure. When we serialize a data structure, a smaller serial representation of the data structure is better. The auxiliary structuring information embedded in a data structure is not part of the stored data. Eliminating the information can reduce the size of the serial representation and facilitate data transportation.

This chapter focuses on serializing common data structures. We discuss the serialization of linear data structures, trees, and graphs. We present methods that produce compact serial representations for the data structures. The methods improve the default Java serialization by reducing the size of serialized object representation.

The serialization technique is based on interface *Externalizable*. We shall not modify the data structure classes presented in Chapters 7, 8, and 9. Instead, a subclass of a data structure class will be externalized. The subclass implements the interface *Externalizable*. The *writeExternal* method of the subclass serializes data elements. It does not include the auxiliary structures such as nodes of a linearly linked list or vertices of a graph in the serial representation of the list or graph. We also implement the *readExternal* method to deserialize the data elements and rebuild a serialized data structure.

The serialization approach for a data structure depends on an output format, which allows a compact serial representation of the data structure. The format allows the data structure to be rebuilt easily. Specifically, we shall present:

- A simple effective storage format for linked lists, which allows a linked list to be serialized into a compact serial representation. A replica of the serialized list can be constructed efficiently. We use a subclass of the *DoublyLinkedList* to illustrate the serialization technique for linear data structures.
- A storage format for trees, which stores data of child nodes along with the number of children for each node of a tree. The storage does not keep any pointer or reference to a child node.
- A graph serialization approach for graphs represented with adjacency vectors. The approach does not serialize adjacency vectors of a graph. The serial representation of a graph can be used to build adjacency vectors in a created replica of the serialized graph.

# 12.1 List Serialization

## 12.1.1 Output Format

Here we use a linearly linked list class, class *DoublyLinkedList*, to illustrate a serialization strategy for linear data structures.

A linear data structure keeps data elements in sequence. The essential relation between the data elements is a linear order of the data elements. We do not need to store information on the relation. We keep the number of data elements of a linear data structure and serialize the data elements one by one into an object output stream. When we rebuild a doubly linked list, we create a node for each serialized data element and link the *prev* and *next* fields of the node with its predecessor and successor, respectively.

## 12.1.2 Class *SerializableList*

We extend class *DoublyLinkedList* presented in Chapter 7 with externalizability. The subclass is called *SerializableList*. To make some variables of class *DoublyLinkedList* visible in its subclasses, we change the access mode of instance variables *length*, *first*, and *last* from private to protected. We also change the access mode of inner class *Node* from private to protected. Thus, the variables and inner class can be accessed in a subclass of class *DoublyLinkedList*.

We now define the subclass *SerializableList* for class *DoublyLinkedList*. The subclass implements methods *writeExternal* and *readExternal* specified in interface *Externalizable*. The *writeExternal* method uses code

```
out.writeInt(length);
Node node = first;
while (node != null) {
    out.writeObject(node.data);
    node = node.next;
}
```

to store the size of a list and serialize the data elements in sequence. The *prev* and *next* fields of a node are ignored by the *writeExternal* method.

When method *readExternal* deserializes a doubly linked list, it creates a node for each data element of the list. It uses the following code to create nodes and link them. The code deserializes data elements and encapsulates each data element with a node.

```
length = in.readInt();
Node node = null;
if (length > 0) {
    first = new Node(in.readObject());
    node = first;
}
```

```
for (int i = 1; i < length; i++) {
    last = new Node(in.readObject());
    node.next = last;
    last.prev = node;
    node = last;
}
if (length <= 1) last = node;
```

The following class, class *SerializableList*, includes a main method for testing the class. The main method builds a linked list, serializes it into a file named *strings.dat*, and deserializes the serial representation. Note that the *writeExternal* and *readExternal* methods of class *SerializableList* are invoked automatically by the Java serialization mechanism.

```
import java.util.*;
import java.io.*;
public class SerializableList
                    extends DoublyLinkedList
                    implements Externalizable {
    public static void main(String[] args) {
    try {
        String[] names={"Cbc", "Bbc", "Abc"};
        SerializableList namesList = new
                SerializableList(names), namesList1;
        FileOutputStream fout = new
                    FileOutputStream("strings.dat");
        ObjectOutputStream out = new
                    ObjectOutputStream(fout);
        out.writeObject(namesList);
        fout.close();

        FileInputStream fin = new
                    FileInputStream("strings.dat");
        ObjectInputStream in = new
                    ObjectInputStream(fin);
        namesList1 = (SerializableList)
                    in.readObject();
        fin.close();

        Enumeration items = namesList1.elements();
        while (items.hasMoreElements()) {
            System.out.print((String)
                        items.nextElement()+" ");
        }
    } catch(Exception ee) {
        ee.printStackTrace();
    }
    }
}
```

```
public SerializableList() { }
public SerializableList(Object[] input_array){
    super(input_array);
}

public void writeExternal(ObjectOutput out)
                throws IOException {
    out.writeInt(length);
    Node node = first;
    while (node != null) {
        out.writeObject(node.data);
        node = node.next;
    }
}

public void readExternal(ObjectInput in)
        throws IOException,
                ClassNotFoundException {
    length = in.readInt();
    Node node = null;
    if (length > 0) {
        first = new Node(in.readObject());
        node = first;
    }
    for (int i = 1; i < length; i++) {
        last = new Node(in.readObject());
        node.next = last;
        last.prev = node;
        node = last;
    }
    if (length <= 1) last = node;
}
}
```

The class *ExternalizableList* is a general data structure class, which can be used to keep any type of data elements. The following example shows how to use the data structure to store customer objects and how to serialize the customer list.

**Example 12.1** The main method of the following class creates an externalizable doubly linked list and populates the list with customer objects. It serializes the list into a file named *customers.dat*. Then, it deserializes the data to create another externalizable doubly linked list. The main method lists the names of the customer objects stored in the created list.

```
import java.util.*;
import java.io.*;
public class ListApplication {
    public static void main(String[] args) {
        try {
```

```
SerializableList customersList =
        new SerializableList(),
        customersList1;
Customer customer = new Customer
        ("John Smith", "Windsor, Ontario",
        "555-2341", 100f);
customersList.addElement(customer);
customer = new Customer("Tom David",
        "London, Ontario", "555-1234", 0f);
customersList.addElement(customer);
customer = new Customer("John David",
        "Toronto, Ontario",
        "555-0123", 20.95f);
customersList.addElement(customer);

FileOutputStream fout = new
        FileOutputStream("customers.dat");
ObjectOutputStream out = new
        ObjectOutputStream(fout);
out.writeObject(customersList);
fout.close();

FileInputStream fin = new
        FileInputStream("customers.dat");
ObjectInputStream in = new
        ObjectInputStream(fin);
customersList1 = (SerializableList)
                        in.readObject();
fin.close();

Enumeration items =
        customersList1.elements();
while (items.hasMoreElements()) {
  System.out.print(((Customer)
        items.nextElement()).name + " ");
}

} catch(Exception ee) {
  ee.printStackTrace();
}
    }
}
```

□

# 12.2 Tree Serialization

## 12.2.1 Output Format

Here we consider the serialization of a generic tree, which is represented by class *Tree* in Chapter 8. The class *Tree* defines an inner class named *Node* and an instance field named *root*. The *root* variable in a tree object keeps a reference to the root node of the tree. Class *Node* uses a vector field named *children* to hold references to the child nodes for a node.

A node is an auxiliary data structure for a tree. It references a data element of the tree with field *data*. When we serialize a tree, if nodes in the tree are not included in its serial representation, the length of the representation will be reduced.

We organize the data elements of a tree level by level in the serial representation of the tree. The child data elements are placed together at the next level. They are preceded with an integer to denote the number of child data elements.

The output format for a tree is illustrated in Fig. 12.1. Node *Wbc* of the tree has two children. The serial representation of the tree includes the two children at the level below node *Wbc*. When the serialized data elements are listed in sequence, we derive the serial representation of the tree shown in Fig. 12.1c.

A *writeExternal* method generates the serial representation of a tree by traversing the nodes in the tree in breadth-first order. The traversal is supported with a queue, which is initialized with the root node of the tree. When the traversal encounters a node in the queue, the method writes its child count to an object output stream, serializes the child data elements into the stream, and places the child nodes of the node into the queue.

As shown in Fig. 12.1c, the serial representation of a tree may have a trailing series of zeros. The length of the trailing zero series depends on the number of leaf nodes in the tree. For example, if a tree has only one node in the lowest level, the trailing series in the serial representation of the tree contains only one zero. The trailing zero series can be replaced with a special value, say $-1$, which signals the end of the list of data elements in the tree. We leave the implementation of a serial representation that has no trailing series of zeros for trees as an exercise.

## 12.2.2 Class *SerializableTree*

The following class, class *SerializableTree*, extends class *Tree* presented in Section 8.1.1 for general trees. It implements interface *Externalizable*. Its instances can be serialized by invoking the *writeObject* method for an object output stream. The *writeExternal* method invoked for an instance of *SerializableTree* converts the tree into a sequence of integers and data elements such as the sequence shown in Fig. 12.1c. The *readExternal* method deserializes the data elements and uses them to build a tree.

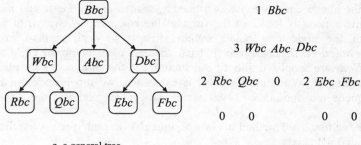

**a**. a general tree

**b**. serialized tree

1  *Bbc*   3   *Wbc  Abc  Dbc*  2  *Rbc  Qbc*  0  2  *Ebc  Fbc*  0  0  0  0

**c**. serial  representation

**Fig. 12.1** The serialization of a tree

Class *SerializableTree* implements method *writeExternal* with code

```
Vector currentLevel = new Vector(),
     nextLevel = new Vector();
if (root == null) {
   out.writeInt(0);
   return;
}
out.writeInt(1);
out.writeObject(root.getData());
currentLevel.addElement(root);
while (!currentLevel.isEmpty()
                    || !nextLevel.isEmpty()) {
    if (!currentLevel.isEmpty()) {
       Node currentNode = (Node)
                    currentLevel.elementAt(0);
       currentLevel.removeElementAt(0);
       out.writeInt(currentNode.degree());
       for (int i=0; i<currentNode.degree(); i++){
          Node tempNode = currentNode.getChild(i);
          Object tempObject = tempNode.getData();
          nextLevel.addElement(tempNode);
          out.writeObject(tempObject);
       }
    } else {
       for (int i=0; i <nextLevel.size(); i++)
          currentLevel.addElement
                    (nextLevel.elementAt(i));
       nextLevel.removeAllElements();
    }
}
```

In the above code, we use two queues, named *currentLevel* and *nextLevel*. Each time a node is found in the front of the *currentLevel*, we write the child count of the node into object output stream *out* with method invocation *out.writeInt(currentNode.degree())*. Then, the data elements in the child nodes of *currentNode* are serialized into the *out* stream, and the child nodes are placed into queue *nextLevel*. When *currentLevel* is exhausted, we move nodes in the *nextLevel* queue into the *currentLevel* queue and process nodes in the refilled *currentLevel*.

The *readExternal* method in class *SerializableTree* interprets a serialized tree. It is defined with code

```
Vector currentLevel = new Vector(),
       nextLevel = new Vector();
int degree = in.readInt();
if (degree == 0) return;
root = new Node(in.readObject());
currentLevel.addElement(root);
while (!currentLevel.isEmpty()
                    || !nextLevel.isEmpty()) {
    if (!currentLevel.isEmpty()) {
        Node currentNode = (Node)
                    currentLevel.elementAt(0);
        currentLevel.removeElementAt(0);
        degree = in.readInt();
        for (int i=0; i < degree; i++){
            currentNode.addChild
                    (in.readObject());
            nextLevel.addElement
                    (currentNode.getChild(i));
        }
    } else {
        for (int i=0; i < nextLevel.size(); i++)
        currentLevel.addElement
                    (nextLevel.elementAt(i));
        nextLevel.removeAllElements();
    }
}
```

The *readExternal* method also uses two queues, named *currentLevel* and *nextLevel*, to interpret a serialized tree. When the method finds a node in *currentLevel*, it reads in the degree of the node with method invocation *in.readInt()*. Then, it reads this number of data elements, uses the data to create child nodes for the *currentNode*, and places the child nodes into *nextLevel* queue with statements

```
for (int i=0; i < degree; i++) {
    Node node = new Node(in.readObject()));
    currentNode.addChild(node);
    nextLevel.addElement(node);
}
```

Thus, the method deserializes the serial representation of a tree and builds a replica of the tree.

The following class, *SerializableTree*, contains a main method for testing the class. Using two queues in serialization and deserialization is for easy explanation. We can modify the *writeExternal* and *readExternal* methods by using only one queue. We leave the modification as an exercise.

```java
import java.util.*;
import java.io.*;
public class SerializableTree extends Tree
                implements Externalizable {
    public static void main(String[] args) {
        try {
        SerializableTree namesTree = new
                SerializableTree(), namesTree1;
        namesTree.root = namesTree.new Node("Cbc");
        namesTree.root.addChild("Bbc");
        Node tempNode = namesTree.root.getChild(0);
        tempNode.addChild("Abc");

        FileOutputStream fout = new
                FileOutputStream("strings.dat");
        ObjectOutputStream out = new
                ObjectOutputStream(fout);
        out.writeObject(namesTree);
        fout.close();

        FileInputStream fin = new
                FileInputStream("strings.dat");
        ObjectInputStream in = new
                ObjectInputStream(fin);
        namesTree1 = (SerializableTree)
                in.readObject();
        fin.close();

        Enumeration items = namesTree1.elements();
        while (items.hasMoreElements()) {
           System.out.print(((Node)
               items.nextElement()).getData()+ " ");
        }

        } catch(Exception ee) {
           ee.printStackTrace();
        }
    }
    public SerializableTree() { }
```

```java
public void writeExternal(ObjectOutput out)
                throws IOException {
   Vector currentLevel = new Vector(),
      nextLevel = new Vector();
   if (root == null) {
      out.writeInt(0);
      return;
   }
   out.writeInt(1);
   out.writeObject(root.getData());
   currentLevel.addElement(root);
   while (!currentLevel.isEmpty()
            || !nextLevel.isEmpty()) {
      if (!currentLevel.isEmpty()) {
      Node currentNode = (Node)
                currentLevel.elementAt(0);
      currentLevel.removeElementAt(0);
      out.writeInt(currentNode.degree());
      for (int i=0;
            i < currentNode.degree(); i++) {
         Node tempNode =
                currentNode.getChild(i);
         Object tempObject =
                tempNode.getData();
         nextLevel.addElement(tempNode);
         out.writeObject(tempObject);
         }
      } else {
      for (int i=0; i < nextLevel.size(); i++)
         currentLevel.addElement
            (nextLevel.elementAt(i));
      nextLevel.removeAllElements();
      }
   }
}

public void readExternal(ObjectInput in)
   throws IOException, ClassNotFoundException
{
   Vector currentLevel = new Vector(),
         nextLevel = new Vector();
   int degree = in.readInt();
   if (degree == 0) return;
   root = new Node(in.readObject());
   currentLevel.addElement(root);
   while (!currentLevel.isEmpty()
            || !nextLevel.isEmpty()) {
```

```
            if (!currentLevel.isEmpty()) {
            Node currentNode = (Node)
                    currentLevel.elementAt(0);
            currentLevel.removeElementAt(0);
            degree = in.readInt();
            for (int i=0; i < degree; i++) {
               currentNode.addChild
                            (in.readObject());
               nextLevel.addElement
                        (currentNode.getChild(i));
               }
            } else {
            for (int i=0; i < nextLevel.size(); i++)
               currentLevel.addElement
                    (nextLevel.elementAt(i));
            nextLevel.removeAllElements();
            }
         }
      }
   }
```

The class *SerializableTree* is a general object container. Its instances can be used to hold any types of data. The following example shows how to use an instance of the class to hold customer objects.

**Example 12.2** The following class contains a main method that uses a *SerializableTree* as a container of customer objects. It serializes the container into file *customers.dat* and deserializes it to build a new container with deserialized customer objects.

```
import java.util.*;
import java.io.*;
public class TreeApplication {
   public static void main(String[] args) {
      try {
      SerializableTree customersTree =
         new SerializableTree(), customersTree1;
      Customer customer = new Customer
            ("John Smith", "Windsor, Ontario",
             "555-2341", 100f);
      customersTree.root =
            customersTree.new Node(customer);
      customer = new Customer("Tom David",
             "London, Ontario", "555-1234", 0f);
      customersTree.root.addChild(customer);
      customer = new Customer("John David",
         "Toronto, Ontario", "555-0123", 20.95f);
      Tree.Node tempNode =
                customersTree.root.getChild(0);
```

```
        tempNode.addChild(customer);

        FileOutputStream fout = new
                FileOutputStream("customers.dat");
        ObjectOutputStream out = new
                ObjectOutputStream(fout);
        out.writeObject(customersTree);
        fout.close();

        FileInputStream fin = new
                FileInputStream("customers.dat");
        ObjectInputStream in = new
                ObjectInputStream(fin);
        customersTree1 = (SerializableTree)
                                in.readObject();
        fin.close();

        Enumeration items =
                customersTree1.elements();
        while (items.hasMoreElements()) {
        System.out.print(((Customer) ((Tree.Node)
         items.nextElement()).getData()).name+" ");
        }
        } catch(Exception ee) {
            ee.printStackTrace();
        }
    }
}
```

□

**Exercise 12.1** Extend the class *BinaryTree* presented in Chapter 8 for serializable binary trees without serializing nodes. (Hint: use integer 0, 1, 2, or 3 to denote that a node in a binary tree has none, has left but no right child, has right but no left child, has both left and right child.)

**Exercise 12.2** Modify the methods *writeExternal* and *readExternal* of class *SerializableTree* by using one queue instead of two.

**Exercise 12.3** Modify the class *SerializableTree* so that a serial representation of a tree terminates with integer −1 after the last node in the lowest level of the tree is written to an object output stream. Thus, a serial representation of a tree will not have a trailing series of zeros.

# 12.3 Graph Serialization

## 12.3.1 Output Format

We now present a format for an object output stream to store the data of undirected, unweighted graph. A vertex in a graph is an object. The vertices of a graph are stored in an array called *vertices* in class *Graph*. We assume vertices adjacent to a vertex are organized into an adjacency vector associated to the vertex. We are interested in the data objects and the adjacencies between the vertices. We are not interested in the vector structure when we serialize a graph.

We can serialize the *vertices* array into an object output stream. For each vertex, we store an integer in the stream to denote the number of vertices that are adjacent to the vertex. The serial representations of vertices that are adjacent to the vertex follow the integer in the object output stream. They are back references to serialized objects from the *vertices* array. Thus, we avoid serializing vectors in the stream.

## 12.3.2 Class *SerializableGraph*

The following class, class *SerializableGraph*, extends class *Graph* that represents undirected, unweighted graphs in Section 9.1.3.1. The class *Graph* uses an adjacency vector to organize the vertices adjacent to a vertex. We leave the serialization of graph objects that use an adjacency matrix to represent adjacencies as an exercise. The class *SerializableGraph* implements interface *Externalizable*.

Class *SerializableGraph* defines method *writeExternal* with code

```
out.writeObject(vertices);
for (int i=0; i < vertexNumber; i++) {
    if (adjacencies[i] == null)
        out.writeInt(0);
    else {
        out.writeInt(adjacencies[i].size());
        for (int j = 0;
                j < adjacencies[i].size(); j++)
            out.writeObject
                (adjacencies[i].elementAt(j));
    }
}
```

The method first serializes the *vertices* array into object output stream *out*. Then, for each adjacency vector, the method writes the size of the vector to the stream and serializes the elements of the vector. When an element in the vector is serialized, the corresponding vertex object stored in the *vertices* array has been serialized. Therefore, the element will be serialized into a back reference handle, which is an integer.

Class *SerializableGraph* defines method *readExternal* with code

```
vertices = (Object[]) in.readObject();
vertexNumber = vertices.length;
adjacencies = new Vector[vertexNumber];
for (int i=0; i < vertexNumber; i++) {
    int k = in.readInt();
    if (k != 0) {
        adjacencies[i] = new Vector(k);
        for (int j=0; j<k; j++)
        adjacencies[i].addElement(in.readObject());
    }
}
```

The method first deserializes the *vertices* array. Then, it reads in the size of each adjacency vector into local variable *k* with expression *in.readInt()*. It deserializes the vector elements with code

```
adjacencies[i] = new Vector(k);
for (int j=0; j<k; j++)
    adjacencies[i].addElement(in.readObject());
```

The vector elements are added into the adjacency vector by the last statement.

```
import java.util.*;
import java.io.*;
public class SerializableGraph extends Graph
                    implements Externalizable {
    public static void main(String[] args) {
        String[] names = {"Cbc", "Bbc", "Abc"};
        SerializableGraph stringsGraph = new
                    SerializableGraph(names);
        stringsGraph.addEdge("Cbc", "Abc");

        try {
        FileOutputStream fout = new
                    FileOutputStream("strings.dat");
        ObjectOutputStream out = new
                ObjectOutputStream(fout);
        out.writeObject(stringsGraph);
        fout.close();

        FileInputStream fin = new
                    FileInputStream("strings.dat");
        ObjectInputStream in = new
                ObjectInputStream(fin);
        SerializableGraph stringsGraph1 =
                (SerializableGraph) in.readObject();
        fin.close();
        Enumeration vertices =
                        stringsGraph1.elements();
```

```java
        while (vertices.hasMoreElements())
        System.out.println(vertices.nextElement());
    } catch(Exception ee) {
        ee.printStackTrace();
    }
}
public SerializableGraph() { }
public SerializableGraph(int vertexNumber){
    super(vertexNumber);
}
public SerializableGraph(Object[] vertices) {
    super(vertices);
}
public void writeExternal(ObjectOutput out)
                    throws IOException {
    out.writeObject(vertices);
    for (int i=0; i < vertexNumber; i++)
    {
        if (adjacencies[i] == null)
          out.writeInt(0);
        else {
        out.writeInt(adjacencies[i].size());
        for (int j = 0;
            j < adjacencies[i].size(); j++)
          out.writeObject
                (adjacencies[i].elementAt(j));
        }
    }
}
public void readExternal(ObjectInput in)
        throws IOException,
            ClassNotFoundException {
    vertices = (Object[]) in.readObject();
    vertexNumber = vertices.length;
    adjacencies = new Vector[vertexNumber];
    for (int i=0; i < vertexNumber; i++){
        int k = in.readInt();
        if (k != 0) {
            adjacencies[i] = new Vector(k);
            for (int j=0; j<k; j++)
                adjacencies[i].addElement
                            (in.readObject());
        }
    }
}
}
```

The class *SerializableGraph* is a general data structure. The vertices in an instance of *SerializableGraph* can hold any type of data objects. In the above main method, the vertices hold strings. In the following example, we use a *SerializableGraph* to hold customer objects.

**Example 12.3** The following class, class *GraphApplication*, uses a *SerializableGraph* to hold customer objects. The data structure is serialized into a data file named *customers.dat*, which is then deserialized to create a new *SerializableGraph*.

```
import java.util.*;
import java.io.*;
public class GraphApplication {
    public static void main(String[] args) {
        try {
        Customer[] customers = new Customer[3];
        customers[0] = new Customer("John Smith",
            "Windsor, Ontario", "555-2341", 100f);
        customers[1] = new Customer("Tom David",
            "London, Ontario", "555-1234", 0f);
        customers[2] = new Customer("John David",
            "Toronto, Ontario", "555-0123", 20.95f);
        SerializableGraph customersGraph =
                    new SerializableGraph(customers),
                    customersGraph1;
        customersGraph.addEdge(customers[0],
                                    customers[1]);

        FileOutputStream fout = new
                FileOutputStream("customers.dat");
        ObjectOutputStream out = new
                ObjectOutputStream(fout);
        out.writeObject(customersGraph);
        fout.close();

        FileInputStream fin = new
                FileInputStream("customers.dat");
        ObjectInputStream in = new
                ObjectInputStream(fin);
        customersGraph1 = (SerializableGraph)
                        in.readObject();
        fin.close();
        Enumeration items =
                    customersGraph1.elements();
        while (items.hasMoreElements()) {
            System.out.print(((Customer)
                items.nextElement()).name + " ");
        }
```

```
System.out.print(
        customersGraph1.isAdjacent(0, 1));
} catch(Exception ee) {
   ee.printStackTrace();
}
```

□

**Exercise 12.4** Extend class *Graph* that uses a matrix to represent adjacencies for undirected, unweighted graphs with a subclass, which implements interface *Externalizable*. The subclass defines the *writeExternal* and *readExternal* methods to serialize and deserialize the *vertices* array and adjacency matrix.

## 12.4 Summary

A data structure can be serialized if the class of the data structure implements interface *Serializable* or *Externalizable*. When the class implements interface *Serializable*, it may define a *writeObject* method, which can be used to serialize non-serializable fields.

In this chapter, we show how to implement interface *Externalizable* for common data structures – linked lists, trees, and graphs. The externalizable data structures have a *writeExternal* method, which generates a more compact serial representation of a data structure than the default Java serialization. The space efficiency is implied by eliminating the storage of auxiliary data structures such as nodes and vectors. The *readExternal* method of the externalizable data structures deserializes the serial representation of a data structure and uses the persistent data to build a new data structure.

## Assignment

A B-tree is a balanced tree data structure for keeping keys. Extend class *B_Tree* defined in Chapter 8 with an externalizable subclass. The *writeExternal* and *readExternal* methods of the subclass are responsible for serializing a B-tree and deserializing a serialized B-tree, respectively. Compare the compactness of the external representation of a B-tree with the serial representation of the B-tree generated with the default serialization mechanism of Java.

# Appendix A
# Binary File Dumping

## A1. Hexadecimal Convertion of Binary Files

A Java class file is a binary file with information represented in bits. The main method of the following utility class, class *dumpfile*, can be used to convert a binary class file into a hexadecimal representation. It creates a data input stream, called *dataIn*, that encapsulates the class file. The method uses a byte array named *line* of 16 bytes long to hold bytes read from the input stream. The read operation is performed with statement

```
bytes = dataIn.read(line);
```

where *bytes* is an integer variable for holding the number of bytes read from the *dataIn* stream.

Each line in the hexadecimal representation is prefixed with an offset from the beginning of the representation. The offset is a four-digit hexadecimal number. The main method converts a byte denoted with *line*[i] to two hexadecimal digits with the expressions

```
Character.toUpperCase(Character.
            forDigit((line[i] & 0xF0)>>4, 16))
Character.toUpperCase(Character.
            forDigit((line[i] & 0xF), 16))
```

The first expression retrieves the first four bits of the byte and converts the binary integer to an upper case hexadecimal digit; the second converts the last four bits of the byte.

Class *dumpfile* can be compiled by a Java compiler. To use the main method of the class to convert a class file, say *Customer.class*, to its hexadecimal representation, issue command

*java dumpfile Customer.class*

The main method of the *dumpfile* class invokes *println* method to print the hexadecimal conversion of class file *Customer.class* on the standard output device.

```
/** Dump a binary representation of a class
 *   file to hexadecimal representation by
 *   converting each byte to two digits.
 *   Usage: java dumpfile <class_file_name>
 */
import java.io.*;
class dumpfile {
    public static void main(String[] args) {
```

```
byte[] line = new byte[16];
DataInputStream dataIn;
try {
    FileInputStream fin = new
            FileInputStream(args[0]);
    dataIn = new DataInputStream(fin);

    int bytes = 1, lineNo = 0x0;
    while (bytes > 0) {
        bytes = dataIn.read(line);
        if (bytes > 0) {
            String liNo =
                Integer.toHexString(lineNo);
            while (liNo.length() < 4)
                liNo = "0" + liNo;
            System.out.print("0x"+liNo+" | ");
            lineNo += 16;
        }
        for (int i = 0; i < bytes; i++)
        {
        System.out.print("" +
        Character.toUpperCase(
            Character.forDigit((line[i] & 0xF0)
            >>4, 16)) + Character.toUpperCase(
            Character.forDigit((line[i] & 0xF),
            16)) + ' ');
        }
        System.out.println("");
    }
}
catch(FileNotFoundException e)
    { System.out.println("No such file"); }
catch(IOException e) { }
}
}
```

## A2. Reading Utf8 Strings

A class file may encode Utf8 strings. To read a Utf8 string, invoke the *readUTF* method for a data input stream that represents the class file. Before the method is executed, skip the bytes that are preceded the Utf8 string in the class file.

The following main method shows an example of reading a Utf8 string. In the main method, expression

```
dataIn.skipBytes(0x2A);
```

is used to skip 0x2A = 42 bytes in class file *Merchandise.class*. Statement

```
System.out.print(DataInputStream.readUTF(dataIn));
```
reads the Utf8 string at position 0x002a in the class file and prints the string on
the standard output.

```
import java.io.*;
class dumpfile {
    public static void main(String[] args) {
        byte[] line = new byte[16];
        DataInputStream dataIn;
        try {
            FileInputStream fin = new
                FileInputStream("Merchandise.class");
            dataIn = new DataInputStream(fin);
            dataIn.skipBytes(0x2A);
            System.out.print(
                    DataInputStream.readUTF(dataIn));
        }
        catch(FileNotFoundException e)
            { System.out.println("No such file"); }
        catch(IOException e) { }
    }
}
```

# Appendix B
# References

## Chapter 1

Object-oriented programming in Java is discussed in [1].

[1] K. Arnold and J. Gosling. *The Java Programming Language*. Addison-Wesley, Reading, Mass., 1996.

## Chapter 2

The Java programming language is specified in [1] and [2].

[2] J. Gosling, B. Joy and G. Steele. *The Java Language Specification*. Addison-Wesley, Reading, Mass., 1996.

## Chapter 5

The Java Virtual Machine description is based on [3].

[3] T. Lindholm and F. Yellin. *The Java Virtual Machine Specification*. Addison-Wesley, Reading, Mass., 1997.

## Chapter 7

For the analysis of the interpolation search algorithms, see [4], [5], and [6]. The sorting methods, binary search, interpolation search and Fibonaccian search are discussed in [7].

[4] A. C. Yao and F. F. Yao. The Complexity of Searching an Ordered Random Table. *Proceedings of the 17$^{th}$ Annual IEEE Symposium on Foundations of Computer Science*, 1976, pp. 173–176.

[5] Y. Perl, A. Itai, and H. Avni. Interpolation Search – A Log Log $N$ Search. *CACM*. 21 (1978) pp. 550–553.

[6] G. H. Gonnet, L. D. Rogers, and J. A. George. An Algorithmic and Complexity Analysis of Interpolation Search. *Acta Informatica* 13 (1980) pp. 39–52.

[7]   D. E. Knuth. *The Art of Computer Programming*, Volume 3, *Sorting and Searching*. Addison-Wesley, Reading, Mass., 1973.

## Chapter 8

Trees have been extensively discussed as a fundamental data structure in the literature. Presentations on trees can be found in [8], [9], and [10].

[8]   A. V. Aho, J. E. Hopcroft, and J. D. Ullman. *The Design and Analysis of Computer Algorithms*. Addison-Wesley, Reading, Mass.,1974.

[9]   D. E. Knuth. *The Art of Computer Programming*, Volume 1, *Funadamental Algorithms*. Addison-Wesley, Reading, Mass., 1968, 1973.

[10]   R. E. Tarjan. *Data Structures and Network Algorithms, Regional Conference Series in Applied Mathematics*, Volume 44. SIAM, 1983.

[11]   R. Bayer. Binary b-trees for virtual memory. *Proceedings of ACM SIGFIDET Workshop*, ACM, 1971, pp. 219–235.

[12]   R. Bayer. Symmetric binary b-trees: Data structure and maintenance algorithms. *Acta Informatica* 1(1972) pp. 290–306.

## Chapter 9

The *distances* method follows an algorithm described in [13]. The algorithm for method *allDistances* is due to [14]. Both algorithms can be found in [8].

[13]   E. W. Dijkstra. A note on two problems in connexion with graphs. *Numerische Mathematik* 1 (1959) pp. 269-271.

[14]   S. C. Kleene. Representation of events in nerve nets and finite automata. *Automata Studies* (1956), Shannon and McCarthy, eds., Princeton University Press, pp. 3-40.

## Chapter 10

The *pathSaturate* method in class *LeveledNetwork* follows an algorithm by Dinic [15]. The original algorithm for method *vertexSaturate* is due to [16]. The method is based on a simplified version of the algorithm described in [10]. The simplified Karzanov's algorithm is called *wave method*. The Dinic's algorithm and wave method can be found in [10].

[15]   E. A. Dinic. Algorithm for solution of a problem of maximum flow in a network with power estimation. *Soviet Math. Dokl.* 11 (1970) pp. 1277–1280.

[16] A. V. Karzanov. Determining the maximum flow in a network by the method of preflows. *Soviet Math. Dokl.* 15 (1974) pp. 434–437.

## Chapter 11

The Java serialization mechanism is defined in *Java Object Serialization Specification* [17], which can be downloaded from http://java.sun.com. The serialization specification describes interfaces *Serializable* and *Externalizable*, classes *ObjectOutputStream* and *ObjectInputStream*. Object stream format and constants for serializations of objects are also defined in the specification.

[17] *Java Object Serialization Specification*. Sun Microsystems, Mountain View, Ca., 1997.

# Index

# W

Printing: Mercedesdruck, Berlin
Binding: Buchbinderei Lüderitz & Bauer, Berlin

# Springer
# and the
# environment

At Springer we firmly believe that an
international science publisher has a
special obligation to the environment,
and our corporate policies consistently
reflect this conviction.
We also expect our business partners –
paper mills, printers, packaging
manufacturers, etc. – to commit
themselves to using materials and
production processes that do not harm
the environment. The paper in this
book is made from low- or no-chlorine
pulp and is acid free, in conformance
with international standards for paper
permanency.